WHERE THE MILLENNIALS WILL TAKE US

Where the Millennials Will Take Us

A NEW GENERATION WRESTLES WITH THE GENDER STRUCTURE

Barbara J. Risman

OXFORD
UNIVERSITY PRESS

OXFORD

UNIVERSITY PRESS

Oxford University Press is a department of the University of Oxford. It furthers
the University's objective of excellence in research, scholarship, and education
by publishing worldwide. Oxford is a registered trade mark of Oxford University
Press in the UK and certain other countries.

Published in the United States of America by Oxford University Press
198 Madison Avenue, New York, NY 10016, United States of America.

© Oxford University Press 2018

Library of Congress Cataloging-in-Publication Data
Names: Risman, Barbara J., 1956– author.
Title: Where the millennials will take us : a new generation wrestles with the gender structure /
Barbara J. Risman.
Description: New York City : Oxford University Press, [2018] | Includes bibliographical references.
Identifiers: LCCN 2017019938 | ISBN 9780199324392 (pbk.) | ISBN 9780199324385 (hardcover) |
ISBN 9780199324408 (updf) | ISBN 9780199324415 (epub)
Subjects: LCSH: Sex role—United States. | Gender expression—United States.
Classification: LCC HQ1075.5.U6 R57 2018 | DDC 305.30973—dc23
LC record available at https://lccn.loc.gov/2017019938

9 8 7 6 5 4 3 2 1

Paperback printed by WebCom, Inc., Canada
Hardback printed by Bridgeport National Bindery, Inc., United States of America

Contents

Acknowledgments

NO BOOK IS written by the author alone, but this one is most clearly a collaborative effort. This project began as a theory book with empirical chapters illustrating the theoretical framework on topics as different as genderqueer youth, women in science, and hooking up. I agreed to teach a graduate qualitative methodology practicum in the sociology department at the University of Illinois at Chicago (UIC) with the goal to also collect data for one chapter in my book. The data were collected primarily by graduate students at UIC, and I owe that class a great debt and thank them immensely for making this project possible. I also thank my colleague and friend Kristen Myers who collaborated on data collection as did some of her students. What derailed the book I planned to write and led to this one was that the data we collected were just too rich, too important to condense into one chapter, and so my proposed book evolved into a book on Millennials. I thank my editor, James Cook, for being gracious enough to accept and encourage a finished project far different than the one promised. I also want to thank the 116 young adults, the Millennials, who took the time to talk with us and so openly share their life stories.

A book that takes as long to write as this one has had the generous contribution from scores of students and colleagues. Amy Brainer, William Scarborough, and Ray Sin were both invaluable as research assistants and as colleagues during the collection and analyses of these data. Thanks to Amy Brainer, Georgiann Davis, Jesse

Holzman, Kristen Myers, William Scarborough, and Ray Sin for reading and providing invaluable feedback on a variety of chapters. Thanks also to Patricia Martin and Lisa Wade, as well as anonymous reviewers, for Oxford University Press for providing me with deep, careful, and very useful reading of my work. I also want to thank the graduate students who have taken courses with me in the last few years for their thoughtful feedback of chapters as they have been developed.

I have had the very good fortune of teaching as University of Illinois at Chicago where my colleagues have been supportive of my research even as I was officially supposed to be focusing on departmental administration. I want to thank my UIC Colleagues and the university itself for granting me a sabbatical during 2015-16 to work on this book. I spent my sabbatical as a Fellow at the Center for Advanced Study in the Behavioral Sciences at Stanford and owe a deep debt of gratitude to the Center for inviting me. My fellowship provided both the quiet peaceful writing study and the energetic intellectually stimulating interaction with the rest of the 2015-2016 cohort. This book would have been far different, and less well written, were it not for my writing group at CASBS. Thanks to my wonderful writing group, including Victoria Bernal, Joshua Gamson, Glenn Loury, Natasha Iskander, Maureen Perry-Jenkins, and Mick Smyer. I also owe a debt of gratitude to my CASBS meditation and yoga groups for helping me stay focused on the task at hand while enjoying the privilege of our time together at CASBS. Over the course of writing this book, I had the opportunity to present ideas as they formed and chapters as they were being written in many university settings, including Southern Illinois University, the University of Trento, the University of Turin, the University of Milan, the University of Genoa, the University of Tennessee, and my own department at the University of Illinois at Chicago. In every setting generous colleagues raised issues that helped the development of this project. Of course, for all the generous help of all these friends and colleagues throughout the years, the final product is mine alone, and I take responsibility for its weaknesses as well as its strengths.

Finally, and most importantly, I want to thank my family. As a mother of a Millennial, I have lived through the evolution of gender politics from my second wave feminism to my child Ashir Leah KaneRisman Coillberg's life experiences. I thank Ashir for all I learned from our journey together. And last, but not least, I want to thank my husband, Randall Liss. I have been working on this book the entire span of our relationship, from 2009 forward. No husband could better embody the possibility of true gender equality. From the moment of our marriage, my husband has devoted himself to supporting my work. Wherever in the world I travel to speak or teach, I have a travel companion. Our marriage exemplifies the fluidity of gender expectations as a man who was a primary breadwinner in a traditional first marriage became a most extravagant caretaker and homemaker in a second marriage. This book is dedicated to Randall, for being willing to fit his own work around mine, to support my writing schedule and professional responsibilities, to lovingly give me the support I needed to successfully be both a university administrator and a sociologist at the same time. Our relationship is proof that the gender structure is indeed changing.

WHERE THE MILLENNIALS WILL TAKE US

1

Introduction

IT'S ENOUGH TO make you dizzy: A woman presidential candidate wins the popular vote but loses the election to a man who brags about grabbing "pussy"; laws are passed to protect transgender people's right to urinate in peace and then political battles rage about repeal; women earn more college degrees than men but remain far behind in average earning power; gay couples can marry but other Americans claim "religious" freedom to discriminate against them; paternal leave is offered by a few businesses, but when men take it their bosses doubt their organizational commitment; the Supreme Court long ago decided women have the right to control their own bodies and 50 years later that right may be challenged. Is gender equality a political football to be debated in Congress or a human right? How can we understand simultaneous advancements in gender and sexuality equity and sometimes what seems to be radical steps backward? Does gender still matter in the 21st century or have we moved beyond the need for a gender revolution?

If you watch a boy struggling not to cry when he scrapes his knee because he is afraid of being called a sissy, you see how gender matters. If you see a transgirl harassed for trying to shower with the other girls, you understand that gender still matters. If you ask a woman who is ignored in a business meeting, she will tell you that gender still matters. If you ask a young mother trying to juggle work and family while her husband assumes that's her problem, you see how gender still matters. If you ask a stay-at-home father if the mothers at the playground accept him, he'll tell you that gender still matters. Gender remains a deeply felt identity with everyday consequences.

But gender is so much more than an identity. It shapes and legitimates inequality in every society. Much has changed in postindustrial societies when it comes to gender, and much has remained the same. Men, as a group, still hold the reins of governmental power, write and interpret the law, dominate the boards of international conglomerates, and expect their mothers and daughters to care for the young, the weak, and the old. Women, as a group, do the work of taking care of other people, whether as mothers and wives, or for pay as nannies, teachers, nurses, housecleaners, or manicurists. Doctors in training are now as likely to be women as men, although the sex gap in physician pay remains. Women can now run for president in the United States, but the Congress and Senate remain overwhelmingly boys clubs. The gender revolution has now been in process too long for it to seem revolutionary. And yet, we cannot claim victory. Freedom from gender oppression is not experienced equally across society. Gender never exists in disembodied space, rather, always in complicated coexistence with other stratification systems such as class, race, ethnicity, and nation-states.

This book arrives on your reading list in a particular moment in history. Is the gender revolution ongoing? Or has the right-wing swing in politics ended our movement forward? Have we reached a cease fire, with some gains for women, some gains for those who defy gender norms, but no revolution? What has changed over time, and what has remained the same? Just where are we now? These are the questions that motivate this book. How I chose to answer them probably reveals as much about me as the topic. As a second-wave feminist, I came into the academy just as it was opening up to women professors. I am a decade younger than the true second-wave academic pioneers, the women who really broke the barricades and took their place in university life. But I wasn't that far behind. Sociology fascinated me from my very first course as an undergraduate (when I was still planning to be a professional flutist) because it helped me understand my life and the constraints I felt as a woman coming of age in the 1970s. Concepts such as role conflict helped me understand the dilemmas of women like me who wanted to be (professionally) the men they were supposed to marry. Women were educated to be part of the world but still understood that trying to be so would conflict with being a wife and mother. Many of the professional women before me felt they had to choose and remained childless. Other women were pushed out of the labor force when their jobs would not accommodate pregnancy or childrearing. Professional women who managed to juggle careers and parenthood often had liberal husbands who were happy that their wives had choices but never conceptualized that parenthood should require them to change their career trajectories at all. As a young, white sociologist, I was aware of these patterns, studied them, and tried very hard to live my principles in an egalitarian, heterosexual marriage where we shared earning a living and caring for our child. While that marriage lasted through most of our childrearing years, I had the good fortune of having a real partner in childrearing, allowing me to build a career as an academic. Now, in my second marriage, my husband is far more domestic than I have ever been, and again, I am lucky enough to come home to gourmet meals at the end of busy work days.

I describe how my life story had led to my interest in gender inequality because I want to openly acknowledge that I write from a particular standpoint. Every writer, every scientist, and every social scientist conceptualizes the world from their life circumstances. It is important for every author to reflect on how their everyday experiences influence their work. Such reflexivity comes natural to me as a sociologist. I am interested in gender inequality because my life has been shaped by trying to escape the constraints of the sexism of the 20th century. I came of age during the women's movement, and a driving force in my life has been to understand gender inequality because I know we cannot change something unless we understand how it operates. This research has been framed by my feminist standpoint and my goal is to provide an understanding of how gender inequality works to help dismantle it.

How we got to this moment in human history, and what to do about it, has been the burning intellectual question that has driven my academic career. Why does our society take the biological material that differs between human beings and create social categories that determine everything from dress styles, to toy preferences, to career possibilities. We even use the biological reality that female bodies birth children to excuse people with male bodies from a moral responsibility to do hands-on caretaking work for their children, parents, or sick friends. Disagree? Well, when was the last time you asked a new father if he was going back to work now that he was a dad? My own research actually began with a study of fathers raising children alone. Could they do a good job, or did their masculinity hamper them? At the time, I was sure that gender differences would just disappear if men and women had the same opportunities and constraints, but my research and others' convinced me otherwise. But that is getting ahead of the story.

In the next chapter, I provide some history on research about gender, as I firmly believe that we cannot understand the present without knowing the journey taken to get here. The main contribution of the next chapter is a way to think about *gender as a social structure*. I offer my own theoretical framework, which has been developing for decades (Risman 1998; 2004), but here I seriously revise it. As sociology took a cultural turn at the beginning of the 21st century, my work has taken some criticism for being too structural. In the revised version of the theoretical framework offered here, I try to correct this weakness. As is often the case, adding nuance, adds complexity. The theoretical model presented here remains true to my argument that we must focus attention not only on gender identity at the individual level but on interactional expectations and macro-institutional issues as well. But at each level of analysis, I suggest that we differentiate between the material (what we can touch, see, and feel) and the cultural (our ideas, meanings, and beliefs). The crux of this argument has been published earlier in *Social Currents* (2017) as it was the basis of my presidential address for the Southern Sociological Society. In the body of this book, I use this framework to organize my research on Millennials.

I then turn our attention directly to those young adults who came of age in the 21st century, most of whom remember 9/11 as history, and have never entered a plane without being frisked, nor lived in a world without personal computers. This is the generation of texting and sexting, of hooking up, and drifting after college. A generation as class divided as the rest of America, more ethnically diverse than any before it, and with such a late average age of marriage that they spend more time than any generation single, without spouses or children. Women are more likely than men to go to college, but still age up into a gender wage gap. Nearly all were raised by mothers who worked for pay, at least sometime during their childhood, and yet the women will face, as did their mothers, a maternal glass ceiling. The world has changed dramatically from their parents' and grandparents' youth, and yet, in some ways, much has remained the same, especially women's responsibility for the daily work of caretaking. Just how does the millennial generation understand gender today? These are young adults between 18 and 30, who came of age in the 21st century, that's why they have been labeled Millennials.[1] Are they children of the gender revolution or its foot soldiers? The research presented here is the first in-depth study of the Millennials and the gender structure they've inherited, how they experience it, and what, if anything, they may do to change it. The question to be answered in this book is how is the gender structure understood today by the Millennials? And will they change it? But before we can jump into that question, we must explore what others have written about both Millennials and what we know about the life-cycle stage we see them in at this moment. In chapter 3, we learn that psychologists have created a new name for this stage of life, emerging adulthood. Sociologists often call the same new stage young adulthood. Whatever we know now about Millennials, they may change as they age, and so we cannot know if we are seeing only a stage in their development or who they remain as a cohort, over their life cycles. In any case, there is a vigorous debate as to whether this generation is self-focused to the point of narcissism or the next great generation.

In chapter 4, I present the methodological information about who we studied, how we gathered the data, and how we did the analysis. The major finding, and the organization for the next few chapters, is that there are distinct strategies used by our respondents, so different that we had to separate them into four groups (*true believers, straddlers, innovators,* and *rebels*) to better understand what was going on in their lives or in the stories they told us about their lives. Some of our sample were *true believers* in the gender structure that they experienced, and they are presented in chapter 5. At the individual level, they were feminine women and masculine men, or tried to be. They grew up in families where they were socialized into traditional gendered norms and continue to be embedded in conservative social networks, particularly literalist religions, where women and men are expected to follow traditional sex-differenti-ated rules, especially regarding clothes and social demeanor. These *true believers* were unique among their peers for being involved in social institutions where they could identify rules that were different for women and men, their church, mosque, or syna-gogue. But these rules did not feel oppressive because they held ideological commit-ments to gender traditionalism, to men's leadership and women's nurturance. They believed gender was a legitimate category to organize social life.

Another group of young people were *innovators.* I present their stories in chapter 6. They were proud of not being bound by gender, by mixing traditionally masculine and feminine personality traits, skills, and hobbies. Many of them, although not all, were raised in liberal households, where girls were encouraged to be anything they wanted to be, to go beyond stereotypes. The young women did not feel that parents, or teachers, had expectations that boxed them into gendered categories, nor had any experienced social institutions, schools, or jobs, that differentiated between women and men. Now it is certainly the case that they may experience sexism in the future, as they try to balance work and family, but few felt such pressure now. The boys, however, did report gender policing when they broke gender norms, but they proceeded nonetheless and reported having found supportive social networks. None of the young *innovators* believed that women and men were that different or that men and women should live different kinds of lives. They held feminist ideolo-gies. The *innovators* did not reject sex categories, and none felt oppressed by being known as women or men, or presenting themselves as such. Another group, the *reb-els* did reject gender at the individual level, entirely. They were like the *innovators,* but more so. You will meet them in chapter 7. They are as proud as *innovators* that they have left behind traditional masculinity and femininity. If they encounter gen-dered expectations, they flaunt them, and they are vehemently against any social organization based on sex category. But they go further, in that they also reject a gendered presentation of the self. Many adopt the identity of genderqueer. *Rebels* do not let the body they have determine their personalities, social roles, the clothes they wear, or which bathroom they use.

In chapter 8, I introduce the largest group of respondents, the ones that are not so sure of themselves. I call them the *straddlers.* In every human group, those who are unsure of where they stand and have inconsistent opinions, are probably the majority. In this analysis, their answers straddle the different levels of the gender structure. They might be very proud that they are neither masculine nor feminine, but some of each, but then believe that men should be tough, and women nurturing. Some seem androgynous, but still endorse traditional views about how men and women should be. Another way these young adults straddle the gender structure is when a guy tries hard to fit into the gender expectations and be tough as he learns to hunt and wrestles. But then, when his girlfriend suggests that since she has a job, and he's still a junior in college, she should cover their expenses, he happily agrees. He may be very masculine on the individual level, but at the interactional level, get him talking about his feminist girlfriend and he's happy to be who she wants, to be the economically dependent partner in their dating relationship. Another example of a straddler is a woman who holds a literalist faith, strongly believes that God has ordained men to be heads of the household, but knows that she is really aggressive, and so plans to find a way to call the shots in her future family subtly from behind the scenes. These *straddlers* realize they live in a changing world and also realize that to be successful, they have to be flexible. Most of them are very gender libertarian, at least to the extent that whatever they believe and how ever they want to live, they do not want to impose their own choices on others. In chapter 9, I compare how these groups of Millennials are similar and different. I find some commonalities, such as a live and let live approach to life, that seem generationally characteristic. Another clear finding is that believing women belong in the home, primarily as domestic wives and mothers, is no longer part of the 21st-century gender structure. Even the *true believers* understand women and men are fundamentally attached to the labor force, although they realize mothers need flexibility to juggle their work lives around caretaking. Clearly, this is progress from the world where I grew up. My parents wanted me to be trained as a nurse or a teacher, just in case my husband ever left me, and I'd be forced into the labor force. In the world of my childhood, no one expected a white, middle-class married woman to work for pay. It wasn't in the cultural script. This is not a world Millennials even remember. But there is great variety beyond the agreement that women and men work for pay, and I trace some of the implications of the diversity toward the gender structure among Millennials.

In the conclusion, I move us beyond the data presented in this book. I return to the question about the gender revolution. Where is it now? I argue that Millennials may want to change it, but their focus on doing so as individuals may hamper their effectiveness. I end with a vision and advice for where I hope they will take the gender structure. I hope that they destroy it. Read on to understand why.

2

Gender as a Social Structure

TO UNDERSTAND GENDER among Millennials, we must first agree on how to conceptualize gender.[1] In this chapter, I present a way to think about gender that goes far beyond a personal identity, that is, *gender as a social structure*. I begin with an overview of how gender has been understood in the past, primarily from the point of view of social scientific research. My contribution is to synthesize past work. I begin with an explanation of previous research and theory and then to integrate them into the revised version of a theoretical framework I've been writing about for most of my career.

To start this journey, we will do a brief overview of the early and evolving biological theories that seek to explain sex differences. We then focus on the psychological theories that conceptualize gender as a personality trait, primarily as a property of individuals. After that, we move to understanding the battle between sociological theories that developed to challenge the presumption that gender was simply an individual characteristic. With this history in mind, I move to the integrative and intersectional frameworks that emerged toward the end of the last century, including my own. Despite the interdisciplinary and often conflicting research published in the last few decades, there is a coherent narrative of increasing sophisticated understanding of gender and sexual inequality. In many ways the research on gender is a case study that illustrates the scientific method. When empirical research did not support theoretical explanations, those explanations were revised, contextualized, and sometimes discarded. New theories emerged. In this chapter, we trace this journey. I end however with my own contribution, a multilevel integrative framework conceptualizing *gender as a social structure* with consequences for individual selves, interactional expectations of others, and institutions and organizations (Risman 1998; 2004; Risman and Davis 2013). We will then use my framework throughout this book to help understand where the Millennials might take us.

THE EVOLUTION OF BIOLOGICAL THEORIES FOR SEX DIFFERENCE

Endocrinologists, medical doctors with expertise on the production, maintenance, and regulation of hormones, have long believed masculinity and femininity were the result of sex hormones (Lillie 1939). William Blair Bell, a British gynecologist, first made this explicit in 1916 when he wrote: "the normal psychology of every woman is dependent on the state of her internal secretions, and . . . unless driven by force of circumstances—economic and social—she will have no inherent wish to leave her normal sphere of action" (1916, p. 129). This statement, as many written at the time, focused only on hormones as constraining factors in women's lives, as if men were not also biological beings. With the rise of science, gendered behaviors began to be justified by sex hormones rather than religion (Bem 1993). But then research showed more complexity, as it was discovered that the very existence of sex hormones in bodies did not distinguish male from female, but rather both sexes showed evidence of estrogen and testosterone, although in differential amounts (Evans 1939; Frank 1929; Laqueur 1927; Parkes 1938; Siebke 1931; Zondek 1934). Not only do men and women both have estrogen and testosterone coursing through their veins, but these hormones have effects far beyond sex or gender, including, but not limited to, the liver, bones, and heart (David et al. 1934). The possibility that sex hormones directly caused sex differences and only sex differences began to be suspect.

An all day long symposium held at the New England Psychological Association focused on new developments in sex research (Money, 1965). New developments included the suggestion that sex hormones during gestation create brain differentiation. That is, hormones in fetal development created masculine and feminine brains, and so were responsible for sex differences but indirectly (see also Phoenix et al. 1959). The brain began to be seen as responsible for sexual differentiation, as well as sexual orientation and gendered behaviors (Phoenix et al. 1959). Although arguments about male and female brains being different originated long ago, there has recently been a recent resurgence of such research (Arnold and Gorski 1984; Brizendine 2006; Cahill 2003; Collaer and Hines 1995; Cooke et al. 1998; Holterhus et al. 2009; Lippa 2005). By the end of the 20th century (see Cooke et al.'s 1998 review article) there was strong consensus that there were differences in male and female brains, but not clear evidence of those consequences (Diamond 2009, p. 625). Some researchers make the strong claim (Hrabovszky and Hutson 2002; Collaer and Hines 1995) that prenatal androgen exposure is strongly correlated with postnatal sex-typical behavior. Brain sex theories of the 21st century continue to maintain that brains are the intervening link between sex hormones and gendered behavior. Meta-analyses find little evidence for the right brain-left brain thesis to explain sex difference (Pfannkuche et al. 2009).

Research on sex-differentiated brains is not without its critics (Epstein 1996; Fine 2011; Fausto-Sterling 2000; Jordan-Young 2010; Oudshoorn 1994). For example, Jordan-Young (2010) conducted an analysis of over 300 brain sex studies and interviewed some of the scientists who conducted them. She concludes that brain organization research is so methodologically flawed that it does not pass the basic litmus tests for scientific research. Studies are based on inconsistent conceptualizations of "sex," gender, and hormones and when conceptualizations of one study are applied to another, findings are usually not replicated. A major deficiency of research on sex differences in human brains is that they lack reliability and depend on inconsistent definitions and measurement of concepts. In addition, much of this research is based on animals who arguably have less cultural influence on their lives than do most people. Fine (2011) reviews a wide range of studies and meta-analyses, and reports that close inspection shows little evidence even when the author claims otherwise. For example, she reviews Brizendine's (2006) claim that female brains are capable of greater empathy. She finds that the research supporting it includes five references, one published in Russian, one based on autopsies, and the others without comparative sex data. Similarly, Fine argues that while brain-imaging data shows some sex differentiation in brain tasks, there is no indication that actual performance on such tasks differed. Much research suggests the magnitude of sex differences are specific to particular racial or ethnic groups, or differ across social classes. For example, we know that skills that are often claimed to be sex differentiated, such as math, often differ quite dramatically across ethnicity and nationality.

In my own research (Davis and Risman 2014), I have explored claims that hormonal levels in utero constrain gender behavior throughout the life course (Udry 2000). We analyzed quite unusual data that measured fetal hormone level, and then measured hormones, attitudes, and behaviors decades later as that fetus became a girl and then a woman. We began this research absolutely convinced that previous findings by Udry (2000) were totally inaccurate because of invalid measurement. But our findings were not so simple as to confirm our original hypotheses. We did find inaccuracies in the earlier research, but despite our predictions, we found statistically significant effects of hormonal levels in utero on self-perception of personality traits often referred to as "masculine" or "feminine." Such effects, however, were far less strong than the earlier research had suggested and far less substantively powerful than the combined effects of remembered socialization experiences, adolescent plans, and adult social roles. This research has strengthened my conviction that we need a multilevel explanation for gender, including attention to individual level of analysis, bodies, and personality. What of women, on average, are more empathetic? First, individuals will, of course, vary tremendously. Second, whether empathy is rewarded is socially determined. The best physician, after all, just might be the one with the best bedside manner. Will she be rewarded for that skill?

In a sweeping review of the science of sex difference Wade (2013) explains that the science in the 21st century has moved far beyond a nature vs. nurture debate. In a truly paradigmatic shift, recent research has shown that environmental and social contexts affect our bodies just as our bodies affect human behavior. The new field of epigenetics suggests that a single gene can do many unpredictable things, and the effects of any genetic tendency depend on triggers in the environment. Research also suggests that environmental experiences, such as famine in one generation, may be detectable in the bodies of their grandchildren. Similarly, while fetal hormones may have some lasting effect on personality, we know that human activity changes the production of hormones as well. Testosterone increases with status. Men who compete in sports show increases in their testosterone, but not so much if they lose the game (Booth et al. 1989; 2006). Testosterone decreases when men are involved with young children (Gettler et al. 2011). What we do now know is that brain plasticity lasts far beyond the first year of life (Halpern 2012).

In a recent book, Fine (2017) also reviews the most recent literature on gender and biology and takes on the myth she labels as "testosterone rex," that is, the assumption that the effect of testosterone on male brain chemistry is what makes young boys into stereotypical males, and that its absence makes girls feminine. She shows that while testosterone definitely affects brains and bodies, it is not the driving force for competitive masculinity. Indeed she demonstrates that women can be as competitive and risk-taking as men. Instead of hormone-shaped brain structure determining behavior, entrenched attitudes are what is difficult to change and restrict women and men from adapting to the new social world. Fine argues persuasively that the social context influences our bodies just as our bodies influence our behavior. One clear piece of evidence is that the sexist strength of social norms slow down human adaptation to postmodern society, whatever the structure of our brains.

Our brains change when we learn new skills and is as social an organ as the rest of our bodies.

Sociologists now have powerful arguments against the naturalization of biological states. Finding evidence of a biological dimension to social stratification can no longer be used to argue that it is inevitable or neutral state of affairs. Nor can it be used to argue that it is irreversible, even within a single generation. The idea that some features of our biology are overwhelming immutable, difficult or impossible to change, is no longer a tenable position. (Wade 2013, p. 287)

Whatever ways biological factors influence human potential, we now know our social environment also influences our very biology. How biological potential is developed, shaped, and given meaning also depends on the social context. It is to this social context that we now turn.

SOCIAL SCIENCE DISCOVERS SEX AND GENDER

Few social scientists were concerned with issues of sex and gender before the middle of the 20th century, even though social activists during the Progressive Era were fighting for women's rights. Sociologists thought the traditional family helped society to function (e.g., Parsons and Bales 1955; Zelditch 1955) and addressed issues of gender when they wrote about women as the "heart" of families with male "heads." At the same time in history, psychologists (Bandura and Waters 1963; Kohlberg 1966) used socialization theory to explain how we could train girls and boys for their socially appropriate roles as men and women, husbands and wives. No one seemed to notice that many poor families and families of color did not have mothers who stayed home but were instead working in the labor force to help earn enough for the family to survive. Beyond sex-role socialization and family sociology, little research or theoretical writing focused on sex or gender, and almost none on inequality between women and men before the second wave of the feminist movement (Ferree and Hall 1996). Of course, then, the field literally exploded, perhaps due to the changing demography of the scientists. As women entered the academy there was more interest in, and attention to, women's lives, and eventually the impact of gender more fully (England et al. 2007).[2] While women still often hit a glass ceiling in academia as in other organizations, research on gender inequality proceeds fast and furiously.

HOW WE MEASURE PSYCHOLOGICAL "SEX ROLES" AND WHY IT MATTERS

Serious attempts to study sex and gender followed the movement of women into science, and the influence of the second wave of feminism on intellectual questions.

Psychologists (e.g., Bem 1981; Spence Helmreich, and Holahan, 1975) began to measure sex role attitudes using scales that had been first used in personality and employment tests (Terman and Miles 1936). These measures assumed that masculinity and femininity were opposite ends of one dimension, and thus if a subject was "high" on femininity, she was necessarily, by measurement design, "low" on masculinity. See Figure 2.1.

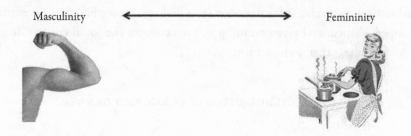

FIGURE 2.1 Unidimensional Measure of Gender

Research began to suggest, however, that measurement of femininity and masculinity as opposites did not accurately reflect actual experience (Locksley and Colten 1979; Pedhazur and Tetenbaum 1979; Edwards and Ashworth 1977). The evidence led Bem (1993; 1981) to offer a new way to think about gender that has become the gold standard in the social sciences; now so taken for granted that she is no longer even cited when these measures are used. Bem suggested that masculinity and femininity were actually two different personality dimensions. For example, an individual could be high on masculinity (which included feeling efficacious, strategic, logical) and also high on femininity (which included nurturance, empathy, warmth). Traditional women would be high on femininity and low on masculinity. Traditional men would be high on masculinity and low on femininity. An aggressive and agentic woman might be low on femininity and high on masculinity, or if she was also warm and nurturant, high on both masculinity and femininity. What makes this new way of thinking about gender revolutionary is that these personality traits are now divorced from the sex of the people that hold them. Women have femininity scores but so do men. Men have masculinity scores, but so do women. See Figure 2.2.

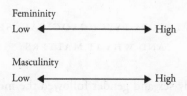

FIGURE 2.2 Masculinity and Femininity as Independent Measures

A decade of debate ensued on the best use of and measurement for this new conceptualization (Bem 1981; 1974; Spence, Helmreich, and Holahan 1975; Spence, Helmreich, and Stapp 1975; Taylor and Hall 1982; White 1979), but eventually it became the new consensus. Many psychologists favored combining the two scales into an androgyny measure, a label used for men and women who were high on both measures. These androgynous people were presumed to be more flexible and adaptive to a variety of social roles. Connell (1995) provides an excellent overview on the measurement of gender, with particular attention to masculinities. Questions can be asked about what kinds of gender expectations now exist, how people learn them, and if they become part of men's and women's personalities.

Recent psychological writing in this tradition (Choi et al. 2008; Choi and Fuqua 2003; Hoffman and Borders 2001) suggests that we should no longer use the words masculinity and femininity but rather move to descriptions of the personality concepts. The scale labeled masculinity measures efficacy/agency/leadership, and the femininity scale measures nurturance and empathy, and so we should label these measures descriptively, perhaps agency and nurturance (see Gill et al. 1987 for a formulation of this rhetorical critique). While I agree this linguistic change is the best trajectory for the future, I continue to use the language of masculinity and femininity in this book to follow the traditions in most social science. Indeed, in the conclusion, I will return to this suggestion and my utopian vision will incorporate the linguistic critique to disassociate these personality traits from labels that bring to mind biological sex categories. I will go even beyond that to suggest we do away with gender as a social structure as well.

The study of masculinity and femininity did not remain the province of psychologists focusing on personality. Social psychologists who studied stereotypes got into the game as well (Fiske 1993; Deaux and Major 1987; Heilman and Eagly 2008). Stereotypes can be categorized as descriptive—simply accurately portraying what "is"—or prescriptive—stereotypes that say what "should" be. Parents who hold prescriptive stereotypes about gender can influence children's development to become like the stereotype. But it is also the case that employers use stereotypes to disadvantage women in traditionally male occupations (Ely and Padavic 2007) and to disadvantage mothers who are stereotyped as unreliable workers. Fiske (2001) argues that when left unchecked, stereotypes create bias that can maintain power differentials and disparities.

SOCIOLOGISTS GET INVOLVED: FROM PERSONALITY TRAITS TO INEQUALITY

When sociologists first turned serious attention to sex and gender, we took the lead from psychologists before us and focused on the differences between individual women and men rooted in childhood sex role socialization (Lever 1974; Stockard and Johnson 1980; Weitzman 1979). Sociologists studied how babies assigned to the male category are encouraged to engage in masculine behaviors. They were offered boy-appropriate toys, rewarded for playing with them, and punished for acting in girlish ways. Babies assigned to the female category are encouraged to engage in feminine behaviors, and were limited to girl-appropriate toys, such as dolls and Easy Bake Ovens (Weitzman et al. 1972). The result of this endemic socialization is what creates the illusion that gender is naturally occurring. And so, the irony of strong socialization practices is that their end product appears to be the free choice of individuals for traditional gendered lives. Yet, the social pressure to conform to stereotypes, which is the socialization process itself, is a form of slow and subtle coercion and social reproduction of inequality. Early feminist research showed that female socialization disadvantages girls (Lever 1974), although even the research itself tended to value masculine traits over feminine ones. More recent research (Martin 1998; Kane 2006; 2012) also studies the ways in which gender becomes internalized into the self. Martin (1998) illustrates how boys' and girls' bodies are gendered by the practices of preschools. Kane's (2012) research on parenting shows that while many parents are concerned with their children being free from gender stereotypes, there is a limit to how free most parents want their boys to be to enact femininity. The implications of this sociological research, as somewhat different from the psychological research discussed above, is the concern with how gender is produced through interaction with children. Sociological emphasis focuses attention on how stereotypical beliefs about appropriate development are transmitted and also how children develop behaviors to avoid stigma. Children learn to be held accountable for developing appropriate gendered behaviors. A similarity between this sociological research and psychological studies is the assumption that at least one key to changing gender inequality is to focus on the raising of a new, and more free, generation.

Critiques of Sex Role Theory

Lopata and Thorne (1978) published a path-breaking and, by now, iconic article in which they argued that sociologists were ignoring the problematic implications of using the word "role" as in "sex or gender role." The word itself implies a functionality between complementary male and female lives. The very rhetoric of "role" requires us to think of a set of relationships with a useful complementarity void of questions of power and privilege. Would we ever use the language of "race roles" to explain the inequality between whites and blacks in American society? Other problems exist with the rhetoric of role as well. The language of "sex role" presumes a stability of behavior expected of women or men whether at home or work, whether young or old, across their racial and ethnic group (See Connell 1987; Ferree 1990; Lorber 1994; Risman 1998; 2004). Why would we expect a female litigator who is brash and aggressive in the courtroom to carry that behavior over with her to the nursery or even to the bedroom? Lorber's (1994) exhaustive review of gender research in the 20th century showed that there simply was no one role for women or men even in American society.

Sociologists rarely talk about gender roles anymore. Kimmel (2008) summarizes a widely held contemporary position when he writes, "sex role theory overemphasizes the developmental decisiveness of early childhood as the moment that gender socialization happens" (2008, p. 106). Sociologists now study gender beyond socialized selves. Whenever I review a manuscript for a sociological journal that uses the language of sex or gender roles, I immediately wonder if the author is up to date with his or her knowledge of the field.[3] In my student's papers (and manuscripts under review), I always strike out the language of "roles" and suggest a more nuanced, accurate concept. My hope is no one that reads this book will make that mistake again. It is not that the sociological concept of "social role" is itself a problem, just the presumption that there is one "gender role" in American society, or any society. Women are not expected to behave the same as mothers and wives, never mind as mothers and as litigators. That does not mean that there are not gendered expectations for litigators, such that when women behave as aggressively as men they are easily accepted as good colleagues. But those same women are expected to behave more aggressively as lawyers than as mothers or wives. Gendered expectations exist in every social role, but there is no one "gender role" that applies to women or men per se, and certainly not to women and men of different race, ethnicities, and classes.

Critiques of Gender Scholarship as White Women's Theory

From the very beginning of the second wave of feminism, women of color have been theorizing about gender as something beyond a personality characteristic, with a focus on how masculinity, femininity, and gender relations vary across ethnic communities and national boundaries. For example, Patricia Hill Collins (1990), Kimberlé Crenshaw (1989), Deborah King (1988), and Audre Lorde (1984) conceptualized gender as *an* axis of oppression intersecting with *other* axes of oppression including race, sexuality, nationality, ability, religion, and so forth. Feminists of color are critical of gender research or theory that positioned Western, white women as the "universal female subject" and race theories for situating men of color as the "universal racial subject." Nakano Glenn (1999) describes the situation as one where "[w]omen of color were left out of both narratives, rendered invisible both as racial and gendered subjects" (p. 3). Mohanty (2003) similarly critiqued feminist scholars for too often presuming that women of the Western, white world represented all women, instead of integrating a global perspective into their theories.

Although scholars labeled the experience, and ultimately the theory, of being oppressed in multiple ways across multiple dimensions with a variety of titles (e.g., intersectionality, womanism, multiracial feminism, etc.), they shared a goal of highlighting how the advantages or disadvantages of group membership, by gender, race, sexuality, class, nationality, and age, must be understood together and not cordoned off as if distinct domains of life (Collins 1990; Crenshaw 1989; Harris 1990; Mohanty 2003; Nakano Glenn 1999). In *Black Feminist Thought*, Patricia Hill Collins (2000) builds on earlier intersectionality work (e.g., Crenshaw 1989; Lorde 1984) by arguing for the "matrix of domination" as a concept that seeks to understand "how . . . intersecting oppressions are actually organized" to oppress marginalized individuals (2000, p. 16). Hill Collins moves beyond *acknowledging* various axes of oppression by challenging us to understand *how* individuals situated in various locations throughout the matrix of domination are differently oppressed. In a recent article, Wilkins (2012) illustrates how to do this, in a study of college students. Her research shows how African-American female college students use stories to construct identities where they come to see themselves as strong and independent black women, creating boundaries between themselves and both white women and black men. The implications of intersectional critiques of sex role theory bring a consideration of social context, and concern with racial inequality, to the study of sex and gender. No longer can research be entirely about "sex differences," as is differences weren't often a legitimation for inequality, and inequality didn't exist only between women and men but also across a variety of other cross-cutting dimensions, such as race, ethnicity, sexuality, and nation-states.

Moving Beyond Individuals

As sociologists began to study gender and inequality, we brought perspectives that focused on social context and found very little existed to help understand gender beyond a psychological trait. Several theoretical alternatives were developed by sociologists, some earlier than others. Those who studied social interaction and the meaning people gave to their face-to-face relationships with others developed a framework that came to be known as "doing gender." In 1987, West and Zimmerman published their now classic article arguing that gender is something we do, not who we are. They argued that men and women are judged immoral if we fail to *perform* our gender as expected, and the violence we see against transgender people certainly supports that argument. Other sociologists, those focused more on the study of inequality in social organizations such as businesses and families, used a structural explanation to understand sex differences at work. In 1977, Kanter's book *Men and Women of the Corporation* applied a structural framework (Mayhew 1980) to gender. Kanter's case study provided evidence that unequal opportunity available to men and women, the existence of elite male power, and the token number of women were responsible for gender inequality at work, not the sex-typical personalities of women and men. These two research trajectories developed independently. In fact, each tradition began by differentiating itself from the then widely accepted sex role paradigm but nearly ignored each other. I trace the development of each tradition. Somewhat later social psychologists brought status expectations research and psychological research on cognitive bias to the sociological study of gender (Ridgeway 2001; Ridgeway and Correll 2004). And finally, as sociology took a cultural turn at the end of the 20th century, concern has followed to understand the macro cultural logics that underpin gender inequality (Swidler 1986; Hays 1998; Blair-Loy 2005). See Figure 2.3 for an illustration of the sociological traditions.

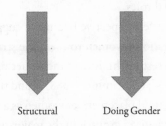

Structural   Doing Gender

FIGURE 2.3 From Sex Roles to Sociological Alternatives

The "Structural" Framework

This focus on structural explanations was a direct reaction to the focus purely on individuals (Mayhew 1980). Sociologists with this view argued that our field's obligation was to study how social structure determined human behavior directly rather than primarily through socialization. Kanter (1977) framed the contradiction between individual versus structural to suggest that the organization of the workplace, not the people employed, was the cause of sexual inequality in wages. Workers who held positions with less formal power and fewer opportunities for mobility are less motivated and ambitious at work, less perceived as promising leaders, and more autocratic bosses when they do enter the lower ranks of management. Kanter found that because women and men of color were then overwhelmingly in positions with limited power and opportunity, they came to portray these negative characteristics. They were then stereotyped as less motivated and effective leaders. In addition, when women and men of color were in leadership positions, they were usually tokens, and the imbalanced sex and race ratios in their workplaces meant they faced far greater scrutiny and negative evaluations. The evidence from Kanter's case study of a major home office of an insurance firm suggested that white majority men who were in positions with little upward mobility and low organizational power also fulfilled the stereotype of an ineffective micro-managing boss. Apparent sex differences in leadership style represented women's disadvantaged organizational roles, not their personalities. Kanter's work had much influence on the study of gender. In a massive meta-analysis of sex differences research, Epstein (1988) supported this purely social structural argument suggesting that most of the differences between men and women were the result of their social roles and societal expectations, and were really "deceptive distinctions" (the title of the book). If men and women were given the same opportunities and constraints, Epstein suggested that the differences between them would quickly vanish. In this argument, gender is more deception than reality. The core of this argument is gender-neutral. The same structural conditions create similar behavior among women and men; it is just that men and women are rarely allowed to fill the same social roles.

This is a politically seductive perspective because it suggests that progress can be made quickly. Change the ratio of women to men, the structure itself, and end sexism. Unfortunately, research testing this idea found something more complicated. In a review of studies about workplaces, Zimmer (1988) found that there was more to gender inequality than the structural placement of women as a subordinate group. Given this gender-neutral theory, whatever group is in the majority would be most powerful, and the group in the minority would be disadvantaged. But when men are the minority group in a workplace, they are not marginalized, they remain advantaged. Research suggested that male nurses become hospital administrators. Male teachers quickly become principals. They ride glass escalators to the top (Williams 1992). Of course, not all men. More recent research suggests that only white men ride his glass escalator to the top while men of color in female-dominated positions are left on the ground floor (Wingfield 2009). Thus, both racial and gender statuses are embedded as disadvantage in organizations. Other research, suggests that male advantage extends to every kind of organization, whether women are tokens or not (Budig 2002).

This new focus on structural explanations was soon applied to research on families. I based my dissertation, "Necessity and the Invention of Mothering," on Kanter's theory. I hypothesized that differences between mothering and fathering were entirely based on mothers being expected to be the primary caretaker. I searched for men who were expected to take care of their kids alone, widowers and men deserted by their wives. I compared them with single mothers, married fathers, and married mothers on their femininity and masculinity, but also on their household labor, childrearing techniques and parent-child intimacy. I hypothesized that the single dads would be just like the single moms. My findings (Risman 1987) were far more complicated. The single dads were more like the moms on some variables. The single fathers described themselves as more feminine (e.g., nurturing and empathetic) than did the other fathers, showing that personality traits are malleable in changing circumstances. But despite men being primary caretakers, there remained statistically significant differences from mothers on a variety of items, including their masculinity scores and parenting measures. They were often more like mothers than other men, but not just like mothers. Other research on families also partially supported structural explanations. In a study based on life histories of baby boomer American women, Gerson (1985) found that women's socialization and adolescent preferences did not predict their strategy for the "hard choices" (the title of the book) made on how to balance work and family commitments. The best explanations for whether women "chose" domestic or work-focused lives were marital stability and success in the labor force. Here the structural conditions of everyday life proved more important than feminine selves but not the only explanation of importance.

Most research about husband and wives testing the importance of structural factors to explain behavior has failed to provide solid evidence for a purely structural explanation for gendered behavior in families. Nearly all the quantitative research suggests that women continue to do more family labor than their husbands, even when they work outside the home as many hours per week and earn equivalent salaries (Davis and Greenstein 2013; Bittman et al. 2003; Bianchi et al. 2000). Tichenor's (2005) qualitative research provides strong empirical evidence that even high-earning wives who earn significantly more than their husbands are compelled by the cultural logic of intensive mothering to shoulder more of the family work. While Sullivan (2006) and Kan et al. (2011) show convincingly that trends have changed over time, with men doing ever more family labor as the decades progress, gender still trumps the structural variables of time and economic dependency when it comes to housework and care work (Risman 2011). If purely structural factors were responsible for gender inequality, we could simply redesign organizations and social roles, and women and men would all of a sudden be equal. The core of a structural argument is gender-neutral; the same structural conditions create behavior, regardless of whether men or women are filling the social roles. The implications of a purely structural theory is that if we move women into men's positions and men into women's positions, their behaviors will be identical and have similar consequences. We would expect male caretakers to "mother" just like women, and female politicians to lead and be followed just like male ones. But this we do not see.

We need to turn to something beyond purely social structural variables to explain the power of gender. This was apparent to sociologists who worked in a more interactionist tradition as well, and their story is told in the next section.

"Doing Gender"

During the same era as the structural frameworks were offered, the importance of symbolic interactionism and face-to-face interaction for the understanding of gender was also becoming clear. In 1987, West and Zimmerman published their path-breaking article in which they argued gender is something we do, not who we are. West and Zimmerman (1987) suggested that we are held accountable to "do" gender and are held to be immoral if we do not do so. They distinguished sex, sex category, and gender from one another in a way that illustrated the importance of how we perform gender to prove our sex category. An individual's *sex* is assigned according to socially defined biological distinctions, usually at birth. *Sex category*, on the other hand, is what we claim to others, and used as a proxy for sex. Sex category depends on performing gender appropriately to be accepted as claimed and does not always coincide with one's biological sex. Sex category is established through what we display on our body, including but not limited to body language, clothing, hairstyles, and appropriate behavior. That is, to claim a sex category, women and men have to *do gender*. By conceptualizing gender as something that we do, West and Zimmerman (1987) drew attention to the ways in which behaviors are enforced, constrained, and policed during social interaction.

West and Zimmerman's (1987) doing gender perspective is similar to Judith Butler's theory of performativity (Butler 1990; 2004). They share a focus on the creation of gender by the activity of the actor. But they differ on the reality of whether there is a "real" self beneath the "doing" of gender. Social scientists study the flexibility of the self, the socially constructed self, but usually presume some version of a self does exist, if only temporarily. On the other hand, Butler (1990; 2004), a philosopher and queer theorist, writes about the self as if it is more imaginary than socially constructed. Queer theorists such as Butler have added to the discussion of "doing gender" in critical ways, helping to sharpen the attention to "performativity."

The "doing gender" framework has become perhaps the most common perspective in contemporary sociological research. By 2016, West and Zimmerman's article has been cited over 8,500 times since its publication in 1987. And yet, gender is not easily described by one version of masculinity and femininity. Researchers have described a myriad of ways that girls and women do femininities, from "intensive mothering" (Hays 1998; Lareau 2003) to "femme" lesbians appropriating traditional emphasized symbols of womanhood such as heels and hose (Levitt et al. 2003), to Latina girls negotiating safe-sex (Garcia 2012), to African-American girls walking a thin line between good and ghetto (Jones 2009). The evidence has moved us beyond gender "roles" to the many ways people do gender. The work by Martin (2003) and Pioggio (2006) highlight the "practice turn" (Poggio 2006, p. 229) in gender studies, adding complexity to the interactionist tradition by showing how gender is practiced in workplace organizations. For example, Gherardi and Poggio (2007) show how interactional dynamics change when the first woman enters a male-dominated and masculinized work setting, exposing the lie that the working behaviors that had been happening before her arrival were gender-neutral.

Men "doing gender" has become its own field of study. Connell (1995) high-lighted how ranking one's masculinity as "hegemonic" creates inequality between men. Hegemonic masculinity is defined as the practice that embodies the culturally accepted "best" and most powerful version of masculinity. Men from marginalized groups, by class or race or sexuality, who did not have access to the powerful social position needed to "do" hegemonic masculinity are disadvantaged gender players, subordinated, if not as much as many women. Historically, homosexual men have been excluded from even the possibility of hegemonic masculinity. But recently, Anderson (2012) has suggested that the homophobia in Western societies has dimin-ished enough that a variety of masculinities now exist horizontally without neces-sarily one being ranked better than others, diminishing the ways that homosexuality stigmatizes men. Clear consensus exists that there are as many masculinities as femi-ninities, and they differ from group to group, and even within one social context.

There has been some criticism, including my own, of the vagueness as to what counts as evidence of "doing gender." Deutsch (2007) suggested that when research-ers find unexpected behaviors, rather than question whether gender is being "undone," they simply claim to discover yet another variety of femininity and mas-culinity. The too wide usage of "doing gender" to explain nearly anything women or men do creates conceptual confusion as we study a world that is indeed changing (Risman 2009). The finding that we may be doing gender even when it doesn't look like we expect is problematic. Fundamentally, we must know what we are looking for when we are studying gendered behavior and then be willing and ready to admit when we do not find it. Why label new behaviors adopted by groups of boys or girls as alternative masculinities and femininities simply because the group itself is composed of biological males or females? If young women strategically adopt tra-ditionally masculine behaviors to fit the moment, is this really doing gender, or is it destabilizing the activity, and decoupling it from biological sex? As marital norms become more egalitarian, we need to be able to differentiate when husbands and wives are doing gender and when they are at least trying to undo it. Similarly, as more opportunities open for girls to be athletic and success oriented, we need to describe how they are remaking their lives rather than merely inventing a label for a new kind of femininity that includes whatever they are doing now. This is not to suggest that we ignore the evidence of multiple masculinities and femininities that do exist and vary by class, ethnicity, race, and social location. Nor should we underestimate those instances when doing gender simply changes form without diminishing male privilege. But we must pay careful attention to whether our research is documenting different kinds of gender or whether it is being undone. After all, if anything people with female identities do is called femininity and anything people with male identities do is masculinity, then "doing gender" becomes tautological.

As the strengths, and weaknesses, of these sociological alternatives became clear, research and theory continued to develop. Three distinct theories have been offered to further understand gender sociologically. Social psychologists brought status expectations research and psychological research on cognitive bias to the sociological study of gender (Ridgeway 2001; Ridgeway and Correll 2004). While the focus here is also on social interaction, as is "doing gender," here the research is often experimental and the concern more directly for the power of social status to shape expectations. Second, as sociology took a cultural turn at the end of the 20th century, focused shifted to the macro cultural logics that underpin gender inequality (Swidler 1986; Hays 1998; Blair-Loy 2005). And finally, as LGBTQ rights have grown, and sexuality studies flourished, scholars have brought queer theory (e.g. Butler 1990) to sociology and renewed our interest in the complicated ties between sexuality and gender (Schilt and Westerbrook 2009; Pascoe 2007). See Figure 2.4 for a summary.

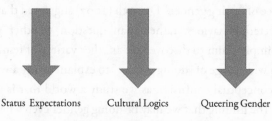

Status Expectations   Cultural Logics   Queering Gender

FIGURE 2.4 (More) Contemporary Sociological Perspective

Status Expectations Framing Gender

The interactional expectations that create gender can neither be reduced to feminine and masculine personalities nor to "doing gender" to meet moral accountability. Some of the reproduction of gender inequality can be traced to how we all use gender to frame what we see, a process by which we subconsciously categorize people and react to them based on the stereotypes attached to the category (Fiske 1998; Fiske and Stevens 1993; Ridgeway 2011). The gender-framing perspective posits that gender exists as a background identity that we use cognitively to enforce interactional expectations of one another. We use gender framing to shape or explain our own behavior as well (Ridgeway and Correll 2004; 2006). We take the expectation that men are good at leadership and women at empathy and nurturance into every new setting. Such expectations create gendered behavior even in settings that are novel and might be expected to allow more freedom from gender.

When gender is used in this way, as a frame for cognition, we invoke established culturally acceptable gender norms as a reference to new situations and new kinds of relationships. Gender then becomes the engine of reproducing inequality between women and men (Ridgeway and Correll 2004). The interactional expectations attached to gender as a status category (Ridgeway 2011) are particularly powerful around nurturing, empathy, and caring. We expect women, and women come to expect themselves, to be morally responsible for care work. Thus, gender remains a powerful cognitive bias at the interactional level of analysis, even when it is not internalized into feminine and masculine selves. We expect high-achieving women to mold their work around mothering (Tichenor 2005), just as we expect poor women of color to love the children they take care of for pay (Nakano Glenn 2010). The presumptions that women are more nurturant than men, and men more agentic than women remain strongly embedded in our culture and well established in Western societies across a wide variety of dimensions (Ridgeway 2011). The implications of this theory are clear. To move toward gender equality we must change the expectations that are attached to the status of male and female. Or perhaps, with more difficulty, erase the importance of status male and female entirely.

Cultural Logics

Acker (1990; 1992) transformed gender theorizing when she applied the cultural logic of gender to workplaces instead of to the individuals in them. Instead of gender-neutral organizational structure, she illustrated how gender is deeply embedded in organizational design. While Kanter (1977) explained sex differences at work as the result of women occupying lower positions in an organization, Acker (1990; 1992) argued that the very definition of jobs and organizational hierarchies are gendered, constructed to advantage men or others who have no caretaking responsibilities. Acker wrote "the term 'gendered institutions' means that gender is present in the processes, practices, images, and ideologies, and distributions of power in the various sectors of social life" (1992, p. 567). Acker contended there is little place for those (historically women) who hold positions as caretakers outside the workplace to fulfill elite ranks of modern corporations, as it is the abstract worker who "is actually a man, and it is the man's body . . . that pervades work and organizational processes" (Acker, 1990, p. 152). While creating opportunity for women to enter the workplace may increase their overall numbers within an organization, Acker argues it will not confront the underlying sexism that blocks women's success. Recently Anne-Marie Slaughter (2015) has made a similar argument. Women cannot "have it all" according to Slaughter because "all" requires you to be a person who doesn't care for anyone at all, not even much self-care. Workplaces that require 24/7 commitment presume that workers have wives, or do not need them. In other words, patriarchy is built into our organizational design. Of course, some privileged women indeed enter masculine spaces by outsourcing their domestic labor to other less privileged women (MacDonald 2011; Nakano Glenn 2010) and so manage a lifestyle that approximates a male experience. Slaughter argues, however, that even very privileged caretakers, like herself, still have to face expectations that no peak periods of intense caretaking should ever impinge on paid labor, and even elite women's lives have to change to accommodate children or elderly parents. This new understanding of gendered work organizations helped push forward a re-emergence of attention to organizational culture.

At the same time, we have seen a renewed emphasis on understanding the importance of culture for understanding all human behavior, including gender, in our more intimate relationships. Swidler's (1986) reconceptualization of culture as a "tool kit" of habits and skills from which people can construct "strategies of action," rather than internalized stable personalities, has had a terrific influence on the study of gender. For example, in a study of diverse women by class and employment status, Hays (1998) found that their belief in the need for intensive mothering set the boundaries of parenting strategies for employed and unemployed mothers. Similarly, Blair-Loy (2005) finds that even very highly paid executives are sometimes pushed out of the labor force by the conflict they perceive between competing devotions to work and intensive mothering. These cultural logics are not only imposed upon women as mothers but also are adopted by women themselves, perhaps through gender socialization and through the adoption of cultural beliefs. Pfau-Effinger (1998) suggests cultural beliefs can best explain the empirical differences by which women in different European countries balance work and motherhood, and that we ignore cultural beliefs about femininity at our own peril. The cultural value of femininity has been renewed as a topic of interest (Schippers 2007). Whether to refocus on cultural beliefs in gender is hotly debated. Rojek and Turner (2000) describe the cultural turn in sociology as merely "decorative" and a distraction from the study of inequality. But I see a return to the meanings and tool kits available to do gender, and to undo it, as very useful in understanding gender as a social structure, which is about inequality, and a topic to which we soon turn. Gender theory has been profoundly influenced by a cultural turn in sociology, by an intersectionality framework, and most recently, by queer theory. While sociologists have offered these alternative ways to understand gender, interdisciplinary feminist and queer studies have also offered insights.

Questions of how gender patterns are racialized; how they vary by nationality, sexuality, and ethnicity; and how they are culturally experienced are now of central concern to the sociology of gender. Queer theory takes us a step beyond an intersectional analysis. Although sexuality has been linked to gender inequality from the very start of second-wave feminist theorizing (MacKinnon 1982; Rich 1980), queer theory goes beyond this by positing sexuality as central to our very conceptualization of gender. Butler (1990) argues that the "heterosexual matrix" and heternormativity is inextricably intertwined with gender inequality. Heteronormativity presumes there are and can only be two genders, and they "ought" to be opposite and attracted to one another. Crawley et al. (2007) show how bodies are gendered by the social processes involved in turning biological sex into gender conformity with presumptions that normality requires opposite genders to desire each other. Schilt and Westbrook (2009) shape our understanding of heteronormativity by examining what happens when trans people disrupt the presumed consistency between sex, gender, and sexuality. In contemporary American society, transgender people who display "cultural genitalia" that allowed them to "pass," to be accepted in their workplaces. In the public sphere, "doing gender" is how one signifies "sex." In fact, transgender men may receive the dividends of masculine privilege in their workplaces after they transition (Schilt 2011). But when transgender people are met in more sexual or even in a private setting, such as a bathroom, violence and harassment often ensues. In fact, transwomen are often killed in intimate encounters. Schilt and Westbrook (2009) argue that these different reactions to transgender people show how gender and (hetero) sexuality are interrelated. They argue that gender inequality relies on the presumption of two and only two opposite sexes, identified by biology alone. As they write:

> This sex/gender/sexuality system rests on the belief that gendered behavior, (hetero) sexual identity and social roles flow naturally from biological sex, creating attraction between two opposite personalities. This belief maintains gender inequality as "opposites"—bodies, bender, sexes- cannot be expected to fulfill the same social roles, and so, cannot receive the same resources. (p. 459)

Westbrook and Schilt (2014) go further to suggest that there are two processes involved in the construction of gender, both "doing gender" and others "determining gender." They argue that determining gender is done both in interaction and also by social policy and legislation. In contemporary society, identity claims to gender are usually accepted in public spaces. But when claims are made to a gender that is not consistent with biological sex ascribed at birth, "public panics" often ensue and biological criterion invoked. These "bathroom bills" where transgender people are required to use the restroom of their birth certificate are examples of the panic that follows determining gender in private spaces. Westbrook and Schilt's theoretical argument is that such panics exist to publically reaffirm a binary, to publically promote the belief that biological sex differences are the primary distinction between women and men, and that this distinction legitimates the rhetoric of protecting women which actually promotes their subordination. It is as if these sociologists, writing years before, had predicted the bathroom bills passed in 2016 by the City of Houston and the States of Mississippi and North Carolina. The panic over private places shows the continuing need to pay attention to how gender and sexuality are intertwined.

Pascoe (2007) furthers the conversation that brings sexuality necessarily into gender studies in her research on masculinity in high school. She focuses how sexuality is an organizing principle of social life that helps construct the very meaning of masculinity. She defines sexuality not only as erotic acts or even as identity but also as public meanings associated with gender. For example, while heterosexuality involves sexual desire, and an identity of being straight, it also confers all sorts of citizenship rights and involves the eroticization of male dominance and female submission. Teenage boys publically claim their romantic power over girls. This is hardly something boys necessarily mature beyond. Even in this day and age, women must wait for men to propose, and this act of waiting to be chosen is the very marker of feminine dependency and subordination (Robnett and Leaper 2013).

Queer theory destabilizes the assumed naturalness of gender and sexual categories (Seidman 1996; Warner 1993) and brings a frame to gender studies that focuses on how social practices produce the categories we take for granted, male and female, woman and man, gay and straight. As Pascoe (2007) writes, "queer theory emphasizes multiple identities and multiplicity in general. Instead of creating knowledge about categories of sexual identity, queer theorists look to see how those categories themselves are created, sustained and undone" (p. 11). This new sensitivity to the construction of categories brings us to the implicit possibility of deconstructing them. And this possibility of moving beyond the categories, beyond gender itself, will be central to my conclusions about where we should be heading in a search for gender equality.

INTEGRATIVE THEORIES

We have thus far covered alternative theories for understanding gender, those focused on how we are socialized to internalize gender-specific traits and those that explain how gender is organized by the expectations of others, either when they are in the room or by cultural stereotypes. We have focused on the alternative case for the power of social structural organization and cultural beliefs versus the power of stereotypes, versus the power of socialization to create gendered selves. At the end of the last century, Browne and England (1997) made a plea to stop thinking about these explanations as either/or. They argued convincingly that every theory presumes some process by which oppression is internalized and becomes part of the self. And every theory about the self requires an understanding of social organization. Theories about gender are not either/or, but have to be, to use a phrase coined by Collins (1998), "both/and." The integrative theories discussed below are all, to some degree, multidisciplinary, and while focusing on gender as a system of stratification, include a concern with how oppression becomes internalized and part of the self. In recent writing, England (2016) returns to this theme, reminding us that powerful inequality is socially structured to get inside of us, and so may become internalized oppression. To study the effects of internalized oppression on individuals is not to deny the social structure, or to "blame the victim," but to acknowledge the power of the social structure to influence our consciousness.

Toward the end of the 20th century, a conceptualization of gender as a stratification system that exists beyond individual characteristics (e.g., Connell 1987; Lorber 1994; Martin 2004; Risman 1998; 2004) and varies along other axes of inequality (e.g., Collins 1990; Crenshaw 1989; Ingraham 1994; Mohanty 2003; Nakano Glenn 1992; 1999) became the new consensus. The labeling of gender as a stratification system makes explicit that gender is not just about difference but also about the distribution of power, property, and prestige. Most social scientists embraced the definition of gender as not merely a personality trait, but as a social system that restricts and encourages patterned behavior and involves inequality. I briefly discuss several of these leading multidimensional gender frameworks (e.g., Connell 1987; Lorber 1994; Martin 2004; Risman 2004; Rubin 1975) before presenting my own gender as a social structure and using it to help us understand how gender operates in the lives of today's Millennials.

A multilevel understanding of gender isn't really new. In her 1975 essay, Gayle Rubin argued that sexual inequality was a kind of political economic oppression, what she termed the sex/gender system. R. W. Connell (1987) pushed the idea further in her book *Gender and Power* with the argument that we must "think of gender as being also a property of collectivities, institutions and historical processes" (p. 13). She emphasized that gender is a process, not a static entity. Connell proposed that each society has a gender order, composed of gender regimes, with gender relations being distinct within each social institution. Thus, a gender regime in workplaces might be more or less sexist than a gender regime within heterosexual families. And within each gender regime, Connell suggested that three domains existed: labor, power, and cathexis. A very useful and important idea emerged from this work: gender regimes within the same society might be complementary, but not always, and inconsistency between them can be the site where "crisis tendencies" emerge and social change more likely.

Lorber (1994) uses the language of social institution to develop an integrative theory about gender. She highlights inequality between men and women in every aspect of life from domestic work, to family life, religion, culture, and the workplace. Lorber concluded that gender, as a historically established institution, has created and perpetuated differences between men and women in order to justify inequality. Although Lorber (1994; 2005) presents gender as a social institution, she believes it can be overcome. I build on her work, as Lorber challenges us to eliminate gender inequality by doing away with it (Lorber, 1994, p. 294). Gender equality can only occur when all individuals are guaranteed equal access to valued resources and, according to Lorber, when society is "de-gendered".

One of the major benefits of multilevel integrative theories is that they move us beyond a warfare theory of science. In a traditional 20th-century scientific model, theories are tested against one another, with winners and losers. Scientists are incentivized to do this kind of research because the holder of the winning theory improves her career. But that doesn't mean that we learn more about the topic. Indeed, in our attempt to understand society that changes constantly, we must move beyond that kind of science. We need to look for complicated answers to complex questions, realizing we are studying processes, not product, as the social world is constantly reinventing itself. The analyses we make may influence the world we study. Indeed, as feminist social scientists we hope so.

My work adds a brick to the wall built by all these scholars who came before me. I am privileged to stand on the shoulder of giants, those first generation of feminist scholars who made possible the study of gender, and those who came after, who built the blocks for me to use to weave an integrative multidisciplinary theory for gender. In this chapter, I have taken you on a quick walk through the myriad theories used to understand gender inequality. As you will soon see, my theory is mostly about assembling parts first conceived by others. I've spent so much time on the research and theorizing that has come before, because I use most of it, but move beyond them with my attempt at integration.

I conceptualize *gender as a social structure* with social processes that occur at the individual, interactional, and macro levels, and with explicit acknowledgement that each level of analysis is equally important, and that the world we live in is like a game of dominoes, when one part changes, it can set off a chain reaction. My hypothesis is that there is a dynamic, recursive causality between individual selves, interactional expectations, and macro cultural ideology and social organization. Change one part of it, and get ready to see that change reverberate. Thus far, I have traced the story about how toward the end of the 20th century, feminist theorists began to move beyond debating whether gender was best understood as internalized selves or externally constrained oppression and began developing theories that encompassed what Collins (1990) describes as a both/and theory of science—multilevel theories for gender as sexual stratification system and not merely psychological characteristics of individuals (Butler 2004; Connell 1987; Ferree and Hall 1996; Lorber 1994; Martin 2004; Risman 2004). Now I weave the previous work into my conceptualization of gender as a social structure. While I have been writing about this for nearly two decades, in this book I am revising the framework by distinguishing material and cultural elements.

I refer to gender as a social structure because this shows how gender is as systemic as politics and economics. While the language of structure suits my purposes, it is not ideal because despite common usage in sociological discourse, no definition of the term "structure" is widely shared. Some might argue that the linguistic term "structure" suggests macro to micro causation, but if so, I intend to disrupt such a definition. I choose to use the word "structure" rather than system or institution or regime to situate gender as central to a society's core organization as the economic structure and the political structure. All definitions of structure share the presumption that social structures exist outside individual desires or motives and that social structures at least partially explain human actions (Smelser 1988). To that extent, nearly all sociologists are structuralists. Beyond that however, consensus dissipates. Blau (1977) focused solely on the constraint collective life imposes on the individual. In their influential work, Blau and his colleagues (e.g., Blau 1977; Rytina et al. 1988) argue that the concept of structure is trivialized if it is located inside an individual's head in the form of internalized norms and values. Blau focused solely on the constraint collective life imposes on the individual; structure must be conceptualized, in his view, as a force opposing individual motivation. This definition of "structure" imposes a clear dualism between structure and action, with structure as constraint and action as choice.

Constraint is, of course, an important function of structure, but to focus only on structure as constraint minimizes structural importance. Not only are women and men coerced into differential social roles; they also often choose their gendered paths within socially structured imagined possibilities. England (2016) shows how this works for low-income women. Poverty directly reduces their access to upward mobility and to the means to control their own fertility. But the social structure, their poverty alone, does not determine their sexual practices. The social structure is internalized as well. These young women report a low sense of efficacy, and little feeling of control over their own lives. Such a sense of diminished efficacy leads to less consistent use of birth control. The consequences of inconsistent contraception are obvious, unplanned pregnancies that further diminish their options. This is a powerful example of how the social structure is internalized in ways that further exacerbate gender inequality.

A social structural analysis, rather than only be concerned with external constraints, must also help us understand how and why actors choose one alternative over another. A structural theory of action suggests that actors compare themselves and their options to those in structurally similar positions (Burt 1982). From this viewpoint, actors are purposive, rationally seeking to maximize their self-perceived well-being under social structural constraints. As Burt (1982) suggests, one can assume that actors choose the best alternatives without presuming they have either enough information to do it well or the options available to make choices that actually do serve their interests. In his view, structure is fixed, but it does provide choices. For example, married women may choose to do considerably more than their equitable share of childcare rather than have their children do without whatever "good enough" parenting means to them if they perceive it unlikely the children's father or anyone else will pick up the slack. While actions are a function of interests, the ability to choose is patterned by the social structure. Burt (1982) suggests that norms develop when actors occupy similar network positions in the social structure and evaluate their own options vis-à-vis the alternatives of similarly situated others. From such comparisons, both norms and feelings of relative deprivation or advantage evolve. Notice the phrase "similarly situated others" above. As long as women and men see themselves as different kinds of people, then women will be unlikely to compare their life options to those of men. Therein lies the power of gender.

In a world where sexual anatomy is used to dichotomize human beings into types, the differentiation itself diffuses both claims to and expectations for gender equality. The social structure is not experienced as oppressive if men and women do not see themselves as similarly situated. As discussed above, when purely structural perspectives have been applied to gender in the past (Epstein 1988; Kanter 1977), there has been a fundamental flaw in the logic. Generic structural theories applied to gender presume that if women and men were to experience identical material conditions, empirically observable gender differences would disappear. This ignores not only internalized gender at the individual level but also both the interactional expectations that remain attached to women and men because of their gender category and the cultural logics and ideologies embedded in society-wide stereotypes. A structural perspective on gender is accurate only if we realize that gender itself is a structure deeply embedded in society, within individuals, in every normative expectation of others, and within institutions and cultural logics at the macro level.

I build on Giddens's (1984) structuration theory with its emphasis on the recursive relationship between social structure and individuals. In his view, social structures shape individuals, but simultaneously, individuals shape the social structure. Giddens embraces the transformative power of human action. He insists that any structural theory must be concerned with reflexivity and actors' interpretations of their own lives. Social structures not only act on people; people also act on social structures. Indeed, social structures are created not by mysterious forces but by human action. When people act on structure, they do so for their own reasons. We must, therefore, be concerned with why actors choose their acts. Actions alter the world we have entered; institutions are powerful but not determinative. And often institutions and the choices they offer conflict with one another. Such conflicts spark individual and collective mobilization that changes the status quo. Giddens insists that concern with meaning must go beyond the verbal justification easily available from actors because so much of social life is routine and so taken for granted that actors will not articulate, or even consider, why they act.

Connell (1987) applies Giddens's (1984) concern with social structure as both constraint and created by action in her treatise on gender and power (see particularly chapter 5). In this analysis, structure constrains action, yet "since human action involves free invention . . . and is reflexive, practice can be turned against what constrains it; so structure can deliberately be the object of practice" (Connell 1987; 1995). Action may turn against structure but can never escape it. We must pay attention both to how structure shapes individual choice and social interaction and to how human agency creates, sustains, and modifies current structure. Action itself may change the immediate or future context. In this theory of gender as a social structure, I integrate this notion of causality as recursive with attention to gender consequences at multiple levels of analysis. Ahearn (2001) succinctly summarizes the reasons that Giddens's theory is so important for understanding both constraints and agency:

> In the theory of structuration is the understanding that people's actions are shaped (in both constraining and enabling ways) by the very social structures that those actions then serve to reinforce or reconfigure. Given this recursive loop consisting of actions influenced by social structures and social structures (re)created by actions, the question of how social change can occur is crucial. (p. 118)

I incorporate his dialectical paradigm into my argument as I am concerned with the structural forces that seem inescapable—and, at the very least, create patterned social behavior—and the structuring of choices that men and women are free to make and the meaning they make of them. I explore the mechanisms by which such constrained choices sometimes change the social structure, and sometimes reinforce it; the reasons for and pace of that change are my central questions. Any concern with the dialectical relationship between structure and agency must by necessity be concerned with the meanings people give to their choices.

The resurgence of cultural sociology toward the end of the 20th century has brought questions of meaning back into theories concerned with the social structure. Swidler's (1986) argument that we conceptualize culture as a tool kit clarifies the importance of culture without defining culture as opposed to structure, but as one important component of it. We have toolboxes of cultural knowledge at our fingertips to help make sense of the world around us; the knowledge exists whether or not it is internalized as aspects of the self. Sometimes this knowledge is so common as to become habit. Béland (2009) has shown how gender scholars (such as Stryker and Wald 2009; and Padamsee 2009) have contributed to understanding the importance of ideas on social policy, as gender ideology plays an important role in understanding cross-national variation.

The cultural component of the social structure—gender as ideological beliefs— also incorporates the interactional expectations that each of us bring to, and also meet head on, in every social encounter. Actors often behave without thinking about it, simply following habits that come to define the cultural meaning of their lives. And yet, they are still knowledgeable agents who can and sometimes do reflexively monitor their own actions. The taken-for-granted and often unacknowledged conditions of action shape behavior, but do so as human beings reflexively monitor the intended and unintended consequences of their action, sometimes reifying the structure, and sometimes changing it. My work builds on Hays (1988) argument:

> A conception of structure as more than a pattern of material, objective, and eternal constraints engendering human passivity; for a conception of agency as more than action that is un-structured, individual, subjective, random and implying absolute freedom; and for a conception of culture as a part of social structure. (p. 58)

As Hays notes, agency depends on structure, including the cultural meanings that are at the core of the social structure. Just as we must constantly acknowledge that structure is a social construction, it is also the case that social structure produces certain kinds of people. Social structure is both enabling and constraining (Hays 1998; Giddens 1984). The cultural trend in sociology (Swidler 1986; Schippers 2007; Hays 1998) helps improve my earlier conceptualizations of gender as a social structure by suggesting to me that at each level of the gender structure we must identify both cultural processes and material conditions. While I will delve into the material and cultural aspects of the gender structure below, I want to differentiate them here simply by referring to culture as ideological processes, that is, meanings given to bodies and legitimation for organizational rules and regulations faced in daily life. Material conditions include bodies themselves and the rules that distribute physical rewards and constraints in a historical moment. Only when we pay attention to both culture and material reality can we begin to identify under what conditions and how bodily difference becomes inequality embedded within a gender structure. See Figure 2.5, which summarizes the model.

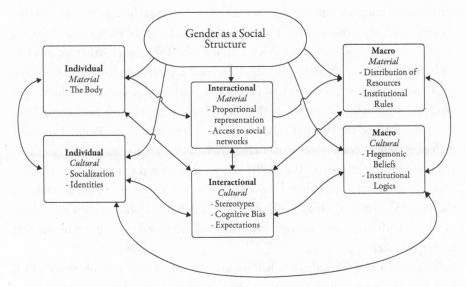

FIGURE 2.5 Gender as a Social Structure Model of Gender as Structure

To understand how gender stratification is produced and reproduced, and sometimes decreased, from generation to generation, we need understand the breadth and depth of the power of gender as a social structure. Thus we should not to ask *whether* gender is best conceptualized as an individual trait, on the interactional level, or as embedded in organizational rules and cultural beliefs. But rather, we need to build a full picture of the complexity of gender as a structure. We need to use empirical research to study the alternative strength of individual selves versus cultural expectations versus organizational design, as explanations for particular questions, or moments in time, or identified dependent variables. We learn more by approaching every empirical question with complexity, a concern for each level of analysis—the individual, the interactional, and organizational, and the recursive relationships between them. We must be concerned with the recursive relationship between cultural and material processes at each level and across levels of the gender structure. As Hay (1994) argues, we need to understand that structure not only limits us but also helps us create a sense of self, gives us tools for action, and therefore makes agency—and social change that might result from it—possible.

Every society has a *gender structure*, a means by which bodies are assigned a sex category from which gender as inequality is built. A gender structure has implications for individuals, their identities, personalities, and therefore the choices they make. The individual level of analysis has long been of interest to social scientists and often presumed to be at least partly the explanation for gender patterns, and therefore inequality. But the power of the gender structure goes far beyond the shaping of selves. Every time we encounter another human being, or even imagine such an encounter, the expectations attached to our sex category become salient to us, and whether we meet such expectations or not, we are held accountable by ourselves and others. This is the power of interactional level of analysis. The gender structure involves far beyond, however, shaping individuals and our expectations for interaction. The legal system, religious doctrines, and often our work organizations are also deeply gendered, with beliefs about male privilege and agency, and female nurturance built into the rules and the cultural logics that accompany regulation. Below I consider each of these levels of analysis separately, although they are all clearly intertwined in any given gender structure. The model is revised from earlier formulations by differentiating material and cultural aspects at each level of analysis. I also now refer to the macro level of analysis as just that, rather than institutional to clarify that I am including both institutional/organizational regulations and the cultural beliefs that accompany them.

Individual Level of Analysis. When we are concerned with the means by which boys and girls come to have a preference to do gender, we should focus on how identities are constructed through early childhood development with explicit socialization and modeling, and how preferences become internalized. The *cultural* aspect of the gender structured does, to some degree, shape the notion of the self. To the extent that women and men choose to do gender-typical behavior across social roles and over the life cycle, we must focus on such individual explanations. Much attention has been paid to gender socialization and the individualist presumptions for gender by psychologists, but sociologists have shied away from it, focusing more on interaction and macro ideology. Continued attention is necessary to the construction of the self, both the means by which socialization leads to internalized predispositions, and how—once selves are adopted—people use identity work to maintain behaviors that bolster their positive sense of selves (Schwalbe et al. 2000). How or how much the gender structure becomes internalized into the self is an important empirical question. We must understand the extent to which cultural ideologies become embedded in individuals; the power of socialization remains a central aspect of the gender structure.

There is also a *material* reality on the individual level. Boys and girls, men and women, and those who reject binary identities are all embodied, with real flesh and blood material objects—bodies—they have to interpret and display. Some part of this may be influenced by genetics and hormones, although this is complicated to study because social roles and experiences influence hormones level as well (Freese et al. 2003; Perrin and Lee 2007; Rosenblitt et al. 2001). To pretend that bodies do not matter is to stick one's head in the sand. How they matter and how they are interpreted must be part of research on the gender structure.

Bourdieu's (1988) practice theory, particularly the concept of habitus, is very useful in conceptualizing the social creation of materiality at the individual level of the gender structure. Young children learn to walk like a girl, and throw like a boy. The gender structure becomes embedded in children's bodies (or not, as when they reject their ascribed gender). The habitus generates the possibility of what actions can be imagined. While some people clearly do reject childhood training, they cannot do it outside the boundaries of their habitus, beyond their imagination. With ever more sophisticated medical intervention possible, people can choose to alter the materiality of their lives, and use technology to embody their identity. Whatever material circumstances of individual lives, whether bodies are born or made, or some of both, the gender structure has defined the possibilities, enabled options, and created constraints.

Interesting important empirical questions remain as to the stability of gendered selves over time to choose or reject gendered options. Men and women who have developed strong gendered identities may choose to fashion traditional sex-specific lives; they have done so with strong guidance from a gender schematic social structure. Men and women may choose to reject those labels, and change their bodies, but they, too, must fashion new selves within the imagined possibilities, the ideational reality, of the gender structure that exists around them. No one is born knowing that lipstick and heels are marks of femininity. In fact, heels were developed for elite men, and face paints have hardly been restricted to women's bodies over time and across cultures. And yet today, heels and lipstick are often part of a transformation to femininity, as girls are taught to be a woman or as transwomen transition to a recognizably female presentation of self. Femininity may be socially constructed, but the desire to adopt gendered selves, or to reject them, is real. The important lesson from the accumulation of research over the 20th century is not that social structure is not powerful at informing individual choices, but that neither the shape of our bodies nor the effects of childhood socialization can explain gender stratification.

We cannot leave a discussion of the individual level of analysis without more attention to both the role of free choice, or agency.[2] While individuals make choices, they are not purely free choices. If agency were simply defined as free will, the constraining role of social context, norms, and power would be ignored. Individuals are profoundly shaped by the gender structure that exists before they do and into which they are born. And yet if human agency did not exist at all, social change would never happen. I use Ahearn's (2001) definition of agency as "the socioculturally mediated capacity to act" (p. 112). Gender structures are in continuous flux, as are all social structures, and individuals alone, or in collectivities, react to and change them. People try to make the best choices they can within the constraints they face. Agency must be conceptualized as broad enough to incorporate both resistance to and reproduction of social life. While Foucault's (1978) attention to pervasive oppressive power is important for feminist thought, I find it more useful to focus on practice theory such as Giddens's (1984) to explain the ever-changing social construction of reality (Berger and Luckmann 1966). We need to be concerned not with the meanings that people make but with how and when behavior is shaped by structure and when human choices reshape the gender structure itself. What helps explain change?

Ahearn (2001) suggests that cross-cultural contact often widens reflexive action, allowing for the possibility of change. Cosmopolitanism opens up wider expanses of imagined choices. One indisputable fact is that social structures do change over time, including gender structures. My goal as a feminist scholar is to understand how and why, so that change that liberates us all from gendered constraints can be instigated and supported. Connell (1987) suggests that "crises tendencies" exist, allowing for cracks in the foundation of the gender structure, when levels of the gender structure are inconsistent. An example of such a crack is when behaviors are required to adapt to new circumstances but beliefs hold static. For instance, when both men and women are employed parents and remain in the labor market when their children are young, but stereotypes still presume that mothers are the primary caretakers and irresponsible employees. Discrepancy exists between women's expectations for equality on the job and their experiences of wage gaps and gender bias. Such a crises tendency exists right now. Circumstances change but gender beliefs lag behind. What happens? We might have a retreat of young mothers from the labor force, pushed out by lower wages, rigid work hours, and sexist husbands. Or we might have millennial women take up the mantle of feminism once again, this time perhaps an intersectional wave of feminism that goes more to the root of the problem, to the gender structure itself.

To infuse the gender revolution with energy, would Millennials need to overcome gendered selves? While that is an empirical question, and one we turn to in the next chapter, it is important to note that gendered selves are not set in concrete in childhood but are always being crafted (Kondo 1990). A few examples will suffice. Jones (2009) shows that young black girls living in Philadelphia's poor and violent neighborhoods learn the cultural trope that ties femininity to their looks, including straight hair and light skin tone, but as they age, they come to understand that to survive they have to be strong and sometimes do that by becoming physical "fighters." These girls encounter and then come to embody racialized femininities that are complicated, complex, inconsistent, and they evolve over time. My own research has shown that middle school girls are encouraged to compete with boys academically and often believe they live in a postfeminist world where they can be anything they want to be (Risman and Seale 2010). But at puberty, they have to revise their ideas about the self and pay attention to being pretty to avoid stigmatization; thus despite successes in the classroom or on the ballfield, they began to accessorize. What others expect of us matters. And so we turn now to the interactional level of analysis.

Interactional level of analysis. Interactional expectations that guide every moment of life are gendered; the *cultural* stereotypes that each of us face in every social encounter are different based on our presumed sex category. The processes most involved at the interactional level of the gender structure are cultural. The culture shapes the expectations of others we meet in our daily lives. Both the "doing gender" and the status expectations we face are squarely at the interactional level. As West and Zimmerman (1987) suggested, we "do gender" to meet the interactional expectations of those around us. Ridgeway and her colleagues (Ridgeway 1991; 2001; 2011; Ridgeway and Correll 2004) show just how powerfully the processes by which status expectations are attached to gender (and race) categories become cross-situational. In a sexist and racist society, women and all persons of color are expected to contribute less to task performances than are white men, unless they have some externally validated source of prestige or authority. Women are expected to be more empathetic and nurturing; men to be more efficacious and agentic. Correll (2004) also shows that cognitive stereotypes about gender can affect women's choices because they assess their abilities within these cultural stereotypes. Such status expectations are one of the engines that recreate inequality even in novel situations where there is no other reason to expect male or white privilege to emerge. Status expectations create a cognitive bias toward privileging men with agency and expecting women to nurture (Ridgeway 2011). Cognitive bias of this sort helps explain the reproduction of gender inequality in everyday life. The most enduring stereotypes around gender are those on the axes of agency for men, and nurturance for women.

We are held accountable to gendered norms, whether we choose to meet those expectations or reject them; the expectations exist. Hollander (2013) has shown the complex nature of the process of accountability. In her analysis, accountability begins with an individual's orientation to sex category (in my terms—at the individual level). We do gender because we are at risk of behavior being negatively evaluated, but to know how to act we must have a priori knowledge of what behavior is appropriate and what is not. That knowledge has been learned so that behavior can happen instantaneously without reflection. Accountability, even at the individual level, is tied to institutions because the beliefs that shape conformity, or rejection, to one's own sex category are shared cultural ideologies. But that is only the beginning of accountability. We all make assessments of our own and others' behavior as to whether it is appropriate to our claimed gender. Finally we face enforcement (from others) with real consequences for future interaction depending on whether we conform to their normative expectations.

Martin (2003; 2006) coined the term to "practice gender" by which she means that a process involving both the actor who "does gender" and the perceiver who gets it. Martin shows that sometimes women perceive men doing masculinity when the men themselves do not intend or admit to doing so. Women can be punished for doing femininity at work, with marginalization, but can also be punished if they do not do femininity, by being perceived as rude and unnecessarily aggressive. Kondo (1990) shows how women mobilize femininity in Japanese workplaces to assert their centrality to the "familial" workplace culture, and by doing so, both gain something, legitimation as culturally appropriate, and lose something, the ability to be equal, by their acquiescence to the marginalized position as women. Practicing gender depends on pre-established understandings and cultural meanings and both reflects and recreates gendered aspects of institutions. To quote Martin (2003):

> Gendered practices are learned and enacted in childhood and in every major site of social behavior over the life course, including in schools, intimate relationships, families, workplaces, houses of worship and social movement. In time, like riding a bicycle, gender practices become almost automatic. They sustain gendered relationships and in turn reconstitute the gendered institution. Over time, the saying and doing create what is said and done. (p. 252)

The interactional level also involves *material* conditions as well; nearly automatically saying, doing, and practicing gender while being accountable to cultural expectations. The relative proportion of others in one's sex category is a material reality that changes the dynamics of interactions, with tokens facing unique challenges, and individuals who shatter homogenous settings facing negative consequences (Kanter 1977; Gherhardi and Poggio 2007). The patterned inequality in access to positions of power and the resistance to integration into social networks creates objective disadvantages to women and to people of color. This disadvantage also clearly extends to those whose gender status is atypical, for example, a woman or a man who presents as androgynous or is anyone who presents themselves as gender nonconforming to the sex assigned at birth. Individuals who do not "do gender" as expected, or don't "do gender" in accordance with their ascribed sex, disrupt interaction by violating taken-for-granted assumptions. Such disruption leads to patterned inequality in access to resources, power, and privilege. It is to the more macro pattern of resources, and the cultural logics that accompany them, that we now turn.

Macro Level of Analysis. The gender structure also organizes social institutions and every type of organization. In many societies, the *material* reality is a legal system that presumes women and men have distinct rights and responsibilities, and those who exist outside a gender binary have few rights—even to exist legally. In societies whose legal systems are based in traditional religious doctrine, male privilege and sex-based rights are woven into the fabric of social control. Even in Western democratic societies, however, some nations still allow for different retirement ages for women and men, thus building gender into legislative bureaucracy. In the United States, most laws are gender-neutral, but private insurance companies are allowed to charge male and female customers different prices. Nearly all countries have myriad laws that discriminate against people whose gender does not coincide with the sex they were labeled at birth. In all societies, the material resource allocation and organizational power still rest, predominantly, in the hands of elite men.

Gender is symbolically embedded in organizational culture as well. Economic organizations embed gendered meanings in the definition of jobs and positions (Gherardi 1995; Acker, 1990; Martin 2004). Any organization that presumes valued workers are available 50 weeks a year, at least 40 hours a week for decades without interruption presumes that such workers have no practical or moral responsibility for caretaking. The industrial and postindustrial economic structure presumes workers have wives or do not need them. Much has begun to change in Western democracies, as laws move toward gender-neutrality. And yet, even when the actual formal rules and regulations begin to change—whether by government, courts, religion, higher education, or organizational rules—the organizational logic often remains, hiding male privilege in gender-neutral formal law (Acker 1990; 2006; Williams 2001). Andocentric cultural beliefs that justify different distributions of resources that privilege men often outlive formal organizational rules and regulations.

Gendered cultural logics exist as ideational processes beyond workplaces. While materialist analyses sometimes skirt or even deny the power of ideas, Béland (2005) argues that we must study changing beliefs to analyze historical changes in politics and policy, including about gender. While there has been debate among feminists who study welfare and gender regimes whether ideology has independent power in determining social policy (Béland 2009; Adams and Padamsee 2001; Brush 2002),

I suggest that ideational processes must be considered as an important part of the macro level of the *gender structure*. Recent empirical research shows why: powerful cultural meanings attached to gender. Budig et al. (2012) find that the effects of motherhood on women's earnings vary cross-culturally depending on gender ideology. If cultural support exists for mothers' labor force participation, then parental leave and public childcare facilities increase women's earnings. But if cultural support exists instead for families headed by male breadwinners with female homemakers, then parental leave and public childcare has no effect, or even detrimental effects, on women's income. Similarly, Pfau-Effinger (1998) compares employment patterns of women in West Germany, Finland, and the Netherlands. She provides convincing evidence that welfare state policy (including childcare availability) alone cannot explain cross-national differences in family structure and women's paid labor. Such policies must be combined with predominant gendered ideology and nationally specific historical cultural values in order to understand the unique historical trajectory of women's paid employment. Ideology matters for gender equity in the labor force and also for equality in other realms.

Pierotti's (2013) research on the quickly spreading rejection of the moral legitimacy of intimate partner violence across the globe is a pivotal example of how gender ideology matters and can change with positive consequences. In the 21st century, the United Nations and a variety of international NGO's have been working hard to define violence against women, including domestic violence, as a human right's violation. Gender development projects and media outreach have tried to reach families and national policy elites. Pierotti traces the attitudinal changes of women in 26 countries over five years to see if these international attempts have led to a convergence toward "global cultural scripts" that redefined violence against women as unacceptable. She found evidence of movement in women's beliefs with significant change in 23 of 26 countries—often very large shifts in attitudes. For example, only a third of women in Nigeria in 2003 thought it was wrong for a husband to hit his wife, but over half did in 2008. In countries where data were available for men, the attitudinal shifts were similar. There were no major material changes: no shifts in demographic, economic, or educational patterns to explain these attitudinal changes across the globe. She concludes that diffusion of cultural scripts about women's rights and violence influenced national policy makers and people at the grass roots. International feminist activists were integral in pushing this agenda, a fact I will return to in the last chapter of this book, in a discussion of social change and utopian possibilities.

Ideologies at the macro level of the gender structure are not fixed, nor are they immutable, but they do exist and clearly have significance in shaping possibilities for feminist social change. The macro level of the gender structure, similar to the individual and institutional levels, must be conceptualized with attention to both material and cultural aspects. We must marry feminist concerns for cultural meaning with institutional analyses of material inequality (O'Conner et al. 1999) for a full understanding of the macro level of the gender structure (Adams and Padamsee 2001).

To summarize, Figure 2.6 is a graphic presentation of the social processes involved in any gender structure, by the level of analysis they occur.

Dimensions of the Gender

	Individual Level	*Interactional Level*	*Macro-Level*
Material:	The Body/body work	Propotionate representation	Distribution of material resources
		Access to social networks	Organisational practices
Cultural:	Socialization	Status expectation	Ideology
	Internalization	Cognitive bias	Beliefs
	Identity work	Othering	
	Construction of selves	Stereotypes	

These are examples of social processes that may help explain the gender each dimension. They are meant to be illustrative and not represent all possible social processes or causal mechanisms.

FIGURE 2.6 Social Processes by Dimensions of the Gender Structure

UTILITY OF GENDER STRUCTURE THEORY

My argument advances the understanding of gender in several ways. First, this model helps impose some order on the encyclopedic research findings that have developed to explain gender. If we think of each research question as one piece of a jigsaw puzzle, being able to identify how one set of findings coordinates with others even when the dependent variables or contexts of interest are distinct, can further a cumulative science. Gender as a social structure is enormously complex. Full attention to the web of interconnection between gendered selves, the cultural expectations that help explain interactional patterns, institutional regulations, and cultural ideologies allows each researcher to explore the growth of their own proverbial trees while remaining cognizant of the forest.

Let me provide some examples. In order to understand when and how change happens in a gender structure, we need to identify mechanisms that create inequality at each level of analysis. If indeed gender segregation in the labor force at this historical moment were primarily explained (and I do not suggest that it is) by gendered selves, then we would do well to consider the most effective socialization mechanisms to create fewer gender-schematic children and resocialization for adults. If we wanted a world with economic equality between the sexes, we would either need to resocialize boys and girls so that girls are no longer any more likely to "choose" low-paying professions than their brothers, or we'd have to accept gender difference and try to institute comparable worth, where jobs equally "worthy" across professions were paid based on some meritocratic criterion. If, however, sex segregation in the labor force is primarily constrained today by cultural expectations of employers and moral accountability of women for caretaking, it is those cultural meanings we must work to alter. But then again, if sex segregation of the labor force exists because jobs are organized so that workers simply cannot succeed at paid work and responsible caretaking, given women's historical responsibility for caretaking and greater probability than men of being single parents, it is the contemporary American workplace rules and organizations that must change (Acker 1990; Williams 2001). The constant recurrence of the debate in American society over whether women can "have it all" suggests these processes are neither well understood nor has consensus developed on which are most important. My hypothesis is that in such a research project all of these social processes are probably in play in the creation of gendered segregation in the labor force. My hypothesis is that a complex problem has complex causes. The empirical question for social science is to sort out their relative weight, at this moment in time, in any given circumstance.

We may never find a universal theoretical explanation for gendered behavior because the search for universal social laws (or a silver bullet) is a fading illusion of 20th-century empiricism. But in any given moment for any particular setting, the causal processes should be identifiable empirically. The complexity of explanation goes beyond one context even at one moment, as the particular causal processes that constrain men and women to do gender may be strong in one institutional setting (e.g., at home) and weaker in another (e.g., at work). The forces that create gender traditionalism for men and women may vary across space as well as time. Conceptualizing gender as a social structure contributes to a more contextually specific version of social science. We can use this model to begin to organize thought about the causal processes that are most likely to be effective on each dimension for any particular question. So one contribution offered here is a means to organize empirical research and findings.

A second contribution of this approach is that it leaves behind the modernist warfare version of science, wherein theories are pitted against one another, with a winner and a loser in every contest. In the past, much energy (including my early work, Risman 1987) was devoted to testing which theory best explained gender inequality by discounting every alternative possibility. Browne and England (1997) show that the argument between individualist versus structuralist explanations for gender is illusory because all theories of gender inequality incorporate assumptions about both internalization and external constraint. Thus, while dueling theories is perhaps an effective technique for building academic careers, with researcher A's career soaring by destroying researcher B's theory, as a model for explaining complex social phenomena, it leaves much to be desired. Theory building that depends on theory slaying presumes parsimony, but this complicated world of ours is not necessarily best described with simplistic mono-causal explanations. While parsimony and theory testing were a model for 20th-century science, a 21st-century science should attempt to find complicated and integrative theories (Hill Collins 1998). The conceptualization of gender as a social structure is my contribution to complicating, but hopefully enriching, social theory about gender.

A third benefit to this multidimensional structural model is that it allows us to seriously investigate the direction and strength of causal relationships between gendered phenomena on each dimension given particular historical circumstances. We can try to identify the site where change occurs and at which level of analysis the ability of reflexive women, men, and those between that binary seem able at this historical moment to effectively reject habitualized gender routines. For example, we can empirically investigate the relationship between gendered selves and doing gender without accepting simplistic unidirectional arguments for inequality presumed to be either about identities or cultural ideology. It is quite possible—indeed likely—that socialized femininity does help explain why we do gender, but doing gender to meet others' expectations, surely, over time, helps construct our gendered selves. Furthermore, gendered institutions depend on our willingness to do gender, and when we rebel, we can change the institutions themselves. I have used the language of dimensions interchangeably with the language of levels because when we think of gender as a social structure, we must move away from privileging any particular dimension as higher than another. How social change occurs is an empirical question, not an a priori theoretical assumption. It may be that individuals struggling to change their identities, as in second-wave feminist consciousness-raising groups or the new lean in circles encouraged by Sandberg (2013), eventually bring their new selves to social interaction and help mold new cultural expectations. For example, as women come to see themselves (or are socialized to see themselves) as sexual actors, the expectations that men must work to provide orgasms for their female romantic partners has become part of the cultural norm. But this is surely not the only way, nor perhaps the most effective way, social change can happen. When social movement activists name as inequality what has heretofore been considered natural (e.g., women's segregation into low-paying jobs), they can create organizational changes such as career ladders between women's quasi-administrative jobs and actual management, opening up opportunities that otherwise would have remained closed, thus creating change on the institutional dimension. Girls raised in the 21st century with the girl-power motif, who know opportunities exist in these workplaces, may have an altered sense of possibilities and therefore of themselves.

We need to also study change and emerging equality when it occurs rather than only documenting inequality. Perhaps the most important feature of this conceptual schema is its dynamism. No one dimension determines the other. Change is fluid and reverberates throughout the structure dynamically. Changes in individual identities and moral accountability may change interactional expectations, but the opposite is possible as well. Change cultural expectations, and individual identities are shaped differently. Institutional changes must result from individuals or group action, yet such change is difficult, as institutions exist across time and space. Once institutional changes occur, they reverberate at the level of cultural expectations and perhaps even on identities. And the cycle of change continues. No mechanistic predictions are possible because human beings sometimes reject the structure itself and, by doing so, change it. Much time and energy can be wasted trying to validate which dimension is more central to inequality or social change. My goal in writing about gender as a social structure is to identify when behavior is habit (an enactment of taken-for-granted gendered cultural norms) and when we do gender consciously, with intent, rebellion, or even with irony. When are we doing gender and recreating inequality without intent? And what happens to interactional dynamics and male-dominated institutions when we rebel? If young people refuse to do gender as we now know it, can they reject the binary itself, or are they simply doing gender differently, forging alternative masculinities and femininities? I end this chapter with a summary of what we know about the gender structure the Millennials whom we will meet in the next few chapters are inheriting.

THE GENDER STRUCTURE FACING MILLENNIALS

What does the gender structure in the United States look like right now for young people coming of age here in urban America? Clearly, there is much diversity across class, race, and ethnicity. But there are some trends. At the individual level, what kind of cultural air do boys and girls breathe as they grow up today? They still live in very distinct worlds and internalize gendered selves (Paechter 2007). But at this moment in US history, girls are allowed more freedom to transgress the gender norms than are boys (Risman and Seale 2010). We are decades into girl power, and there are a whole set of programs and policies to encourage girls to study science, technology, engineering, and math (STEM) disciplines. Athletes can now be popular girls and often are (Bystydzienski and Bird 2006). Boys, however, are still not given the latitude to be girly, and certainly not encouraged to be so (Kane 2012).

The research on gendered personality traits shows this has consequences (Twenge 1997; Twenge et al. 2012). Women have become more efficacious over time, they feel more in control of their lives, are more confident about being leaders, that is, they have become more "masculine" on the measures of "sex role" inventories. Men, however, have not changed. They have not, on average, become more feminine. My own early research suggests that when men do caretaking work, they do develop more nurturing, empathic selves, usually referred to on sex role scales as "feminine" (Risman 1987). But this has yet to show up in quantitative studies. So we have a society where women are allowed to develop some masculine characteristics and are even rewarded in adolescence and early adulthood for doing so. Girls are now more likely than boys to be valedictorian of their high school classes, to attend college, and to graduate (Diprete and Buckmann 2013). The culture has changed, but more for young women than men.

But what about the material aspect of the individual level? What are the ways in which boys and girls come to embody their gender? Boys still learn to be rough and tumble, to develop muscles. At the same time, while girls are encouraged to be athletes, they are still raised to care tremendously about their looks, their weight, their clothes (Risman and Seale 2010). In my own research on middle schoolers, the girls seem to focus excessively on their bodies, as if their bodies could carry the weight of expected femininity, even if their behaviors did not. Female bodies become a primary means to "do femininity" in a world where girls are encouraged to be competitive with boys in every other sphere of life. Girls (at least heterosexual ones) compete for boys with their looks and with boys in the classroom for grades. It remains a very dangerous place for a feminine boy, or indeed for any child that is gender nonconforming (Dietert and Dentice 2013; Rieger and Savin-Williams 2012). Although change is uneven. Some lucky nonconforming youth have supportive parents (Meadow 2012). If some young adults feel freer now to challenge gender stereotypes, the cultural expectations they face are surely involved.

At the interactional level of analysis, what are the cultural expectations young people face today? Surely cultural norms have changed from the breadwinner/homemaker model. Now both women and men are expected to remain in the labor force throughout their lives even while jobs that pay a living wage are becoming scarce for those without college degrees. What seems to be new is that employment is now a criterion for marriage for both women and men, and that means far more working-class women remain single as they become mothers than in the past. Sharing the family work, the childcare and the housework, is still more an ideal than a reality. But we should not forget that as an *ideal*, it is new and different from previous generations (Gerson 2010). Still, the cultural beliefs around "intensive mothering" remain strong, and "intensive fathering" isn't even a phrase yet coined. Some research suggests that women plan careers that will be easy to disrupt for parenting before they even have boyfriends (Cinamon 2006). These women rein in their ambition even before they enter the labor force because of the fear of future work-family conflict. While the cultural norms now encourage women to enter the labor force, and even when they do so with great ambition, a great deal of evidence shows they encounter cognitive bias. For women who enter traditionally male fields, bias is often encountered early and overtly (Garcia-Retamero and Lopez-Zafra 2006). Women who advance in every field walk a tightrope; to be effective they must be able to lead, but if they are too directive, they shatter stereotypes about femininity and are disliked or devalued (Eagly and Carli 2003; Ritter and Yoder 2004). Many women hit a maternal wall, when they run up against workplace norms that require a 24/7 commitment and they have a child to pick up at daycare at 6:00 p.m. Of course, these anti-family norms hurt some men as well. If men use family-friendly policies, they are often considered less dependable and promotable (Rudman and Mescher 2013). Much has changed in gender expectations from a breadwinner/homemaker model among parents today, but much has lagged behind in the organization of work (Moen et. al. 2016). We continue to have biases both based on gender itself and against people who have caretaking responsibilities, which of course historically has meant against women.

It is harder to isolate the material aspect of the interactional level. Perhaps the most easily observable one is the circumstance when women or men are the token in the room. In some communities, a father caring for his child during the day at the playground is one of a kind, and often ignored by the mothers around him. Women in predominantly male occupations are still often encumbered with expectations that they represent all women or all women of their race or ethnicity (Dyson 2012). Of course, the most serious kinds of disruptions happen when people do not meet the expectations held for them at all, when people identified as one sex at birth change their gender, or when someone cannot be categorized at all and presents themselves as between the gender binary. This has been become more acceptable, especially in public places (Westbrook and Schilt 2014). But as laws began to protect transgender people in places where same-sex segregation is expected, such as bathrooms, we have seen a great deal of political opposition and what sociologists call "moral panic" (Westbrook and Schilt 2014). The country is in the middle of a cultural war about gender expectations for those whose gender identity does not match their birth certificate. Do we allow them to follow expectations based on gender identity or not?

At the macro level, what cultural ideology is most dominant in the United States today? Ideological worldviews are defined by what people think ought to be, not what is. And of course, there are many points of view in every family, every state, and they differ by class, race, and every other social dimension. And yet, there are some commonalities that we share as a society. Here's my read of the most basic shared threads in gender ideology at the moment. Mothers are now expected to financially support their families, always when they are single, and usually even if married. Married and cohabiting men are usually expected to at least partly share family and paid work, but it is still women's job to be good mothers first and foremost. A man that isn't employed is not marriageable. And it may now be the case that a perhaps woman that isn't employed isn't marriageable either. Gender equality is at least now often an espoused value. And yet, since cultural values remain sexist, caregiving work is undervalued and badly paid.

At the material level of enforceable law and policy, the United States is almost entirely gender-neutral. Husbands and wives no longer have differential rights in divorce, and labor laws are increasingly gender-neutral. Employment ads cannot openly declare men or women wanted, although there are surely more subtle ways to signal which gender employers prefer. All combat roles are open to women, although as of this writing only men must register for the draft. The one set of institutions that still openly and legally have different organizational rules and regulations for men and women are religious denominations. In some religious groups, like Catholics, orthodox Jews and Muslims, women cannot rise to leadership positions as clergy. In many conservative denominations, women have to dress modestly, presumably so as not to sexually arouse the men they encounter. Religious rules remain the last bastion of accepted regulated gender essentialism in Western societies. While no law or policy determines wages, the real effect of sexism is still seen in gender wage gaps in every field, although men without college degrees have fared so badly in the last few decades that women in their communities are closing the wage gap, not because women are doing so well but because the men are doing so badly (McCall 2015).

The gender structure remains very powerful today, even if it has changed, and women have many more options than in previous centuries. England (2010) has argued that the gender revolution has stalled, and it is in this context that the Millennials enter adulthood. In the next chapter, we shall see what we know about young people today, and how they are experience our gender structure. There is very little information about Millennials and even less about their experiences with the gender structure. With this book, I hope to change that.

3

Millennials as Emerging Adults

FROM HERE FORWARD, I use the framework presented in the last chapter, *gender as a social structure*, to help understand the life experiences of Millennials. I begin by contextualizing this generation within a historical context. I then review what we know about their stage of life within a human development framework. I integrate what we know about the transition to adulthood at this moment in history with the research on a new developmental stage of life known as "emerging adulthood" (Arnett 2000; 2015). And finally, I then turn our attention to the research already done on Millennials, especially the debate captured by the conflicting titles of *Generation Me* (Twenge 2014) and *Millennial Momentum* (Winograd and Hais 2011). *Generation Me* portrays self-involved youth while the *Millennial Momentum* introduces a new civically engaged generation that will re-energize America. I draw on a new article by Milkman (2017) to illustrate that at least some college-educated Millennials have begun to create social movements after the 2008 financial crises. I conclude by pulling together what little is known about Millennials and the gender structure from previous research.

HISTORICAL TRENDS IN THE TRANSITION TO ADULTHOOD

There has been a trend since just after World War II for the transition to adulthood to take ever longer every decade and to be more varied and more individualistic. In much of the 20th century, adulthood was reached when young people left school, found a full-time job, and then moved out of their parents' homes to marry and have children. This happened at the completion of high school or college and in a predictable order. School ended, jobs began, followed by marriage and family—all in quick succession. Shanahan (2000) reviewed the literature nearly two decades ago and reported then that the orderly pathway to adulthood created by industrialization was fragmenting, with an "individualization" of the life course. How long this modern, industrial predictable pattern actually existed is an open question, but what is clear is by the end of the 20th century, things had changed quite dramatically. By now, this orderly and relatively quick transition from adolescence to adulthood seems a distant memory of a far more simpler time.

The increasing length and variability in the process of moving into adulthood is tied to the sweeping changes in both the economy and the family in the 20th century. Over time, a greater proportion of young people went to high school and then to college. The majority of Americans are now in high school until they are 18, and nearly half are still in school into their mid-twenties (Furstenberg 2010). More than 10% are still in school between 25 and 30, and another 5% are still finishing their degrees well into their 30s. No wonder it takes so long for young Americans to enter the labor force full time. In addition, entry-level jobs are less and less likely to pay a living wage. With many years spent in education accompanied by low-paying entry-level jobs, it takes longer to feel financially secure enough to support anyone beyond oneself, let alone become a parent. By 2016, more young adults lived with their parents than with a romantic partner (Pew Research Center 2016). But this is truer for some people than others. Waters et al. (2011) edited a book as part of an effort funded by the MacArthur Foundation to study transitions to adulthood. They show that the local context matters. Transitions to adulthood are smoother and earlier in rural and small towns than in large metropolitan areas. Those living in cities with vibrant economies may drift from job to job but still remain optimistic, while those living in cities with sky-high rents have a far harder time establishing lives independent from their parents. Immigrants, particularly those who use higher education as a route for upward mobility, are the most comfortable with remaining in their parent's home well into early adulthood. Overall, 40% of young adults will "boomerang" home sometime after their first attempt at independent living. What that edited volume shows, most of all, is that becoming an adult is a gradual process and that there is no longer one normative pathway. Similarly, Arum and Roksa (2011) showed, not surprisingly, that most Millennials are still adrift two years after college graduation.

Many Millennials wait longer to create their own families than did previous generations, beyond the period of drifting during their 20s. Today's young people were raised in an era when divorce was common, and most are very careful about their own marital choices. They are unlikely to marry before each partner is economically viable (Settersten and Ray 2010). And so, that means a very long period of extended singlehood, and for those who do not become financially stable at all, marriage is often delayed beyond parenthood. The pressure to marry to become sexually active is now a historical artifact and has little relevance to the lives of Millennials. Once cohabitation became acceptable and sex outside of marriage normative, there is little pressure to get married at a young age. The median age for marriage in 2016 was 29 for men and 27 for women (Pew Research Center 2014). College-educated people often wait to marry until well established in their careers—into their 30s. Couples now may be the same or opposite sex, but what they have in common is waiting to marry until economically secure. This allows for long periods of self-development, often remaining at least partly economically dependent on their parents. In fact, nearly half of young people live with their parents into their early 20s, and that remains as high as one out of ten into their 30s (Furstenberg 2010). There is growing variability in age at marriage and parenthood by economic class.

Adult children often live on their own, boomerang home, and eventually set off again for independence. Young people often move to attend college, for jobs, and are free to travel, living beyond the traditional constraints of family and neighborhood. Americans prefer to live on their own, and often find that inter-generational households produce some tension, although this is less true in immigrant families. Giddens (1991) suggests that such freedom brings with it the start of an individuation of the life course. Rather than there being one way to grow up, there are nearly as many paths as there are people. Growing up is harder to do in the 21st century, and this was true even before the Great Recession faced by Millennials in 2008 (Furstenberg et al. 2004). But what exactly does growing up mean in today's world?

Furstenberg and other researchers (Settersten and Ray 2010) developed a set of questions used in the 2002 General Social Survey, a nationally representative survey about transition to adulthood. They found that 95% of Americans defined adulthood as finishing school, establishing an independent home, and full-time employment. In the past, Americans believed that marriage and parenthood were part of the package of adulthood, but that has changed. Using longitudinal Census data for the last century, as well as 500 in-depth interviews with young adults in 21st-century America, Furstenberg et al. (2004) suggest that it is not until approximately 30 years of age that most young people today actually achieve the independence required for this new definition of adulthood, including having finished school, becoming self-supporting, and living independently (i.e., without their parents) with a full-time job (75% by age 30). If we included marriage and parenthood in the definition of adulthood (as in the past), less than a third of men and half of the women would be considered adults by their third decade! The length of time it takes to finish school, find full-time work, and become financially independent in America has elongated in the 21st century. While some other countries have a clear institutionalized pathway from education to work, that simply doesn't exist for most young people in the United States (Shanahan 2000). Each Millennial is on their own to find a path between school and work.

But some patterns do emerge when trying to understand this generation. In 2007, before many of the Millennials graduated from high school, it was already the case that 20% of all men and 16% of all women were still living at home between 25 and 29 years of age. The rates were even higher for black people—25% of black men and 20% of black women. The rates are far higher for the children of immigrants (both those who arrive to the United States as very young children and those who are second generation). While these racial and ethnic differences in family types have existed across generations, perhaps the most striking new pattern is the dramatic class differentiation between the kinds of families being formed today (Cherlin 2014; Furstenberg 2010; Cohen 2014). Since so many Americans now believe marriage should wait until after financial independence, it is easy to understand why it is currently much more common among the middle class. Indeed, for many working-class women, of all races, parenthood now precedes marriage (Martin et al. 2017).[1] It is far harder for single women to move out of her parents' home when they have drifted into single motherhood and depend upon kin to help both financially and with daily childcare.

Why does it take so long to reach adulthood in the 21st century? The cost of college and ever-increasing student debt leaves even the young people from affluent families dependent on their parents for many years. The less lucky ones drift around looking for decent jobs to earn a living wage in a society where entry-level work often doesn't pay enough to support oneself, never mind becoming a contributing partner or a parent. Perhaps also our expectations have changed. Americans now desire a stage of independence between adolescence and adulthood, and while this is a relatively new cultural invention, we have come to take it for granted. Of course, women without full-time jobs, financial dependence, or homes of their own do drift into motherhood. Does that make them adults, as they are now responsible for someone else? Or does young, single motherhood simply create more challenges for the transition to adulthood? This transition now takes so long that some psychologists suggest it must be regarded as a new stage of human development.

EMERGING ADULTHOOD: A NEW DEVELOPMENTAL STAGE?

Millennials are coming of age in this historical moment when transition to adulthood is a long, complicated, and terrifically varied experience (Arnett 2000; 2015;

Furstenberg 2010). Arnett (2000) introduced the concept of "emerging adulthood" as a theory of development from the late teens through the 20s. He argued that a new developmental stage has emerged in modern America for which there is no normative path. It is not until the age of 30 that two-thirds of Americans have finished school, married, and become parents. Arnett claims the only unifying feature of these years is residential instability, that is, emerging adults move around a lot. Another unifying feature of young people today is that they are quite clear that they do not yet consider themselves adults.

A particularly new, and perhaps uniquely American, aspect of the data presented by Arnett (2015) is that emerging adults today define their life stage, emerging adulthood, less by what they do than how they do it. Arnett reports on a variety of research projects he and his colleagues conducted with young people between 18 and 30 years of age, including three nationally representative samples and 300 in-depth interviews. From this research, they have identified three major psychological tasks for this new stage of emerging adulthood: "accepting responsibility for oneself, making independent decisions, and trying to gain financial independence" (p. 15). All the emotional work during this new developmental stage appears individualistic, focusing on identity exploration in every sphere of life. Arnett (2015) summarized the distinguishing features of emerging adulthood and wrote about testing alternative selves, and trying out alternative identities and relationships. His list of distinguishing features of this new life stage included identity exploration; instability not only in residence but also in love and work; subjective self-focus; feeling in-between; and optimism about the ability to create the life desired. While Arnett does not focus on gender, he does claim there were few differences by sex, race, or ethnicity. Still there were some differences between men and women in his findings worth noting.

In Arnett's research, men and women report their lives as more alike than different, and that includes marital timing and searching for a mate. They want to have completed their individualistic quest for identity before partnering. When they do look for a mate, they want someone who is their equal and has a similar worldview. Both men and women feel the pressure to marry by age 30, but mostly only women feel the societal sanctions looming if they do not. One quite major difference between men's and women's lives at this age, although Arnett does not focus on it, is that more than half the women who become mothers before 30 are single. Clearly men are freer to fully experience this period of emerging adulthood, by focusing primarily on themselves, than are women. Transition to motherhood disrupts emerging adulthood, at least as defined as focused on self-exploration, and thrusts one, at least partly, into an adult social role.

Carving an identity is the work of this emerging life stage, and Arnett does report that in his research there were a few statistically significant differences between men and women. Young women report experiencing anticipatory work-family tensions. Women sometimes feel their ability to choose from broad career opportunities limited because they want to be mothers. This affects their occupational choices. Arnett claims, without any critical analysis of the gender presumptions involved, "for many women in emerging adulthood, choosing a career direction means not simply making a choice that clicks with their identity but making a choice that will allow them to balance their dual identities as workers and mothers" (2015, p. 176). Nowhere does Arnett question why employment must require a choice between paid employment and parenting for women, nor why men don't have to worry about anticipatory fatherhood as they focus on developing their potential. Still, for both men and women the focus on self-development is the prime directive for emerging adulthood. Those who do attend college find themselves enveloped in an institution designed as a "safe haven" (2015, p. 166) for identity exploration. Some of this exploration is about careers, some about sexuality. Broido (2004) finds that millennial college students are more likely than those in the past to self-identify as non-heterosexual and agrees with Torkelson (2012) that emerging adulthood now includes identity struggles about sexualities and gender. A unifying theme is the desire for meaning and authenticity. When seeking full-time work, college educated or not, nearly all want to find work that has meaning for them—that will reflect who they really are. Whether this will be possible in the end, of course, is another issue.

Both sociologists and psychologists have discovered the new social processes of the elongated transition to adulthood in American society. Sociologists showed us that the path from adolescence to adulthood is both longer and more individuated today than in the past (Furstenberg et al. 2004; Fussell and Furstenberg 2005; Furstenberg 2010; Shanahan 2000). Arnett and his psychologist colleagues focus on what happens during this elongated process and have shown that the psychological tasks actually are so complex they comprise a new stage of human development: emerging adulthood. The Millennials you meet in the next chapters are currently experiencing this prolonged life stage between adolescence and adulthood. How are the Millennials managing emerging adulthood? We turn now to what previous research has identified as generational, or cohort, characteristics of today's emerging adults.

MILLENNIALS: EMERGING ADULTHOOD IN THE 21ST CENTURY

Academic research (Donnelly et al. 2015; Twenge et al. 2012; Eagen et al. 2013; Pew Research Center 2014; Ely et al. 2014; Broido 2004) shows that Millennials are not only the most ethnically and racially diverse generation in American but also the most liberal. Furstenberg (2017) cautions us not to accept psychological generalizations for this diverse generation, as they are likely to be as divided by race, ethnicity, and religion as generations before them. Still, there are some trends worth noting. They are the most educated and the least religious generation yet. It is impossible for those before them to imagine how Millennials weave their social lives into an ever-increasing number of online social networks. Despite the length of time it takes to transition to adulthood, these emerging adults are very optimistic about their futures. Even when 37% of Millennials were unemployed in 2010, they still claimed to be sure they would eventually meet their economic goals. Perhaps they believe they can meet their economic goals because their priorities are not that materialistic. The highest priority mentioned by Millennials was being a good parent (52%). The next most common priority was to have a successful marriage (30%), and only 15% reported having a high-paying career as an important goal. They seem to be pursuing intrinsic goals of personal well-being rather than having financial priorities, at least at this point in life.

Whatever their personal goals, the Pew data show that Millennials get along well with their elders, even if many of them lean more left than their elders. Millennials are less supportive of assertive national security policy and more supportive of progressive domestic social agendas than any other generation. They are also more likely than any other group to identify as Democrats. Based on a 2013 annual survey, called American Freshman, of over 165,000 full-time, first-year students enrolled in 234 different US colleges and universities (Eagen et al. 2013), we know that these students' social views are liberal; for example, 87% of the women and 79% of the men support the right of gay men and lesbians to adopt a child. More than two-thirds endorse the idea that wealthier people should pay more taxes than they currently do, although they are not more likely to support gun control than older Americans.

There is some controversy over whether Millennials are liberal when it comes to gender politics. Donnelly et al. (2015) find that by 2010, seven out of ten high school seniors agreed with a variety of items that measured approval of women's equality within the family, including supporting the mother's employment. England has argued that much change occurred in the 20th century, but that the gender revolution is now stalled (2010). There is little published research on this topic, but in a recent series of online publications debate has ensued. Pepin and Cotter (2017) report complex and contradictory trends. They find there is a split in Millennials' attitudes regarding gender equality: they continue to support equality in the labor market but have become less progressive than the generation before them when it comes to gender equality in the home. They argue that Millennials hold a new ideology that Pepin and Cotter term "egalitarian essentialism," which means that they believe men and women are equal, but that there are some essential differences between them, especially women's increased interest and skill in nurturance. Their analysis is based on longitudinal data from a survey (Monitoring the Future) of high school seniors from 1976 to 2014. Egalitarian essentialism is the belief that women and men should have equal rights and opportunities but that the sexes have different skills and desires, and that the home and family are and should remain feminine spaces. Carson (2017) argues that Millennials might be more traditional when it comes to gender equality in the family because they have observed their parents, whether two workers or single mothers, struggle with workplaces that do not have family-friendly policies, leading some of them to want to return to a past where family life was less stressful. There might be little reason to explain a trend toward traditionalism because not all research has found the same pattern. Research conducted by myself, Ray Sin, and William Scarborough (2017) finds no such trend among Millennials. We use nationally representative data (the General Social Survey) and find that Millennials are staying the course and endorsing equality as much as those before them. We do find that the big swings in attitudinal values toward support of egalitarian families happened before Millennials were born. They inherited liberal gender values from their baby boomer parents.

Other research also finds gender attitudes are complicated among Millennials. Ely et al. (2014) report on a study of students pursuing a master's of business administration at the Harvard Business School, surely one of the most elite educational settings in America. In this elite, career-oriented program, a third of Millennial men anticipate equally sharing family tasks, considerably more than any past generation. This is a good thing, since three-quarters of female millennial MBA students' expect their careers to be just as important as their partners. Still there are still sex differences in these elite graduate student responses. Two-thirds of these men expect their wives to take primary responsibility for childcare, but only 42% of these elite women expect to do so. Clearly, many of these women will do well to marry someone other than the men in their class. Yet, it is still the reality that four out of ten women working toward a graduate degree in business at Harvard, the most elite of institutions, still anticipates primary, not shared, responsibility for parenting.

Beyond these descriptive data about Millennials, there is a raging debate among academics on how to characterize the Millennials as a generation. Are they the self-focused "me" generation, or are they the next best hope to save the world? On one side is psychologist Twenge (2014) with her book *Generation Me*, and on the other political scientists Winograd and Hais (2011) with their analysis of Millennials as a generation who will re-energize America via civic engagement. As we wade into this debate, we must remember the caution sociologist Furstenberg (2017) offers that we refrain from over-generalizing psychological trends to entire generations.

My findings support that caution, but before we dive into my data, we must attend to the debate about whether Millennials are going to make a difference in the world around them by political engagement or are they self-focused narcissists.

Winograd and Hais (2011) hang their argument on a theory by Howe and Strauss (1991; 1997) that suggests generational identities rotate over time. Strauss and Howe suggest that there are four generational archetypes. Each generational type has a distinctive attitudinal and behavioral set of traits: idealist, reactive (to the idealism of their parents), civic-minded (who want to change the world through political participation), and adaptive (tending toward conformity). The theory implicitly rests on a Freudian notion of children growing into adults that react in a predictable fashion to their parent's childrearing philosophies. According to Strauss and Howe, these generations cycle every 80 years, four archetypes with 20 years per generation. Winograd and Hais apply this schema to Millennials. If baby boomers were an idealist generation, then the oldest of the baby boomers birthed Generation X, who are "reactive" and whose response to being raised by laissez faire liberal parents was to become individualistic, alienated, and pragmatic. The children of the younger baby boomers and the children of Generation X are the Millennials, and they will be—according to this theory—civic-minded, "focused on revitalizing the nation's institutions and dealing with the long-standing issues deferred during the idealist era that is now passing from the scene" (p. 25). Winograd and Hais argue that because of their place in this generational drama, Millennials will believe in government's ability to help design a better world. The authors cite data that suggests Millennials use less drugs than their parents, have fewer unplanned pregnancies, and fewer abortions. They are "pragmatic idealists" who are far more approving of civil rights on issues of race, gender, and sexuality than previous generations. Most Millennials (92%) find nothing at all objectionable about interracial dating and nearly half support affirmative action. In this way, they are the live and let live generation. And yet, having experienced the job market during the Great Recession, they look to government for help. Almost two-thirds agree that government should guarantee everyone a place to sleep and food to eat. The data that provided evidence for this argument are from nationally representative surveys.

As political scientists, Winograd and Hais's (2011) focus is on politics. They cite the enthusiasm of Millennials for the Obama presidency in 2008 as support for their argument about the civic mindedness of this generation. While the Bernie Sanders presidential candidacy was long after their book was published, the Millennial enthusiasm for his candidacy would no doubt by used by these authors to support their hypothesis. In the 2016 presidential race, more than 80% of the Millennials in the Iowa Democratic caucus supported Senator Bernie Sanders, and so it went throughout the 2016 Democratic primary season. Millennials, at least white ones, both women and men, overwhelmingly voted for Sanders against the first woman to win a major party nomination for the presidency. Millennials were overwhelming enthusiastic about a self-declared socialist who supports free tuition for all, which is evidence for the argument that today's emerging adults support governmental activism to solve social problems. But, they chose the left-leaning man over the feminist, and that may suggest that their gender politics are not as progressive, or as salient, as other values. Using exit poll data (Edison Research National Exit Poll) from the 2016 presidential election, Kawashima-Ginsberg (2017) shows that Millennials were the age group most likely to support Democratic candidate Hillary Clinton, but fewer of them voted for her than for Obama in either of the two most recent presidential elections. Here, too, we see a split among Millennials: two-thirds of all non-whites voting for Clinton, but only half of white women, and a third of white men. White men who are not college educated were likely to vote for Trump, and as a group they were more likely to vote in 2016 than ever in the past, while other Millennials voted less than in the past. Once again, we must be cautious about presuming Millennials are all cut from the same cloth.

Winograd and Hais cite the increasing educational success of women and the closing economic gender wage gaps between younger Americans to predict that both women and men of this generation will demand more work-life balance as they age. And yet, Winograd and Hais note the self-reliance of Millennials, who believe that individual initiatives (as well as government programs) are necessary to solve problems, which created the slogan "think globally, act locally." These authors suggest that Millennials makeup a "generation raised on technologies that enable it to customize each choice and . . . is not about to embrace programs that offer one size fits all solutions." In this view, Millennials are individualists who believe their civic responsibility is both to apply creative, customized solutions to social problems and to work with government to make changes. They are the "next great generation."

According to sociologist Ruth Milkman, the Millennials are a new political generation, although she makes no claims to their greatness. She builds on Mannheim's theory of generation (1927) to suggest that the Millennials comprise a new political generation with shared experience that set them apart from previous ones. The experiences Milkman suggests shape their political activity involve being digital natives who are more educated than previous generations but face precariousness in the labor force. Millennials were also raised in a world presumably concerned with gender and racial equality and yet still face discrimination. Milkman argues that this set of experiences has led to a generation who weave intersectionality into their social movements. In the years since 2008, Millennials have led social movements involving immigration (the Dreamers), racism (Black Lives Matter), economic inequality (Occupy Wall Street), and sexual violence on campus. From this research, we do not know if most Millennials will become politically engaged, but at least some have concerns beyond themselves.

Could these be the same Millennials that Twenge (2014) has written about? She claims her respondents in *Generation Me* are "more confident, assertive, entitled and more miserable (book sub-title)" than any before them. According to Twenge, this is a generation told they could be anything they wanted to be, yet they grew up to face widespread unemployment and limited opportunities. This is a generation that feels entitled to material comfort and the right to find meaningful work, yet they can't pay off their student loans or find an affordable place to live. She critiques the self-esteem movement that shaped their parents and teachers' childrearing philosophy, that is, to raise a generation more concerned with feelings than accomplishments. She argues that parents and teachers tried very hard to raise Millennials to think well enough of themselves so they could do great things. But then they grew up and "after a childhood of optimism and high expectations, reality hit them like a smack in the face" (p. xi). Twenge argues that this is a generation who has been taught to feel good about themselves, and does so, whether their accomplishments justify those feelings or not. Twenge draws her findings from a decade of research, including more than 30 studies based on nationally representative surveys from 11 million young Americans, as well as qualitative data from her own students at San Diego State University. The strength of this research is that there are often generational comparisons from surveys done annually so that Millennials can be compared with baby boomers at the same age. Overall, Twenge finds a cultural shift toward individualism that has shaped the Millennials as a generation. She admits that this has some positive outcomes, such as their support for equality and tolerance. But it also has disadvantages for society, and for themselves, if attention to their own feelings devolves into narcissism.

Twenge writes that the major childrearing philosophy of Millennials' parents was to "just be yourself." This has led to a live and let live philosophy since everyone believes they should be true to themselves. This rhetoric is compatible with claims to equal rights across gender, racial, or sexual minorities. Millennials are far more likely than their elders to support a diversity of family types, supporting the right of gay people to marry and have children, single women to become mothers, and accepting cohabitation as just one more kind of relationship. Interracial dating is no longer unusual or stigmatized, and when couples decide to marry, the norms around weddings have been totally discarded as each couple chooses their own style to best represent who they are, with destination weddings and online invitations as accepted as the traditional church wedding with cream-colored printed invitations. All of this freedom to be oneself allows individuals not only to shape their own lives but requires them to also accept the lives others choose as well.

The freedom to focus on the self also has a dark side, or so Twenge argues. If one's moral responsibility, and right, is to be true to the self, do others matter as much? Or does this generation drift into moral relativism where no one has any responsibility to anyone else since everyone has the primary responsibility to be true to oneself? Twenge supports this argument about narcissism with findings that show the Millennials (who she calls Gen Me) are far less likely to follow social rules, as they do not believe there is one way to do anything. She claims the consequences for rejecting social rules are far-reaching, including everything from bad manners, to cheating on exams, to avoiding service in the military. Millennials simply do not care about others as much as about themselves. More evidence provided for this claim about selfishness comes from several sources. In a direct test of the "next greatest generation" argument, Twenge used a nationally representative sample of high school and college students to compare their civic orientation (desire to make the world a better place) against the boomers when they were young. Not a single measure (out of 30) of civic orientation was higher among the Millennials than among the baby boomers. She also cites research by Christian Smith based on a survey and in-depth interviewers in which he found only 4% of Millennials were engaged civically or politically, even at the height of the first Obama presidential campaign, during the summer of 2008. In fact, the vast majority of respondents in the Smith study (69%) claimed no interest in politics. As of 2016, however, white Millennials did indeed seem very interested and involved in the candidacy of Bernie Sanders, which does not support this argument of a totally self-oriented generation. Or perhaps what their support for Bernie Sanders showed was a generation self-interested in free college tuition and loan forgiveness.

What does interest Millennials then? Twenge finds that they are mostly interested in themselves. Millennials are fond of selfies and invented sexting, which Twenge uses as evidence of a generational narcissism that has grown out of the "it's all about me" self-esteem mentality with which they were raised. She argues there is an increasing obsession with physical appearance. Indeed the willingness to use invasive medical procedures to improve one's body is justified by the goal of higher self-esteem. Twenge argues that today's emerging adults believe in themselves but not much else. They see a world where external happenings, from 9/11 to the Great Recession to terrorist attacks, determine the course of their lives, rather than their own efforts. This kind of externality can be adaptive, protecting the self-esteem in a cruel world. But it can also lead to cynicism and alienation, and even depression. The belief that external forces determine the course of one's life doesn't bode well for committing fully to a partner or even to meeting one's own goals.

The academic literature discussed above provides us with some hard facts and some widely conflicting analysis. Millennials live at a moment in history where there is no one quick or easy route to adulthood. Indeed, there is so much time between adolescence and adulthood that psychologists have defined it as a new stage of the life course, emerging adulthood. Young people are supposed to spend time at this moment in their lives thinking about who they want to be, to find themselves. Academics are debating whether Millennials are narcissistic or civic-minded. More research might help shed light on the issue, and I have found a genre on research worth looking at, even if it isn't academic. The people who market products are also researchers and have studied how to sell products to this new generation, with profits resting on the results. Before we end this chapter, let us take a look at what marketing companies have learned about the Millennials.

In 2010 Prosumer Report focused on a gender shift in Millennials, asking "Are women the new men?" This summary gives a flavor of their findings:

> The Millennials are a generation like no other. They are more mobile, more multicultural, and more fluid adopters—and adapters—of new technologies than any generation before. They live in a world without roadmaps or commonly recognized authorities, creating their own content, communication channels and life paths. They differ from earlier generations in at least one other important way as well: In much of the West, they have grown up in a "postfeminist" era, with women broadly acknowledged as men's equals—if not always treated as such. The civil rights protests and demonstrations these young people have witnessed in their lifetimes haven't been about women versus men, but about the rights of immigrants or people with minority sexual orientations. The notion of "women's liberation" is a dusty artifact, of no relevance to young people other than as a source of humor or historical context. (p. 1)

Their research also suggests that what everyone wants is to be "happy." And nearly three-quarters of the Millennials in this report state they are currently happy. Perhaps this is due to a shift from the goals of earlier generations that focused on success and power to more ephemeral goals of love and friendship. These are goals that are more likely to be reached by personal effort and more widely available. These are also goals that address their reported fear of "being alone."

As part of a large international sample, Prosumer Report included descriptive information about gender attitudes from 500 American Millennials. Most of the women do not see their choices limited by gender and do not believe the choices they make have implications for women as a group. The majority of women and men disagree that males should be the ones to lead and initiate romance, and less than 20% of the women and 30% of the men think that a man should earn more than his female partner. While slightly more than half the men believe women should be feminine and men should be masculine, less than half the women believe this. Women see themselves equal to men and yet are still far more likely to weigh work-life balance against salary when considering the benefit of a career. While both men and women see marriage as a merger of equals, men feel the expectation to remain in the labor force throughout their lives, while women feel they have choices (perhaps really responsibility?) when juggling career and childrearing, for example, through part-time work or leaving the labor force temporarily for motherhood. This marketing research suggests that because women report choices about their lives, and men do not, it will be the women who call the shots in their families. How so? Well, if women remain in the labor force, they expect husbands to compromise on work goals and share homemaking and childrearing. But if women "choose" to focus on motherhood, they expect men to shoulder primary responsibility for the families' economic well-being. According to this argument, men now have "masculine miasma," struggling with new undefined definitions of masculinity. Heterosexual men are uncomfortable with the new reality that their lives are dependent on the choices future wives make about juggling family and work; they must wait for a partner to make choices before making their own major career decisions. Whether these marketers are correct will be tested in the years to come. In may also be that men don't feel the need to constrain their choices by parental duties, and women are the ones that feel dependent on husbands to have the luxury of choice. Still, both sexes claim that gender distinctions are no longer "set in stone" and men and women are more alike than different in these data. The report ends with a recommendation to marketers that the new model should be a "couples paradigm" showing the couple as a successful brand working together to manage day-to-day life.

Another marketing study, the "Cassandra Gender Report" reports similar findings about gender fluidity. This report produced by the Intelligence Group, a research-based consumer insight company, also suggests that Gen Y and Z (other labels that include most Millennials 14-24 years of age in in 2013) strive for a gender-neutral world in which products and messaging are universally appealing. More than half of their respondents claim they would rather shop in a unisex store than one that caters specifically to their sex, and fewer than half prefer gender-specific products. Nearly half of the women in their 900 person online survey are "cool with men wearing makeup" and nine in ten are "cool with women proposing to men." Three-quarters of the women would rather be tough than dainty. It is the men who feel increasingly ignored, and a quarter of men believe males are portrayed inaccurately in ads, including as incompetent fathers. The marketing data seem to support Twenge's argument that today's emerging adults focus on personal goals, such as being happy, more than being successful. These descriptive data also suggest a great diversity of positions toward gender normativity. These data support the argument that at least some of this generation critiques the very existence of norms that differentiate how men and women should live. There is not much evidence, however, about the civic engagement of Millennials in commercial data. Clearly knowing about the gender structure matters more for selling products than knowing about political engagement.

So in the end, what do we know about Millennials? They are coming of age in an era when it takes a long time to transition to adulthood. They will experience the reflexivity of the new life stage we now call emerging adulthood. As of now, they are more liberal than previous generations. Some proportion of them has begun to critique gender norms about dress and self-presentation, although surely this is still probably a minority position. They are more diverse in every way we measure, by race and ethnicity, and gender and sexual identities. But there are still traces of gender traditionalism, with women feeling more responsible for choosing work that can be juggled around parenthood. This generation was clearly raised to be authentic, to be true to themselves. Whether that includes wanting to create a better world for themselves, using traditional politics, remains to be seen. Perhaps the past literature can best be summarized as characterizing Millennials as self-indulgent, narcissistic, individualist do-gooders. The research is contradictory as to whether they are as gender progressive as generations before them or whether the work-family struggles of their employed parents have made some of them yearn for a time in the past when families were more traditional. Still, other research suggests this generation is more critical of gender norms constraining their choices than any generation before them. It is with that summary that we move on to meet the emerging adults in this study.

The qualitative data presented in the rest of this book is not comparative across generations. It is based entirely on the life stories of 116 Chicagoland Millennials who were between 18 and 30 years of age in 2013. Most were college students or recent graduates. It is the first data ever collected to deeply probe how this generation deals with the gender structure in its entirely. Our interviews covered the individual level of analysis with deep questions about sense of self. We also asked about gendered expectations they hold for others, and how they experience what is expected of them during interaction with family and friends. Their stories include whether they experience the gender structure as oppressive, and if so, how. We also asked, and they answered in great depth, what their ideological beliefs were and whether we should have norms that differentiate the lives of men and women. We asked about the experiences of gender embedded in institutional rules and regulations. This research will add depth and breadth to what we know about Millennials and *gender as a social structure*.

4

Getting the Stories

DATA COLLECTION AND METHODOLOGY

GIVEN THE HISTORICAL power of *gender as a social structure*, it is fascinating to watch the ever-increasing visibility of Millennials who reject some part of the gender rules by which they are expected to live. We don't really know very much about how young people today understand the gender structure or their place within it. While we have some attitudinal data, there has been no research that examines all levels of the gender structure simultaneously. Do most women still try hard to be feminine and men to be masculine? How do Millennials think about gender norms? Do they "do gender" to meet the expectations others hold for them? How often and how do they rebel? Given the lack of longitudinal data, we cannot know if Millennials feel more oppressed by the sex categories themselves than generations before them, but we do know we have increasing numbers of gender nonconforming youth. We do know that this is the first time in history that young people are publically demanding to be identified without a gender at all, rejecting the "gender binary" outright, advocating policy-based changes, such as gender-neutral bathrooms. Saltzburg and Davis (2010) refer to youth who rebel against gender categories as "poetic activists" (p. 87) generating new meanings and new interpretations.

Change is in the air, and with all the winds blowing, the very meaning of gender is up for grabs. Surprisingly, we have very few studies that ask how Millennials understand, enact, or rebel against the gender social structure. To tackle this question, I agreed to teach a doctoral seminar at my university, the University of Illinois at Chicago, that would be a hands-on experience in qualitative data analysis for graduate students. A team of graduate students and I collaborated on the development of a life history interview schedule, with a major component dedicated to measuring concepts at each level of analysis in gender structure theory, as discussed in chapter 2. This is in no way a representative study of Millennials. Rather, it is an in-depth study of an ethnically diverse, mostly working-class sample of young people who live in and around the city of Chicago. They were 18 to 30 years of age when we collected data in 2013. It is a first attempt at understanding how Millennials are experiencing, adapting to, or rebelling against the gender structure.

WHAT DID WE ASK AND HOW DID WE ASK IT?

Our goal was twofold. First, we wanted to understand the lives of today's young people, Millennials, holistically. We used a traditional life history narrative interview in which we asked questions about their experiences across different life contexts, from school to romantic relationships to career goals. The second goal was to understand how they experienced the gender structure, beliefs about themselves, the expectations they faced, their worldviews, and their understanding of institutional gendered constraints. The questions were explicitly designed to allow us to explore gender at the individual level of analysis; at the interactional level; and at the macro level of both their experiences of institutional rules and regulations, and cultural beliefs. This research is designed to illustrate the usefulness of conceptualizing *gender as a social structure*. We use the theory to organize our analysis, although we did not organize the interview schedule, however, by level of analysis. Rather, we began the interview with questions about their family of origin, and then schools, and neighborhoods. We asked about their experiences in childhood with parents and siblings, successes and failures at school, their extracurricular activities, their neighborhoods, and about their hopes, dreams, and expectations as children, teenagers, and young adults. The full interview schedule is in appendix 1.

We expected that beginning the interview with a life history narrative would help our respondents open up and talk about something familiar and easy for them. We then moved to the very detailed and elaborate module about gender. A small group of doctoral students specializing in the sociology of gender met with me for an entire semester before data collection began to develop the interview schedule. Our goal was to create an interview format so we could collect data about how respondents understood each level of the gender structure. We searched for short provocative readings to instigate conversations about gender beliefs. We settled on three prompts: a short article about a Swedish preschool that had banned gendered pronouns, a vignette we wrote about a gender nonconforming young woman's struggles in a public bathroom, and a magazine ad involving a boy with painted toenails that had caused a controversy. We also asked many questions about their own lives, experiences, and beliefs.

The respondents first read an article about a preschool in Sweden that uses no gender pronouns, and we asked a series of questions about their thoughts on attending such a school and whether they would like their own children to do so.[1] We wrote the following vignette about a woman who presented herself in very traditional masculine attire and was harassed in a women's bathroom:

> *Lisa is a woman in her early 20s. With her hair cut short and wearing clothing that she bought from the men's department, Lisa is frequently mistaken for a man. While traveling, she stops by a roadside restroom. As she enters the restroom, another woman mistakes Lisa for a man, telling her that "this is the woman's restroom" and threatens to call security on Lisa if she doesn't leave. After encountering this situation numerous times, Lisa begins avoiding public restrooms and locker rooms altogether.*

We asked questions about whether they had ever witnessed such a scene, what they thought each actor should do and what they might do if they had seen it.

We then showed them the picture in Figure 4.1 from a J.Crew advertisement that caused some controversy when it was released. Our questions focused on why they thought it had caused some public outcry and how they felt about it personally.

SATURDAY
with jenna

See how she and son Beckett
go off duty in style.

quality time

"Lucky for me, I ended
up with a boy whose
favorite color is pink.
Toenail painting is way
more fun in neon."

FIGURE 4.1 J.Crew Ad 2010

The interviews ended with a series of questions about how the respondent saw themselves as similar or different from other boys and girls when they were young, and about following and breaking gender norms throughout their life through to the present.

In the spring of 2013, I then had the pleasure to co-teach a graduate methods course with a then senior graduate student, Amy Brainer now on the faculty at the University of Michigan at Dearborn, and with the collaboration of a colleague, Professor Kristen Myers, who is a professor of sociology and director of the Center for the Study of Women, Gender & Sexuality at Northern Illinois University. Professor Myers also taught a course using the same interview schedule on her campus. We had the able research assistance of then graduate student Ray Sin, now an associate behavioral researcher at Morningstar, Inc., who remained a vital part of the process right through the writing of this book.

WHO DID WE INTERVIEW, AND HOW DID WE FIND THEM?

We began by recruiting students from introductory sociology courses. We also had a theoretically guided recruitment strategy to target spaces where we might find young people who self-consciously rejected gender binaries, whatever language they chose to describe themselves. Our recruitment included LGBT centers in universities across Chicagoland, and as far as Indiana and Dekalb, Illinois. We also used a snowball method where we had student interviewers follow leads in their social networks and communities, and included a few interviews with people who lived as far away as California if they happened to be visiting locally. While most of the sample who were critical of a gender binary describe themselves as queer or genderqueer, others used language such as between the binary, or neither man nor woman. We heard a colorful array of identity labels used by these young people to describe themselves: queer, butch lesbian, genderqueer, uncertain, transman, transwoman, on the LGBTQ spectrum, nongendered, androgynous, ambiguous, and gender-neutral. We had more than a few respondents inform us that identity labels they had used in the past had been different and that they might use new ones in the future.

In this convenience sample, we interviewed more women than men. The sample was racially and ethnically diverse, and included six transgender respondents. In fact, this is a majority-minority sample including many immigrants, children of immigrants, and first-generation college students. Our sample for analysis was 116 Millennials, most but not all, college students or recent graduates. We have slightly less than a third male and the rest female interviewees. We had three transwoman and three transmen. Among the females, 43% are white, 9% black, 22% Asian, 17% Latina, and about 8% are other, mostly from the Middle East. The males are nearly equally split between being white (36%), Asian American (24%), and Latino (27%) with just three black males (see table 4.1). Two-thirds of the trans respondents are white and the remainder are split equally between black and mixed race. Genderqueer respondents claimed a queer gender but always told us their sex as the one ascribed at birth and so are included in this table in the male or female sex category. The self-descriptions of the sex given by transgender respondents were the sex they now identified with, and so they are separated as a category in table 4.1.

Seventy-two percent of our sample identified as heterosexual: 57 women, 26 men. We had 11 people who identified as gay: 2 lesbians, 4 gay men, 3 female genderqueer, 1 transman, and 1 transwoman. Twenty-two respondents provided us with a series of other sexual identities, including bisexual, bi-curious, queer, pansexual, other, and refuse to be labeled.

We have a great deal of ethnic and racial diversity among respondents. Our sample is majority-minority because the University of Illinois at Chicago, from which a large proportion of the respondents were drawn, is such a multicultural student environment, with many students who grew up in the city, and there are immigrants or the children of immigrants. Ethnic, religious, or racial differences that emerge in the findings are interwoven into the major analyses. We lack much range on class diversity because we have few young people raised in upper-middle class environments; most are first-generation college students. Still, it is important to remember that this sample excludes the poorest of American Millennials who do not graduate high school and those who do not enter four-year colleges. This research project adds to the literature at least partly because it is an unusual majority-minority, ethnically, racially, and gender diverse sample. It is a sample of young adults who grew up mostly in working-class families but have managed to succeed enough academically to enter a four-year university.

One defining aspect of this research is that our sample is atypical because we actively recruited individuals who consciously rejected some aspects of the gender structure, including some who totally reject gender as a binary. What we know from psychological research on youth who do not present themselves as normatively gendered is that they are at great risk for bullying by their peers, sometimes rejection by their parents, and mental health issues (D'augelli et al. 2008; Dietert and Dentice 2013; Ehrensaft 2011; Garofalo et al. 2006; Grossman et al. 2005; 2006a; 2006b;

TABLE 4.1
SAMPLE DEMOGRAPHICS BY RACE AND SEX (*N* = 116)

	White	Black	Asian	Latino/a	Middle Eastern	Mixed	Total
Female	33 (43.4%)	7 (9.2%)	17 (22.4%)	13 (17.2%)	4 (5.3%)	2 (2.6%)	76 (100%)
Male	13 (38.2%)	3 (8.8%)	8 (23.5%)	9 (26.5%)	0 (0.0%)	1 (2.9%)	34 (100%)
Transmen	1 (33.3%)	1 (33.3%)	0 (0.0%)	0 (0.0%)	0 (0.0%)	1 (33.3%)	3 (100%)
Transwomen	3 (100%)	0 (0.03%)	0 (0.0%)	0 (0.0%)	0 (0.0%)	0 (0.0%)	3 (100%)

2011; Grossman and D'augelli 2006; Horn 2007; Kane 2006; McGuire et al. 2010; Rieger and Savin-Williams 2012; Wyss 2004; Young and Sweeting 2004). Rates of mental illness and suicide attempts are far higher among gender nonconforming youth than their more conforming peers (D'augelli et al. 2008; Dietert and Dentice 2013; Grossman et al. 2005; Grossman et al. 2006a; Grossman and D'augelli 2006; Wyss 2004; Young and Sweeting 2004). Indeed, research suggests that gender non-conformity among youth is more responsible for bullying than being gay (Rieger and Savin-Williams 2012; Horn 2007; Pascoe 2007). Horn (2007) reports that straight boys who are not gender-conforming are less accepted by their peers than gay boys or girls. We tried to be very sensitive to painful issues when they arose in the interviews.

It is important to clarify the conceptual distinction, while acknowledging empirical correlations, between breaking gender norms, sexual desire for same-sex others, and adopting a genderqueer identity. Some of the respondents in this study self-consciously reject gendered expectations but otherwise define themselves as a heterosexual woman or man. Others identify as gay and report same-sex desire but fulfill gender expectations without discomfort. Some genderqueer females identify as lesbians, and others hold queer sexual identities that also reject binary categorization. Others reject any sexual identity label at all. Some of the respondents live between the gender binary, rejecting some aspects of their physical selves and yet do not hold a genderqueer identity. The relationship between gender and sexual identity is complicated but analytically distinct for social scientific inquiry. By including young people who are self-consciously rejecting gender conformity in our sample, we can empirically treat gender more as a continuum than a simple dichotomy.

Each respondent chose where they wanted to be interviewed. The most typical place was either in the sociology department at UIC or a coffee shop. But there were also interviews at respondent's apartments and at university LGBT centers. Interviews lasted from slightly less than an hour to more than three hours. I personally interviewed many of the genderqueer and transgender Millennials, and the rest of the nonconforming respondents were interviewed by my faculty colleague or a doctoral student specializing in the study of gender. Other interviewers included students from my graduate seminar, students from Kristen Myers's undergraduate senior capstone research class, and my own research assistants. This led to a wide range of interviewing interactional styles and some inconsistency in probing techniques and transcription quality. To deal with these issues, we had on-going interview training and weekly meetings to talk about interviews completed. In addition, one of the faculty investigators read at least one early transcript from every interviewer and provided in-depth feedback to ensure quality control in the future. We routinely read and discussed each other's transcripts to ensure compatibility. Most of the interviewers were women, and we cannot know if the sex of the interviewer affected the results. On the one hand, it is clearly a weakness of the study that the interviews were completed by many different interviewers. On the other hand, having many interviewers also strengthens the data. The diversity of interviewers adds reliability because these interviews could not have been shaped by a bias that a single interviewer might bring to the project. In addition, a major strength of our technique, face-to-face, semi-structured interviews, is that, although we all asked a common core of questions, the interviewers allowed for conversational flexibility so that respondents were able to focus on matters central to them. We know the data tap the respondents' powerful feelings from the personal, complex stories they shared with us, which was often poignant, compelling, and moving.

DATA TRANSCRIPTION AND ANALYSIS

Most interviewers transcribed their own interviews, although research assistants transcribed my interviews and those by senior collaborators. All 116 interviews were done in person, taped, and transcribed. Each interview transcript was accompanied by field notes taken immediately after the interview to document visual information and body language as remembered by the interviewer. We also recorded interviewers' subjective responses on the field notes, carefully labeled as such. All transcriptions were then loaded into one hermeneutic unit for analysis within the qualitative computer assisted program Atlas.ti. The first round of coding used a complicated, conceptual coding scheme adapted directly from the gender as a social structure model presented in chapter 2. The coding scheme was pretested, by four different coders, and revised based on the interviews themselves. My senior research assistant, Ray Sin, carefully managed the data, corrected any coding that was unclear or inaccurate, and managed the computer program for analysis. I conducted all the analyses using gender as a social structure to organize the findings by individual, interactional, and macro levels of analysis. The coding scheme is available in appendix 2.

Using an iterative data-analysis technique, starting with theoretical concepts, and then revising coding schemes as necessary, we coded four distinct aspects of the narratives about gender *at the individual level* of analysis, as experienced in everyday lives: (1) their sense of having feminine or masculine selves; (2) their feelings about their bodies; (3) their understanding of their own behaviors as gender traditional or as rejecting gender norms. We also asked questions about their individual ideology about gender. We proceeded to code data at the interactional and macro levels as well. *At the interactional level*, we coded for how the respondents perceived the expectations about their behaviors and presentations of their bodies from parents, peers, and the community. We also coded for when they felt constrained, when they acquiesced, when they resisted, and who either policed them or supported their resistance to gendered norms. *At the macro level*, we coded how they perceived culturally accepted worldviews about the gender structure and whether they believed the cultural logics that organized society were conservative or liberal about gender equality. We also asked what institutions, if any, they believed restricted their behavior or limited their options because of their sex or gender, and how. It is the case that most of these young people have yet to grapple with balancing work and family, workplace discrimination against caretakers, or even workplace discrimination against women. And so, their understanding of macro-institutional constraints is often hypothetical and not based on personal experience. At each level of analysis, we paid attention to identifying both material and cultural phenomenon. The analysis includes attention to individual, interactional, and macro levels of analysis, but all data are based on narrative life interviews and thus from the perspective of the individual respondents we interviewed. While we did not organize the life history narrative interview around each level of analysis, it was constructed to be sure that questions that focused on each level were included.

Our first finding, and an unexpected one, was that there was simply too little consistency in personal narratives to sharply distinguish our sample into gender conformists and nonconformists. My research plan had been to compare the youth who openly rejected the gender binary with the men and women who conformed to the gender structure, what others have called "gender normals" (Schilt and Westbrook 2009). What I found was too much diversity within the "gender normals" to identify just one "normal" for this cohort of Millennials. A preview of one major finding is the lack of consistency across measures of gender even within one level of analysis, such as at the individual level of defining the self. There was even less consistency between personal actions, beliefs, and general worldviews. The lack of consistency was, at first, very frustrating. However, eventually I realized that the variety of ways we have traditionally understood and measured gender simply doesn't reflect the reality of experiences among Millennials. Even among the vast majority of our sample who do not question the gender binary, women were just as likely (more actually, but only slightly) to describe themselves via anecdotes about doing activities considered traditionally masculine as men. Most women seemed to enjoy telling us about all the ways they break femininity rules. This was true even when they were enthusiastic about other stereotypically feminine pursuits such as shopping or fashion. Men were far more likely to be consistent and normatively masculine, but a significant minority of men also described themselves as somewhat feminine, proud to break gender norms. Many men used libertarian ideology in support of gender equality and personal freedom for all, but then they described hegemonically traditional selves. Sometimes men with very traditional beliefs routinely broke gender norms in their behavior. There were some true gender conformists in the sample, but they were the minority.

As the analysis progressed, it became clear there was too much interesting information about gender and Millennials to focus only on those who try to live between the gender binary and simply compare them to the rest of the sample. The interviews with women and men who do not reject the binary were too fascinating to be treated as mere comparison data. Another unexpected but clear finding was that the genderqueer youth and the transgender youth had very different stories to tell. Even among the transgender young adults, life histories, beliefs about their own bodies, identities, or ideologies about gender varied tremendously. My focus expanded from trying to primarily understand gender nonconforming young people to a focus on the *gender structure* and Millennials more generally.

A PREVIEW OF THE FINDINGS

My plan for this book changed during its writing. Originally, I planned to write a theory book using the data to briefly illustrate concepts from my theory of *gender as a social structure* in a chapter. As often happens during the research process, the coding of the interviews and the initial analysis led to new insights and new directions. The inconsistency in responses to questions about gender among the majority of respondents led me to realize that the chaos of their responses cried out for more analysis. And so the direction of this book changed.

A major finding of this research is that most of the Millennials in this sample have complex and inconsistent relationships to the gender structure. While most of the females assigned as girls at birth in this sample do not reject the category woman, they vary widely in how much they conform to gender norms and the degree to which they rebel against them. These Millennials vary tremendously in how they understand and position themselves in reference to the gender structure. As I read and reread their interviews, I came to see they fall into four different groups in relationship to the *gender as a social structure:* the *true believers*, the *straddlers,* the *innovators*, and the *rebels.* I discuss each briefly in this chapter and devote a full chapter to each.

The first group is *true believers* (n = 30). On every level, they accepted, endorsed, and lived gender traditionally. They believed men and women are essentially different, were expected to and conformed to expectations appropriate for their sex category. They accepted the cultural worldview that men and women should live different lives, and while they could identify institutional rules and regulations that existed because of their sex, they did not experience those rules or regulations (particularly religious ones) to be oppressive. Twenty-one of the 64 women are *true believers*. Nine of the 29 young men are *true believers*. Less than a third of this sample is truly and fully gender conformist.

Most of the Millennials in this sample are *straddlers* (n = 48). By this I mean that they have one foot in a traditional gender structure and the other foot in a world without clear gender rules. At one level of analysis they sound like *true believers*, but at another they sound rebellious and reject the gender structure. For example, they may have both internalized some aspects of traditionally gendered selves at the individual level but also reject the constraints they perceive from others' expectations. Sometimes—though certainly not always—they reject those expectations and rules, and rebel. Others claim feminist worldviews, rejecting gender inequality and any institutionalization of gendered regulations, yet hold traditional expectations for an opposite-sex partner on a date. They *straddle* the gender structure because they are *innovators* at one level but traditionalists at another. Of the 64 young women, 31 fall into this category, with inconsistent behaviors, some adoption of traditional femininity or gendered norms while rejecting other parts of the gender structure. There is often inconsistency between their behaviors and beliefs. Fourteen of the men are *straddlers*. There are also three transmen and one transwoman who fit in this category. These transgender respondents, like the other *straddlers*, sound inconsistent when they talk about themselves and their place in the gender structure. Most transgender respondents in this group critique the stereotypes around gender but then often refer to how different boys and girls really are, in their experience, and how they fit in better with the group they were not assigned to at birth.

Slightly less than 20% of the women and almost a third of the men in the sample are *innovators* (n = 21). *Innovators* consistently reject the gender structure at each level of analysis and reflectively try to change it. *Innovators* reject constraints perceived to be based on their sex category and adamantly reject what they understand to be sexist inequality whether it appears as ideology or institutional rules and regulations. They do not reject the idea of a gender binary, nor do they question being women or men. Instead, they want to end the presumption that because of their sex they should be appropriately gendered masculine or feminine. Their stories focus on the constraints of gender stereotypes about activities and expectations regarding their personalities, with little critique of gendered expectations for the presentation of their bodies.

What differentiates the *rebels* (n = 17) from the *innovators* is their critique of the categories of gender. The *rebels* often hold a genderqueer identity but not always.

These Millennials are those who either feel driven by internal psychological need or political commitment, or both, to queer gender, to blend the masculine and feminine while rejecting the reality of the binary itself. The *rebels* reject the expectation that because they are labeled female at birth, they must present themselves as women, or if labeled male at birth, as men. Some play with gender presentation day by day. Some *rebels* usually appear masculine although remain identified as women and report often being mistaken for men. Others reject gender categories entirely. The two transwoman in this group also reject the notion that as women they must be feminine or that identifying as one sex or the other should require certain kinds of personalities or create gendered expectations for life patterns. All *rebels* report far more gender policing than any other group. People living between the binary are far more susceptible to societal pressure to conform. Only two of the *rebels* (the transwomen) desire to live as a sex not ascribed at birth, but all want to be free from the constraints of presenting their gender according to their biological sex.

These categories are only ideal types designed to help impose some order on complicated life stories. Perhaps the most clear way to conceptualize this typology is on the degree of consistency in their responses about the self, expectations of others, worldviews, and experiences of institutional constraints. The *true believers* are mostly consistent supporters of the gender structure and the status quo between women and mén. The primary trait of *straddlers* is their inconsistency; when you read their interviews it is often hard to believe the transcript represents one person's story because of the incongruity between one section of the narrative from the next. The *innovators* and *rebels* are both consistent in their critique of the gender structure. The *rebels* go further than the *innovators* because they disregard the material constraints of gender at the individual level, as well as the cultural ones. They want to dismantle the gender binary itself or at least decouple it entirely from biological bodies.

The proportion of the sample in each category is meaningless. It is important to remember that these percentages describe only this convenience sample where we consciously searched for gender nonconformists to diversify it. The sample is also majority-minority and primarily urban college students, many of whom are children of immigrants. This is not a random or generalizable sample. There is absolutely **no** relevance for proportions of Millennials for the general public, nor is it even representative of Millennials who are college educated. Rather, as with any qualitative research with a volunteer sample, these analyses are designed to help understand the variety of experiences of today's Millennials and are not generalizable. In the last chapter, I will use another, very different kind of college sample, with quantitative measures, to guestimate how common each category is on college campuses today. It doesn't matter how many Millennials are in each group. The *rebels* surely are a small minority, but their very existence is changing cultural norms. Many universities, and conference hotels, now offer all gender bathrooms. Some college instructors ask their students to provide preferred pronouns when they introduce themselves, and some young people use pronouns that are new to the English language, plural "they" or ze. Just as the majority of women in the 1970s didn't identify as feminists, but they changed America, so too, the proportion of young people who are *innovators* or *rebels* is irrelevant because their existence makes waves. The empirical research reported here is designed to help us understand the Millennials who are pushing back against gender, as well as those committed to retaining traditional gender norms, and those who are confused about themselves and the gender structure itself.

The data analysis chapters that follow are organized by these four categories because they reflect the respondent's positionality vis-à-vis the gender structure. Chapter 5 tells the stories of the *true believers*. Chapter 6 focuses on the *innovators*. Chapter 7 is about the *rebels*, and chapter 8 presents the *straddlers*. In chapter 9, I compare and contrast these four groups, returning to the major analytic task of this book, using the framework of *gender as a social structure* to better understand Millennials' today. Chapter 10 provides a conclusion with an argument for why we must move beyond having a gender structure at all if we want to move toward a more just world.

5

The True Believers

IN THIS CHAPTER, I tell the story of the *true believers*. I introduce these 30 Millennials, about a quarter of the total sample, and provide a short portrait of them. Before doing so, I want to introduce you to two of the *true believers* individually. No two respondents are the same, but a short biographical sketch of two young adults can help make vivid the concepts discussed in this chapter.

Let me introduce Amy Smith and Chad Whitelow.

Amy is a heterosexual young women who describes herself both as white and Middle Eastern, but when asked what she would check if she could only check one box regarding her racial/ethnic background, she answers white. Her parents migrated from the Middle East, and she was born in the United States. She was raised in a religious Muslim household. As a young girl, Amy always liked wearing dresses and skorts (skirts with shorts attached underneath). But in the sixth grade she decided to start dressing more modestly with long shirts and pants, and skirts that reached the knees or longer. It was at that age she also decided to wear a head scarf.

Her parents consciously enforced traditional gender norms. While growing up, the majority of the housework fell on the shoulders of Amy and her sister, and by high school they were expected to do almost all the cleaning. Her parents, mostly her dad, expected her and her sister to behave differently than her brothers. For example, whenever Amy would swear or say anything negative, such as "this sucks," she remembers her dad would reply, "that's so ugly coming out of a girl's mouth!"

Amy's family lived a sex-segregated existence: her brothers would play together, distinct from Amy and her sisters. Her brothers were allowed to stay out later than Amy and her sisters, even if the girls were only at a friend's house. Amy believes her parents enforced this double-standard because they understood girls to be different from boys; girls were more delicate. While growing up, whenever Amy went out, even if she was with girlfriends, her parents would instruct her to take one of her brothers with them for protection. This made it difficult for Amy to go out at all since all of her friends were girls, and some of them, too, were supposed to avoid interacting with the opposite sex. The requirement that she was to avoid boys made it impossible for Amy to participate in typical school activities such as homecoming, prom, or any other parties. Amy was also not allowed to date, and she respected this restriction. Amy told us she and her siblings all expect to have arranged marriages, and any dates, if they do have them, will be with the persons that they are considering as marriage partners and would be set up by their parents.

None of this feels restrictive or oppressive to Amy. She believes that girls and boys are different and those differences should be maintained. She elaborated: "I don't think guys should be as feminine as girls, and I don't think girls should be as tough as guys." She continued, telling us that girls should not dress like guys and that gender norms should not be violated. Still, she does not think that girls should be restricted from playing with traditional boy toys such as Legos or video games. Nor does she anywhere suggest that other people should follow her beliefs, as they are firmly grounded in religious ideology.

And now let me introduce Chad. He is an African American heterosexual male and was raised Lutheran. His interests are predominately stereotypically masculine pursuits such as sports and hanging with his male friends. In high school, Chad was a member of the organized group Gentlemen of Distinction, where he remembers "we acted as gentlemen . . . [and] showed our gentlemen-ness personalities to the women that were in high school. You know, we would do things like pass out roses, carry books for the young ladies, and stuff." In college, Chad joined the Black Male Initiative, which he found to be very meaningful because of the brotherhood that he developed with other black men.

While growing up, Chad's parents tried to instill traditional gender norms. His mother wanted him to learn how to treat a woman as a lady, in addition to being financially successful in life, and his dad wanted him to learn how to protect himself. These values are still very important to him, and he told us that he discusses with his friends how to treat women better. Chad believes that masculinity is something that is passed down from other men. Important life lessons, he claims, were taught by his older brothers, who were in turn, taught by their older brothers. Male camaraderie is very important to him.

Chad believes that there are immutable differences between men and women. He explained: "I sternly believe in a male, you know, being a strong presence and not overly emotional or overly—I'm not fond of a male having female traits or a female having too strong of male traits." At times, Chad seems to endorse the idea that men are superior to women because they are physically stronger. In fact, throughout the interview, he tries his best to distant himself from anything not strongly coded as masculine. For example, he feels the need to justify having had a manicure so it does not attenuate his toughness; he wants it known he did not get a colored polish. And he told us that he drew the line at getting a pedicure—that seemed to be pampering oneself, a too feminine activity. Despite this, he does not want to be seen as prejudiced against people who do not conform to gender rules. He told us about knowing a girl who looked masculine in the seventh grade, and how he treated her like a boy because that's how he thought she wanted to be treated. Like other *true believers*, he did not want to be seen as imposing his view on others.

In this chapter, I introduce 30 *true believers* and focus on their understandings of the contemporary gender structure. They are *true believers* because, at the macro level, they believe in a gender ideology where women and men should be different and accept religious rules that enforce gender differentiation and segregation. In addition, at the interactional level, they report having been shaped by their parent's traditional expectations, and they impose gendered expectations on those in their own social networks. At the individual level, they internalize masculinity or femininity and embody it in how they present themselves to the world.

I begin with their ideologies about how society should be on the macro level, and how they understand the world around them and cultural norms. I start here because for this group, the pathways between familial worldviews, parent's socialization patterns, and their own identities and beliefs are transparent. Their parents have raised them according to religious ideologies based on essentialist gender beliefs, and they have internalized and accepted those beliefs and live by them. These Millennial *true believers* are, however, tolerant of other people's choices. At the macro level, one major theme emerges, with two branches. The major theme is *gender just is and should be*. The men and women provide somewhat different reasons for this; the women cite God's will as explained in their literalist religious worldview, while the men are more likely to use the rhetoric of biological essentialism. At the interactional level, one theme emerged: having experienced intentional *gender specific socialization* with gender policing to enforce it. At the individual level, three themes emerged. These respondents were proud to have *internalized gender as personality traits* and to carefully *follow gendered behavioral norms*. They also are quite unhappy with their bodies (*not good enough bodies*), although this is not unique to them.

These themes span cultural meanings: beliefs in gender difference, memories of socialization into doing gender, and the consequent internalization of femininity or masculinity. At the materialist level, they also lived far more gender-segregated lives than other Millennials and could name institutional (usually religious) dictates that created male and female structures of constraints and opportunity. They also strove hard to embody, in a very material way, the femininity or masculinity that they want to present to the world. Figure 5.1 illustrates the themes that discussed in this chapter.

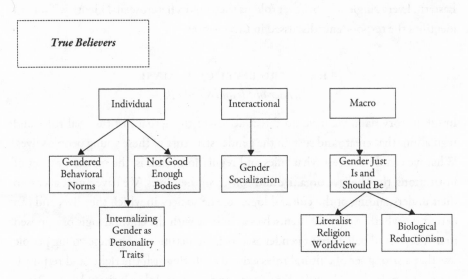

FIGURE 5.1 Themes for *True Believers*

True believers were usually raised in fundamentalist or literalist religions either by Evangelical Christian, Catholic, or Muslim families. Of the 30 *true believers*, 18 are either immigrants or the children of immigrants, a ratio not very different from the sample as a whole. The women are more likely to ascribe their traditional gender beliefs to religious doctrine than the men. In their interviews, nearly all the women referenced their religious upbringings and beliefs as explanations for their opinions about gender and sexuality. Now, not every woman raised in a literalist religious household is a true believer, some had rebelled and therefore appear in other chapters, but not one female true believer had been raised by secular parents or in a progressive faith tradition. The men in this category are more religious than others in the sample, but the men more often told us that their beliefs about gender are based on essentialist biological understandings of sex rather than religious doctrine. It may be a quirk of the sample, but it is worth noting that unlike the women, these men did not tell stories about religious backgrounds having major impacts on gendered expectations. Most men seemed to have left their parents' literalist conservative beliefs behind as they left high school. There were only two men who framed their gendered beliefs from a faith position; the rest of the male *true believers* gave nonreligious reasons for endorsing the gender structure.

Among *true believers*, there are 6 Latino/a's, 4 blacks, 12 Asians and Asian-Americans, and 5 whites. Men from all racial and ethnic groups were represented, while nearly half the women were Asian or Asian-American, including women from both India and Southeast Asia. There are three women, including Amy who you met earlier, who either identified their race as Middle Eastern or mixed white/Middle Eastern. Every single true believer told us they hold a heterosexual identity. Table 5.1 identifies the respondents discussed in this chapter.

THE MACRO LEVEL OF ANALYSIS
Gender Just Is and Should Be

In life history data, we have no direct access to the actual institutional rules and regulations that create and sustain the gender structure of these young people's lives. What we can do is assess what rules and regulations, that is, the material aspect of institutions, they believe organize and constrain their lives. We have direct access to their understanding of the cultural logics of the society in which they live, and can determine whether they see themselves as in sync with the cultural logic or opposed to it. The overall belief about gender as a social structure among these young people was that a strong set of cultural rules existed to distinguish the rights and responsibilities, the roles, and the rules for women and men; and that it should be so. There were only four comments in all of these narratives that were coded as liberal cultural beliefs, equally split between men and women. Three of these comments were about formal equality in the labor market, such as equal pay for equal work for women and men. One of the men critiqued the strict rules about the colors of pink and blue, and endorsed the right of men to cook, because he enjoyed doing so. All the rest of the responses about their cultural worldviews were easily coded as "conservative" beliefs. For example, they had strong beliefs that there are and should be appropriate and distinct socialization techniques for boys and girls and that men and women should dress and act in sex-appropriate and sex-differentiated ways. While not all of these young people are overtly homophobic, few support equality for gays and lesbians, and many worry that changing gender norms could lead to more gay people or "confusion" about sexual identity among youth. I found few differences in the responses of the men and women *true believers* at this level of analysis and therefore have presented their answers together. The women and men talk about the same religious rules that constrain women and men differently, although women talk about experiencing (legitimate in their eyes) constraints while the men do not.

TABLE 5.1
PROFILES OF *TRUE BELIEVERS*

No.	Name	Sex	Sexual Identity	Race	Religion	Immigration Status
1	Amalia Asad	Female	Heterosexual	Middle Eastern	Islam	Child of immigrant
2	Amy Smith	Female	Heterosexual	Mixed	Islam	Child of immigrant
3	Angela Smith	Female	Heterosexual	Asian	Hindu	Native-Born
4	Antonio Garza	Male	Heterosexual	Hispanic	Catholic	Native-Born
5	Cara Steward-Huez	Female	Heterosexual	Black	Christian	Native-Born
6	Carmen Tan	Female	Heterosexual	Asian	Christian	Child of immigrant
7	Chad Whitelow	Male	Heterosexual	Black	Christian	Native-Born
8	Chris Moore	Male	Heterosexual	Asian	Catholic	Child of Immigrant
9	Cori Trevor	Female	Heterosexual	Hispanic	Catholic	Child of immigrant
10	Darshana Nayar	Female	Heterosexual	Asian	Islam	Immigrant
11	Diana Boulom	Female	Heterosexual	Asian	Catholic	Native-Born
12	Elizabeth Chen	Female	Heterosexual	Asian	None	Immigrant
13	Howard Knoll	Male	Heterosexual	Black	Christian	Native-Born
14	Jane Garcia	Female	Heterosexual	Hispanic	Unsure	Child of immigrant
15	Jennifer Edwards	Female	Heterosexual	Asian	Christian	Immigrant
16	Jonathan Poem	Male	Heterosexual	Asian	Christian	Child of Immigrant
17	Manha Abbasi	Female	Heterosexual	Middle Eastern	Islam	Native-Born
18	Maribel Ramirez	Female	Heterosexual	Hispanic	Catholic	Native-Born

(continued)

TABLE 5.1
(CONTINUED)

No.	Name	Sex	Sexual Identity	Race	Religion	Immigration Status
19	Martha Brodowski	Female	Heterosexual	White	Catholic	Immigrant
20	Matteo Calderon	Male	Heterosexual	Hispanic	Catholic	Child of Immigrant
21	Megan Hu	Female	Heterosexual	Asian	None	Immigrant
22	Miranda Lambert	Female	Heterosexual	White	Catholic	Child of immigrant
23	Mona Queracy	Female	Heterosexual	Asian	Islam	Child of immigrant
24	Racquel Gonzalez	Female	Heterosexual	Hispanic	Christian	Child of immigrant
25	Richard Parker	Male	Heterosexual	White	None	Native-Born
26	Robert van Buren	Male	Heterosexual	White	None	Native-Born
27	Sara Richards	Female	Heterosexual	White	Christian	Native-Born
28	Sarah Belele	Female	Heterosexual	Black	Christian	Native-Born
29	Sarah Smith	Female	Heterosexual	Asian	Hindu	Child of immigrant
30	Tariq Valiani	Male	Heterosexual	Asian	Hindu	Immigrant

The following quotes illustrate a cultural worldview that includes the belief that men and women are and should be different kinds of people. The responses of *true believers* to the story about a Swedish school that did not use gendered pronouns were particularly illuminating. Only one of these respondents would have wanted to attend this school or would consider sending their children to such a place. For many, the explanation had to do with raising children out of step with the rest of the world. But for others, trying to create an egalitarian society without gender difference was appalling. As Jennifer Edwards argued, we must raise boys and girls to know their appropriate place.

> I think the child should know the rules and behavior of his or her gender . . . each gender should play their roles according[ly], and for that, they should know how they ought to be. So I think that is very important for everyone to know and realize . . . I think boys should take the lead in most of the things. They need to know what they are doing. They should be much more independent. Girls should also be the same way but not be too domineering.

Martha Brodowski doesn't accept the language of "stereotypes" when discussing socializing children. Instead she says in no uncertain terms that children are

> supposed to learn about their gender but not be taught that it is like a stereotype, like mentioned in the article . . . . You're not stereotyping anything. That is how it was and that is how it is supposed to be.

Among these *true believers*, gender and sexuality are conflated and presumed to be tightly bound together. We can see this in Carmen Tan's reaction to the Swedish school article:

> It might make them confused about what gender they are. I feel like if it's a guy, they should call him a guy and if it's a girl, they should call it a girl. I don't know . . . I guess it's because of my religion, and I just think it . . . I don't approve of homosexuals. And this just [is] confus[ing], it might make them grow up to be gay or lesbian. It's not that I disapprove, but it's just like, um, the Bible says that um, it should be like a guy and a girl to together, so they have offspring.

These respondents worry that allowing boys to play with dolls and to answer to ongendered pronouns in the Swedish school might lead to more gay men (which is presumptively framed as negative). This quote by Miranda Lambert begins with her quick statement about the preschool article, "I was shocked." She wrestles with her belief in freedom of choice and her acceptance of gay friends against her strong but vague cultural belief that encouraging choices about gender behaviors will encourage homosexuality, of which she disapproves despite having gay friends.

> It's almost like . . . forcing the boys to become or to act like girls, and almost . . . leading to boys becoming gay or something, which I was never against that. I believe in free love, like I have a couple of gay best friends, and they're honestly the best, and I don't know, but it just makes me, that made me mad.

Megan Hu's comment sums up their opinions about the Swedish preschool very simply. She said, "It is weird."

There is a constant tension in these young people's answers between tolerance for other peoples' choices and condemning people who do not conform to social norms. The following quotes are in response to the J.Crew ad where a mother is painting her son's toenails pink. In this quote from Richard Parker, we see the J.Crew ad in tension with his belief in individual freedom of choice, thus he disapproves. Richard says:

> Uh, I think it's wrong, but unless the kid wanted to do dress up or whatever. Then I suppose it's ok. But if the mother's beliefs or views are influenced onto the child, then it could be wrong . . . I mean, some guys paint their fingernails and toenails like women, but that's their choice. Will I do it? No.

Carmen Tan and Elizabeth Chen are worried about the relationship between pink nails and the child being mistaken for, if not becoming, gay, of which they both clearly disapprove. Chen said

> When they're kids it's fine, but if it's an adult, it might make people mistake that person as gay. I think it is not good. Because he is like really a young age. If older people do this, then little boys might get sexual orientation confusion.

Jonathan Poem can't even understand the reason for such an ad:

> I don't see the purpose of it. Why? What are they trying to tell? Why would they put that? As a guy, as a grown up, I think it's kind of weird for guys. It's just for me that 'cause I'm not used to those things, I don't have friends that actually do that stuff.

Similarly Amy Smith criticizes the mother in the J.Crew ad:

> The mom is trying to make the boy into the girl, which is not right. Because it's not like he wants to do it, very, you know, his mom is doing it. I don't know . . . I think the mother shouldn't be painting a little boy's nails, because when he's older he's going to want to do it and then people are going to judge him differently.

There was also clear disapproval among the *true believers* of the woman named Lisa in our scenario about gender atypicality in restrooms. Lisa presented herself as a female who had short hair and wore men's clothes and was being harassed by another woman while entering a women's restroom. The comments here too waver with the tension between the rhetoric of "freedom of choice" and strong disapproval of Lisa's choices. Jennifer Edwards identifies with the woman in the story giving Lisa a hard time. Jennifer had trouble believing that a woman who breaks so many gender norms about self-presentation is "really" a woman.

> I would mistake her as well. If she tells me that she's a female, I would still not believe it because she really looks like that. She has cut her hair like that, she has dressed like that. It is difficult to believe.

Matteo Calderon first couldn't believe it was for real and asked if the woman was just "doing an experiment." He had to be sure that it wasn't an "experiment" of some sort before he could respond. If it was for real, he told us:

> If she wants to change her gender then she needs to know that she can't use the woman's restroom if she wants to look like a guy. She should know the causes that comes with it—just like if an ordinary guy walks into a female's bathroom, you're going to get the same response—if you look like a guy, you're going to get treated like a guy. That's how society works.

Martha Brodowski went even further than disbelief in her reply to the story about Lisa with her comment, "it's insane." Among these *true believers*, gender and sexual preference are believed to be necessarily tied together, and wrapped in a bow with appropriate bodily presentation.

While the rhetoric of the importance of "freedom of choice" was muted here compared with the other young people in this sample, it did exist. Despite these very conservative views, most of these young people felt that if other people do not agree with their ideology "that's their choice." Although when it came to gender and sexuality choices, these *true believers* often added a caveat that people who deviated from what they considered appropriate gendered norms are "weird" and would have to live with the consequences. Still, no one wanted to deny anyone else their freedom of choice to be "weird."

This strong streak of gender conservatism does not extend to the world of work, where nearly all the women intended to succeed after they finished school. Neither women nor men believe that a woman's place is in the home, barefoot and pregnant. They do not even espouse, at this moment of their lives, support for marriages headed by male breadwinners with domestic, at-home wives. This is not to say that none of these women will become stay-at-home mothers when the pressure of balancing work and family squeezes them, but few told us about plans to do so at the time. Of course, this sample is predominantly young people in college and so is biased toward those seeking higher education and upward mobility. Still, it is very interesting that the workplace is no longer coded as masculine, or made for men, by these Millennials. What was once considered breaking gender norms, such as working in a professional job dominated by men, is no longer understood as such. There also seems to be an agreement that pay should be the same for women and men who do the same job, and everyone should be free to choose their own field. The following quote reveals this acceptance clearly. Sara Richards told us she was surprised to find men in her classes but was glad they could choose a female-dominated profession if they wanted to.

> Being a social work major you would think that that was something only girls would do. But we had a handful of boys that were in the most of my classes and that graduated with me. So I think the world is changing and accepting that boys do things that girls do also, and I think that's interesting and it's exciting to know that the world is changing like that.

The gender structure at the macro level involves not only worldview but also understandings of whether social institutions and organizations impose actual material rules and regulations, rewards and penalties differently for men and women. No one in the sample talked about organizational constraints on gender except for their religious congregations. We must remember, at this stage of life, they have yet to experience workplace discrimination or the institutionally created incompatibilities of parenting and employment. Here we have many stories among the women about religious institutional rules that regulated their behaviors as women with some but not much irritation at the constraints. Men told very few stories of institutional constraints, even religious ones. Many of the Muslim women talked about not being allowed to have boyfriends and even being discouraged from having boys as friends.

Muslim women often told their interviewers that they chose their own dress. Some chose to wear a hijab when their mother had not, others did not wear a hijab when their mothers had, but all dressed modestly and believed that women and men should follow the different rules culture set for them. Evangelical Christian women also talked about the need for women's modesty and their avoidance of skimpy clothing. Perhaps the best example of this acceptance of different rules that cultures require of men and women is stated by Mona Queracy regarding apparel rules in Islam.

> Like for example, there's a bunch of things, like a way girl and a guy dresses. For a girl in my religion we have to cover, we have to be modest, we have to cover our hair, our private parts. For a boy, he has to cover his private parts, he has to cover up to his . . . there is a specific area like for girls it is from knees to breast and for boys it is knees to his navel. And so we have different rules that are for boys and that are for girls, but it is supposed be like there is a reason why girls have to cover up to their breast because we have breasts and boys don't. So just things like that like there are different criteria for boys and girls because we are different. They are not there to make us unequal; they are there because that is just how we are.

The bodily reality that men also have hair and breasts does not seem to challenge the logic of sex-specific rules as accepted by *true believers*.

The anecdotes about institutional gender-typed rules and regulations were always about religious regulations and often included stories about sexual norms. Two female *true believers* talked about how their religious beliefs compelled them to break off friendships when they learned a friend was gay. But by far the most common story told by Christian conservative and Muslim women was about the rules against any fraternization with boys, including a ban on dating and avoiding physical contact with the opposite sex. Most report requirements to dress moderately. None of this is surprising given the stories the young women tell about the interactional expectations they face in their everyday lives. As Mona Queracy succinctly tells us:

> Well the way they raised us was that whatever Islam prohibited, they [our parents] prohibited, and there are a lot of things, the list can go on forever. The main things were like the way you dressed, the way you act.

The one major tie that binds these *true believers* into a cohesive group is a conservative worldview as traditionally defined—a belief in conserving the cultural patterns that now exist. They value the beliefs inculcated by their parents, families, and religious leaders, and simply want to recreate the world as it is today for tomorrow.

Cara Steward-Huez's comment illustrates this basic conservatism, that is, the desire to freeze social norms just the way they are:

> I'm one of those people who likes to stick with certain things. Stick with certain ways of life and the normal way of life.

For *true believers*, the traditional expectations for women and men seemed to have worked in the past and are both enshrined in religious belief and believed etched into our biology. *True believers* support the continued existence of distinct roles for women and men. And yet, they wrestle with the seeming contradiction within their belief systems; they claim to support freedom of choice as an American ideal and yet condemn others who make different choices when it comes to gender and sexuality.

THE INTERACTIONAL LEVEL OF ANALYSIS
Gender Socialization: Policing Expected

In this section, I analyze the data to answer the question of what kind of gendered standards did these young people believe they were held to by their families and their peers. What did they believe their parents and their peers required of them to behave appropriately as men or women? I begin with a discussion of parental expectations and enforcement strategies for gendered behaviors. These *true believers*, especially the women, are remarkably different from the rest of the women in the sample, recounting far more parental gendered expectations. The women tell far more stories than the men of parental expectations and constraint, although the men have a few, albeit very different ones. More than half the stories in the entire sample about gendered expectations by parents were told by female *true believers* even though they made up less than 20% of the participants. The women spoke of having earlier curfews than their brothers and a heavier housework load. There was a marked difference in how the stories were told by *true believers* compared with the other groups because most of the rules their parents enforced were accepted as legitimate, even though sometimes they reported feeling hemmed in and pushed back a little.

The women *true believers* told far more stories about parental rules and regulations than did any of the other respondents in the sample. These 21 women told us more than 90 stories about their parents' explicit gendered expectations. The most common gendered parental rule was a stricter curfew for daughters than sons, justified both with reference to physical safety and to discourage sexual activity. Both the men and the women told us that curfews were far stricter for the girls in the family. The second gendered norm enforced by parents was higher expectations for domestic labor during high school and college for daughters than sons. While parents of *straddlers* and *innovators* also often had different rules for sons and daughters, they were usually weakly enforced and often ignored by the children. Not so in these families. Parents of *true believers* strictly enforced gendered norms, with clear and open conversations, usually justified by religious ideology. These young people did not protest but rather followed the cultural logics that required girls and boys to live different kinds of lives. Nearly all the *true believers* were raised in religious households, conservative Christian native-born families or by religious immigrant parents from all over the world, from the Middle East to India, Mexico, and Poland. They do not talk about finding these childhood restrictions constraining because they share their parent's religious beliefs and adopt their cultural practices as they endorse these rules and regulations and recount them without identifying their gender specificity as a problem.

Nearly every one of these female *true believers* remembered childhoods where parents were both considerably stricter with them than their brothers and stricter than they believed parents of other American girls. Amy Smith's parents were very active in a religious community, and her father was an imam. Amy was not allowed to go to the prom, homecoming, or middle school dances, but this did not matter to her at all. In fact, she told us that the one time she went to a Halloween party she was sorry because she didn't like the "atmosphere." She explained that perhaps her parents

> tried to seclude us maybe a little bit . . . . I mean we were the first generation being raised here so they didn't want us to mix with Americans that much, 'cause they didn't want us to lose our culture and pick up the bad habits I guess.

The immigrant status of many of these women becomes significant because they frequently compare their upbringing with native-born Americans. For example Manha Abbasi told us her parents insisted on her being "modest," which meant that she had to wear capris and long sleeves. She could wear "nothing revealing." They didn't like her going out without a chaperone, and she said, "I didn't mind, I thought it was good. I felt that way too." Amalia Asad compared herself with her brothers; she was one of the young women who most chafed at the different expectations.

> I remember thinking I wish I was a guy sometimes because they always had it easier with like my parents, but I think the fact that they could always kind of go out where they wanted, and mom didn't have to like worry about what they're doing because you know how guys can go from place, to place, to place? I think I've always wanted to be a guy in that sense . . . a girl's reputation that

is like you have to be really good and actually listen to your parents and stuff. I think that, just the freedom, I think guys always had more freedom than girls growing up.

For most of these women, restrictions on dress and curfew felt legitimate, but resentment sometimes crept into their voices. This especially happened when talking about being expected to clean up after their brothers. For example, Manha Abbasi told us that her parents expected that since she was a girl, "you clean, you cook, you do those things" while her brother sat "around and did nothing." Amy Smith also told us that her parents expected the girls to help cook and clean up around the house when her brothers' didn't have to help out at all. Maribel Ramirez told us about her responsibilities growing up and how they related to her parents' hopes and dreams for her. While living at home, her chores were

helping my mom out . . . since all my brothers were there I had to, like, clean after them and do everything, wash, cook, clean while she was at work.

Comparisons with brothers sometimes were conveyed with a little jealousy. Amalia Asad wished she could see movies at the mall or go to school dances like her brothers. Darshana Nayar complained that her brothers were allowed to stay out later, and her parents refused to let her ride the back of her brother's motorcycle.

Even the daughters of very traditionally religious parents told us that they were expected to participate in both domestic and professional worlds: to be the "housewife kind of girl" who marries relatively young but also excels at school in order to get a good job, and, remarkably often, "preferably in the medical field." Amalia Asad told us her parents wanted her married by now (at age 20).

I should have been married by now, but I'll tell a lot of my friends, "Well, I'm already past the limit." We all joke about it. They all try setting me up with people, I kind of take it as a joke. I never really take it seriously, but my mom wanted me married soon. So to this day she pushes it so.

Amalia's parents expect her to go to graduate school, but, at the same time, they do not approve of her living away from home until she is married. Amalia believes her parents' ideal would be for her to attend graduate school while living with a husband.

There was also some sense of regret expressed by women whose parents didn't believe they should date or whose parents resisted their desire play soccer or engage in outdoor adventures. Cara Steward-Huez regrets her parents denying her the opportunity to be a cheerleader.

My parents didn't condone gyrating and dancing and the shorts. The outfits that they wore were really skimpy. My parents were like, if you can't wear something else, then you can't do it. I wanted to participate in it because all of my friends were a part of it but I couldn't. . . . I was sad, it was once again I felt like the outcast. And it bothered me because it was like, why can't I be like everybody else? My parents would always say, you're not like everyone else, you need to accept who you are, and don't try to be like everyone else.

Cara's parents held very strict beliefs and used interventionist strategies in both their daughter's life and Cara's daughter's life. Cara was one of the few parents in our study, and her parents were very involved in their granddaughter's life. For example, they talked to their granddaughter's kindergarten teacher when they found out another little girl had kissed her at school. They wanted to investigate whether the child had learned that unacceptable (to them) behavior at home. They needed assurance that no lesbian couple had enrolled their child in their Christian preschool. Cara didn't sound convinced that this was a serious issue but acquiesced to her parent's concerns. This kind of overt gender socialization, and disapproval of homosexuality, is reported far more often by *true believers* than by the rest of the sample.

Even these true believer women occasionally rebel. But examples of rebellion against gender norms are revealing. Amalia Asad laughs when she admits she spits sometimes. Amy Smith swears occasionally despite her parents' admonishments. Cara Steward-Huez wears her baseball cap backward in a college classroom despite her parent's disapproval. Sarah Belele had a boyfriend in high school who sent his picture to her phone (she left the exact content of the picture mysterious), her mother found it, and then "World War III" happened—she didn't get her phone back for a year. Only one woman, Miranda Lambert, defies her parents in a more drastic manner: despite their ban on sex before marriage, at 20 years old, she's been having sex with her boyfriend for two years. Miranda might have been classified as a straddler because of this sexual intimacy, but she was a true believer in different kinds of lives for women and men despite ongoing sexual activity with a boyfriend. (These categories are, after all, ideal types, and so decisions had to be made for ambiguous cases.)

Most true believer men were easily categorized as such. They told disproportionately more stories than other men in the sample about fathers socializing them for hegemonic masculinity. When the men talked about parental expectations, it was often about learning to be a masculine man. Parents signed their sons up for baseball and soccer and basketball. Fathers passed on masculine skills in craftsmanship and car maintenance. One father was glad to finally have a son who would pass on the family name. Another young man, Chris Moore, talked about being raised to be in charge of the women in his family:

> Since I'm the only male in the family, my dad has high expectations of me, and I know what it expected of me, like, whenever, when I take charge of the family, I'm supposed to be that male figure, the strength, the backbone of the family, so whenever we're introduced with problems or whatever, usually it should go through me. So positively I mean the way I was raised I understand what was expected, and so, like, I'm still learning, but I know how to handle situations.

Similarly, Matteo Calderon told us his father passes on knowledge about how to take care of the house to him because he's a son and still living at home:

> Since my brother moved out of the house and has his own family, he wants me to know everything he knows in case he passes away or something. That's how I learned how to fix a car when I was ten years old . . . . And fix houses and plumbing and everything. So the buildings that they rent, every single time something breaks, he always sends me so that I can learn. And that's pretty much how my summer, my winter, every day of the week goes.

Not only does Matteo's father want to be sure he can do the masculine chores of fixing cars and houses, but he also taught him to repress his feelings.

> At the time [of his grandfather's death] my dad told me not to cry. That guys don't shed tears. So it was really hard on me after that day on. . . . Yeah, even now. I've seen my uncle die, my cousin nearly died, my friend nearly died. I never shed a tear.

Other men reported being taught not to cry as well. Still, there were far fewer stories about gendered socialization among the men than the women in the true believer group. Perhaps the rules in these families still treat the boys as the unmarked category; rules for the children are rules for boys, with special rules for girls. And so boys don't code their upbringing as much about gender and have fewer stories to tell. The more subtle means of making them masculine may not be noticed as easily as the conventions their sisters experience—earlier curfews, clothing dictates, and assumed domestic chores—to make them feminine.

We only have the stories our respondents share with us. And so we can't observe firsthand the effectiveness of powerful socialization techniques and parental policing. We do know that this kind of overt gender socialization is reported far more by *true believers* than by the rest of the sample. They were expected to follow gendered rules and they do. They spend more time in gender-segregated environments than most others, and so there is a material consequence of following parental expectations, they socialize mostly with same-sex others. While most attend gender-integrated public schools, much of their free time is sex segregated.

While both women and men report parental gender socialization, men report less peer policing than do women. When women report peer policing, they talk about Millennial women outside their close communities stigmatizing them for looking different. These women recounted stories of being made to feel different by others outside their close networks because of their dress, whether a hijab or simply out-of-fashion modest apparel. Amalia Asad commented on how different she dressed from those outside of her culture.

> But I know that whenever a lot of girls would wear shorts and stuff like that I would be different. Because as a girl we're supposed to be more covered up in our culture, and to them it was like, "Oh, if it's hot, you wear shorts and a tank," so I always felt different in that sense, but I always thought that what I was doing was normal because my mom was always covered. But for them, they [the girls she knew] would always question me, not that I felt uncomfortable, but I was like, "Oh my gosh, I should be wearing shorts," but I couldn't. So I always felt different in that sense.

Darshana Nayar does not usually wear a hijab. When she does, she feels as if the people around her stare. When she finishes recounting this experience, she looks down quietly.

> But sometimes I go to pray, to a mosque, and when I'm driving I'm covered, and you see a car next to you, and they just look at you different. Like, if you weren't wearing anything, they wouldn't look at you, but now that you . . . I dunno . . . It feels weird, but I don't feel bad about it. I would keep doing it, but I just don't like doing it.

When these young women report feeling punished for "doing gender," it is for looking different, and more conservative, than other Millennial women. They report others reacting negatively to a hijab or critiquing their dressing standards as too modest.

The true believer men very rarely buck masculine tradition and so do not set themselves up for peer policing. Their sex-segregated social lives involve some gender policing by peers but not nearly as often as others in the sample. They don't remember peers policing their gender violations very much because they don't violate the rules to trigger reactions. When they did mention stories about peer pressure, they provide examples of other conservative men policing them for very small acts of deviance such as driving a car that is (feminine coded) pink, having a neat, well-organized bedroom, or being a good listener. Several young men admitted to occasionally playing with their sister's dolls as children. Chris Moore told us his sisters would chase him away: "Why, are you playing with girls' stuff? You should be playing with guys' stuff." He suffered teasing from male friends as a teenager when he played volleyball, a sport they believed too feminine. Even now, as an adult, Chris faces interactional sanctions for driving a little pink car inherited from his sister. He fears the looks of derision, being somewhat embarrassed by it. But the car gets good gas and it was free, so he has come to terms with ignoring the sarcasm. In one particularly poignant tale, we see how great the sensitivity is among these men when even slightly entering feminine terrain. Chris told us that having older sisters meant he had learned to talk easily with women, and so became one of the "go-to-guys" for female friends to confide in. Some of his buddies found out and teased him, saying that he was "too feminine." Chris decided that they were just jealous because he could interact so well with the girls. In this social world of *true believers*, simply being a good listener was enough to create negative sanctions from male peers. Only one man, Tariq Valiani told us a story about a serious gender violation, crying, for which his high school friends ridiculed him.

> I guess, in high school I cried once, and I guess people considered that feminine, stop being a girl and crying.

These *true believers* are quite distinct from the other men in this sample because of their far fewer stories about peer pressure. We cannot know if that's because they didn't want to admit to gender deviance to mostly female interviewers, and thus wouldn't discuss what happened when they broke gender norms. An alternative possibility is that they have succeeded so well at being stereotypically masculine that they have faced very little peer policing, with little deviance for anyone to notice or stigmatize. They convey a great concern not to exhibit behavior that might conceivably be considered feminine, and so provide examples of very minor gender infractions, when they mention any at all. Among the men in the larger sample, only the *true believers* recount very few moments of breaking norms. They follow the rules and are keenly aware that the slightest deviation will have consequences. They take pride in meeting the expectations for manliness and believe men and women are and should be very different.

In sum, these millennial *true believers* tell many and varied stories about explicit gender socialization, mostly by parents. In their families of origin, different rules for sons and daughters are not openly challenged; instead, they are usually considered legitimate, justified by religious doctrine. While occasionally such rules chafe, they do not often report feeling constrained because they share their parents' worldview and accept their place in the gender structure. Nor do they report many instances of peer policing as they rarely deviate from social expectations within their own communities. Yet, even with strong family and peer pressure, all of these respondents claim, as does everyone in the sample, that whatever pressures they face, in the end, whatever they do is their own free will. Now, we move on to discuss who they believe they have come to be as individuals and the choices they make.

THE INDIVIDUAL LEVEL OF ANALYSIS
Gendered Behavioral Norms

To understand how these young people describe their personalities, the extent to which they had internalized gendered norms into their very sense of self, we coded in several ways. First, we coded descriptions of activities that could be identified as female-typed (shopping for clothes and accessories, taking ballet classes) or masculine (playing in the dirt, physical aggression). We then coded their personal goals and noted if any were stereotypically masculine or feminine. We then coded any answers that indicated how they saw their personalities as feminine or masculine.

The first step I took to analyze the data was to look at what activities they tell us they do. The *true believers* had very different personal life stories from others in the sample. These *true believers* adhered far more strictly to gendered norms and told far fewer stories about breaking them. Both women and men told us about living gender stereotypical lives. Their lives were different, and so will be how I present their stories. The 21 women told us many stories about activities they enjoyed that were easily coded as feminine, including shopping, fixing their hair, liking to play with Barbie dolls, accessorizing, and getting their nails done. The women told stories about enjoying the very first time their mother dolled them up in a fancy dress. A few representative quotes will suffice. Angela Smith told us she was like other girls because she liked playing with dolls and always wanted to be a princess for Halloween. Martha Brodowski similarly told us she was like other girls because she liked

> doing girly stuff, clothes, looking nice, bracelets, earrings, just doing girly stuff.
> Cooking.

Mona Queracy told us she was

> always kind of a girly girl, so I always liked to dress up and, like, wear dresses and nice clothes and jewelry. Every time my mom would do makeup, I would come stand by her and ask her to put some on me too.

In the narratives of the female *true believers*, we heard very few stories of nonconforming gender activities, and most of these were spiked with contradictory comments about also liking traditionally gendered ones. Most of these gender violations were hardly radical rebellions. One young woman, Amalia Asad told us she was sometimes called a tomboy in elementary school because she dressed "like a boy" and could run well. The lesson she took home, however, was to be sure she looked feminine at other times. Racquel Gonzalez loved to play with toy cars, and Sarah Belele likes to play football and watch basketball. Another young woman, Cara Steward-Huez tried to play basketball with her cousins, in her parentally required skirt, but was told "girls sit on the sideline . . . and cross their legs," and so she did. Cara told a story about her major experience breaking a gender norm: wearing her baseball cap backward with gym shoes. She recounts

> I was like, I want to buy some gym shoes, and even now my mom looks at me, she's like, why do you have gym shoes on, why you're a girl. You're not supposed . . . . She likes casual flats.

So how do these women *true believers* handle the apparent contradiction between believing they should refrain from masculine activities and occasionally doing something mildly beyond traditional femininity? For Cara, the solution was to decide that her rebellious act was no longer gender nonconforming because wearing her hat backward and gym shoes on a college campus was not noticed by her classmates. She believes it's now acceptable for women to dress like this on campus, although she still refrains from doing so near her family, as it would be considered rebellious and disrespectful. Driving a car with a stick shift was the only example of gender nonconformity Martha Brodowski remembered ever having committed. Martha's justification was that even though driving a stick shift in America is not considered feminine, everyone did it in Poland, where she grew up, and so it wasn't really masculine. Two women loved toy cars as girls. Both found acceptable ways to play with them by using vehicles in make-believe games with their Barbie dolls, reducing the perceived gender atypicality. The smallest variation from stereotypical femininity is considered gender nonconformity among these young women, including being "nature friendly" and liking to play outside. In nearly every act of mildly breaking a gender norm, these young women resolved the contradiction between their beliefs and their behavior by reframing what is feminine and coming to believe their behaviors were indeed feminine after all.

None of these women understood a college degree or a high-paying job as inconsistent with essentialist beliefs about gender difference or even male supremacy. Even among true believer Millennials, education and job success were not conceptualized as breaking gender norms at all, but rather as being done in the service of the family, to help support parents and future children. Their occupational goals included ER doctor, "anything in the medical field," biologist, social worker, nurse, and physician's assistant. Most of their occupational goals did involve helping people, and in that sense fall within a feminine purview. Only one woman, Cara Steward-Huez had a nontraditional career goal, playing for the WNBA, but her discussion of it sounded more like fantasy than a plan, "I've always thought about that. Wow, not be a basketball player's wife but just to be the actual player." Whatever their occupational goal, working for pay is taken for granted even by the most religious of these young women. Nearly all wanted to finish their education and get a job before settling down. As Jennifer Edwards said, "I first want to concentrate on my studies . . . I just don't want to distract myself too much."

Like the women, every man told us some stories about activities coded appropriate for their sex, in this case coded as traditionally masculine. These nine men told us 37 stories between them. They told us about childhoods where they were in the Boy Scouts, played a variety of sports from baseball to football to lacrosse and golf. They lifted weights and enjoyed video games. They liked playing with action figures and toy guns. They took out the trash. They learned to do hard manual labor, fix cars, and renovate houses. Many, but not all, reported physical fights, some take martial arts, and most work out at the gym.

These young men believed that boys and girls were different, and they tried hard to live this truth in their lives. Richard Parker told us he liked "playing hard and getting dirty and being outside kind of thing. I don't know, what boys do, ride bikes and stuff." He wanted us to be clear that he didn't stay inside and play with dolls. Antonio Garza told us, "In high school I was in JROTC [Army], and there were times we had to go to events like the forest and camp out and do stuff like that." Chad Whitelow said:

I like action figures and cars, and stuff like that. You know, I always wanted wrestling toys and stuff like that. I mean, I would, I played with dolls when I was with my female cousins and stuff, because I didn't have any action figures with me—but if I had two Barbies, they would be fighting. [laughs] I think it was only like a little bit of violence that made me realize that I was a boy.

Half of these men admitted to some activities that were not typically for men; I wouldn't necessarily have identified these behaviors gender atypical if the young men themselves had not been so sensitive to conformity that they labeled them so. Jonathan Poem admitted to wishing that leggings were made for men because they looked comfortable for working out and sleeping. Matteo Calderon had once painted his girlfriend's nails for her and recounted it as breaking a gender norm. Robert Van Buren had a manicure, although without polish. He also loved his sister's Easy Bake Oven and shared it with her. Antonio Garza once had long hair, which he deemed important enough to mention as a gender norm violation. Chad Whitelow recounted wearing makeup to complete a college classroom assignment to break a gendered social norm. This was the only time he remembered ever having broken a gender norm. These true believer Millennials try hard to limit behavior to normatively male activities both because they desire to meet parental and peer expectations and because they have become strongly gendered men.

Internalization of Gender as Personality

Perhaps so few of these men broke norms, and weak norms when they did, is because they had strong personal investments in a masculine identity. All of these men talked explicitly about masculinity and the nine men told 23 independent stories about their masculine sense of self. For example, Chris Moore talks about lifting weights:

> I mean in high school that's when I started lifted weights and stuff because, even though I had a girlfriend, there were still sometimes where I wanted to, I wanted to be intimidating, I don't really know why, I think because I wasn't really looking for anybody at the time, but I wanted to be intimidating so nobody would mess with me and it worked.

Jonathan Poem explains that men don't need to talk about their emotions:

> I think we don't have to say much, we don't have to express our feelings that, like, you're my best friend. We don't have to say that. We just know, like, how we feel.

Tariq Valiana agrees with Jonathan when he says "guys aren't meant to be that emotional," and I know he was talking about himself because he was proud that when he didn't get the girl he wanted, he got mad and took a break from dating, he didn't let himself cry. Although Chris Moore admits to crying when his older sister started preschool, leaving him alone at home (which means he must have been a toddler.) Howard Knoll claims that growing up without a father made him "stronger." Robert Van Buren similarly describes his endorsement of a masculine self-identity; he just doesn't do nurturance "It's awkward for me to try to comfort somebody. I just really don't know what to say."

Like the women, and despite much concern about displaying and defending masculine selves, half of these true believer young men admitted to having some feminine attributes or having had them as children. Chad Whitelow tells this story about how nurturing he is, but embedded within is his declaration of the masculine characteristic of repressing one's feelings. He elaborates:

In high school, a friend of mine, a really close friend of mine, her mother, her little sister were all stabbed to death, and everybody at school was real hurt and sad and down. You know, of course, I was hurt too, but I felt like it was my duty to not show that hurt and kind of mend everyone else's feelings. There was a point in the day where we were all out in the hallway, you know we were all in the same class, and some of the young ladies had to step out, and I got some guys together to make sure they were all right. We went outside, and I don't remember exactly what I said, but I know I said something and with all these tears, everybody started dying laughing. Like they were just cracking up. One of the girls walked up to and said, "Chad, that's the reason why I love you. 'Cause you just know exactly what to say." I just felt like that's my duty to make people happy because I hate it when people are sad around me, or you know, not feeling one hundred percent.

Richard Parker similarly tries to soothe hurt feelings "when a friend is down, I sometimes can be gentle towards them, treating them kindly, I suppose to keep them, to keep them from being further down. I don't know." What is striking to me about these men's stories about their feminine sides is that they are childhood memories or embedded in the more masculine ideal of repressing one's feelings to help others, to be chivalrous. So while they admitted to some feminine behaviors or personality traits, they did so in the context of having overcome these childish indiscretions.

One strategy used by *true believers*, if they occasionally stumbled into doing something typically seen as inappropriate for their sex, was to hold onto a very strong identity as feminine or masculine. For example, 12 of these women told us stories that indicated a self-conscious and reflective pride in owning a very feminine personality and identity. Amy Smith was very clear that she had no friends that were men because "girls stuck to girls." Angela Smith agreed that she only hung out with girls and simply is a "girly girl." Cori Trevor identifies herself as a very nurturing person who always takes care of other people:

When a friend is going through something emotional I try to help them out. In any way I can. I try to bring their mood up. If I'm not able to, it makes me feel kind of responsible because I wasn't able to help out.

However strict their gender socialization, all of these women believe they eventually make their own decisions about dress standards, modesty, and behavior. And while they all believe in the gender structure as it is, they do make a variety of different personal decisions about their clothing choices. The following quote by Mona Queracy shows very clearly both the expectations that the Arab women in the *true believers* sample faced and also the freedom they feel to make their own decisions about whether to wear the hijab. Mona's mother does not wear a hijab and was "really shocked" when Mona decided to do so, after being inspired by an Islamic studies teacher at her private school.

> Well, for a woman to wear a hijab it is kind of like . . . it is said to be mandatory because it makes you modest. There are a bunch of purposes for it but it is also, like everything else in life, whether you chose to follow it or not, it is your decision . . . . Forcing somebody to wear it or like forcing someone to believe what they do not believe is not allowed . . . . The point is if you accept it within you, then that is the only reason it will matter. But if you're doing it just to please people, you are not going to get any reward for it. You're unhappy; there is no point of it. . . . But it is your personal choice and personal views and people should be okay with that, but obviously culturally and socially people are mean about it.

Darshana Nayar told a very similar story but with a decidedly different outcome

> Back in India, if I tried to look like this [points up and down her body], my parents wouldn't approve. My grandma wouldn't have it either. So, I used to just cover myself, and I didn't mind. But then I moved here, and if I was completely covered, people look at you differently. And my parents didn't force me to cover myself. They were just like, "It's up to you. If you wanna wear a hijab, go ahead. If you don't wanna wear a hijab, it's up to you also." So, I started out wearing just regular jeans and T-shirt, and then I started working. I was making more money, I went shopping more.

Amy Smith provides a glimpse of how despite very strong socialization and cultural expectations she eventually came to the conclusion that whatever she chose is her free choice, even if that choice came at the beginning in the sixth grade when she was clearly still under her families influence.

> I decided to wear the head scarf when I was in sixth grade . . . . I never thought about it, but my mom wore it, so I mean it was just like a thing that eventually

you're going to like—and all our friends did at that age so I mean, it's kind of an early age for most people, but I just had to do it 'cause my sister was doing it. So I wore it, and then I still wore like normal jeans, and like shorts and sweaters, nothing changed. But then when I got to my junior and senior year of high school maybe I started dressing like more modestly . . . . As a kid you don't really think about it, and my parents were never strict about what we had to wear. And they didn't even make us wear the head scarf, like my dad had to tell me like a million times, "Are you sure you wanna wear it? 'Cause once you do, you can't take it off," and I was like "No, I want to do it." They were never strict on that it was our choice.

While the choice was her own, the rule that once she made it as a preteen, she must always live with it was not.

Still, not every true believer sees herself as naturally feminine, modest, or subordinate, sometimes they have to work at it. Cara Stewart-Huez is a complicated woman, included in the group of *true believers* because of her essentialist views about gender and her religious articulation of them. But she is also aware that she has an aggressive side to her personality, and so she has decided she will have to manipulate a husband into believing he is in charge even though she plans to be. She believes a man must be the head of the household, or, at least, he must believe he is. And so, she's got a strategy worked out,

I'm a go-getter. So when it comes to something that I want, even with me, my friends will say that I'm the one out of the group where if I see a guy and I like him I will go and I'll talk to him before he even has an opportunity to approach me. So I'm aggressive in that sense, even with things I want out of life. If I want a particular car, I'm aggressive to the point where it's like I'm going to go get the car, and I'll have the car or have whatever it is that I want. . . . I'm the more dominant one in the relationship. So it's not so much that I call the shots, but it's like a vast majority, it's like a mind game almost I think in relationships. When you are the aggressive one because in the man's mind he thinks that he's the dominant one, but it's like when you're the aggressor you can make the person feel like they're the dominant one, but in actuality it's like you are controlling the situation from their mind. Physically they may be in control, but mentally it's like you're in control.

Powerful women may be disallowed in Cara's world, but she knows she needs to be one, and so plots how to hide her influence and trick her man into believing he's in charge.

Other true believer women also prided themselves on leadership skills gained in clubs at school while still defending their strong identity as feminine. Diana Boulom talks about a Cambodian Thai club and how leadership skills learned there helped her in an all-female sorority at college.

> I was forced to be president, and then I was president again in my senior year.
> So it kinda gave me leadership skills which helped me with joining the sorority.
> Because in the sorority, you really need leadership skills to handle everything.

Sara Richards talks about debating her high school biology teacher, defending her belief in creationism, as an example of learning to be strong and to stand up for her beliefs. She then tested her leadership skills by standing in for the youth pastor at a church conference when he became ill. In both cases, she honed skills stereotypically considered masculine in the service of a traditional religion that taught her men should be in charge.

While these women are proud of their leadership skills, and even sometimes being aggressive, none of them explicitly admitted to being masculine in any way. The true believer women tell no ironic stories about gender constraints nor recount proud tales of breaking norms. They try hard to fit into their role in society, to be polite, nurturing, feminine women. When they do something slightly beyond the bounds of feminine stereotypes, they work hard to redefine their activities as gender appropriate or create a manipulative strategy to hide their power or leadership.

Not Good Enough Bodies

Before we leave the section about identities, it is important to discuss how these Millennial *true believers* talk about their bodies because that topic came into conversations in response to direct questions but also throughout the interviews even when questions were not targeted to the issue. Both women and men sound alienated from their physical selves. No one seems to be able to do gender well enough with the bodies they have; the ideals are far beyond the material reality they have to work with.

These women use the body very consciously, to do gender appropriately. Sometimes they even use their looks to counteract somewhat less traditional behavior. For example, because Amalia Asad could run so fast and beat the boys in races, afterward she went home to "do my hair or something." These 21 young women told 42 negative stories about their bodies, and nearly every respondent told at least one. Many believed themselves too fat, especially in high school. Although a few were concerned they were too thin. One young woman really wanted a smaller "butt," while another told us it was "a black thing" that she wanted more "booty." One had breasts she believed were too small and dreamed about an implant her family would never allow. Women thought their feet were too big or their face too scarred with acne.

There was real pain in their voices as they talked about their bodies, much of it focused on concerns with weight. Cara Stewart-Huez told us:

> I was a chubby kid, so I struggled with my self-esteem and my weight. For you to have this particular set of friends and you have to go make new friends knowing that, you know you're a fat kid and people may not look at you that way. It was hard.

But Cara tells us she got a "boost of confidence" when she lost 30 pounds. Cori Trevor tells a similar story, she lost 30 pounds and got a big boost to her self-confidence in the eighth grade. "I intentionally did it so I wouldn't be made fun of anymore." Racquel Gonzalez also talked about having "issues" with weight until she started getting good at soccer and swimming which resulted in her losing weight. Maribel Ramirez answered the question about how she felt about her body growing up with a simple answer, "bad." Sara Richards told us how she felt about her body growing up and replied, "We didn't have the best relationship." Sara's comment seems to sum of the feelings of the majority of these female *true believers*.

As with all the females in this sample, weight loomed large in the *true believers'* self-concept and self-esteem. Since many of these women are immigrants or daughters of immigrants, their stories about their bodies often had a cross-cultural twist. Darshana Nayar recounts how being slightly overweight in India didn't really matter but that all changed when she came to America.

> Back in India I was fine with it. I was a little bit—I wasn't completely overweight, but I considered myself overweight. But, I was fine with it. But here, when I moved here, I saw other girls, they were much more skinny than me. I dunno, it just made me feel less confident about myself. And then—but I didn't do anything about it. I was like, "Oh, whatever, I don't care." And then, even in high school when I graduated, I was still kinda fatter. But then it was just—I still didn't care. And then when I started commuting, I started losing a lot of weight. And then now, I'm fine.

We find strong evidence that these women had negative emotions about their bodies: only four narratives included any instances of positive comments about their physical self, and all four were how much better they felt about themselves after losing weight. These data clearly indicate real pain that suffused these young women's lives in their pursuit of an appropriately feminine, thin, but curvy, body.

Many of the men (six of nine) also told us about feeling badly about their bodies, especially when they were younger. The complaints were mostly about being too short, and either too thin or too chubby. There was not the passionate pain in their stories that we heard from the women. These men don't seem particularly self-reflective about their bodies. Only one young man actually mentions anything he really liked about his body and that was embedded in a comment about losing weight. The most frequent scenario recounted was growing up and out of caring about weight. The men who were uncomfortable being short, however, didn't seem to get over worrying about it. As Matteo Calderon informs us:

> I hate being short . . . because people don't take me serious . . . mostly on the female side I guess . . . . If I could change anything about myself I would change my height.

And yet, Matteo also believed he enjoyed an advantage from being short, that is, not looking too threatening in his tough neighborhood.

> I looked like a kid, like a small boy not my age. That helped me because—I guess if you look like a gang banger then problems will come to you pretty much. So I guess me looking like younger than my age, I guess I don't look like a threat to people. So that helped me a lot . . . I guess for like the bully and everything, I'm short, so no one ever really picked fights with me or anything.

The men and women *true believers* remembered being explicitly socialized by their parents to be feminine women or masculine men. The men remember their fathers especially as training them to be stoic. Both women and men are proud they meet their parental expectations and have become the young adults their parents want them to be, rarely breaking gender norms. The women try hard to hide any aggressiveness, and to be the warm, traditional, and caring young women, who present their bodies with a modesty required by their religions. The men try to become the tough guys they are meant to be, both by internalizing masculinity as an identity and by trying hard to have tough bodies, to embody masculinity at the material level.

BACK TO THE FUTURE
Conserving the Gender Structure for the Next Generation

These young *true believers* have the comfort of great consistency in their lives. Their parents raised them to live gendered lives, and they do so, but not only do they comply with parental expectations, but they have also internalized self-identities that embrace traditional masculinity or femininity, and they endorse worldviews that naturalize essential differences between the sexes. Their ideology matches their practice and their internalized identities. Smooth gender sailing as long as they stay on the pond that is their community.

The male and female *true believers* are indistinguishable when they talk in the abstract about their cultural understandings of the gender structure. They both believe in a world where men and women know their place and live inside it. They react negatively to possibilities of social change in feminist directions and disapprove when people break gender norms in their behavior or self-presentation. While they use the rhetoric of free choice for themselves and others to conform to the gender structure or not, they seem quite willing to use interactional strategies to punish gender nonconformity when they encounter it. So they believe in free choice, but they also police gender.

These young people face strong parental pressures to adopt feminine or masculine behaviors, self-presentations, and selves. The women talk about their parents' explicit goals to ensure that they become domestic, respectful, and modest. The young men remember being taught to be tough, emotionally repressed, and skilled at masculine tasks such as home and car repair. Both men and women face explicit and deliberate gender socialization, but the women have far more stories to tell than the men, having faced more daily restrictions and constraints. While some of the women occasionally chafe at the greater freedoms of their brothers, few really complain or try to change the rules their parents enforce. Neither men nor women tell very many stories about their peers policing their behavior because deviating from gendered scripts is a rare occurrence, and when they do, it's a mild kind of nonconformity.

It is important to understand that whatever effect gender socialization might have played in these young adult lives, they are quite committed to making their own decisions and experience their choices as personal agency. This is a hallmark of all the respondents in the study, the almost religious belief in their ability to be individuals and make free choices about their lives, including gender norms.

These men and women are both very different kinds of people and hold a very similar position vis-à-vis the gender structure. They both have gendered self-concepts and a desire to "do gender" traditionally, that is, to conform to a gender structure where women are modest and feminine and men are the leaders, emotionally tough, and resilient. None of these young people talk about being coerced into the lives they lead, rather they talk about wanting to conform. They have been raised to live within the confines of gender, and they have internalized gendered selves and reiterate worldviews that legitimate gender difference and inequality. They work to present appropriately gendered bodies, whether that means dieting or working out at the gym, and are proud to display all of their gendered personalities. In their cultural schemas, men have freedoms, rights, and responsibilities that women do not. And women have responsibilities to be the kind of nurturing people that society needs, but the same is not required of men.

Religion is the one institution that men and women *true believers* identify as having rules and regulations that do and should differ by sex. These rules extend to dictates about dress, modesty, dating, and marriage. They structure the material differences between the sexes. Women talk a great deal more about religious rules than do men, both because they are more impacted by restrictions and, in this sample, they are more personally religious as well. For every woman who is a true believer, faith in literalist religions is the explanation for accepting the current gender structure. Men raised in literalist traditions are also *true believers*, but they talk more about essentialist biological differences between the sexes than about religious dictates. Men and women clearly hold different investments in the gender structure, with women giving up freedoms available to men, but perhaps gaining protections within traditional religious subcultures (Kaufman 1991; Stacey 1990; Haddad, Smith, and Moore 2006). Men simply retain the benefits of male privilege. What becomes clear from the data, if not surprising, is the link between literalist religions, heteronormativity, and homophobia. Those with a sacred explanation for sex differences conflate sexuality and gender normativity. They worry about reducing gender socialization, and they reject the possibility that men and women might be more alike than different because they fear that reducing gender difference may mean more people becoming homosexual, which is seen as negative by these *true believers*.

We cannot know definitively where their worldview comes from, but we do know that these young women's and men's parents raised them within these literalist faith traditions and are believers themselves. Using these life history narratives, we can trace the respondent's stories from their parent's cultural logics and their religious organizations' rules and regulations (the macro level) to the expectations they faced during parental gender socialization patterns (the interactional level). And thus far, as they enter adulthood, their parents appear successful at raising children who adopt their traditional gender structures and become the adults their parents hoped for. These kinds of data preclude a serious conversation of causality but do provide provocative hypotheses: here it appears as if the macro worldviews of parents are transmitted to children through their socialization practices, and these young people have adopted their parents' worldview. They do not feel oppressed by religious gendered regulation. Thus, the hypothesis based on their stories is that the causality flows from macro through interactional to individuals.

And yet, even among these *true believers*, we begin to see adaptation to the modern American cultural ideologies of free choice, individualism, and upward mobility for both sexes. We had no respondent, male or female true believer, espouse a gender norm that suggested college-educated women must identify being a wife and mother as a career goal. Of course, women who go to college are self-selected toward independent workplace success, and some may become full-time mothers, for a short time or perhaps as a lifestyle. Still, traditionalists a generation ago were far more likely to believe a woman should plan a life devoted to her family. These young people, while holding close to the gender structure of the past, are also changing it simply by living in a world where women are free to choose their careers and succeed at them. So, in that sense, we can see how a gender structure is dynamic. Even *true believers* face competing cultural logics, and, by doing so, both support and begin to change the contours of a gendered worldview.

If once upon a time, the women's movement grew out of youth rebellion, these Millennials suggest that today the politics of gender are far more complicated and that cohort replacement does not necessarily lead to increasing equality for women. These young people are opposed to gender-bending, that is, allowing women to move beyond traditional femininity or encouraging men to acknowledge feminine aspects of themselves. In this way, they differ tremendously from the rest of the sample. While they take for granted a woman's right to a career, they do not conceptualize that as about gender. They see that as simply endorsing the American dream of supporting their families' goals for upward mobility, and in today's world that takes the income of both husbands and wives. In the next chapter, I introduce the *innovators*, whom I think of as the "traditional" feminists in this study. Like the *true believers*, they too hold a consistent set of beliefs. In their case, however, they reject the gender structure, at least culturally, as far as it stands for differential rights, roles, or responsibilities for women and men. They firmly believe that men and women's lives ought to converge for full equality between the sexes.

6

The Innovators

IN THIS CHAPTER, I tell the story of the *innovators*. I introduce these 21 young adults, about 20% of the total sample, and provide a short portrait of them. Before doing so, I introduce you to two of these *innovators* so you can have a snapshot of two real people to think about as you read the chapter.

Let me introduce Ed Macias. Ed is a 24-year-old, native-born man whose parents were born in Mexico. While growing up, he was never interested in sports. Instead, his passion has always been fashion. He was chosen "best dressed" in his high school yearbook for all four years. Looking back from young adulthood, he tells us he knew he was gay for a long time, but hid his identity during his teen years by acting stereotypically heteronormative and masculine. He married a woman, and they had a child together. He then came out of the closet and divorced his wife, with whom he remains close friends, and continues to co-parent.

Growing up, Ed looked up to his brothers and felt pressured to be as "macho" as they were. His family constantly policed his behavior, asking him to "man up." Even though he tried to live up to stereotypically masculine gender ideals, he still detoured around at least some gender norms. For example, his parents confronted him on his decision to switch his major from interior design to cosmetology. But he stood his ground and refused to acquiesce. Similar to other *innovators*, Ed believes traditional gender norms should be eliminated. His experience growing up led to this position, as he felt pressured to present himself as traditionally masculine and spend time with the boys in his family, even though he preferred the company of girls. Now he feels that everyone should be allowed to express gender as they choose, and he has persuaded his family to accept his sexuality and his interest in some traditionally female activities, including his occupation. He still appreciates a good sports game as a spectator.

Let me introduce Lucy Holmes. Lucy is a 21-year-old white woman who identifies as heterosexual. She was raised as a Catholic but is now an atheist. Lucy's parents enforced strict rules on their children while they were growing up. Lucy and her siblings were not allowed to date or wear revealing clothes. Lucy, however, claims that she broke every single rule that her parents set for her throughout her childhood and adolescence. Lucy describes herself as "really independent" and claims not to rely on anyone but herself for anything. Ironically, this desire for independence is a quality she remembers her parents instilled in her, and so while they had strict rules, they also encouraged self-reliance.

Lucy desires to be free to do anything a man can. Her reaction to the article about the gender-neutral school was very positive. She found the school particularly appealing because she had to attend a school where boys and girls were not treated equally. She explains that she never wanted to be an all out tomboy but rather a girl who does "guy stuff." She believes that restricting children to certain behaviors or activities based on gender lowers their self-esteem. She has always broken gender norms, refuses to follow any expectations she might face because she is female, and she would like to live in a world without gender distinctions.

These young people, and the rest of the respondents in this chapter, are *innovators* not simply because they self-consciously reject aspects of the gender structure (though they do) as many *straddlers* were critical of some aspects of the gender structure as well. They are *innovators* because they are consistently critical of the gender structure; at the macro level of ideology they reject gender essentialism and sexism; at the interactional level they feel constrained by expectations and try to define new ones for themselves and others; and at the individual level they articulate oppositional attitudes toward gendered expectations and constraints into their very sense of self. The *innovators* reject the gender structure, both the cultural and material components, at the macro and interactional levels of analysis. But at the individual level, they only reject the cultural beliefs in sexism but not the material embodiment of how they present themselves as gendered persons. They do not reject self-presentation as male or female as do the *rebels*, introduced in the next chapter. To highlight the complexity of these *innovators'* lives, I want to note that the categories are porous, especially between *innovator* and *rebel*. One of the male *innovators*, Daniel Penn, talked explicitly about deciding whether to identify as genderqueer and, by doing so, to reject gender categories. He told us, "There are times I wanted to identify as queer. I feel conflicted because the work that I do [anti-sexist and anti-violence activism] requires there to be binaries: requires there to be male and female, masculine and feminine, and that's why I feel stuck. That's why I do it" (i.e., continue to identify as male and not genderqueer). We do not know if Daniel will continue to identify as a man or move toward a genderqueer identity in the future, nor whether any of the others will adopt new or different identities tomorrow. If Daniel had currently identified as genderqueer, I would have categorized him as someone who was rejecting the gender structure in its totality, including the gender binary itself, and so his story would be in the next chapter with the *rebels*. This analysis—as any cross-sectional research—presents one moment in time. Daniel's analysis of his identity shows us how sometimes picking a gender identity is a journey.

I begin this chapter with a focus on the individual level of analysis, what these young people tell us about their sense of themselves, how gendered (or not) they perceive their activities, goals, and personalities. I begin here because unlike the *true believers*, these Millennials do not seem driven by their ideological beliefs; their worldviews are more taken for granted than at the center of their lives. Nor are they often purposefully challenging gender expectations, for themselves or others, although they sometimes do indeed ignore them. Instead, they are innovating primarily in their personal lives. And so I begin here, with how they see themselves and their choices. There are four themes that emerged from reading these narratives. First, all these *innovators* are proud of their ability to *mix 'n' match* gendered behaviors. When it comes to *mix 'n' matching* their personalities, however, the stories diverge by sex. The women are as proud of mix 'n' matching their personality traits from a grab bag of traditionally masculine and feminine as they are about their mixing up their behaviors. The men, not so much. The men are acutely aware that hegemonic masculinity can be oppressive to women. They do not want to benefit from unearned privilege; and so they withhold enthusiasm when discussing their own masculinity, sometimes even apologizing for it. They may not reject masculinity entirely, but they do reject hegemonic masculinity. When it comes to the second theme, *the body*, a summary is simple: both women and men, nearly all of them, dislike their bodies, and many explicitly tie that to societal expectations that flow from gender norms. Even when they felt little pressure to follow gendered behavioral norms, they still feel coerced to follow the rules about presenting their bodies in heteronormative gendered ways. They may not always try hard to do so, but they feel the pressure. They may not bother to perfect gendered self-presentation, but they do not openly rebel against it either. Like everyone else in this research, these *innovators* want to get a good job and support their families, but with the added twist that some of them want to find careers that will allow them to change the world, which makes sense since their ideological beliefs are anti-sexist.

I then move to the interactional level. In that section three themes emerge. The first applies only to the women: the *you-go-girl* memories of parents who did not limit behavior because they were girls. The young men remembered quite different boyhoods, which included shaming from their families whenever they broke gender norms. The second theme about peer *gender policing* was apparent in both the men and women's narratives, but spoken of differently. The women felt policed not for what they did, but how they looked as they approached and navigated puberty. The men's stories involve parents and peers, and focus on a variety of behaviors that were perceived as effeminate, from body language to choice of sports. The men were shamed for what they did, not for how they looked. The men's stories were far more painful than the women's, as gender policing was perceived to be an attack on their sexual identity as well. Friend, families, and church members sanctioned boys for breaking gender norms in an attempt to prevent them from becoming, or acting, gay. For both men and women, the stories about painful gender policing are told as history, with nearly all of these young people claiming that by now, as young adults, they've chosen *supportive social networks* and so no longer face expectations to become more normatively gendered.

Finally, I end this chapter with their understanding and attitudes toward the contemporary gender structure at the macro level, how they understand the world around them and the cultural norms, their experiences of the sex-specific rules and regulations within institutions. What do they understand to be cultural beliefs about the role of women and men in society and the extent to which they subscribe to it themselves? Institutional constraints have yet to be felt at this developmental moment in their lives, but ideologically they understand that discrimination exists and are committed to *undoing gender* in all social institutions. Here the stories of the women and men are very similar. In Figure 6.1 these themes are presented graphically.

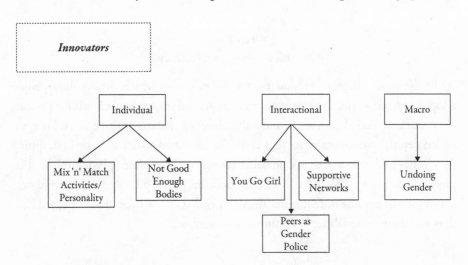

FIGURE 6.1 Themes for the *Innovators*

Before we begin the analysis, a short description of these *innovators* as a group is in order. None of the *innovators* were very religious, although one young man was still an active member of a nondenominational Christian church where his mother was the pastor assigned to college youth. Among the *innovators*, there are four Latino/as, three blacks, one self-identified mixed race (white and black), two Asians, and the rest are white. *Innovators* come from various racial and ethnic groups in this volunteer sample. What makes the *innovators* quite different from others in the sample is the diversity of their sexual identities. About half (11 of 21) are heterosexual, 6 identify as gay or lesbian, and the rest use a variety of labels including queer, bisexual, and unsure.

There were 12 women *innovators* with a diversity of sexual identities. More than half are heterosexual, two were lesbians, one was unsure of her sexual identity, one bisexual, and one had a sexually queer identity, but not a genderqueer one. Slightly more than half are women of color (two Latinas, one Asian-American, and two black). The rest are white. The white women were less likely to claim a religious affiliation. Of the seven white women, only one reported as Christian, the rest reported no religion. Of the five women of color, four identified themselves as either Catholic or Christian, and one reported no religion. None were currently very active religiously.

These male *innovators* were equally split between men who identified as straight and those who identified as gay, with one man still unsure of his sexual identity. Five are men of color (one Asian, two Latino, and one black, and one mixed-race black and white) and four are white. Four report no religion, one is Jewish, two identify as Catholic, and two as Christian. None were currently very active religiously (Table 6.1).

WHO I AM?

Or the Individual Level of Analysis

As in the other chapters, to understand the extent to which these young people adopt gendered norms as their own and internalized masculine or feminine personality traits, we coded data at the individual level of analysis in three ways. First, we coded descriptions of activities that could be identified as female-typed (shopping for clothes and accessories, taking ballet classes) or masculine (playing in the dirt, physical aggression). We then coded their personal goals and noted if they were stereotypically masculine or feminine. Third, we coded any answers that indicated how they saw their personalities as feminine or masculine.

TABLE 6.1

PROFILES OF *INNOVATORS*

No.	Name	Sex	Sexual Identity	Race	Religion	Immigration Status
1	Abby Hernandez	Female	Heterosexual	Latina	Catholic	Child of immigrant
2	Benny Goodman	Male	Unsure	Asian	Catholic	Child of Immigrant
3	Brad Burns	Male	Homosexual	White	None	Native-Born
4	Courtney Thompson	Female	Queer	White	None	Native-Born
5	Daniel Penn	Male	Heterosexual	Latino	None	Child of Immigrant
6	Dorothy Jones	Female	Unsure	White	None	Native-Born
7	Ed Macias	Male	Homosexual	Latino	Catholic	Native-Born
8	Evan Scott	Male	Homosexual	White	Jewish	Native-Born
9	Keisha Fuller	Female	Homosexual	Black	Christian	Native-Born
10	Lucy Holmes	Female	Heterosexual	White	None	Native-Born
11	Lynn Johnson	Female	Heterosexual	White	None	Native-Born
12	Marckie Harrison	Male	Heterosexual	Mixed	Christian	Native-Born
13	Mary Wade	Female	Heterosexual	Asian	Catholic	Immigrant
14	Masen Schrock	Male	Homosexual	Black	Christian	Native-Born
15	Nitsa Snow	Female	Heterosexual	White	Christian	Child of immigrant
16	Ramona Connell	Female	Bisexual	White	None	Child of immigrant

(continued)

TABLE 6.1
(CONTINUED)

No.	Name	Sex	Sexual Identity	Race	Religion	Immigration Status
17	Sasha Payne	Female	Heterosexual	Latina	None	Native-Born
18	Shikela Nike	Female	Homosexual	Black	Christian	Native-Born
19	Steve Jones	Male	Heterosexual	White	None	Immigrant
20	Steve Molder	Male	Heterosexual	White	None	Native-Born
21	Storm Geddon	Female	Heterosexual	White	None	Native-Born

Mix 'n' Match Activities

These Millennials have thought a great deal about the role of gender inequality in their lives. They told many stories about how they were both masculine and feminine and behaviors that were both traditionally done by men and those done historically by women. They all refused to simply follow gendered expectations at the interactional level and endorsed feminist visions of gender equality, whether or not they used the "f" word, "feminist" itself.

Among women *innovators* there were far fewer stories about feminine activities in childhood than masculine ones. They told more than double the number of stories about male-typed than female-typed activities in childhood. Only half of these women talked about feminine pursuits in any detail, but every woman in this group told at least one story of masculine pursuits, and many told three or more stories about activities usually done by boys. These women integrated feminine and masculine activities as they talked about what they did as children and now as young adults. Many of the pursuits they spoke of were not easily gendered, such as being in the band or choir and loving to watch TV and go to the movies. They often seemed to choose less gender-typed activities. For example, the team sports they participated in included swimming and water polo, two of the less stereotypically gendered sports.

Their feminine pursuits included liking to play with Powerpuff Girls and Barbie dolls. Several talked about doing housework for their parents, and one even wanted us to know she liked making everything neat. They talked about enjoying children and how much they liked to interact with kids came up over and over again. They took singing lessons, did yoga, slack line, ballet, Spanish dance, and belly-dancing. They joined Girl Scouts. They talked about makeup, ear piercing, belly-button piercing, and loving to shop. They had been members of dance teams, pom pom squads, and one had been a cheerleader in school and then with a professional team. One woman just loved the Spice Girls. One of the 12 women described her self-presentation style as "girlie girl," but that didn't stop her from self-consciously choosing masculine pursuits and even using her good looks to surprise people with her interests and strongly articulated positions.

These women ranged tremendously in how enthusiastically they adopted feminine activities. A few examples will illustrate the range of stereotypically feminine activities these women report. Mary Wade is the only woman in this group to describe herself as girly and this is how she does so:

Oh, I am very girly. Like . . . girly. Right now, you probably don't think so, because I didn't prepare [not wearing makeup for the interview], but . . . when I was young, I remember that I got in trouble because I saw my aunt, and you know she's also very girly, she had makeup on and everything. And I asked my mom to buy me a powder, and I was eight years old, you know a press powder . . . I wear skirts, I wear shorts, I wear high-waisted shorts. I wear bright clothes. I mean not all the time, I wear neutrals, and then like a pop of color here and there, I'm not that in your face color kind of girl. But I do wear jeans, skinny jeans. I wear heels . . . not in school . . . I have a lot of heels at home.

To Mary, and several of the other young women, to be "girly" means to look feminine rather than to restrict oneself to female-typed activities. Ramona Connell wanted us to be sure we knew that she "liked playing dress up and things like that . . . painting my nails." She told us, "I enjoyed the girly things just as much as I enjoyed things that were deemed for boys." Others, like Lucy Holmes, talked specifically about gender-typed play, "I really liked dolls, I still have my baby dolls from when I was little."

Most of the young women, however, color their feminine pursuits with at least a dash of reflective criticism. Storm Geddon remembers loving dresses, begging for them, but then never wearing them.

I was a little tomboy, I was, and so I needed the shorts and the jeans and the T-shirts, you can't, you know, be climbing around on stuff without them. But I'd go to the store with my mom and be like, I want that dress! I want that dress! And she'd get them for me, and I'd never wear them! And she just finally gave up on me and be like, "No! We're not getting any more dresses! You're not wearing them!" But I loved them! I liked, you know, all the stereotypically girly stuff, I liked, I thought it was pretty, but it just wasn't practical! Okay? I was a lot more in shorts and pants and overalls, I loved my overalls, I miss overalls, not even gonna lie.

Abby Hernandez tells a similar tale of both embracing girl's toys and rejecting them at the same time, but with an interesting twist of a mother who did not herself like or encourage doll play.

My cousin liked the Powerpuff Girls, and when I played dolls with my cousin I kind of liked it, but since I had this reputation of being active, I got bored after a while, but I did like it. I did enjoy playing dolls with her, and I remember I wanted to play dolls with my mom. And I think it's because of my mom, my mom doesn't like playing dolls, she doesn't like colorful things, so I think maybe it was because of how she is that I didn't like the color pink, that I didn't like playing dolls. Because I would be like, "Mom, play dolls with me." She would get bored.

These innovator women often spoke of consciously being able to go back and forth, moving between masculine and feminine pursuits. Most were lucky enough to have parents who did not socialize them for traditional femininity. Many had parents who were liberal, feminists mothers who allowed flexibility in play. But the liberal-family influences often were limited to nuclear families, with extended family somewhat harder to please. Courtney Thompson talks about her self-presentation:

> Depending on if I am going to an extended family party, then I dress more feminine than if I am hanging out with my own friends or going out somewhere.

Ramona Connell explains how she uses gender presentation to confuse people, looking feminine and acting in ways that a girly girl isn't expected to act.

> I'll go into guys' bathrooms. I don't really care. [ten-second pause] Like, I'll dress up and be a girly girl, but I'll throw off my heels and get down and dirty in some mud if I want. I feel like when people see me they expect me to act a certain way, and then when I don't, or the way I talk. I use a lot of swears. And I'm very blunt and straightforward. I don't skip around the bush, and I feel like sometimes when, in those certain situations when people are taken aback by it.

Abby Hernandez offers an interesting insight into a definition of "girly." As she ages, she shops for a wide variety of gym shoes to go with her mostly masculine wardrobe. A collection of shoes for her gym clothes was close enough to be defined as at least sort-of feminine for Abby. She said:

> Whenever I got more into high school, I started looking more into different styles of gym shoes. Before it was just like sneakers, any type of sneakers, as long as their gym shoes. But then I was like mmm Converse, or I like these gym shoes or these type of sneakers, these are better looking or whatever, that I can remember. And then just different kinds . . . I guess I got more girly tom boy . . . as I got older.

These women enthusiastically tell stories about their activities that are traditionally male, many even sound boastful. They are proud of being independent and tough minded. Ramona Connell tells of an anecdote caught by video camera when she was three and a half years old. She was opening presents at her sisters' birthday party. Her father told her to "back off" and she responded, "*You* back off *my* back, Daddy!" She goes on to say, "And from then on my parents just knew I was gonna be my own person and do whatever I want." Ramona told many other stories, including being kicked out of men's restrooms, which she used because she didn't see the point of waiting when there was a long line for the women's room. She also liked tackle football.

Nearly all of these young women considered themselves tomboys or did so earlier in their lives. Many never liked dolls, disliked dancing, and couldn't sit still long enough to enjoy reading. Almost all of them enjoy playing competitive sports, and most did not like Barbie dolls or Pony Pals. They spoke of remote-controlled cars, kickboxing, boxing, car mechanics, G.I. Joes, BB guns, and played trumpet. Many had stories of past or current very short hairstyles or sporting Mohawks. Some loved cars, video games, hanging with and playing sports with boys. They liked playing in the dirt, fishing, and hunting. Some mentioned hating cheerleading and volleyball, while others engaged in both activities.

Mary Wade, the self-described girly girl also describes her masculine activities.

I'm thinking when I was nine, ten years old. I helped my dad, I would like ask him what the parts were and what each thing meant, and what it meant to do this and that. I helped him. Switch brakes, you know, because it's hard to do on his own, especially with a car jack. So he calls me, "Give me the wrench, give me this, give me that, these parts . . ."

Later Mary continued talking about one of her favorite activities.

I started taking martial arts classes actually. I started taking kickboxing and boxing classes. You would see, there's not a lot of girls there. Well, actually in the kickboxing class, there were a lot of girls. But in the boxing class, it was guys, and then me and my cousin. Just two of us both girls. So people would be like, oh you're the only girls . . . but yeah, I did like boxing . . . I stopped because it was getting expensive.

There were so many stories about enjoying masculine activities that a small sample will have to do. Lynn Johnson tells us, "I love cars, and I love fixing cars." Nitsa Snow explains, "I would play with boys and stuff at recess because they'd play more fun games than the girls that would just be sitting around so in grade school I played football and kickball with the boys." Dorothy Jones told us, "I had Barbies, but I never played with them. I would play with my neighbor. I was really good friends with this neighbor boy. I would play with his like remote-controlled cars and like his N64 and like all his stuff.

The tomboy theme was predominant in these young woman's stories. As Dorothy Jones said simply, "Like I said I was a tomboy so I would play with all the boy stuff and like I would wear boy clothes. I would wear T-shirts . . . That's what I wanted to do so I did it." Abby Hernandez tells us she was a tomboy by age four: "I guess when I was little at the age of four or five, I had already decided not to wear dresses or skirts ever, again. [laughs] I was a big tom boy, so I grew up wearing pants, sweatpants, jeans, shorts, things like that, and gym shoes, all the time, gym shoes." Similarly, Courtney Thompson reported that she just liked boy clothes. She laughed and said, "I was the biggest tomboy." Dorothy Jones sounded very much like many of these other young women *innovators* when she said:

> I mean I just was never into the girly stuff, I guess. Like going to dances or dancing with boys and I didn't wear any makeup or get dolled up for school or anything . . . I've always been a tomboy. I wear men's clothes, men's shoes, literally because I have big feet and there aren't a lot of cute womens' in my size. I think it's stupid you can't be who you want to be.

Ramona Connell sounded quite like the others with her comment, although she admits that the ridicule from others did hurt because she both wanted to be comfortable in her clothes and to "fit in."

> I was a big tomboy. . . . Just cause, you know I had short hair. All the boys had the same haircut as I did. And I'd wear cut off T-shirts and baggy pants and gym shoes and stuff and you know. So, I did get made fun of for it, but I didn't really care. I did, 'cause I wanted to fit in, but at the same time it was all just about comfort. It's what I liked.

Abby Hernandez indicates how being a tomboy changed, as she presented herself somewhat more feminine in high school: "I guess as I grew older I started wearing more things that related to girl stuff, you know, like necklaces, earrings, or like the way I dressed was more girly, it was still casual, still no dresses, only special occasions like graduation, things like that, picture day, I wore dresses, and then they would be like, 'Oh my god, you're wearing dress' [in a funny voice] then that's it."

There were many stories from these young women about spending time in the company of boys growing up, sometimes because of the sex ratio of the family and sometimes by choice. Ramona Connell, the young woman who spoke of liking to paint her toenails also liked BB guns.

> My cousins and I would line up G.I. Joes and shoot them with BB guns and stuff. And I was always a better shot than they were. I grew up predominantly

with all male cousins. That's probably where some of my aggressiveness came from . . . I played with male things.

Nitsa Snow told us that

other than the girls on the swimming and water polo team I mostly hung out with guys because I didn't—I don't know, girls are just too much drama. I couldn't do it, I couldn't deal with it. I'm very low drama, so I don't like confrontations or anything like that, so I hung out with a bunch of guys during high school.

Courtney Thomson said, "I would rather hang out with all the guys than the girls. The girls would play all these club games, like Pony Pals. I wasn't into that. Doing things and running around and being active, that's what I liked to do." Similarly Keisha Fuller told us she enjoyed "playing basketball, playing it with all the boys, just being outside really; anything that had to do with outside . . . I like being outside." Dorothy Jones too enjoyed playing with boys more than with other girls, "I liked to go outside and play sports. And at recess I liked to play with the guys. I didn't really associate that much with girls when I was younger. The neighborhood girls I played with were more like me [tomboys]."

These girls often lived in families that allowed them freedom to express themselves and refrained from overt traditional gender socialization. For example, Nitsa Snow told us that her "dad has always been really outdoorsy so we would go fishing with him, and he would take us shooting and stuff like that. So I guess it wasn't very typical." Similarly, when Lucy Holmes wanted to play team sports with boys, her parents encouraged her.

I wanted to play on an all-boys basketball team. My parents put me in there; they didn't care. My sister played football on an all-boys team. It never mattered so, but when people found out. I don't know what outsiders thought about it, but when my family found out like my grandparents didn't care. They were like "Oh, you play basketball!?" And then they would come to my game and they would laugh because I was horrible.

Even when these *innovators* felt pushback from families, they continued their active tomboy ways. Sasha Payne said:

Me and my sisters were always tomboys. We were never like girly girl. My dad would try to dress us up in dresses but we'd come home like fully head to toe full of dirt.

Sasha Payne also told us of some pushback for her masculine activities, this time gaming activities.

> I played a lot of video games and that was kind of frowned upon playing all these video games. I had all the systems that came out. I love video games even till this day. Now it's more socially acceptable . . . I've always done it cause I love them . . . I didn't care about makeup, and hair products, and having like new stuff, and I didn't care if my shoes were raggedy and I didn't care about stuff. All I worried about was going home and finishing that damn video game.

Occasionally these young women *innovators* criticized traditionally feminine pursuits. Storm Geddon always "hated pink" and still does. Storm had desperately wanted to join the Boy Scouts so she could go camping and do outdoor activities. She complained about what happened when she joined the Girl Scouts instead. "That was boring, I hated that. We did not do anything scouty. Selling cookies is not scouty!" Keisha Fuller wants us to be very clear that even though she likes to do many masculine activities and even looks masculine sometimes, she is definitely not transgender. It is important to notice that she never faced stigmatization for her choices from family or friends:

> I never really felt like a, I ain't never felt like a boy, like I ain't never had gender issues stuff like that, so I never felt like a boy. I just know that I like boy things, and I knew that when I was like probably like eight or nine. But it wasn't a big deal you know my family or my neighborhood, like nobody made a big deal out of it because I wanted remote-control cars or because I wanted to play in the dirt, nobody made a big deal out of it; that I didn't want to wear dresses and it wasn't a big deal, which is why it was so easy for me you know living, I mean given my lifestyle, my sexual preferences. I never had, I didn't have a problem.

Thus, while these girls more or less mixed up masculine and feminine pursuits, and styles of self-presentation, they did not wish to be boys or have a desire to be anything but young women. More importantly, they express the ability to be free to do things without considering if their behavior was traditionally labeled feminine or masculine. To sum up this feeling among these women, Shikela Nike's words are perhaps most succinct, "I like to do stuff that boys do."

The men were also reflective about their activities. While they recount childhoods that involve much traditional masculinity, they also boast about everything they do that is not stereotypically male. They seem to enjoy telling stories about their gendered norm breaking. For these nine men, we coded 28 stories about traditionally masculine-typed activities, and 43 stories about activities that are stereotypically

female. All the men told some stories about both gender conforming and nonconforming activities.

The activities that they told us about showed how they were "like other boys,"
including enjoying getting dirty and playing in mud as kids. They also liked Hot
Wheels, Power Rangers, Transformers, and math and science. One reported hating arts and crafts. As they aged, they became interested in business, computers,
attracted to technology and machines, read science fiction, had fist fights, played on
and managed team sports. One played college varsity football.

A few examples should suffice to illustrate their traditional masculine pursuits. Brad Burns told us he "liked Transformers and video games, and I liked to
four wheel, and you know play in the mud. All that stuff. A lot of the guy things."
Similarly, Steve Molder enjoyed tinkering with computers and fixing things, taking
things apart. Daniel Penn remembers wanting "to keep this sort of hyper masculine,
sort of like, presentation performance." Ed Macias remembers trying very hard to
stay tightly within a masculine box so no one would suspect he was gay, "I wasn't
out, you could say, so I would always follow that boy status. I never did anything
girly, never did anything that would resemble a gay boy you could say." Interestingly,
later in the interview Ed said he still "likes doing my manly stuff . . . I enjoy watching
sports, I enjoy, you know, hanging out with guys . . . a lot of girls don't tend to like
sports and stuff like that." The homosexual, heterosexual, and unsure men were all
just as likely to talk about having some masculine activities now or in the past.

But all of these *innovators* were proud that their activities involved nontraditional
gender activities as well as masculine ones. As children, this included hanging out
with girls and enjoying Barbie dolls, glittery slippers, and girly clothing. Many of
them had taken on, or been assigned, domestic and caretaking labor within their
families, including caring for babies, washing dishes, doing the family laundry, and
cleaning the house. As they aged, some still preferred the company of women. Other
activities they talked about were preparing to be good fathers, avoiding violent arguments, crying when sad or stressed, enrolling in women's studies classes, and working
in men's initiatives against sexism. These men talked about being comfortable with
better paid girlfriends handling the expenses for their dates, and some of them cited
disliking football as evidence they weren't hegemonic guys. Several reported painting their toenails. One young man talked about always hugging his friends. Some
enjoyed breaking gendered norms just to disrupt the everyday scene, such as wearing heels to the grocery store. Others had real interests in ballet, or modern dance,
or simply wanted pierced ears. What they shared in common was little fear about
breaking gender norms, at least as young adults. Evan Scott tells us his experience.
Notice how carefully he tries not to presume any activity should be gendered and
apologizes for falling into the trap of doing so.

I have definitely painted my fingernails. And, I mean, I haven't gotten any ridicule. I mean, sometimes when you get older it becomes the cool thing to do. But, I mean, I think it's kind of cool to paint your fingernails every now and then. But that's from a guy perspective, I mean, look at me, I just fell into a gender thing! Um, I'm, sorry, I like it, and I know some people who do, so I mean, go for it.

Steve Molder tells us he paints his fingernails "hot pink," recounting no serious pushback for doing so. Steve also hugs his friends when he sees them and realizes he is "more aware of my emotions than most men." He mentions no particular stigmatization attached to this behavior.

Other activities these men report enjoying are being a member of a dance troupe and spending time and energy shopping because fashion matters to them. Two mentioned how much they really wanted to be fathers, and many of these young men helped with traditionally feminine domestic chores in their parents' homes. Enjoying stereotypically feminine aspects of themselves did not necessarily mean that they rejected traditionally masculine activities, although occasionally that was true. Marckie Harrison said:

I wanted to be a dancer in high school, and then I decided to pursue it and ended up being a dancer and a football player . . . I really was positively affected by the Orchesis Dance Troupe. I had grown up being more of the jock, so doing something as like expressive as dance was nice for me to get more out of my creative and theatrical side of me out.

Evan Scott and Daniel Penn talked about their childhood and how they developed caretaking skills. As Evan Scott told us:

My mom she was really sick, so she worked, and I used to take care of the house, like I used to wash the dishes, wash everybody's clothes, keep the house clean, and I did most of the housework. When I moved with my grandmother, I had chores like cleaning the bathroom, typical things.

Rather than resenting this work, Evan came to see himself as a nurturer and talked about really wanting to become a father. "I want to have children one day. It doesn't matter how really, I just love children." As a gay man, he hasn't yet figured out the "how" of it, but he is very committed to parenthood. Similarly, Daniel Penn recounts taking care of his young cousin because of the boy's parents' alcoholism and incarceration.

If I stay home, whether it's during the summer or the breaks, now my cousin goes to school, but when he didn't go to school, I would babysit. I didn't require him to pay me or anything like that, because I was doing it out of love and making sure that this kid, my cousin, had someone to take care of him. And so a lot of that responsibility arose knowing that his mom was, um, in rehab, and was incarcerated, and still is in rehab now, and so that's the reason she's not in the picture as far as family. . . . He's the closest thing I have to being a sibling. So I take care of him.

While both straight and gay men talked about breaking gender norms, gay men seemed to find it easier to do. The following stories from gay men illustrate how they understand homosexuality as allowing them the freedom to be both masculine and feminine, to be *innovators*. Masen Schrock was quite explicit about this.

As a gay man, because you know, you can do more things [breaking gender norms], but I thought about doing drag at one point in time, I just didn't have the drive to do it.

Masen was pretty clear on what he did and didn't like to do and quite unfazed by whether his desires would be seen as effeminate.

When I was eight, my mom tried to get me to play football, and I was like I didn't want to run around or have someone tackle me. . . .When I was sixteen I got more into feminine clothing and more flamboyant than most guys, and it was seen as being feminine.

Evan Scott also played with male- and female-typed toys as a boy and labeled the female toys and clothes as "the homosexual side" of himself, whereas straight *innovators* simply prided themselves on breaking gender norms. Evan stated:

I played with Barbies, and I had these toy slippers that I played with when I was younger . . . but I did play with Hot Wheels and stuff like that and that's when I started to identify myself as a boy. But the dolls and the slipper things was just me being wacky, just like the homosexual side of me coming out.

Brad Burns goes even further when he told us his alter ego is called "the Lady . . . I definitely have the girl demeanor, the attitude, the hip, the finger pointing, the inner diva I guess."

Now, from these quotes, it might seem as if only the gay men truly broke gender norms. But that is inaccurate. Daniel Penn tells us, similar to Ed Macias, that he didn't like football because he didn't "like one person dominating someone else's body tackling." Daniel also sometimes used his body in ways that are often stereotyped as feminine. He told us "the way I sit sometimes, I'm very like cross-legged, like very leg-over-thigh I think: which I find to be a very lot more comfortable." Daniel's nickname as a boy was "Ed-girl" because he liked hanging around with girls better, even if that was justified by his assuming a "protector" role (which is, after all, masculine).

> I hung out with a lot of girls. And it was more so . . . from a protector sort of like . . . avenue . . . the guys throwing rocks at girls. And although there wasn't an attraction, a reciprocal attraction there was still that "you're a nice guy" you know, "you're a good guy" so that at least reinforced hanging out, continuing hanging out with girls. The picking on . . . the being picked on part occurred when a lot of the guys noticed that what I was doing. I was going against the gender norms, going against this, at a young age, very hyper masculinity, throwing rocks. . . . The nickname that I got was "Ed-girl" at a young age.

Daniel talks about his most recent relationship with a girlfriend in which they both ignored gender norms with no problem at all.

> I didn't have a job at the time, I, so I didn't have any money. So the money that I would have, if I asked for any, would be from my mom. But Vicki had a job, she had a car, she lived with her parents, but soon they moved out shortly after graduating. So it just made sense. And the way she would explain it, "I have these resources, why am I not taking advantage of these? Let's make this work together. We're in communion. We're in it together. Let's share in this." And for me, I think what sort of triumphed these gender roles was my necessity, my class-identity necessities. I have no car, no money, but this person—who is the opposite gender—has these things and can fulfill that necessity. As far as, as well as, the typical gender roles or gender necessities within my relationship. So I was okay with her picking me up. I was okay with her paying. I was okay with her buying me things or so on and so forth.

Gender was not, however, the only status attribute that was on Daniel's mind. He wanted to participate in a fundraising event usually peopled by women, a bake sale. He was not deterred by his gender, but, as a working-class Latino man, he worried that he would be perceived as dangerous knocking on neighbor's doors:

> So I said okay I want to do that but sweets and goods and cakes and that kind of stuff seemed kind of more of a feminine thing. Like baking goods . . . who bakes

goods . . . women do. . . . But I also felt really conflicted because at the same time it's transcending my gender, but I couldn't transcend my class. So although I wanted to sell these cookies and goods and so on and so forth . . . who in the apartment complex would be willing to buy it if they have three or four jobs and they're not even home or they don't have enough money to buy it, let alone their own groceries. . . . Plus it looks really strange, a man of color, a Latino going door to door [makes knocking sound] selling cookies when a lot of the kids in the neighborhood are mischievous or would be pulling pranks. . . . It made me look very suspicious. Why is this kid outside knocking at my door selling cookies? What is he doing?

This quote highlights the everyday ways in which gendered norms interact with racial categories and class dynamics. While there are too few of any one "type" of young person in this to identify patterns by race and class, I highlight these issues as they came up in interviews.

Both male and female *innovators* are proud to mix masculine and feminine activities. They boast about breaking gender norms, but then again, the questions may have led them to do so, being excited to brag about what makes them different from others. More importantly, a key observation is that they neither feel constrained to "do gender" in stereotypically masculine or feminine ways nor compelled to reject them altogether. Instead, as *innovators*, they felt free to "do gender" in multiple ways, without aligning themselves exclusively to masculine or feminine pursuits. To *innovators*, gender is akin to a bricolage, mix 'n' matching masculine and feminine pursuits, and, in doing so, they hope to reduce gender expectations.

I now move to describe their narratives about their personalities rather than behavior. Here the stories differ by sex. The women are proud of themselves for integrating what has stereotypically been considered masculine into their selves. While the men are also proud to have crossed the gender divide and to describe themselves with feminine characteristics, like nurturance and sensitivity, they worry about sounding too masculine, or at least hegemonically masculine, because they do not want to be perceived as sexist. These men do not want to hold onto masculinity that is based on unearned privilege or in any way might recreate gender inequality.

First, I describe the women's responses. These women told more stories about being feminine than masculine, but just barely. They describe themselves as loving, accepting, helpful to others, and considerate of other's feelings. Some of them say they are not confrontational or forceful, and some don't feel aggressive at all. One considers herself a pushover, and several of these young woman talk about loving children. A few examples below are stories of the ways these women see themselves as feminine. Ramona Connell tells us "I'm very loving and accepting of everyone. So, I'm just always affectionate." Lynn Johnson says, "I'm kind of a pushover . . . I don't really see myself as being pushy." Lucy Holmes explains because she is worried about other people's feelings, she doesn't want to share her innermost self: "I want help other people. That's why I don't want to tell them my stuff, I don't want to burden them," which ironically creates a self that avoids emotional contact, which might be called masculine.

Something these young women share with other women in the sample, and many of the innovator men, is loving children. Lynn Johnson exclaims, "Children are awesome! And they're cute!" Sasha Payne gushes:

Oh, I love kids. I love them. I love the sassiness. The truthfulness. They're so damn cute, you know, until they get to a certain age where then you just want to kick them. My nieces and my nephews, I'm just really good with kids. I have a way of talking to them and they listen to me. Even at my job trying to clean their teeth, you know how hard that is . . . ?

While these women described themselves with the feminine traits discussed earlier, they also offered stories about their masculine side. They nearly all use the word tomboy, but the word most often used to describe their masculine self was aggressive. They used the word aggressive to mean a variety of attitudes, from the tendency to get physical in an argument to pursuing male dating partners, to dominating verbal disagreements. Other terms they used to describe themselves included bossy, mean, and forceful. In addition, Mary Wade, the self-described "girly girl" reports she kicks and hits a punching bag as a way to overcome stress.

Ramona Connell's story is an example of how these young women consider themselves aggressive. What is interesting here is the lengths she went to in order to exhibit her aggressiveness: the one game a year when the cheerleaders played the football squad.

I've always been very aggressive within sports. I'm not afraid to drop a shoulder, if I need to tackle someone. And then in high school we did powder-puff, and I would get very aggressive with that. And I broke my foot, actually, playing powder-puff, and I wanted to continue playing on it. They did this thing where the football players taught the cheerleaders how to play football, and the cheerleaders taught the football players how to cheer, and the dance team was involved and the band. So, all of us played a part against each other. So, all of my friends were our coaches and stuff, and they were like, "Hell, yeah, Ramona. You're like badass." And stuff like that.

Lucy Holmes also talked about being aggressive but this time in pursuit of a boy she liked, "He was a year older than me and I was super pushy with him. I would chase him around and force him to give me kisses, and he hated it. I am pretty sure he likes guys now." Abby Hernandez gives yet another example of aggressiveness. She was willing to fight when necessary. She remembers that one of her cousins "threw something at me or something like that, I punched him, I was aggressive when I was little. But that's all I remember. I don't think I was a bully though, just with disagreements."

The one respondent who self-identified as a "girly girl" in childhood recounts also being "bossy," mean, and physically fighting. She wavers between seeing this as horrible or something more positive, that is, sassy.

> I'm bossy! I was a bossy child [emphatically], and I was also very mean! I would admit that. I was, I was a horrible child! [laughs] I mean, not really, but there were certain parts . . . I was very, kind of strong. I remember, there was this guy, he would bully me, he bullied a lot of people. And what I did was, I got so sick of him . . . it was second grade, too. . . I slapped him, and then I like, reached my hands, I had long fingernails, and so I got his shirt and I guess it got red . . . I was kind of sassy. I kind of like that.

A good summary of how women describe themselves with terms traditionally labeled as masculine can be seen in Keisha Fuller's statement when she told us she likes to "speak my mind, you know just never let anyone like beat me down, mentally, physically."

There was no obvious relationship between a woman's sexual identity and her self-described masculinity or femininity. All of these *innovators* mixed and matched their descriptions of themselves from masculine and feminine stereotypes. The women were pleased with the persons they had become and bragged about integrating the feminine and the masculine aspects of themselves. Not so the men.

These men talk more (in pure counts of stories) about their masculine than feminine personality traits. But there is a surprising twist to this story. They boast about being vulnerable, nurturing, caring, and loving. They are proud that they openly cry when in pain and are compassionate and sensitive to the needs of others. Let's begin with a few examples of how these young men embrace their feminine side. As we've seen before, Brad Burns said he has a "girly side . . . an inner diva." He continues and stated that he is

> definitely . . . I am more of a girl, I am more emotional, I have a temper, and I like to get flowers and all that crap . . . I just need someone who can take care of me if I would ever need it. I mean I don't like saying there is a guy or a girl

role in a gay relationship, but I definitely want a man to take care of me, kind of like a girl thing, but I am not a girl.

Once again, just to make it clear that not only gay men talk about embracing their feminine side; for example, Daniel Penn, a man with a heterosexual identity, said he would talk to his mother "in a very flamboyant and a very feminine way." Someone else explains just how caring he is by telling us he likes to hand write all his thank you notes. These men are boastful about their ability to express their feminine side.

While the men are proud of integrating feminine characteristics into their personalities, there is a surprising twist to this story, as they do not boast about being masculine. Instead, they sound almost apologetic for much of their masculinity. When it comes to describing masculinity, which they do more often, they talk about being assertive and aggressive and sometimes having violent tendencies, but usually with a reflexive, self-critical tone. They worry about the negative implications of hegemonic masculinity. When they talk about their own masculinity, it is hedged with apology. These young men talk about their masculinity, with many caveats, explaining that they don't embrace male privilege. Daniel Penn sometimes feels possessive of his girlfriend, and he doesn't think he should. Similarly, he worries about being too assertive in conversations.

> Sometimes when I get very aggressive and very assertive trying to get my point. And it's only out of frustration of not being able to communicate how I feel and communicate my needs.

Brad Burns, who earlier told us how he was an "inner diva" also has a very masculine side to his personality.

> When I finally found my voice, I wanted it to be heard. So if I have an opinion about something, if I am very passionate about it, which is everything, I will let you know about it. When I get really excited, well just normally I am loud so people take that as "woah."

In fact, Brad was one of the only men to have been in a fight serious enough to involve the police. He said:

> I got into a fight with my partner, five years ago. I was twenty-one, we were arguing about his drug use, and it went into a gas station yard where things got heated. Long story short, he slapped me, so I started punching him. The police came, saw me punching him and pulled me off him.

Not all the men in this group were so self-conscious about gender privilege, so conscious of the positive aspects of feminine personality traits, and so very critical of masculine ones. But most were aware of the ways in which what is labeled femininity is usually repressed in men and are on a mission to change that. Indeed Daniel Penn tries to be a change agent in his everyday life.

> How I dress and how I perceive myself, how I speak very eloquently, it also touches race and class. It's like [others think], "I don't expect you to speak very eloquently, particularly about love and emotions. You talk about love and emotions. Like guys don't talk about that stuff." I know that that's the initial reaction, but I think even as the conversation develops, people find more comfort in that. It's like, "Oh, it's okay to talk about my feelings? It's okay to talk about relationships? It's okay to cry? It's okay to do this, this and that?" And I allow for that to occur. I feel comfortable enough for that to . . . for people to push-back for people to say "Why do you call your girlfriend partner or why do you sit that way or why is it that you care about this stuff so much?" I'm able to give an explanation about it. It's a learning moment. I feel like a lot of liberation for one person is tied to the liberation of other people. The liberation of one aspect of yourself, one identity is tied to another aspect . . . . I'm okay with making people feel uncomfortable.

Overall, these millennial men were proud of having integrative selves, adding characteristics often attributed to the opposite sex to their sense of selves. The women were proud of what they did, their male-typed activities, and the masculine traits they had integrated into their personalities. The men were also proud to enjoy female-typed activities and to have adopted feminine aspects into their personalities, but they hedged when talking about their own masculinity, worried they might fall into the trap of being seen as a sexist, hegemonic guy. Overall, one interesting observation is that what they reject is not sex categories. What they reject is prescribed gender norms dictating what a man and woman should be. Instead, *innovators* incorporate both masculinity and femininity into their sense of selves and, by doing so, they show that there is no one way to be a man or a woman. They reject the cultural toolkit that would have them fashion gendered selves and try hard to create personalities and activities that transcend the masculine or the feminine.

Not Good Enough Bodies

However comfortable these male and female *innovators* are with their behaviors, or personalities, they dislike their bodies as much as the rest of the sample. Just like everyone else, they are acutely aware of their real or imagined deficiencies compared with ideal types. In addition, however, some are also self-reflexive about the ways in which their self-presentation, their bodies, and clothes are constrained by gendered norms. Sometimes they simply refuse to comply, sometimes they acquiesce, but these *innovators* are often aware of gendered expectations as limiting their freedom. They feel the material requirements of gender embodiment as a constraint, but they do not rebel against the categories, rather they try to adapt as best as they can.

Every man told us about something he really didn't like about his body; most told us at least two stories. Every account of the body that initially seemed positive was really ambivalent, usually a remark that they liked their body better after having changed it somehow (e.g., losing weight or gaining muscle). Some of the men felt they were too fat, while others felt too skinny. The other body parts criticized were chests, arms, teeth, and face. Some men felt they were too short—too much like a "runt."

A few examples of these stories will suffice. Masen Schrock told us he was "picked on because I was short, calling me a midget." Daniel Penn thought he was too fat, so he remembers,

> In middle school, I would starve myself. I would starve myself in order to lose a lot of weight. So a lot of the weight just came from puberty and like getting taller, and I would purposefully skip breakfast and lunch in order to lose weight: in order to be looking like a conventional male ... male athlete ... male figure.

Similarly, Brad Burns told us he

> didn't really think about my body all that much until high school. I was always tiny, I was a runt until my junior year of high school. I was short and skinny and really runty looking. Which is why I think I got bullied and was an easy target. There wasn't a lot of confidence in my body yet.

Others told stories that were far more ambivalent, with negative feelings that sometimes got resolved, mostly having to do with weight. Evans Scott told us, "I didn't like the way my face looked, but I will say I was pretty lean, 'cause, well, I was in marching band which kept me mostly fit at the time. And, I did a lot of gym activities, and that kept me in shape, so I was pretty comfortable all around." Benny Goodman's story is less linear, "I spent a lot of time feeling uncomfortable about it [his weight]. I guess that changed senior year when I went to a tennis camp for a summer and then started to lose more weight. Then this year has been really hectic being an RA

and the increased work load, and I've kind of gotten back to being uncomfortable."
Steve Molder was what he considered "pretty fat" for most of his youth, and he was
"picked on" for it. He was quite clear—"I did not like it [his body]."

Sometimes skin tone and the discrimination it engendered created even more dislike for aspects of the physical self. Daniel Penn said:

> I disliked my skin tone. I disliked my hair. I disliked my accent . . . . And this is
> at, maybe, grade school, to be honest, grade school, and seeing that the popular
> kids are the guys that had women around them who were often white com-
> plexion, very, very stylish hair and often—not even blonde, it was very dark,
> and stylish hair with gel and that sort of thing . . . athletic, which would resem-
> ble like the body image of certain physique. And a lot of that I did not have.
> Growing up I was very chubby. I had glasses. Then I had a really thick accent.
> And I had a really thick dark skin. . . . But a lot of things as far as body image
> and physical appearance, I very much disliked. I very much disliked.

Nearly every story that had any positive body message in it at all was framed by
overcoming negativity. For example, Masen Schrock told us, "I was always short,
growing up I was always small compared to other kids. I'm okay with it now. I love
that I'm small." Evan Scott said, "I didn't like the way I looked for a little while
because I had weird buck teeth in middle school. I know, depressing. I didn't like
the way my face looked, but I will say I was pretty lean." Steve Molder eventually
felt better about his body image "It has improved because I've lost quite a bit of
weight.

In sum, these young men remember a great deal of discomfort in their bodies as
children and young adolescents. Some of them claim to not care so much about
what others think anymore, and so are more comfortable in their skins as they age.
Others appear to allow their weight to be the measure of how comfortable they
are in their bodies. Most claim to be more comfortable with their bodies now than
when they were younger.

The stories the women told us about their about bodies were nearly—although
not quite—as negative as for the rest of the female sample and very similar to the
male *innovators* stories. Among these dozen women, negative comments were three
times as likely as positive ones. In fact, only seven women told us anything positive
about their own bodies, and five of those also told us about their negative feelings
as well. But there were two women who felt really good about their bodies, Lynn
Johnson and Shikela Nike. That's the good news. The other ten told stories about
dissatisfaction with a variety of their own body parts. These young women disliked
their bodies at least partly because it brought them a sexist male gaze and teasing

from peers, a theme I return to in the section focused on the interactional level of analysis.

The seven women who spoke positively at all about their bodies liked their short haircuts and how their figures had blossomed. Two of these women actually felt self-confident about their bodies just as they were. Lynn Johnson tells us "I've always been pretty." Shikela Nike said, "I am pretty self-confident [about her body]." The rest of these women tell stories about being happy with their body *now* after previous discontent. There were two paths these women talked about as ways to overcome discontent with their bodies: losing weight or taking college classes in which the social processes of defining attractiveness and policing women's bodies are analyzed. Ramona Connell shows us the first option, coming to like one's body after weight loss, "I, just one day, started losing weight. All the baby fat and whatever. Now I'm fine with it." Courtney Thompson told us about the positive impact learning about the social structure had on her life:

> I'm a lot more accepting [of my weight]. Going to school and taking sociology classes and seeing how this systematic structure of society operates and enforces our everyday behavior, I definitely take that into consideration more, and I try to be more accepting of everything, with myself.

Far more often we heard stories of disliking one's body than accepting it or appreciating it. All but two of the women told us negatives anecdotes about their own bodies. The most common problem was feeling too fat, with at least half the women mentioning it once. But then several people were also worried about being too thin, and one worried about seesawing between too thin and too fat. But weight was hardly the only complaint. Women worried about frizzy hair, "too big" bodies, too short bodies, having triangular necks, and ugly underarm and body hair. One woman even worried about having uneven labia.

Much of the painful feelings came from comparing oneself with peers and teasing by peers. Keisha Fuller complained:

> I didn't like how small I was, how skinny I was, like all the other girls that I was hanging around with, like, you know, they were growing, you can tell that their bodies and breasts and butt and stuff. Mine wasn't. I was really skinny, so I didn't like that.

Courtney Thompson said, "I definitely didn't like my hair for a really long time. It's really curly so it can get really frizzy, and I didn't like that." But Courtney's discontent only grew in college: "I wouldn't say it was till college that I was really focused on my body. I like gained weight from drinking a lot and partying. It was a struggle accepting this body, this bigger body. I felt the pressure of society to be thin and beautiful." Dorothy Jones didn't like being a "bigger" person, "I disliked it because I was always the bigger kid so I got bullied for being like fat and everything." But Dorothy ignored the teasing mostly as a child, it was later that it really affected her:

> As a kid I didn't really think about it, as I said I was always bigger. I've always been bigger. . . . But as a kid I didn't really worry about it, and I was always active in sports so that kind of helped. And then when I was like around twenty years old, I wasn't as active anymore and everything and I was at school and I was going out and partying and I had really bad self-esteem because I had acne and then with my weight, I was gaining a lot of weight. Then something kind of clicked [snaps], and I decided to make a change. So that's when I took Accutane and lost a ton of weight . . . . I was like I can make a change and like help boost my self-esteem. It's up to me, I can make that choice.

These young woman experience life not only as female but also within the context of their ethnic and racial groups. Mary Wade was convinced that the familial concern with her weight was because she was larger than most other Filipinas. While these data suggest that women from every ethnic group feel pressured to be thin, Mary insisted her familial pressure was based in ethnicity.

> Ooh, my body, I was always insecure about my body, even now I am. [short laugh] I just . . . because I was always like a bigger child, and a lot of Filipino kids are like, skinny, so I was always criticized for being fat. It used to be horrible before, used to be horrible, I would cry when people would call me fat. You know, even my uncles and aunts would criticize me, and my older cousins would. And it was bad, like, for me . . . I really, you know, I didn't look good and stuff. Then it got worse and worse, and even my parents would start telling me about it . . . . Even when I was young, you know, they would mention it jokingly, and then when they realized that I was in high school, and I was still not skinny, they started to become more insistent. They would be like, "Why are you eating? You're eating too much, you've been eating," and I'm like, "No, I actually haven't eaten all day."

Like Mary Wade, Ramona Connell is convinced her problem with a hairy body is based on her ethnicity, in this case, her Palestinian heritage, despite waxing and hair removal is commonly used by women from all groups.

I am half Palestinian, and I sweat. I have Irish-Swedish hair all over my body except under my arms and down there [looks at her groin]. And, ughh, God I hate it. But it's just, you know, I was a cheerleader for so long, so I got in the habit of having my armpits on display. Ughh. I have the thickest, nastiest hair under there. I'm sorry that's too much information.

Both the men and women *innovators* spoke of disliking their bodies. The women in particular are clear that gendered expectations require much work and attention to mold what is natural into what is acceptable as feminine. At the material level of the gender structure, these Millennials are dissatisfied but getting by. Both women and men report that they have overcome negativity regarding their bodies. Although their stories seem far less clear that all the psychological discomfort is behind them.

Career Plans?

Neither the men nor the women spent a great deal of time talking about their professional or life goals, nor did I see any particular pattern in whether they were gendered or not. For many, just getting to college was a major life goal for themselves and for their mostly working-class and/or immigrant parents. As Daniel Penn said:

I had been ingrained with the idea of getting a college degree, and that I finally have access to get a college degree. I was very happy when I read an acceptance letter . . . it made me happy to know that they were happy. That I was succeeding at something they had been telling me for the longest time. I graduated high school, now I'm moving on to the next step. The emotion is still being replayed every time I go home. "Oh, we can't believe you're going to college. We're so proud of you. Let us know how we can support you." That kind of thing.

Career choices for the men included being a politician, a high school math teacher, a therapist, or a beautician. Career choices for the women were not so different: teacher, doctor, massage therapist, and sex therapist were the occupations explicitly mentioned in the interviews. Mostly, these young *innovators* wanted to go to college and get a job that allowed them, as Brad Burns articulated, "to get a really nice job and not have to struggle with money." Similarly Mary Wade had the basic goal of upward mobility "go to college, finish, get a job, start a family."

Many of them had a social-change agenda as one of their life goals. As Ramona Connell said:

I want to go into sex therapy, that's my end goal. And then possibly do—I've been working with the Gender and Sexuality Center here at my university and

I really love it—so, I kind of want to go into school psychology and work with younger kids, LGBT, kind of helping them find themselves, find their own identity and being comfortable with it.

Daniel Penn too hoped to find a way to make a living making social change. Others talked about raising children without gender expectations as their way to contribute to a better world in the future.

Most of these *innovators* do not talk about pursuing high-status careers. They want to have good, solid jobs with financial stability so they are able to support their families. On this, they seem very much like the rest of the sample.

WHAT'S EXPECTED OF ME?
Or the Interactional Level of Analysis
You Go Girl

This theme obviously emerged only in the women's stories. These millennial women had far fewer tales to tell about gender policing than any other women in the sample. In fact, there were only 32 narratives coded for both family and peers expectations, and about half of those were stories of feminist-leaning expectations. These *innovators* talked about their parents cheering them on as athletes, accepting their same-sex sexual experimentation as adolescents, and whatever sexual identity they adopt as young adults. Several mentioned support for their decision to cut off long hair for short boyish styles. This quote from Ramona Connell sums up the predominant feeling of these women:

I mean, my mom and dad were very open people with letting me be who exactly I wanted to be.

Lucy Holmes told us similarly:

Because I was never girly and neither was my sister. My parents lived on a farm, so we did farm work. So our parents were never like "girls do this" and "guys do this." From an early age my mom was like "girls do this and guys do the same thing."

Yet, most of these young women also received some mixed messages from family members, if not necessarily from parents. Abby Hernandez, for example, felt very accepted as a tomboy and while occasionally denied a specific "boy" toy, she was usually offered something similar even if in a pink color. Abby told us:

I guess because my mom knew that I was more of an active type that I only sit there for like five minutes, so she did get me a soccer ball, she did get me a basketball, but I think that's always been open to both genders. But that's all I remember, I was more identified with the cars and stuff like that. I also wanted the little cars, one of my aunts actually bought me that, the cars, the little convertibles where you sit and you drive, but they bought me a pink one, I never like the color pink, but they bought me the pink one, I don't think I minded when I was little though . . . . They all knew that I was very tomboyish.

Courtney Thompson similarly told a story of mostly acceptance, with only a few traces of gender policing. She referred to how accepting her parents were of her sexual identity, even though they are still somewhat uncomfortable with her masculine presentation style.

I think coming out was a big point in my life. I feel accepted by my parents, and I feel like they love me no matter what, but I also feel, and I don't know if this is just me projecting my personal feelings, but sometimes it's like a code switch thing. If I am around the house and I'm going out with my friend, I'll dress how I feel most comfortable, and if I am going to a family event, I feel like I have to put on a little bit more of a performance and wear girlier clothes . . . . My mom and dad are cool. My mom sometimes will ask, why are you wearing that? Those clothes are so masculine. I mean that doesn't bother me, well it bothers me on some level. Other members of my family have expressed very homophobic viewpoints. I think sometimes, my parents would never say this, the vibe I get is that they are embarrassed. I still kind of conform to what I think wouldn't embarrass them.

Several women mentioned that chores were gendered in their parent's home with boys being asked to take out the garbage, and brothers having later curfews. But only one of these women talked in length about parents insisting on actually enforcing traditional gendered behaviors. Sasha Payne's father was very strict about boys, in an attempt to restrict sexual activity, and tried to police her and her sisters' behavior by insisting they wear dresses, but they never complied.

Oh, wow, my dad was like super strict about boys. I mean even cousins coming into the house . . . 'cause me and my sisters were always tomboys. We were never like girly girl. My dad would try to dress us up in dresses, but we'd come home like fully head to toe full of dirt. You know because we got black, playing football or basketball or something like that and my dad was really upset.

Sasha's story of even attempted, if failed, gender policing was more the exception than the rule among women *innovators*. Most report having been encouraged to be all they could be, ignoring gendered restrictions. With this cross-sectional data, it is impossible to know if it is due to the relative absence of gender policing that they became *innovators*, or if they had experienced gender policing, they would have still forged ahead. But from their narratives, it is clear that they felt free to experiment with how to integrate both masculinity and femininity into their sense of selves.

Peers as Gender Police

The male *innovators* could not have reported more different childhood experiences of gender nonconformity than the female ones. All but one of these young men told stories about either families or friends, and usually both, criticizing their nonconforming gendered behaviors. The vast majority of this criticism was openly homophobic, rather than simply concerned with policing behaviors that were deemed feminine. This was remembered especially vividly by the men who identified as gay, but it was also true for the one young man still unsure about his sexual identity and for one of the straight men as well. Even the stories told by straight men about gender policing itself, with no memories they labeled as gay bashing, still have the scent of homophobia. These nine men told approximately 50 stories of gender policing by peers, parents, and other family members, an average of five stories each.

The stories of childhood criticism, bullying, and gender policing are dense with pain. These men were sanctioned by their parents and extended family members for activities ranging from gesturing with their hands too much when they talk, to not dating in high school, to acting too "flamboyant," for spending too much time with female friends, as well as for any indication that they might be gay. Benny Goodman recalled a conversation with his father about how he used his hands when he talked. Benny told us:

> Like if I talked and did this [makes hand gestures] and stuff like that. I usually don't do it though. I guess at one point I did that, and then my dad said something . . . "try not to make so many motions when you talk," but he didn't offer any context behind that, but that's all he said . . . I thought ok, whatever. I'll just stop doing hand motions because it felt kinda weird anyway.

Daniel Penn told several stories about the ways his extended family tried to police his sexuality even as he felt supported by his nuclear family. His extended family was worried that because he was not dating, he might be gay. He felt the pressure of heteronormativity early in life.

Even my family members, like, whenever I would go to Mexico with family, because obviously I want to spend time with them, they want to get to see what's life over there in the States, they would constantly ask, like, "Are you dating anyone?" "What does your girlfriend look like?" "What does your girlfriend do?" And I remember I would even lie, like, "Yea, I'm dating someone," just to reinforce the fact that yes, I am interested in women, and yes, I am the male and male as defined by dating women so on and so forth. So, it was extended family, it wasn't so much immediate family at all. It was people that I considered friends.

Sometimes Daniel Penn had to contend with negative reactions from his immediate family as well:

> I would speak to my mom in very flamboyant and a very feminine way. And to her it's like, "Don't do that, it's ugly. Don't do that, you look ugly doing that." But I knew what I was doing, and it knew it would make her mad and piss her off. . . . But there was a clear sort of like negative reaction to that sort of flamboyancy.

Ed Macias did not face overt homophobia as a teenager because he stayed in the closet to avoid it. He consciously behaved in stereotypically masculine ways to avoid being suspected of being gay. His early life was shaped by fear of homophobia.

> When I was growing up, I pretty much did everything a regular boy would do because I wasn't out, you could say. So I would always follow that boy status. I never did anything girly, never did anything that would resemble a gay boy you could say.

In fact, he worked so hard at being a regular guy, he married a woman. Still, he was sometimes informally sanctioned for not being one of the guys; he enjoyed hanging out with the women at family gatherings.

> Usually all our family events tend to be, oh, girls on one side, guys on the other, drinking and stuff like that. I always tended to go more towards the girls. And pretty much everybody questioned it, you know. Either it was my cousins, my brothers, you know? They always were like, "Oh, you're with the girls." Or "Oh, you're always hanging out with them for every family event that we have." I felt more comfortable around the women than the guys for some reason.

There were several stories about these young men being treated badly in the church. Members of their parent's congregations often stigmatized these young men, in ways the respondents interpreted as homophobic. Such stories paint these houses of worship as intolerant rather than sacred spaces.

Some men did tell stories about more accepting families. Marckie Harrison's father encouraged him to take ballet. Steve Molder's mother didn't care much when he borrowed her high heels to wear to the grocery store. Parents seemed more supportive of gendered rule-breaking for boys they did not suspect might be gay.

Still, these nine male *innovators* had to be very tough to face the sanctions they experienced in boyhood. Whether they are gay or straight, and the sample is split right down the middle, they faced negative interactional encounters when they challenged gender norms. The straight men don't take these negative social reactions too seriously, sometimes they even enjoyed provoking people. That is, the heterosexual men were privileged to have sexual identities that they did not feel needed to be hidden nor were they at risk for being bullied because of them. The men who were openly gay as teenagers both feared and faced homophobia as well as gender policing from parents.

Both men and women report policing from peers but men win, hands down, for the number and intensity of their stories. Men reported gender policing on everything from body language to liking to dress fashionably. While the women remembered little policing to act girly, they remembered a great deal of policing about the presentation of their physical selves as feminine, often mistaken for boys when they were younger.

As sad and as harsh as the stories of how these young men's parent's shamed them for gender nonconformity, such experiences seemed far less often and to be less cruel than the gender policing these *innovators* recount from peers. Boys were ridiculed for everything from liking "boy bands" to not being "tough" enough.

Boys were presumed gay for dressing well or being "trendy." They were made to feel uncomfortable if they disliked team sports that men usually play or wanted to play a sport usually played by women. Friends made it clear that basketball is manly while volleyball is girly. Steve Molder managed his social world in this way, "Even if I wasn't the toughest, I would act like I was because that was expected." Ed Macias had to worry about what he wanted to do, dress well, and what he didn't want to do, play sports. He continued:

> Well I pretty much consider myself trendy. That's one thing people look at like, "Oh, why is that guy dressed so good?" or "Why is that guy wearing that?" you know? And that's when they start going into, "Hey he must be gay!"

Daniel Penn grew up in the kind of neighborhood where joining a gang was a choice many of his friends made, perhaps the easiest choice to make. In retrospect, using language clearly gained on campus, he sees the choice he made as one about adopting an alternative masculinity. He averted the expected way he would become a man.

> There was, sort of like, an economy in hyper masculinity as far as gangs.... And it was like a transcendence of that masculinity. It's like okay, alright, you will gain your power and authority through gangs and drugs and alcohol. You can very much get it through education and that sort of authority and that sort of power.

While Marckie Harrison had parents who supported his freedom to choose activities and even encouraged him to try new activities traditionally done by women, he still had to face his friends' responses.

> I took ballet my senior year in high school, you know, my dad wanted me to do it, and my friends knew me well enough to not even think twice about it, you know, but I did get some crap for it all in fun though.

The accounts of interactional responses to gender nonconformity above are primarily to gender deviance, but the underlying tone at least implied, if not overt, is concern that gender nonconformity indicates, or may lead to, homosexuality. While the topic of bullying gay boys because of their sexual identity is not the primary story in this chapter, the narratives told by the young men who identified as gay are important here because they opened up so fully about their painful teenage years. Gender nonconformity and homosexuality are so conflated in our society that the young men in the study do not distinguish the experiences. Many of the men tried to undercut the pain in their stories by assuring us that when their peers taunted them, they were, after all, just joking. But the jokes didn't seem very funny when repeated to us. As Brad Burns began his story, I've been jokingly pushed into the girl's bathroom because I was gay and that's where I belong, but it was a joke. Brad then graphically recounts being bullied every day but tries to laugh it off because he was being teased for something that was, after all, true. But the pain in the story can't be hidden so easily.

> You get bullied every day, you get called gay, but it was true. [laughs] Can't blame them I guess. I guess I could have been more outgoing, but I guess that goes along with not being very comfortable with yourself yet.... The kid called me gay, and I slapped him in the face, and then the teachers came and broke it up. But it got pretty physical for a minute; we got sat down and talked to.

The kid ended up having to apologize to me. Then they switched our schedules around so we weren't allowed to be in the same classroom.

Gender policing by peers seemed most vicious when it was explicitly aimed at gay men or men suspected of being gay. Two of the young men in this sample remained in the closet throughout their adolescence to avoid what they saw happening to others. The straight men had far less to lose and were more likely to either play with the irony of their gender rebellion or to become personally invested in anti-sexist social change that allowed them and others freedom from gender stereotypes.

The women's behavior was far less policed than the men by their peers for their behavior, but gender policing did happen to them as well. One young woman felt pressured by friends to lose weight. Another was still angry that she wasn't allowed to join the Boy Scouts. Some were proud of having broken dress codes in elementary and high school. The most serious policing these women reported from peers was about being judged for their sexual behavior. Lucy Holmes told us the consequences of being a "serial dater" in high school:

> Everyone would make fun of me. They would call me a slut or say stuff like that. And I definitely wasn't a slut, I just liked dating. But because I went through guys like water, whereas my guy friends would have a new girlfriend every other week and no one batted an eye. But because I had a different boyfriend everyone flipped shit.

While there were women's stories about constrained behaviors because of gender norms, those stories were not nearly as emotionally laden, nor told with the angst, as the ones we heard from the rest of the women in the study, and not even in the same ballpark as the powerful stories told by the innovator men. Many of these women's peers accepted traditionally male behaviors and even encouraged them. Overall the stories about gendered behavioral constraints among women were relatively few and without gravitas. Instead of pain, the stories about breaking gender norms were told with pride. Courtney Thompson was told she couldn't play baseball with the neighborhood boys because she was a girl, but her brother stood up for her and told them, "So what if she's a girl, she'll still beat you." She ended up playing.

These women *innovators* report remembering few expectations that they behave within feminine boundaries as little girls. Where the pain can be heard in some of these women *innovators'* voices is when it comes to gendered expectations for their self-presentations, that is, being sanctioned for breaking presentation norms. All but one of these women told stories about feeling constrained norms of bodily presentation and policed for breaking them, at least once. As children, most were dressed in pink and forced to wear dresses whether they wanted to or not. Most were pressured to learn to use makeup and walk in heels. The feminine socialization was, ironically, often imposed for the expressed purpose of professional success. Abby Hernandez remembered:

> My mom, just like this, if you want to be a professional you have to . . . learn to apply makeup, you need to look presentable, you need to sometimes wear skirts and heels, and sometimes you need to wear dresses, or what if you have a specific event that you need to go to or a ball, all that kind of stuff. She's like you need to learn how to dress.

Nitsa Snow told us her mother doesn't like her to wear a sweater not designed for a women's body even hanging around the house.

> If I wear a guy's sweater I have from J.Crew, it's just a lounging around sweater, they'd [her sisters] be like "Why are you wearing that? You should look nicer". . . And my mom. Like she said I should try harder.

And yet, what is interesting here is that most of these women told contradictory socialization stories about self-presentation with mothers who wanted them to wear makeup and fathers who believed high heels were too girly. Or fathers that insisted on dresses while mothers insisted they could pick their own clothes. The socialization they remember as constraining is usually about their looks, not their activities, and often inconsistent. For example, Mary Wade remembered:

> There's pictures of me as a kid all dressed up in dresses, and I remember getting all dolled up for one picture, and I remember thinking like this is annoying. Why do I have to do this? And then I was like okay this is what a girl does and boys dress like this and boys play with that . . . . I was about five or six . . . . I just kinda accepted it, cuz you know as a kid you don't really realize it, but I thought it was annoying that I had to put on tights and shoes and all that stuff.

But then again, the socialization in Mary Wade's family wasn't consistent because her father was concerned she would grow up too girly:

> When I was a child my dad got mad at me for this, too. I'd always try to get wedges or high heels for kids . . . my dad was kind of like, you shouldn't be too girly. . . I think it's just he didn't want me to be like the shallow . . . I don't

know the word for it . . . ditzy, I guess . . . is it ditzy? I don't know, you know like very girly.

Some of these young women had parents with very liberal gender ideologies. When she was young, Ramona Connell's mother told her she could wear boys' clothes if she wanted. "You can wear whatever you want. You can pick out your outfit to do that. It's all up to you. If you want my help, I'll help you, but if you don't, you can wear whatever you want." And when she hit puberty, her father told her, "You don't need to wax your legs." But even with open-minded parents, the larger social context matters. Ramona talked about an incident she never forgot, the sting of being stared at.

I was young, what looked like a little boy and I was just hurling sand balls at other kids on the playground. And we were having a sand fight. And my cousins were like, "Ramona, Ramona!" As soon as I came over, I remember forever this woman's face distinctly. She looked at me, and then tapped her friend and was like [her eyes were wide], "That's a little girl! [looks at me, whispers, and points to a corner of the room] That's a little girl!"

One common refrain from these female *innovators* was being mistaken for a boy in childhood. One consequence of liberal parents allowing girls to dress comfortably, as they wished, was that others often mistook these young women for boys in their childhoods. Abby Hernandez remembers family members taunting her.

I remember when I was in Mexico, I was dressed in a soccer uniform, because in Mexico soccer is a big deal, so I think one of my uncles or one of my aunts bought me a soccer uniform from one of the teams. . . . I was wearing it and my cousin was also wearing some soccer get-up or something like that. And a lady said, "Do you boys want to do something?" and I was like, "What, I'm not a boy." [laughs] I guess because I was dressed that way she thought I was a guy and I was acting, I was running like a guy, I was playing soccer, you know I was always more identified as a tomboy. I don't know I guess that's something, the way I dress, the things I like to do, I'm not girly, I don't like makeup, yeah, that's something that people picked out . . . my mom used to be "I have a boy," even my uncles they tease me, they're like, "Oh, you know her dad wanted a boy or whatever and they got a boy" [using a mock deep man's voice], and I'm like, "Thanks" [sarcastically and laughs a little] because I still identify myself as a girl just a sporty girl. That's the kind of stuff I was picked on.

Similarly, Courtney Thompson recalled:

> I mean in general when I was a kid I wore boys clothes and had the short hair so everyone thought that was weird. Once when I was like four my uncle asked me if I wished that I was a boy. I got really defensive and it's weird because it still gives me an angry feeling. I can still remember it so vividly.

Storm Geddon remembered being mistaken for a boy, and then a lesbian, as well. Notice how she claimed that dressing like a boy never really made a difference, but then told a story about the mistaken identity being a problem:

> I cut my hair into a Mohawk before school started, I didn't really wear, you know, girly clothes, I don't know what I was wearing that day. It was, I was walking with one of my friends, we were arm in arm, down the hallway, like after gym or something. And it was some random comment I heard from behind. "Oh, those two are lesbians," um no. Not really, but okay, dude. It's just weird and I was like, that's really random. I don't know, okay, there's nothing to suggest that happening right now, but, I don't need you jumping to conclusions, that's helpful in your life. . . . So, I, I looked like a boy for a good year, I did. So, I dressed like a boy, there wasn't a whole lot of reaction, just pretty much ignored. I think they all thought I was a stoner, anyway.

Many of these women had been mistaken for boys as a child, but by now, they had found peer groups that supported their self-presentation styles. Keisha Fuller has friends who really like the tattoos on her arms. Lynn Johnson got her haircut very short multiple times. Her parents don't mind. In fact she said:

> They like it. The first time I did it, it was for a friend who had cancer. They wouldn't let me shave my head all the way, but they let me get a pixie cut and I just really liked it. And now I got it cut again, so. . . . The snooty people in my class thought I was, they didn't really say anything, but I could tell they were judging me like hardcore. And then my friends loved it, like they thought it was adorable.

While these women did not report many gender constraints on their behavior, they did report much pressure to look like a lady now that they are grown. They had to learn the skills of feminine self-presentation, how to apply makeup, walk in heels, and buy and wear appropriate clothes. Indeed, just as for other women in the sample, looking professional was defined as wearing makeup and doing femininity. What makes these women quite distinct is that they all tell stories about rebelling against gendered expectations wherever they find them. They criticize gendered expectations and reject whatever doesn't feel comfortable.

Supportive Social Networks

By late adolescence, most women and men *innovators* had located friendship groups and peers that support their freedom to behave and dress how they wish and to avoid gender stereotypes. On the interactional level, these Millennials started rejecting gendered norms as children and continue to innovate as they age. They remain, however, comfortable being women and men who reject norms, and do not reject the gender binary itself.

By the time we interviewed the women, none felt contemporary pressure from friends or families because of their gendered behaviors or personalities. Their families had usually been supportive since childhood. They now reported being comfortable in a network of supportive friends. Nearly all have located friendship groups and peers that support their freedom to ignore gender norms. Of course, these female *innovators* do not challenge the gender binary with their self-presentation. Some may avoid dresses, hose, and makeup, but all are easily recognizable as women.

Given the harsh experiences of these men in their childhoods, it is worth noting that they also have succeeded in finding supportive social networks. Their search for, and development of supportive networks, seemed more difficult, and so I will delve more deeply here. As young adults these men now face new and more feminist expectations from lovers, sisters, teachers, parents, friends, and sometimes anti-sexist men's groups on campus. These male *innovators* have successfully chosen supportive environments. Five of the nine young men tell stories of feminist expectations from contemporary peers. In these men's stories about the present, gender nonconformity is not usually stigmatized, sometimes not even noticed. The *innovators'* friends and family today do not necessarily care about gender norm violations, and may even expect them to be men with feminist, if not feminine, sensibilities.

Daniel Penn's story is worth telling in some detail. He joined a college peer group that supported gender exploration and started dating a woman who identified strongly as a feminist. Daniel began to be reflective about masculinity and struggled with how nurturing fit inside his maleness.

And that sort of opened the door so to explain my emotional and sort of nurturing and caring aspect and loving aspect. And what does it mean to do all that and still be a man? Can men do, are able to do that? Can men be sweet and

caring and nurturing? How is that received and how is it perceived? I learned a
lot of that with the person I was seeing at the time.

This same girlfriend had graduated, had a job, a car and money, while Daniel was still
a broke college student. She expected him to be financially dependent on her because
it made sense. He has come to feel quite comfortable being taken out on dates and
generally to ignore gendered expectations in romantic relationships. Daniel's redef-
inition of himself was also instigated by his work with an anti-sexist, anti-violence
men's group on his college campus. His new reputation is as an anti-sexist man and
he is very proud of the activist group with which he is involved.

So there's a lot of introspection and question who you are as a man, and what
does that mean as far as relation to other folks . . . specifically, women and
LGBT folk. And so, so it's a very, it's a preventional program that's prevent-
ing gendered violence. That's one component of it. And the second component is an action component—to say the least, now that you know this
information, this stuff, what are you gonna do about it? . . . People on campus
know me for men's initiatives. "That's the guy that talked about masculinities
and gender and violence and all this stuff." I hold pride in that. I hold pride
in that.

Rather than cave in to traditional expectations because they faced ridicule or stigma,
these men sought out new peer groups where gender conformity was neither
required nor expected. And they often use their newfound confidence to change the
expectations of those around them. For example Steve Jones said, "I sometimes carry
pink stuff or sometimes I sit with my legs crossed, but it doesn't matter, I don't care."
Masen Schrock found that confidence as well, "When I was sixteen I got more into
feminine clothing and more flamboyant than most guys, and it was seen as being
feminine." He was comfortable pushing that boundary. Steve Molder was "mildly
entertained" by wearing heels to go food shopping and painting his nails pink.
Daniel Penn would sit cross-legged, leg over thigh, because he found it more comfortable. Daniel Penn consciously pushed the boundaries for the people he worked
with. As he told us:

Yeah. I think using the term *partner* referring to my relationship, people are
very often shocked. Even colleagues at work are . . . not so much in the diversity
office where I work but in the information hub, when I refer to the person I am
dating and my partner they're like, "What do you mean, do you mean guy, do
you mean girl . . . you mean girl right?"

Both the men and women *innovators* recounted gendered expectations in their past, whether from parents or peers. And yet, as *innovators*, they have rejected conformity and have overcome expectations when they so desire. To do so, they have consciously chosen new social networks where their behavior and presentation of self are considered appropriate. They no longer feel policed by their peers, or, in most cases, even their families.

WORLDVIEWS AND INSTITUTIONAL CONSTRAINTS
Or the Macro Level of Analysis
Undoing Gender

Neither women nor men *innovators* talk very much about the constraints they face at the organizational or institutional levels. Almost all are too young to have faced issues of work-family balance or—if female—to have hit a glass ceiling. If they have experienced cognitive bias in their lives until now, they do not know it. This is news, evidence that for some Millennials at least, the educational institutions and religious congregations they have experienced do not enforce gender segregation or discrimination, at least not that our respondents could articulate. The only stories they tell of institutional or material constraints they've experienced are about single-sex sports teams and youth groups. Several of the women wanted to play football, and one still was angry she couldn't join the Boy Scouts, which had camping trips she coveted while the Girls Scouts offered crafts and cookies. Two of the men had wanted to play volleyball.

When painful stories about discrimination were recounted, they were primarily about homophobia, rather than gender nonconformity. But because homophobia and heteronormativity are so closely tied with gender normativity, especially for men, it is quite difficult to disentangle these stories. One of the woman's family refused to accept her girlfriend. A male innovator was convinced he was treated harshly by the justice system because the physical altercation for which he was charged was with his male partner. The material experience of discrimination for gender nonconformity was inextricably linked to homophobia in everyday life.

When it came to worldviews and cultural beliefs about the gender structure, the women and men were very similar, they all believed it should be dismantled. These young people understand the contemporary cultural logic of gender to support inequality. And their goal is to challenge the worldview that now exists. There was no ambivalence among these *innovators*. None held essentialist or conservative beliefs about gender. There was a general agreement with Courtney Thompson that the Swedish school without gendered pronouns was "awesome." These 21 *innovators* told us approximately 36 stories about their beliefs that challenged the gender structure.

They told very few stories that could conceivably be used as support for any norms that distinguished men from women. They did not endorse a gender structure with distinct roles and expectations for men and women. They did not endorse institutions whose rules or regulations differed for men and women. All the *innovators* felt strongly that the controversy caused by the advertisement where a young boy was wearing pink nail polish should not have happened: they supported the freedom for boys to do, be, and wear whatever they wanted. Steve Jones explained, critically, why it was so controversial in our society: "because we live in a society that is very homophobic and so strict with the gender roles, and that's why it caused controversy." Mary Wade would like to send her children to a school that used no gender pronouns. She asserted:

> I think it's great how they're trying to make kids learn those things. Make them realize that gender shouldn't be the basis of things, I think that's kind of cool. Because you know, we're used to thinking, especially about the crying, girls get more comfort than guys do. I think that's interesting how they're trying to treat them the same way. Because it shows that women are not as weak as you think they are.

A few had some worries about how far they could go raising gender-neutral children in today's world and protect their children from being stigmatized. For example, Steve Jones reflected on whether he would want his future children to attend the Swedish school that used only gender-free pronouns in a world that did not.

> I don't know, it seems like a good school. It seems like a step in the right direction, and it's a little bit risky because I feel like when those kids leave that school and go into our society which is so delineated between male and female that they might struggle with some of those social issues with what boys do and what girls do.

Daniel Penn wants not only a gender-inclusive school but a radically de-gendered one that also pays attention to other kinds of social inequality such as race and class.

Despite these minor caveats, Ramona Connell expresses these young *innovators'* ideology eloquently as she explains, "just to have an open mind and an open heart about the world. You don't need to discriminate against anyone." Courtney Thompson told us, "I just think that both girls and boys should be treated the same, even when it comes to the aspect of boys being emotional. Not all boys are tough and aggressive and not all girls are nurturing." Evan Scott's explanation about the controversy about a boy painting his fingernails pink added another thought shared by most of the *innovators*, "people are, most of us are closed-minded in this century." Mary Wade thinks it is "kind of cute" to paint a boy's fingernails. Nitsa Snow, a licensed nail technician, doesn't think it's a big enough deal to talk about very much. Storm Geddon agrees about the controversy, "I think it is stupid. It's just a little boy who likes to get his nails painted," something she does to her younger male cousin without any reaction. Keisha Fuller agrees that a school without gender pronouns would be a good thing.

> I think the goal that they are trying to accomplish is teaching the kids about . . . like indirectly teaching them about equality . . . about gender equality. I think that is pretty cool.

Overall, these young millennial *innovators* sound very much like traditional feminists. They want equality between women and men, with a focus on rights and responsibilities, freedom from stereotypes. And not very much concern about destroying gender binaries at all.

Feminist Future Envisioned

So how did these *innovators* come to these worldviews so critical of the gender structure? Feeling constrained by the gender structure predisposes one to have a critical gaze, but how that develops into innovation is still an interesting question. For these men and women, the answers seem varied, but most felt gender norms personally oppressive at some time in their childhood or adolescence. At least some personal experiences helped solidify ideologies consistently critical of the gender structure. Both men and women believed that norms that differentiated boys and girls, men and women, were wrong. For those raised with strict gender socialization, there was regret that they hadn't had the opportunity to grow up with more freedom. Many of the women had grown up in liberal homes where they were encouraged to be all they could be. All the *innovators* wanted to allow future children to grow up without gendered restrictions and were critical of gender policing, whether they had experienced it personally or not. Whether these young *innovators* were openly radical or quietly resistant, they were opposed to the gender structure that required different lives for women and men, although they did not conceptualize their innovation as rejection of the gender binary. They wanted to undo gender, so that being a man or woman wasn't confined by gendered expectations.

The men and women *innovators* told somewhat different stories about who they are and want to be on the individual level, how they experience their sense of selves. When discussing the meanings they give to their individual lives, men and women value their innovative selves. Both men and women enjoy male and female typical activities, and feel comfortable mixing and matching the masculine and feminine aspects of their personalities. The women are very proud to mix and match behaviors and personality traits. The men are also very proud of integrating female typical activities and personality traits into their sense of self and feel as if they are better people for doing so. The men, however, were also hesitant to proudly proclaim masculine personality traits, however, because they were acutely aware of the sexism embedded in traditional hegemonic masculinity and wanted to escape reproducing it. At the individual level of the gender structure, the women and men *innovators* talked a great deal about how their bodies were not quite good enough, but those discussions were only loosely linked to gender. And yet, the bodies they had, and were not quite good enough, were being measured against gendered standards. While they were somewhat critical of the material level of the expectation of gender embodiment, they did not rebel against the gender binary nor reject self-presentation differences for women and men. All these *innovators* rebelled against the internalization of cultural femininity and masculinity into their definition of self and strove for integrative personalities beyond gender binaries.

Most of women *innovators* did not remember experiencing oppressive gender socialization but most, as children, had been routinely mistaken for boys. Still, by now they have chosen supportive friends and feel remarkably free from gendered expectations for their behavior. They were still pressured to look like "ladies," but most women *innovators* did not report finding this overwhelmingly oppressive. The men *innovators* had been fiercely policed from childhood onward by friends and family members. The interactional sanctions faced by men for atypical gender behaviors could not really be distinguished from simultaneous negative reactions to actual or presumed homosexuality. The men's families, friends, and members of their churches so conflated gender typicality and heterosexuality that even the slightest indication of gender nonconformity, from ballet classes to volleyball, brought sanctions experienced as shaming for both behavior and sexuality. These interactional sanctions were most painful for the gay men, because they felt punished for being who they really were. For the heterosexual men, the gender policing led to irony and in-your-face gender bending and/or anti-sexism social movement activity. At the interactional level of analysis, the cultural expectations for male *innovators* were felt as far more narrow than for women.

All *innovators* rebelled against interactional sanctions and had found new peer groups where they and their choices were respected. These groups included feminist organizations, LGBTQ centers on college campuses, gay neighborhoods in urban centers, and carefully chosen partners, friends, and online communities. At the interactional level of analysis, traditional cultural expectations were far more painful for men than women. But all these *innovators*, by definition, rejected traditional gendered expectations. All the *innovators* were agentic in seeking out peer groups so that the daily experiences in their material worlds were more supportive than not. Their social networks were carefully tended to be filled with like-minded others. These *innovators* manipulated their physical material worlds, by assembling supportive social networks, and so no longer felt the daily sting of social disapproval. It is unknown whether the women *innovators* will face strong sanctions when they enter the job market with well-documented cognitive gender bias against females who are strong and powerful actors.

With cross-sectional interview data, I cannot make strong arguments about how these young people came to experience the gender structure as they do or how they might change it. Their stories, however, lead to some hypotheses. As Millennials, they grew up during the ongoing gender revolution. Many had parents who seemed to have feminist ideologies. These Millennials had access to the Internet from early adolescence, and many spoke about discovering ideas and communities online. Others spoke directly about reading feminists, for instance, Judith Butler, or learning about the social construction of gender in college classrooms. These cultural products that were already easily accessible during Millennials' adolescence helped legitimate their innovative behavior as they rejected gendered expectations. The macro level of feminist cultural ideology that was in the air made their individual paths easier. Some of these *innovators* were very conscious that their lives actually helped make a new world to "undo" gender as a heteronormative expectation. Their stories suggest to me that the cultural production at the macro level helped legitimate feelings of constraint at the individual level. At the same time, many of the women were raised by parents who were baby boom mothers, perhaps with feminist ideologies. With support from both existing cultural ideas and feminist-leaning parents, these Millennials make their own agentic decisions to be *innovators* and to consciously try to change the interactional expectations for themselves and for others.

All the *innovators* share the cultural commitment to a society where being labeled a male or female at birth does not require any set of behaviors or any stereotypical personality characteristics. All share a goal to change the interactional level just by being who they are. All share a cultural worldview antagonistic to the traditional gender structure. These *innovators* do not reject their sex, they just desire sex and gender to be independent from each other, so whatever sex is labeled at birth has little repercussions for the rest of one's life. In the next chapter, we move on to a smaller group of respondents, with a stronger and deeper critique of the gender structure, the *rebels*.

7

The Rebels

IN THIS CHAPTER, I tell the story of the 17 *rebels*. Before doing so, I introduce you to three of them so you can have a snapshot of real people to think about as you read the chapter ahead. I introduce you to the only male self-identified genderqueer in this sample, one of the females who considers herself between the gender binary but does not use the language of genderqueer and a transman.

Let me introduce Cary Van Pelt. Cary is a white, bisexual youth who has progressive politics, as does his liberal family. He identifies as a male and genderqueer. While growing up, he enjoyed the company of girls more than boys. In high school, he became involved with theater, film clubs, and the gay-straight alliance, which provided him with creative and social outlets. He reports having been bullied through his school years but could not remember—or did not want to share—the details, except for one specific occasion where other kids in school threw rocks at him. Overall, he felt like the odd kid in school and admitted poignantly that the mental agony from isolation was more painful than the physical abuse from bullying.

He recalls attending a Halloween party dressed in female clothing, platform boots, a velvet scarf and red lipstick as a high point in his life. It was his excuse to begin experimenting with makeup. He found it liberating because it was the first time he wore makeup in public and documented it on Facebook. He now considers himself very feminine and likes to wear makeup and colorful clothing. He proclaims, "there is nothing about a dick that makes you more inclined to black and blue and less inclined to red and yellow. I think that is insane." He is still comfortable with his male body and doesn't consider himself transgender. He claims that his family has always supported his gender and sexual nonconformity, but still he does not feel comfortable letting them know he wears makeup regularly.

Even though Cary feels comfortable traversing gender boundaries, he is terrified of the police. Specifically, he is very fearful of being pushed around or beaten up, motivated by the possibility that violence will be directed at him because of his gender nonconformity. He does not hesitate to point out that the education system indoctrinates everyone to "categorize people into male and female camps" while suppressing the freedom to express themselves however they wish. He would have liked to attend a gender-neutral school like the one in the article we had him read. Overall, Cary is very cognizant of the limitations that the gender structure imposes generally on him and confronts it head on, even though he feels threatened at times for doing so.

Let me next introduce Clover Johnson. Clover is a 23-year-old white female. Although she does not explicitly use the moniker genderqueer to describe herself, Clover's interview parallels those who self-identify as genderqueer. Clover was raised with strict religious guidelines. At about age 16, she started rebelling against her parent's religiosity and the expectations associated with it. Until then, she was not permitted to watch movies or go to school dances because those activities were seen by her parents as the work of the devil. She and other kids at her church formed a group that openly and actively challenged the church's teachings to such an extent that she earned the reputation of the kid that says "no to the man." Clover talks about breaking gendered norms early in her life. She was never a girly girl in childhood, always more of a tomboy. When she was in fifth grade, she and a few girl friends were denied the right to try out for the football team. They organized a petition, seeking the right for girls to play on the male football team. They did not gather enough signatures to change the rules, but the petition drive itself clearly shows Clover's rebellious spirit already in evidence in elementary school.

Clover was the first girl to go through puberty in her class, and she hated her early physical maturation, breasts that made her look like a woman before any of the others girls in her class. She particularly hated the attention from boys and the jealousy masking as dislike from the other girls. She repeatedly tried to hide her body by dressing like a boy and wearing loose-fitting clothing. Many of the other students would make fun of her presentation of self, calling her either a boy or a dyke. This continued throughout middle school. By high school, she started to dress more feminine and started to wear "girlier" clothing and growing her hair longer. But then when she left high school and started working, she chopped her long hair off, shaved part of her head, and dyed the rest of her hair blue. She switches her appearance from feminine to masculine and back to feminine with much aplomb and with little current opposition from her friends, coworkers and, by now, even her family. In college, she spearheaded a movement to install gender-neutral bathrooms on her campus. Clover has strong opinions about the gender structure. She is totally dedicated to removing any rules, expectations, and beliefs that jam people into one or the other category. She believes in eradicating the attachment of gendered expectations to social roles. And she refuses to be pigeon-holed into one gender category or the other.

Finally, meet Salem Bee. Salem was assigned as female at birth and grew up a girl in a complicated family system. His parents had not been married when he was conceived, but Salem believes they were married before he was born, although divorced soon after Salem and two siblings were born. Most of his childhood was spent with his mother as a single parent, but then a stepfather and his three children entered their household, temporarily, until another divorce. Salem is not close with anyone in the family; his mother knows he is a transman but has not allowed any of the siblings to be told. Salem intends to graduate with his now legal male name and stop the charade with his family. Salem remembers always being uncomfortable with people, and therefore shy and withdrawn. In retrospect, he is sure that his problems were a result of not being comfortable as a girl. He was bullied by other girls for not being feminine enough and took refuge in anime and video games. There were bouts of serious depression in his adolescence. His mother wasn't strict about "gender roles" and was perfectly happy with him playing with Tonka trucks and rolling in the dirt. She even protected him from other women who tried to insist he play with Barbies. But as Salem became a teenager, his mother tried but failed to encourage a more feminine self-presentation. The "Internet was my safety net" is how Salem tells us he got through adolescence. He always wore hand-me-downs from an older male cousin and so felt comfortable in his self-presentation during girlhood, until puberty happened and he hated the secondary-sex characteristics that emerged. He always had mostly male friends and hated that his peers rejected him as a buddy when he became in their eyes a "chick" who should hang out with other girls. Salem didn't want to hang out with the girls. As a young child going forward, Salem wanted to be a fighter pilot and joined ROTC as a freshman in college with full support from his parents. But that year, living in a female dormitory, and being a female in ROTC was a very unhappy year, and he dropped out of ROTC and stopped living in a sex-segregated female setting. Salem started playing male characters in online role-playing games, and then discovered what the T meant in LGBT while searching on the Internet. Salem told us:

I started doing research because that curiosity goes again. Do other people feel like this? Am I just weird? What's going on? I run across transgender. I sit there and read it and BAM it clicks. I'm like, yes. So then I realize that [his campus] has an LGBT resource center. It took a lot of guts for me to come up here.

Very soon thereafter, Salem began to transition. His best friend now is a trans-woman, and he's deeply involved in the trans community on campus. He dreamed about joining the military someday in the future, if it allows transmen. The interview was done before the short time that such a possibility existed.

While Salem was absolutely sure that men and women in his experience were very different in their personalities, and in the activities that drew them together as friends, his ideological beliefs in the abstract were quite the opposite. He was enthusiastic about the Swedish school, and if he ever had children (which he doesn't now want), he'd absolutely want to send his kids somewhere like it. He thinks "it's silly to teach kids this is how gender is .... I think it's really silly to have a gender binary when gender is fluid and is a spectrum." Once Salem Bee transitioned, his mother started to critique his new self as not masculine enough, and Salem put his foot down saying, "I'm okay with being a feminine man." While Salem is terribly uncomfortable with his breasts and will not leave the house without wearing a binder, he is not trying to be a "traditional man." As he says, "I consider myself first and foremost a gentle man. I'm okay with not being a macho man. That's not who I am." Sam rejects rigid gender norms even as he lives in a gender different from the one attached to the sex ascribed at birth.

Before proceeding with the analysis, let me provide some description of who these *rebels* are as a group. Thirteen of these respondents are white, two are Asian (both immigrants), one Latina, and one black. White *rebels* are overrepresented in comparison with the rest of the sample, although approximately a quarter (4 out of 17) are young adults of color. The majority of these respondents report no religion (including spiritual but not religious). Two are Christian and one Jewish. One of the persons with no religion was the child of an evangelical Christian minister. There was no relationship between ethnicity and having a religion, with two whites and one black claiming religious identities. Unfortunately, the samples are too small to make any meaningful intersectional comparisons.

Ten of these 17 *rebels* identify as genderqueer. What this means is that they jettison gender as a binary, rejecting womanhood and manhood, femininity and masculinity, as they are currently defined in the gender structure. Only one genderqueer respondent stated that she had rejected a sex category of male or female (although I do know that several have decided to do so since our interviews). Only two respondents made mention of gender-neutral pronouns during their interviews, and neither of them had yet to switch to using alternative pronouns in their daily lives. No one asked us to refer to them in the plural (as they instead of he or she) or by any of the possible gender neutral pronouns now being used by some in the genderqueer community (*ne/nirs, ve/vis, ze, zir*). One respondent had asked close friends to use nongender pronouns at the time of the interview, but not colleagues or family; and the other had experimented in a support group, but at the point when we interviewed her, she had chosen to use female pronouns in public. There are clearly many genderqueer people, including some of these respondents a year after our interview, who reject pronouns related to their gender rather than simply to their sex. But given the fluidity of identities in this sample, and the reality that we have not systematically tracked the respondents, my decision here is to use pronouns the respondents were publically using at the time of the interview. I use male and female pronouns for genderqueer respondents, as they did themselves when we interviewed them. I refer to these respondents as male and female but *not* as women and men, because it is the gender structure that turns female bodies into women, and male bodies into men. A few of these female respondents had changed their first names in real life to sound more androgynous, or masculine, and others did so for this study. As always, I use the fictional names chosen by the respondents. There were three other respondents who rebelled against the gender structure, by changing their bodies either physically or by consistently living androgynously but who did not self-identify as genderqueer. Two were masculine lesbians, and one, Clover, who you have met, simply disliked the word genderqueer, but described herself expressly as living between the gender binary, which is what the others used as a definition of that very word. The final three are transgender respondents, two transwomen and a transman. The transwomen were assigned male at birth, raised as boys, and now identify as females and are living as women. They do use female pronouns, as do I when I refer to them. They identify their sexual orientation as pansexual and queer respectively. While these transwomen do live as females, they have not adopted a traditionally feminine self-presentation. For example, Alice wore work jeans and a T-shirt with black suede shoes with purple streaked hair. The transman was assigned a female at birth, raised as a girl, and now identifies as male and is living as a man. He uses male pronouns, as I do when I refer to him. These transgender respondents do not endorse the reality of a gender binary for either themselves or others. As might be expected given the salience of gender issues in these young people's lives, their interviews are longer and richer, with many more stories about gender, both conformity and breaking norms, than the other respondents in the sample. In fact these 17 respondents told us 149 stories about gender conformity and 308 stories about breaking gender norms. That is, they told us almost twice as many stories about nonconformity than conformity. All talked deeply and at length about gender issues in their lives, indicating deep reflection about gender issues (Table 7.1).

TABLE 7.1
PROFILE OF *REBELS*

No.	Name	Sex	Sexual Identity	Race	Religion	Immigration Status
1	Ali Kang	Female Genderqueer	Homosexual	Asian	None	Immigrant
2	Alice Weeks	Transwoman	Pansexual	White	None	Native-Born
3	Amy Baker	Transwoman	Queer	White	Buddhist	Native-Born
4	Andy Jones	Female Genderqueer	Queer	White	None	Native-Born
5	Cary Van Pelt	Male Genderqueer	Bisexual	White	None	Native-Born
6	Clover Johnson	Female Genderqueer	Bi-curious	White	None	Child of Immigrant
7	Eugene Martin	Female Genderqueer	Queer	Black	Christian	Native-Born
8	Frankie Adams	Female Genderqueer	Pansexual	White	None	Child of Immigrant
9	Jes Simpson	Female Genderqueer	Homosexual	Asian	None	Immigrant
10	Nick Cohen	Female Genderqueer	Queer	White	Jewish	Native-Born
11	Noelle Garcia	Female Genderqueer	Queer	Latina	Spiritual	Native-Born
12	Rainbow Bright	Female Genderqueer	Homosexual	White	Christian	Native-Born
13	Rhyn Black	Female Genderqueer	Queer	White	None	Native-Born
14	Salem Bee	Transman	Homosexual	White	None	Native-Born
15	Susie Cue	Female Genderqueer	Bisexual	White	Spiritual	Native-Born
16	Suzie Jones	Female Genderqueer	Queer	White	None	Native-Born
17	Theodore Black	Female Genderqueer	Refused	White	None	Native-Born

I begin this chapter with the individual level of analysis because these young people have not simply adopted the identities their parents offered them, nor do they acquiesce to social expectations. They are *rebels*. At the individual level, the themes that emerge are complicated. The first theme that emerged in this sample is how these rebellious Millennials try to live between the binary of male and female by *rejecting the societal expectations for presenting* their bodies. A few have changed their very embodiment, with breast reduction, others changed their body language and their clothes to present themselves as between male and female, bound their breasts, or switched back and forth between presenting as more masculine or feminine. The transwomen are both transitioning and using hormones, as yet undecided of the surgeries in their future. Nearly all these *rebels* provide many heart-wrenching stories of being policed for atypical gender presentations of self, by families, by peers, and by strangers. The second theme that emerged was that these *rebels mix 'n' match* from traditionally male and female activities and personalities. Most had always done so, and all felt that they had grown out of whatever conformity had constrained them when younger. A few of the females had been *rebels* from early childhood and had no memory of enjoying anything feminine. Most of these young people remembered very little policing about what they did or their integration of masculine and feminine selves as children. This was not true for the transwomen who remember their parents trying to force them to be more masculine boys. All the respondents were very conscious of not internalizing or portraying a hegemonic masculinity that could be seen as sexist.

At the interactional level these narratives were very different from everyone else in this study. These interviews were chock full of stories about *gender policing*. The first theme is how painful and ubiquitous they report others policing their bodies. For those few who have "come out" as genderqueer, even supportive social networks freeze up when faced with accepting a genderqueer identity. Friends often fail to understand what it means to live "between the binary." The transwomen faced policing and then rejection from family members as well. The next theme identified at the interactional level of analysis was the *rebels'* constant commitment to *pushing back* against the gender binary. When expectations constrained them, they addressed the issue rather than sidestepped it. When it comes to using a bathroom, sometimes they confronted strangers who questioned their gender identity, other times they found bathrooms that were empty. The point is that they identified the problems they faced and found ways to change the environment or at least came up with a workable solution to the problem. These *rebels* are efficacious. If they do not feel comfortable in their culture, or in their bodies, they either try to change the world or themselves. Their responses to individual problems push the boundaries of interactional expectations, and so they are attempting to change gendered expectations as they live every day. The final theme is about the *supportive social networks* they have assembled. All of these *rebels* report that their close networks are now supportive; this appears to be primarily explained by their efficacy. While most people live within similar social networks, finding like-minded others is easier for those in the majority than the minority. For those in a minority, finding like-minded others takes work. These young people have rejected those who reject them and have constructed safe and embracing social networks.

Finally, I end this chapter by addressing their attitudes toward the contemporary gender structure at the macro level, how they understand the world, cultural norms, and their experiences of the sex-specific rules and regulations within institutions. The first theme here was *feeling oppressed by social institutions*, by the real material rules that exist in today's institutions and organizations. All of these *rebels* identify at least some institutional and organizational constraints on their everyday lives. The institutional oppression ranged from dancing lessons where girls had to stay on point to the requirement that female weight lifters wear short skirts. Clothing stores in particular were viewed as places of exclusion, and bathrooms places of ostracism. They all held *change the worldviews*—which is the second theme—at the macro level of culture. They held radical positions about gender, desiring a world where the sex assigned at birth wouldn't influence social norms at all. Some were actively involved in efforts to remove institutional gender constraints (e.g., advocating gender-neutral bathrooms) and the larger public discourse. Others believed that simply living between the binary was itself a political act. These Millennials highlight the possibility for individual and collective agency to push back and perhaps change the gender structure as we now know it.

Figure 7.1 illustrates the themes that emerge in the analysis of these *rebels*.

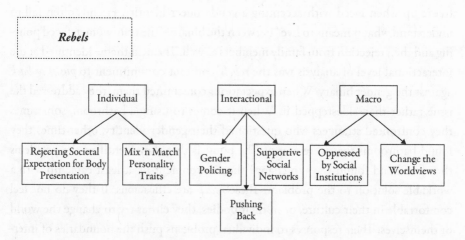

FIGURE 7.1 Themes for the *Rebels*

WHO I AM?
Or the Individual Level of Analysis
Rejecting Norms for Presenting Bodies

Most of the 17 *rebels* explicitly and self-reflexively lived in some fashion between the binary of masculine and feminine. This was the predominant narrative in their stories. They refused to be constrained by categories. As Eugene Martin told us, "I never really felt like a girl. I tried to be one for a while but it never felt . . . it never felt comfortable. But I didn't really think of myself as like trans either. I just knew that I wasn't comfortable putting on this show." Later Eugene tells us clearly that she is both female and genderqueer, "I've presented as female for so many years. I identify as queer, and I've grown attached to that label." The two transwomen I categorized as *rebels* also reject the notion that simply because someone identifies as female, she must be feminine. They too reject gender as a simple binary.

Fourteen of the 17 *rebels* do not try to pass as members of the sex different from the one they had been labeled at birth. They either self-identified with the word genderqueer or rejected the concept of embodied masculinity and femininity as applied to them. All 17 *rebels* rejected the gender presentation that matched the sex they were assigned at birth. Most of these *rebels* distinguished between their sex, male or female, and their gender, especially their gender performance. I refer to the genderqueer respondents as male or female, but not men or women as a way to distinguish between their sex and their gender. The transwomen both replied their current biological sex was male and might be changed in the future, but that they identified as female gender, and so I refer to them as female and as women. All had journeys where they held different gender identities in the past, and many were open to changes that yet might come. As Frankie Adams told us:

> I did research for my partner who's trans, and it was more so I could learn and be accepting of my partner. And then the more research that I did, the more that it seemed to become a checklist for me. I was like okay, okay, these apply to me as well. And so then, then I like explored a boy identity for a couple of years. . . . But more recently I've just realized that it depends on my mood, on the day . . . like for the most part, like, I don't really ever identity as female or like as a girl, I mean, I mean I might identify as feminine or masculine or like you know or like butch or femme but not really like boy or girl . . . just because like, you know, the way that I see it, the way that I have seen and experienced the world, no one is like the norms that is like boy and girl, but everyone. It has a little bit of the other. I mean even biologically everybody has some testosterone, everybody has some estrogen. So I feel like it is more like a mix of ·

that. So I definitely feel like gender, I would say like, the closest way I can put it into words now or the best way that I understand my identity in this current moment of my life is like gender-neutral, but I can lean more feminine or more masculine depending on the day.

While most of the *rebels* had experienced this kind of fluidity with both gender and sexual identities, this was not true for all. Three of the genderqueer young adults identified as females with preferences for masculine activities and presentation styles from their earliest memories. They identified themselves as having masculine interests and the desire to escape feminine attire from early childhood, and began identifying as butch lesbians in adolescence. The two transwomen had always felt different from others along a gender spectrum, and both had identified as gay men before they discovered they could change the gender they had been identified at birth. In terms of sexual identities, four *rebels* identified as lesbians, and the rest offered a variety of sexual identities including bisexual, queer, pansexual, bi-curious, or refused to be labeled. The most common sexual and gender identity (7 of 16) was "queer." Most of these *rebels* rejected both sexual identity and gender binaries. A quote from Alice Weeks, a transwoman, reflects many a rebel's sentiment.

> I identified as bisexual for quite a while, but I don't believe that there are only two genders or two sexes. Just from my own experience and meeting trans people. I know that people follow along a wide spectrum from very masculine to very feminine and everything in between or neither or both. So for there to say that there's like two different types of people that I'm attracted to just didn't really cover the wide variety of just identities that I was dating at the time. I was like, you know what, this doesn't fit. Queer is a much more fitting identity for the kind of people that I'm attracted to.

The topic that most engaged these respondents was a conversation about how they experience their bodies and present themselves to others. This topic came up often and in a variety of places throughout the interview, even when it was not clear how it related to the question at hand. While many of the other respondents in this research project spoke negatively about their bodies, the issues for the rest of the sample were mostly related to perceived attractiveness, often but not only related to weight. Such general negative comments about attractiveness were also made by the respondents; many of them also reported dislike of their bodies regarding attractiveness. For example, Frankie Adams and Clover Johnson both complained about being too heavy at one point of their lives. Andy Jones told us she once had an eating disorder. Clover Johnson didn't like the size of her breasts or the hairiness of her arms. Noelle Garcia didn't complain about her weight but rather her body hair and her breast size. She told us:

> Well I used to shave like my whole body because I was really uncomfortable with hair, and I used to have like really hairy arms and I would get picked on a lot in like seventh grade.

Still, bodies mattered a great deal more to these *rebels* for their gendered identities. Most of the stories these respondents told about gender nonconformity focused on their discomfort wearing gender-typical clothing and performing gendered body language. Most, but not all, of these Millennials remembered quite a lot of freedom to choose between masculine and feminine self-presentations, as well as a wide range of activities during childhood. But a few, especially women with strong preferences for only male clothing and also the two transwomen, reported a great deal of parental pressure to conform to gender-appropriate clothing and behavior. The policing of bodily presentations became widely felt as truly oppressive during and after puberty.

Every rebel complained about the kind of clothes manufactured for people with bodies like theirs. The genderqueer respondents often wore clothing of the opposite sex to create an androgynous persona, combining female bodies and male clothes. Nick Cohen remarked:

> When I wear men's clothes, I don't look like a man and I'm okay with that. I don't want to look like a man. If I took testosterone or had surgery, I would start passing as a man, and I don't want to actually pass as a man. That's not my goal. I like being androgynous. I like being in the middle and having a feminine body and wearing men's clothes on it is exactly where I want to be. In the androgyny.

The female rebel genderqueer respondents were split on how comfortable they felt with the physical aspects of their biological sex, including breasts and genitals. About half were comfortable in their bodies but felt constrained by how they were expected to perform femininity via clothing and body language. The others reported varying levels of discontent with their genitals or secondary-sex characteristics such as breasts or the tonal range of their voices. The half who described discomfort with their physical bodies reported discomfort began with the onset of puberty, as breasts developed and menstruation began. For some the unease that developed at puberty was attributed to the sexist male gaze that accompanied the development of breasts. Clover Johnson said:

> I went through puberty in fifth grade. 'Cause I remember getting to sixth grade and being the only girl with boobies. Uhh, I just remember being confused at first. Like . . . first I was on the playground having a good old time, just doing this and that and the next morning I wake up and I'm like two feet taller. I seriously went through puberty overnight. Yeah, went through puberty overnight. I woke up one day with a pizza face, C cups, and I was a foot taller in my bed, and I was like, "What is happening?" and I just remember getting all this attention from all the boys at school, like, I remember going to school and all the boys suddenly knew my name and wanted to talk to me . . . I remember hating being like a female figure, not being a female, but being a female figure for men, like in that sense. Being just a figure to look at. . . . so, boys would start paying attention to me all the time, and I didn't like that at all, so I was like what the fuck is wrong with my body? Why are people paying attention to me?

At this point in her life cycle, Clover had decided to embrace being female and genderqueer and now avoids a sexist male gaze by dressing in what she describes as an androgynous fashion, boyish enough that she is sometimes mistaken for a man when she uses restrooms.

For some of these *rebels*, though discomfort begins in puberty, the discomfort remains an enduring source of pain. Eugene Martin remembered

> in fourth grade I had to start wearing bras. And then in fifth grade I started my cycle and I cried. So it was when my body started changing that I began to hate it. . . . I'd like to lose weight. Try to get rid of my hips. Sometimes I toy with the idea of like starting to T but like not transitioning, quote unquote, all the way. Just enough to stay androgynous: like super androgynous. But I don't know if that's possible.

For others, positive aspects of their bodies compete with their discomfort. Frankie Adams, who had spent a few years experimenting with a transboy identity eventually decided that she was more comfortable with a genderqueer identity, despite some dislike of her body. How she felt about her breasts was one of the reasons she decided not to remain in her previous transgender identity. She spoke about the physical pleasure her breasts provided during sexual play.

I've definitely considered top surgery. Like mastectomy. And the reason that I didn't really consider it before was because I really enjoy the sensitivity of my nipples in play, like in bed . . . and I'm not as like strictly boy identified as I used to be. It's a lot more fluid.

Theodore Black was still debating her sexual identity, whether to identify as gay or queer and was still unsure how that related to her gender identity. She answered without hesitation that her sex was female although she had always been masculine in appearance. While she currently identified as genderqueer, she was considering whether to identify as a transman and live as a male. She reflected on the trade-offs of adopting different gender and sexual identities. She seemed to prefer being gay as at least a part of her identity but wasn't sure that would be possible living as a man, and that was part of her decision-making.

I've been considering being transgendered so technically living as a male. I've been considering going on hormones and obtaining surgeries, but if I were to do that I probably would not identify as gay. However, I kind of haven't gotten to that level yet where I actually know.

For now, Theodore described herself as genderqueer, having no gender or being both male and female in some ways, and for now she is comfortable enough to live with her body as it is, as long as she binds her breasts.

Jes Simpson was less comfortable in her body as she grew into puberty than anyone else in this sample except for the transwomen. Her articulate interview shows the pain she endured from the beginning of puberty, which ended only when she had top surgery a few years before our interview.

Middle school was a pretty tough time for me because puberty came . . . because before that I felt okay with my body because all of the secondary-sex characteristics hadn't shown up. So I didn't really think much about it. But as soon as those things showed up and I became very anxious and I really disliked my body and I was very self-conscious and always very just nervous and uncomfortable and awkward and um . . . I broke a lot of dress codes at that time because I didn't want to wear dresses, and I didn't want to tuck my shirt in, I wanted to pull it out so that I could cover my curves. And then I wanted to wear gym clothes all the time. I didn't want to wear dresses, but the school that I went to was very strict about this dress code so I got picked on a lot.

Eventually Jes found a way out of this conundrum:

> As soon as I, like, knew that I could simply get rid of that [breasts], I didn't have to change all the other parts. I felt like I could make peace with all of the other characteristics.

The two transwomen, Alice Weeks and Amy Baker, had experienced distress with their bodies throughout their lives, while the transman, Salem Bee, did not experience discomfort until puberty. Alice Weeks remembered a childhood where she had been overweight, physically inactive, and by the second grade had begun to dislike the "fact that I was a boy." In elementary school what Alice didn't like about being a boy was having "to follow masculine gender roles." She didn't want to play sports with other boys, and so mostly remained a loner spending time reading. Alice didn't feel uncomfortable in her clothes though, jeans and T-shirts were worn by boys and girls alike. It wasn't until after puberty that Alice began to rebel against her gender. She found her voice lowering a crushing moment and felt bewildered when she began to develop facial hair. Several bouts of mental illness followed, including severe depression and in-patient commitment for suicidal tendencies. Alice remembers these "treatments" as further traumatizing because of the gender segregation of the facilities themselves. Once she moved out of her parent's home, she came out to herself as transgender, and soon thereafter moved to a college town and began transitioning. She now has a female driver's license, although still a male social security card, but lives as a woman. Alice uses hormones to help change her body and has done so for five years. As she became a woman, she spent a few months "crazy exploring femininity" with makeup. But soon thereafter, she once again began to live mostly in jeans and T-shirts. Occasionally she wears makeup, but refers to the purple streak in her hair as being "goth" not feminine. Salem Bee was most miserable when living in a female dormitory in college, but once transitioned, he was comfortable being a feminine man and had no intention of trying to "macho" up his body language.

All these respondents, some quite comfortable with their secondary-sex characteristics and some not, shared discomfort about clothing styles and expectations for body language being so gendered. Some of these respondents tell stories about going back and forth between more feminine and masculine self-presentations, either over time or from day to day. Others have adopted masculine or "boyish" self-presentation styles as the only way to feel authentic and comfortable in their skin. Below, I first present data from the respondents who report a more fluid sense of self, and then present data on those who rejected gendered expectations early in childhood and have remained consistent throughout their lives.

Most of these Millennials went through stages of changing their dress patterns and presentation styles over time. Some began dressing in boy's clothing, changed to "goth," and perhaps back again, switching to more gender normative clothes for a time in high school, and eventually mixing up male and female styles. Other *rebels* pick and choose from male and female articles of clothing and presentation, day by day or even article by article of clothing. Others were quite consistent in presenting themselves masculine enough to be confused for males, although they often described themselves as androgynous. When these young people adopted what they understand to be androgynous styles, they seemed to me to equate androgynous clothes with those usually worn by men. No female rebel primarily presented herself as feminine all or even most of the time. The two transwomen do not present themselves as traditionally feminine women but as female. The following quotes illustrate the majority pattern of respondents who change their self-presentations over time. Clover Johnson remembers when she started dressing like a boy and stopped again.

> I felt very masculine and that I should have been a boy anyway, but I still really like guys. So I was like, maybe I should just be a gay boy. And I sort of, seventh grade is when all of that confusion came to my mind. And that's when I started dressing like a boy and chopped off all my hair and, you know, really started acting more like a boy. Not really acting, just embracing more of my boyhood. . . . Like, if you did not know me and you just had met me, you would think I was transing to be a boy. Like, pre-op about to be a boy transitioning. And at one point, in eighth grade . . . no, no, in ninth grade, it was like the beginning of ninth grade and the end of eighth grade, I just stopped. I don't even know where or why or how it happened. It was just no . . . I just no longer felt the need to hide my body, I guess. 'Cause the whole reason I was dressing was like to hide my body. I didn't want people to see my boobs or my curves. And I also just didn't want to be thought of as a female. Like, I wanted to be treated like one of the dudes. The best way to do it was to be one of the dudes. But I also felt like that was hiding a part of me.

Andy Jones remembers starting to dress like a girl to hide her discomfort with being one, and then realizing she was doing that and stopping what she came to see as a charade.

> It was when I was nineteen that I realized, "just fake it. Just pretend you're a girl." And that was the first year I bought my first pair of dangly earrings and it was all downhill from there, and grew my hair out long and became very affected feminine and then just kept doing that . . . and kept doing that long after I realized that I was not actually a girl, like came to verbalize the fact

I didn't know the word genderqueer yet, but I knew that I was neither male nor female or possibly I was both. And that's sort of how I try to articulate it. . . . I was so like desperate to fit in, and I had to try even harder . . . when I was very much in denial about this part of myself, I dress extremely feminine. All the time in dresses, high heels, lots of makeup, long blonde hair, . . . Yeah, it was sort of, I mean, it was an act. It was drag. And then I realized that I was torturing myself. So I sort of got away from that, and now I'm somewhere between. I still like wearing, you know, dresses and stuff sometimes, but my general day-to-day appearance is pretty androgynous.

Yet another pattern among these young people's struggle with how to perform their gender is illustrated by Susie Cue who wrestles with claiming an androgynous identity while realizing she receives pleasure that comes with sometimes dressing in gender-appropriate ways. She describes herself as androgynous, insisting that she is neither a woman or a man and so beyond the binary.

I don't want to deny my feminine side quote unquote. But I also don't want to deny my masculine side quote unquote. And a lot of times when it comes to the feminine side, it has to do with the appearance. So I mean I don't want to look at the feminine side as being a negative. It is not . . . I mean I can see the negatives in putting on makeup and stuff because it portrays an unrealistic view of people. But also I think everybody putting it on is okay, everybody not wearing it is okay. So it's kind of I will not wear makeup when I don't want to wear makeup, and I will wear makeup when I want to look pretty. Or look accentuated I guess . . . I've considered identifying as umm . . . what's the word, it's with an *a*. . . . Like dressing gender neutral. But I like dressing like a girl.

Similarly, Rhyn Black told us:

At this point I'm pretty much comfortable doing whatever I want. There's days that I wake up and I feel like extremely feminine and I want to wear a dress and a ton of makeup, and there's days that I feel extremely masculine and I want to wear man's pants and a plaid shirt button down. It really just depends.

But she, too, struggles, like Susie Cue, with the disconnect between her identity and how people perceive her when she does dress in feminine ways.

The expectation, I think that it's especially difficult for me when I'm presenting as a girl. It doesn't change the fact that this is how I feel about my gender, but other people don't see that. When I'm wearing a dress and makeup, my queerness is virtually invisible to people. That's kind of hard sometimes because I think that, you know, I feel like it's a part of myself that doesn't get recognized.

Rainbow Bright has pretty much left behind feminine dress and wears primarily pants and shirts. This is her complicated story of self-presentation. She has considered breast reduction but not a total removal because she identifies "as mostly like a woman so I guess like having something there would confirm that a little bit." Yet, despite her discomfort with her breasts and rejection of feminine dress, she still wears a bikini at the beach.

I go to the beach, I like to wear a bikini at the beach even though it's very not like me, it's because I like sun. I like to tan. You know what I mean? So I wear like a bikini at the beach and people are always like, "Wow! Where did you come from?" . . . yeah, that's like the only place that I'm like okay with them [i.e., breasts], I guess. I'm still a little uncomfortable, I guess, but I'd rather like be in like a bikini than wear like a long T-shirt on the beach when everyone else is like half naked. You know what I mean?

These rebel respondents range from total ease with their physical selves to severe discomfort with their bodies, leading to breast removal and hormone use. Yet, none perform traditional heels-and-hose femininity with any regularity, although some do occasionally. Others have only been comfortable in masculine dress from their earliest memories. Three of these female *rebels* had adopted masculine interests and sense of selves as very young children and have never wavered. Many of these female respondents were mistaken for boys when they were young, and some still are routinely presumed to be men. The transwomen had troubled childhoods, realized early that they were uncomfortable as boys and transitioned to women without adopting the belief that women had to be particularly feminine. The relationship between body and identity is far more complicated for these respondents than for any other group in this study. Bodies and identities are at the core of much of the conversation with these young adults, and that differs tremendously from most of the rest of the sample.

Mix 'n' Matching

While they all talked a great deal about how their identity was embodied, they also told many more stories about breaking gender norms than following them. And yet, they told stories of following gender norms as well. What was clear from the interviews is that they incorporate both traditionally male and female activities into their repertoire and they integrate personality traits from both masculine and feminine stereotypes. I move here to the second theme of these stories, how they *mix 'n' match* and integrate the masculine and feminine into their behaviors and personalities. In this way, the *rebels* and *innovators* are quite alike. I start with stories about conforming to the sex they were assigned to at birth and then those that are about rule-breaking. I then discuss how they talk about their personalities. It is important to note that while gender identity and rule-breaking were salient to all, they are not obsessive about gender issues. Most talked a great deal about many activities that were not gendered either masculine nor feminine, such as watching movies, driving cars, playing air hockey, playing instruments in the orchestra or band, or signing in the chorus. Others loved going to concerts, listening to music, or spending time writing. Some were involved in theater productions as actors or crew. Some were artists. Others were involved in 4H, Academic Bowl programs, and student government. Gender matters, but it is not the whole story of their lives.

The stories about gender conformity focused primarily on activities during childhood and early adolescence. And they were not really strongly gender coded at all. Female *rebels* told us that they sometimes enjoyed housework, loved music, had sticker collections, enjoyed chatting on the phone with girlfriends, thought "boys were stupid," liked hanging out at the mall, and going shopping. One respondent, Susie Cue, remembers making a "baby name book" with her friends where they found names of future husbands and babies. Some hated any kind of sports. Others were jocks who played mostly in traditionally female sports such as soccer and softball, although two played rugby as well. One reported an eating disorder, several others told stories about dieting. They reported being good at jump rope and dancing from sun up to sun down. Some like tap dancing, others jazz. Several reported liking to share their feelings with others and being good with people. Alice Weeks remembered discovering video games and realizing they were both something she enjoyed and acceptable for boys to play with, and so they became a big part of her childhood.

Many of these stories about gender conformity are offered with a post-hoc, critical, feminist gaze. For example, Noelle Garcia was homecoming princess for two years in her high school. However, when she told the story in retrospect, she criticized her earlier self as "very gendered and stereotypical." Clover Johnson tells us several stories about her female activities. She loved to jump rope, and was very good at it, while she detested competitive sports. She also describes how she used femininity, told now with a critical lens, to try to turn a friendship with a man into a romantic relationship.

I would like hang out with him all the time and just give him those little batty eyes [looks up and blinks quickly], and he probably had no clue what was going on. It wasn't until one day in the seventh grade where I was like, "Hey, I like you." And he was like, "Oh . . . oooohhhh. Okay. Do you wanna be my girlfriend?" And I was like [nods emphatically], "Yeah."

Similarly Rhyn Black described her adolescence:

I had crushes on boys. I liked having long hair. I wore dresses . . . I still really was a girl. I was like I am going to be a ballerina; I wanted to wear pink sometimes.

Susie Cue "liked to dress up, you know, take pictures of myself like dressing up and all that." Andy Jones remembered things she considered feminine in her childhood like shopping, bright colors, and animals.

The one male genderqueer respondent, Cary Van Pelt, agreed with the rest, that there was much about his childhood that was traditionally gendered, in this case gendered masculine. In fact, he didn't remember getting involved in anything feminine for the first 13 years of his life. As Cary told us:

I enjoy some very masculine things. I had action figures as a kid. Occasionally, I'll play with dolls because my sister was lying around, but mostly I play with superheroes. Video games are also very male. Shooting and blowing up. A lot of the activities that I was into were very male, and I had that in common with a lot of males. . . . I didn't care about my appearance. . . . That was why I thought something very deep in me changed a couple of times in my life once I moved into Indiana sometime in high school. . . . I don't have any memory of the first thirteen years of life, actively getting involved with feminine stuff.

Many, if not most, memories of gender conformity were full of contradictions. For example, Rainbow Bright told us that during her

senior year of high school, I know that I went to a dance and I wore a dress and that was probably the last time I wore a dress. And probably wasn't comfortable in it then.

But she also liked to wear a self-revealing bikini at the beach. Several respondents told us about both conformity and rule-breaking in the same story. For example, Nick Cohen said:

I loved to wear princess dresses. I loved dressing up and being girly as a kid. But I also was very athletic and embraced the name tomboy. I don't know. I guess

I like to think that I was gender independent from the earliest point on, but on a regular basis I would wear boys' clothes and baseball caps and run off and hang upside down on the monkey bars, but I loved playing dress up, and I loved wearing big frou-frou princess dresses and tiaras and makeup and all of that too.

Rainbow Bright similarly both embraces and rejects traditional femininity with this quote.

I like fashion and stuff like that. It's not the same fashion that other girls like but I do like . . . men's fashion. But I guess like it's the same thing as like a girl would look at like women's fashion magazines and stuff like that. I really follow like men's fashion blogs and stuff. I guess it's kinda like same interest just different content.

While we heard many stories about gender-appropriate behavior in childhood, often couched in a critical gaze looking backward, we heard far more stories about gender nonconformity from early childhood until the present moment. The two transwomen remembered disliking boy's activities and being more social like the girls. The one male rebel respondent is very clear that once he reached adolescence, he often liked activities and products that were culturally defined as feminine, although mixed in with traditionally male desires. He liked

glamour images, like, pin-up pictures or forties or golden-age of Hollywood actresses and stuff like that . . . I like the seventies glam rock music and the late seventies to eighties new wave music. That's the kind of things that I'm interested in.

Most of these female *rebels* remember their childhoods with pride because of their stereotypically male behaviors. I move now to provide examples of the kinds of activities they remembered as being nonconforming in their childhoods distinct from discussion of their physical selves. Some of these female *rebels* reported taking the lead with boys sexually, while some preferred math and science to English. Most do not remember being policed or even facing criticism for these kinds of choices, although there were exceptions. Many of these females had parents who supported their choosing activities that interested them without regard for gender stereotypes. These young females reported with pride enjoying stereotypically masculine activities from childhood on. For example, Clover Johnson remembered a great deal of "boyish" behavior in childhood. While her mother didn't think girls should have BB guns her father disagreed.

I got a BB gun for my twelfth birthday; I was never into girly things. I always wanted things that I could use, so I wanted tools to use for things. Or, like art supplies. Like, things that I could make something with. So, I would always ask for . . . I always liked my brother's shit, too. So I would want like action figures. I always loved Star Wars. I wanted like Star Wars action figures. I just always liked boys' shit. I remember like, back when my dad was teaching me how to fire a gun when I was a kid, he would like take me to the shooting range and like my brother learned how to shoot a gun. We all would just hang out in the backyard with bows and arrows and guns and just fire at bottles all the time. Just what you did. So I remember for my twelfth birthday, I wanted a BB gun because I wanted to be just like my brother. He had BB gun and he would like sit in the woods all day long, like shooting at tree trunks and like shooting at bottles, and I thought it was so cool. So, I like asked my dad for a BB gun, and I think it was why my dad and I are so close, because I would ask him for these things and he would be like, "You're the best daughter ever." Like, "Dad, for this Christmas I want a new hammer!" He'd be like, "Okay, baby." Umm, so I asked my dad for a BB gun, and he was like ecstatic. He was just over the moon with joy that I wanted a BB gun.

Clover continued by describing how different her childhood was from other girls and how her parents not only supported, but also insisted, on her atypical experience.

Working on the farm as a kid, I had a lot of fun. And I like physical labor. I like physically building things. And I like physical work. Something I was raised with. I don't feel like a lot of girls like to do that. Like to physically lift up heavy things and build shit and like, learn how to fix things. I'm always all about fucking fixing things. And any time anything breaks I want to be like the handy man that fixes it. Girls are like [high pitched voice], "Just call someone." Like, I feel like, I dunno. Just things like that. Masculine traits, I guess, things that [in deep voice] men would do. Like, I like to get my hands into, I want to like learn how to fix it, I want to know how it works. Like, I used to work on cars with my dad all the time. I know how, like, an engine works. And how a motor runs, so because of that usually I can look at things and sort of kind of figure out how to fix something if it gets fucked up, usually not, I try though. But I feel like that's something a lot of girls just don't even entertain that thought. . . . . I like those things, like yeah, mechanics and electronics or like getting my hands dirty.

Others also tell stories of male-typed preferences for toys and activities. Eugene Martin remembered primarily masculine interests in childhood without memories of being punished for her interests.

Well I was a tomboy . . . . I had an obsession with flashlights, and I collected flashlights and stickers, and I was a weird kid. [laughing] I would take things apart and put them back together or try and put them back together. . . . I just felt like I had interest in the same things [as boys], like jumping off of bunk beds and like wanting to be the boy Power Ranger. I don't know.

Eugene continued with a story about breaking a gender norm—taking up wrestling—and was proud to have broken that barrier because, within a few years, girls were half the wrestlers in the program.

My afterschool program was part of a park district here in Chicago, and we would compete against other park districts in our like district. I did wrestling which I actually, the first year that I did that, I was the first girl to go. And like they did like a little physical thing, and the doctor told me take off my shirt, and I was like that's kind of weird. I think I was like eight or nine maybe. And like his assistant was like, "That's a girl." [laughs] But then the next year that I went, there was maybe like a quarter girls, like twenty-five percent. And then the next year was like pretty evenly. Yeah, so I thought that was pretty cool.

Of course, not every one of these young people was accepted so easily with their gender-atypical activities. Cary Van Pelt, the one male rebel who identifies as genderqueer, remembered being different from other young men in his school, and uncomfortably so. He told us:

I never had any affinity for any sports, except basketball, only slightly. I kind of enjoyed basketball. I enjoyed basketball when playing it during recess. Any sort of competitive, structured environment around the sport, except basketball, I detested. . . . I was in Catholic school where football was very important, and my complete lack of interest or enjoyment in that really socially set me apart almost as much as being Protestant in a school full of Catholics.

The parental and peer responses to gender nonconformity varied widely. The transwomen report much angst and unhappiness in adolescence as they rejected much male activity and with such vehemence that parent's attempted to coerce them to behave more appropriately. Even here, however, Alice Weeks remembered her mother allowing her great leeway to enjoy feminine activities, but her father tried to pressure her into baseball and hockey. She hated baseball, but, to her surprise, she really enjoyed hockey as a young boy. Unfortunately, as Alice entered puberty she felt acutely different from the other boys and became less comfortable playing with them. Salem Bee, a transman, remembered parental support for his long-standing desire to join the military and be a fighter pilot. The majority of these female genderqueer respondents remembered their gender-atypical behaviors and preference for activities accepted by peers and parents. The female *rebels* tell us the same thing as the *innovators*, girls are allowed to push boundaries into boyland. However, for the *rebels*, they hit a wall because when they refused to adopt feminine presentations of self in adolescence, they began to feel pressure to conform.

These *rebels* have successfully disconnected—in their own minds—femininity from female bodies, and masculinity from male ones. In this section, I present how these young people spoke of feminine and masculine personality traits and how they mix 'n' match them. The females do not routinely talk about themselves using primarily masculine personality traits. Even those who do report masculine traits concurrently report feminine ones. For example, Clover Johnson, who described a childhood and young adulthood defined by masculine activities, told us, "I've always been really good at getting along with people, like I've always been a really good people person."

These *rebels* seem very sensitive to the negative aspects of hegemonic masculinity, aggressiveness, and domination, and do not want to replicate such traits in their own personalities, even if they want to appear masculine physically. Once again, these *rebels* share this dislike for hegemonic masculinity with the *innovators*. As Eugene Martin told us, she didn't want to be treated like a "bro":

> I don't want to be treated like I'm a bro, 'cause I'm *not* . . . . Besides the obnoxious way they dress, they're just obnoxious people in general. Not all straight men, just bros in particular. Like, they kind of like elevate themselves, where it's like you have to be masculine like in this weird chauvinistic way.

As the male respondent, Cary Van Pelt is also very aware of hegemonic masculinity and proud to have left it behind. Eugene Martin wants to be seen as masculine but is very insistent that she is not aggressive as she coins the phrase, a "gentle masculinity." All the while, she is very conscious of not putting down other females, of not being chauvinistic, or adopting too harsh a misogyny as part of masculinity.

> I think of myself as having a more gentle masculinity . . . . I don't really think of myself as an aggressive person, and I think that a lot of times masculinity is associated with aggression. And, I kind of like being a gentleman even though, in some ways, it's probably misogynistic of me. I think it's a better

type of misogyny. . . . Well, I guess I think of one of my friends who was kind of hooking up with a bro a few years ago, and we would just kind of like ignore her otherwise and I guess I think of myself as being more attentive and more emotionally available. This is just like expanding, not necessarily on being a gentleman but just how to be myself. Just *not* douchey; to sum it up.

Eugene continued with a description of self that is quite feminine.

I can be kind of touchy feely. It really just depends on the person. I don't know if that is always true . . . . I'm not a forceful person . . . . Actually I'm kind of viewed as a soft pushover . . . I'm passive aggressive. I'm so passive aggressive. [laughing] Like with my friends and stuff. Yeah, don't call me back. I'm not going to text you back for like two days. [laughing]

Similarly, Rainbow Bright wants us to know that however comfortably masculine she may look, "I'm not aggressive like at all really. Like usually, even like when . . . I don't like confrontation like at all. So if someone else is trying to like, you know, pick an argument with me or do anything like that, usually I just let it go off my shoulder, which sometimes annoys people more if I don't fight back." Rhyn Black also used a very feminine metaphor to describe herself, at least in the past, "I mean I was kind of an emotional butterfly, or I mean, a social butterfly." Nick Cohen also is very reflective about masculinity, and while she does embrace androgyny in looks, she is grateful for not having been raised as a man in a sexist society, "I didn't have the indoctrination of tough masculinity; I did have the socialization of caregiving and constant emotional communication." She continued, "while I like to dress transmasculine, I really like to be the one asked out on a date." Alice Weeks characterizes herself as forceful, with a strong personality, but also affectionate and sympathetic.

As the earlier quotes imply, the most common self-descriptions reflectively support an identity full of complexity, as both feminine and masculine or in between the polarities, with a self-described androgynous self. For example, Susie Cue complained:

I have friends who refuse to recognize that I like to be more androgynous in my personality I guess. Or friends who refuse my masculinity or some friends who refuse my femininity . . . I think life is more of a balance between the two . . . I don't want to deny my quote unquote feminine side. But I also don't want to deny my masculine side quote unquote.

Similarly, Jes Simpson, who is often mistaken for a man, dresses in male-typical fashion, and has had top surgery, realizes that at least some of her personality can be described in what are traditionally feminine terms.

> I like to share feelings, and I like to like observe. So I do feel like I do have some characteristics that would be considered as more feminine by the social standard. Yeah because I am thoughtful and I am observant and I'm . . . yeah, I like to talk about things.

Overall, these respondents mix and match when they talk about their personalities. The females do not simply adopt characteristics of the opposite sex. Rather, they are keenly aware that despite their androgynous or even masculine self-presentations, they do not want to adopt masculinity that is boorish, aggressive, or dominating. They do not want to own a masculinity that privileges them nor demeans women. They seem to embrace the feminine skills of emotional reflection and sharing, even as they often adopt more masculine self-presentation styles. Nor do the transwomen adopt a feminine presentation geared toward a male heterosexual gaze.

These respondents' life goals do not seem very different from those of the rest of this sample. Like others, they don't actually talk very much about their career goals. Frankie Adams is in cosmetology school, while Nick Cohen is disappointed with herself because she's not yet in graduate school. Andy Jones is an environmental attorney currently looking for work. Most of these respondents, like all the rest, simply want to finish school and get a job that allows them to live comfortably. Some talk about wanting to be parents, although others are clear they do not desire children. But there is one difference in how they talk about their goals from others: their goals often include making the world a safer place for people who fall between the binaries of sex and gender. For example, Clover Johnson asserted:

> I want to have a butt load of babies, I wanna have little forest babies like I was— they're gonna have gender neutral names, there's not gonna be any such thing as girl things or boy things in my house.

In summary, these *rebels* embody the ability to live between the gender binary. At a very material level, they reject gender and mark that with their bodies. Some choose this identity for primarily political reasons as they reject gender itself as an unnecessary and stratified category. For others, the sexist gaze that the female form brought them felt intolerable. A genderqueer identity for these females often signals a rejection of the gender binary, a stand against the constraints of gender inequality. But not all who are gender nonconforming do so for political reasons. Others remember desiring to do activities and wear clothing traditionally assigned to the other sex from early childhood and came to rebel against the gender structure simply by following a path that felt authentic from earliest childhood. They often felt dissatisfied and pained by their bodies, from puberty forward, or began to feel less comfortable with the secondary-sex characteristics of breasts or menstruation. The transgender respondents struggled with great pain and mental illness in their journey from their assigned sex to their current gender, but now feel themselves authentic. All of these *rebels* have an identity that detaches traditional femininity and masculinity from male and female bodies. Whatever route they traveled to be *gender rebels*, all felt gender dress-norms constraining. It was the rejection of gendered presentations of their bodies that matched their biological sex that seemed to create the most serious stigma in their lives.

When it comes to behavior, many remember gender traditional behavior in their past, although they often recall it with a hint of irony or critical analysis. Overall, they are very self-conscious about *mix 'n' matching* feminine and masculine personality traits and behaviors. None of the *rebels* reject the feminine aspects of their personality. Nor did any of them adopt hegemonic masculinity with its implication of female subordination. Most did not recall instances of social stigma because of their adoption of activities usually done by the opposite sex, or because they embraced aspects of their masculine and feminine selves. Rather, the stories told below, about interactional stigma, are mostly about how others react to their bodies. Like the rest of this sample, these young people wanted to graduate, get middle-class jobs, and support their families. But here too, as among the *innovators*, many have social justice goals for the future.

WHAT'S EXPECTED OF ME?
Or the Interactional Level of Analysis

The first and predominant theme at the interactional level of analysis was their experience of other's *policing their bodies*. All *rebels* reported childhood experiences that included gender nonconformity, but the reactions to that nonconformity from parents, peers, and their communities varied tremendously. They told more stories of being policed for their nonconforming behaviors, including both activities and their presentations of self, than any other group. The second theme in these stories is totally intertwined with the first, and that is *pushing back* against gender policing. Generally, these young people do not give up and acquiesce—they stand their ground. They told 207 stories about rebelling against these constraints and very few stories (n = 29) about acquiescing to interactional expectations. At the interactional level, when these young people faced gender-conformity expectations, they usually rebelled. If they faced severe repression in their families of origin, they sometimes waited until they moved out of their parent's home to become who they want to be. All had pushed back at norms as children and young adolescents even if sometimes they complied under duress. The third theme was their efficacy in creating *supportive social networks*. They may have faced severe gender policing, but they did push back and are living the lives they chose, surrounded by supportive intimate networks.

Policing Their Bodies

When analyzing interviews with the *rebels*, we cannot easily divorce gender-atypical behaviors from self-presentation because these stories are told as one. And yet, negative reactions to gender-atypical dress and presentation styles were ubiquitous, while negative reactions to gender-atypical activities were more unusual. That is, many of these young people faced little sanctions for breaking gendered-behavioral norms, but they all faced at least some sanctions for how they presented their bodies. I begin with a discussion of the wide variety of interactional responses these young people encountered for their gender-atypical activities and self-presentation as children. In this discussion of gender policing, I start with a focus on families, then move to other adults, peers, and finally to strangers. I then move to the nearly universal reactions these young people encountered if they "came out" or openly self-identified as genderqueer or trans, informing friends and family that they exist either between the gender binary; as neither men nor women were transitioning their gender category.

First, let's discuss the diversity of experiences in families of origin. Not all these young people faced parental pressure to conform to gender stereotypes. About half were raised by families open to their following atypical interests and styles of self-presentation. But the other half were policed severely by at least some family members. Even liberal parents quite accepting of young girls who wanted to break gender norms and dress in masculine attire became less understanding when informed by their daughter (the one male genderqueer had not done this) that she no longer identified as a woman, was not really a transgender man either, but was between the binary. At that point, even very liberal families often respond with dismay, as did the parents of the transgender respondents. Most eventually came around.

There were many gender-traditional families, or at least extended families with gender-traditional members who tried to socialize these genderqueer young people into femininity (or in one case, masculinity) as soon as they started to behave in ways that defied gender stereotypes. Suzie Jones remembered:

Yeah, when I was in my house with my mom and my step-grandma, I was running around and like jumping up and touching the top of the door, like the frame of it, and was just being kind of rowdy. . . . And I think if I were a boy, they would just be like, "Oh, she's . . . or he's just running around," but since I was doing that, my step-grandma took an issue with it, and she kept giving me books about how to be ladylike and polite and things like that.

Eugene Johnson also remembers a grandmother who punished her for urinating like a boy; it had such an impact that Eugene began to fear doing anything that might be seen as boyish. She told this story about her childhood.

> I potty trained myself apparently. And I remember peeing standing up a lot, but my grandma had a long talk . . . she spanked me first and it was just like . . . she warned me a few times, but than one time she just spanked me. And it was like girls don't stand to pee, they sit down. And so I just always felt like I had to. It got to the point where I was afraid to ask for anything with the word boy in it, like it was an overreaction on my part but actually I think I've told you this before but I was afraid to ask for things like Chef Boyardee or play with my cousin's Gameboy. [loud laughter]

Eugene's family continued to try to socialize her into femininity as she aged, but eventually her mother came to accept her as she was.

> Growing up sometimes we would have to go to church and I would have to . . . I was forced to wear dresses then or for picture day . . . . I would just cry or plead with my grandma or mom about it, but then as I got older and living with my mom more, my mom just kind of tolerated not wanting to wear dresses.

The one male in this genderqueer sample did not begin to break gender norms consciously until adolescence and still chooses to hide part of himself from his family. While he believes they will not mind when they found out he is genderqueer, he clearly feels the need for secrecy about his decision to wear makeup. Cary Van Pelt told us:

> I've kept my profile on Facebook to be that photo of me with makeup on (at Halloween), because that is the only way I can have a profile photo of me kinda dressed how I want to be but also have an explanation for it. . . . I'll probably keep that one until Halloween at which I would probably have another one with me. . . . I'm not totally ready for my family and parents to see, although they'll be cool. But I'm not totally ready for them to see that aspect of me.

Noelle Garcia remembered arguing with cousins about their traditional expectations that women cook for them. She tell us about a cousin of her posting on Facebook that

> "girls these days, knowing how to roll blunts but not flautas." And I was like, what? . . . "why do girls need to know how to roll flautas and why can't guys do it?" and this other guy like responded it to it like, "No, girls should know how to cook" and blah blah blah, and I just got really offended . . . I can't really remember what I said but I pretty much talked about equality.

Jes Simpson came from a traditional family and faced perhaps the strictest gender socialization of any of the genderqueer youth. As Jes recounted:

> As early as I could remember, I hated it [wearing dresses] and we always had conflicts over buying clothes and she would take me to a department store and ask me to pick whatever I liked and I always went for boy's clothes. And then she would disapprove and then bring me . . . drag me to the girls department and then try on different dresses. And then I would run away, I would run away . . . she would just make me wear them. It's not like I really had a choice to. . . . She knew that I didn't like them and I didn't want them but she would make me. . . . Well actually it's like a tug-of-war. It went back and forth. Sometimes I'd win and sometime she'd win. But this battle, I would say, until I became financially independent, that I was able, when I was like actually able to . . . had full autonomy to shop and to live as an independent person from my mother.

While most families with traditional gender values were concerned both with gender and sexual nonconformity, that was not true for all. For example, Jes Simpson tells us all the gender policing was really about gender and not her identity as a lesbian.

> She's fine with my sexual orientation . . . that doesn't bother her at all. . . . One time she said to me, "I know that there are many kinds of lesbians . . . why can't you just be a beautiful lesbian?"

One more example of the kind of pressures faced by these genderqueer youth from traditional families will do. Noelle Garcia told us:

> Okay, well every year, since I was a little kid, like all of my uncles and boy cousins get together and play football for, uh, it's called the Turkey Bowl.

And growing up with my dad, he always played football with my brother and I. I remember always wanting to play, but they wouldn't let me because I was a girl. They didn't want me to get hurt or anything. It was just really messed up. But yeah, I remember being really hurt by that because they let me play [football with them] outside of that Turkey Bowl. But like when the big event came like I wasn't allowed to . . . after a while I just didn't want to play anymore. I was just like whatever. And then after I joined rugby in college they were like, "Oh, you should play with us." And I'm like "Oh, yeah."

Until the Turkey Bowl invitation, Noelle's family had disliked her playing rugby at all but eventually they came to see it as an advantage for family games, although by then she had been so offended, she refused to play. The two transwomen faced great sanctions from families when they came out. While Amy Baker remains alienated from her family, Alice Weeks has since been so accepted by her family of origin that her father currently lives with her and her two (polyamorous) partners. Salem Bee, a transman, is not very close to his complicated family, but his mother was supportive when he came out first as gay and then later as trans.

Other families were very supportive of their girls' gender nonconformity. Ali Kang told us her family didn't mind that she was more interested in boyish activities, and because she was, they understood that she would rather dress like her brother.

But I don't think my parents really cared though since I had like an older brother, they, you know, we were closer so I got influenced from him . . . . Also growing up I actually am the more athletic one among four. My older brother doesn't really do any sports. He's like a geeky person. He likes all the computer stuff, you know, mechanic stuff. So that's where he's passionate. So I did sports, and they think that if I dress more, you know, more masculine and all of that it's totally appropriate. It's not weird. And the good thing about that is we can always share clothes. [laughs]

Rhyn Black also reported parents who encouraged her to do anything and wear anything she so desired. As Rhyn told us, "I did most of the stuff that I wanted to do. My parents were really cool about letting me try out different things that I was interested in." Rhyn went on to say that her parents were supportive whether she cut off all her hair or had nose rings, and they welcomed her to "the club" when she announced she'd lost her virginity in high school. They never restricted her activities or androgynous dress. Susie Cue told us, "My mom was pretty proud of me for being different." Nick Cohen's mother had forbidden Barbie dolls because they promoted a negative body image and was furious when Nick's aunt sent an older cousin's collection. Nick went on to say that her father allowed her to do much more physical risk-taking activities than did her friends' parents.

> My dad was totally on board and let me do whatever I wanted as long as I wasn't literally going to like fall and kill myself. But that included climbing trees way higher than the other girls would . . . I remember once on a hike when there was, you know, a fallen tree that had fallen probably five or six feet above was like perched like probably like six feet above the ground over like a little ravine. Just high enough to feel scary and dangerous and adventurous for a little kid but low enough that even if I had fallen, the worst that probably would have happened would have been a broken bone . . . exactly the sort of situation that I loved . . . . The other dads got furious. . . . The other dads stopped it like, "No, you can't let her do that. You can't let her do that. Our daughters will see and will want to too." So the other dads forbid me from going and climbing on this log because they were afraid that their daughters would follow and might hurt themselves.

Whether these young people have critical or supportive families, they have all faced significant pressure from other adults and authority figures in their social world, sometimes teachers, often bosses, occasionally doctors, or members of their church. Sometimes these adults in authority positions were critical because they presumed gender nonconformity was an indicator of, or might lead to, being gay. Other times, gender nonconformity itself was enough to create censure. I focus here on the policing that was primarily about gender nonconformity although this was particularly painful for the respondents when it was also accompanied by homophobia. Many of these young people remember teachers pressuring them to "do gender" more traditionally. Eugene Martin remembered her preschool teachers encouraging her to switch playing from Legos to dolls. Jes Simpson remembered pressure from teachers through her school experience:

> They would be like you should grow your hair out. You shouldn't act like a boy all the time. You need to be more modest, you need to do this and that. . . . And one thing that I hated the most was that they always would say, but I never really understood what it meant, was that you need to learn to love yourself. Have some self-love or have some self-respect when I did very boyish things. . . . I got picked on by teachers, by classmates.

A few of these respondents had suspicious encounters with medical professionals. Eugene Martin told us that a doctor had tried to "feminize" her with hormones without her consent. She recounted the experience this way:

> I don't know if this is significant or not but I had that strange situation with a doctor who had lied about my blood work. About my hormone levels and he wanted to treat me for a condition using female hormones but I refused. And he said that was the only way and basically released me from his care because I wouldn't . . . because I didn't comply . . . . So I started going to an LGBT-friendly place, and that's when my doctor than told me, "Oh, your blood work and all that is normal. You actually have higher levels of testosterone." So I thought, oh how weird because maybe that's why he wanted to give me the female hormones and not like tell me. But now in healthcare I think now I've found some really friendly, good doctors. Who, like they're just sensitive to queer issues.

These young genderqueer *innovators* had trouble not only with doctors but at workplaces as well. Salem Bee, a transman, remembered being constantly asked if he needed help simply doing his job stocking shelves at a supermarket when presenting as female. Once he transitioned, he was left alone to do his work. Ali Kang told us she had to dress more feminine during an internship at a financial firm or she would have been let go. Frankie Adams believed she had trouble finding full-time professional work at all because of her self-presentation as masculine. Nick Cohen explained:

> There have been issues with dress codes in professional settings. My first real professional job doing the same things I'm doing now but with a different company. . . . They [had a] very explicit, strict dress code that was different for men and women. And there was initially some conflict with my boss when I started following the men's dress code [he would not allow a female to wear a tie]. . . . But the strict dress code said that men wore ties every day so I couldn't wear men's clothes without a tie because it wasn't formal enough, and I would be dressed down than everyone else. The agreement that we came to was that if I wore a sweater vest or a sweater or a suit jacket over my button up every day then I would be considered formal enough without wearing a tie.

Whether these young people were sanctioned by the adults in their lives or not, every one of them tells anecdotes about being policed by peers, from their early years in elementary school onward. Most have by now found peer groups accepting of who they are, but that doesn't lessen the pain in the stories about the past. Clover Johnson was home schooled for a year or two and remembers being an outsider from the moment of her arrival in elementary school. She recalled, "On my third or fourth day of second or of third grade, I was finally put into real school, one of the girls was like, 'Why are you so dirty and why don't you wear dresses?'" Noelle Garcia remembers usually playing with the boys, and so "they would call me Marvin like instead of like [Noelle], and I don't know they just came up with that." Cary Van Pelt remembers what happened one day as he was showing a teacher affection.

> I was hugging my teacher and my leg popped up and everyone was laughing. It was cute. It wasn't in a negative way. It would have been nothing if I were a girl.

He then explained that he continues to face many such micro-aggressions. "There are lots of examples of those, even in my day-to-day behaviors. Look at my hands like this and that. I talked with my hands a lot, people think that is considered very camp." Cary Van Pelt had no idea what being gay meant the first time he was bullied with it as a homophobic taunt. Still, Cary believed that the exclusions from peer groups were far more painful than the taunts.

> Exclusion always felt like a much deeper knife than torments ever really did . . . . I have been reluctant to label anything as bullying . . . I was always the odd kid. I got called gay a lot. The first time I ever knew what the word gay meant. . . . Always the boys in class. The girls never really did. I think because the girls always liked me because I was nonthreatening.

Eugene Martin also told stories filled with pain about feeling isolated from peers both in high school and at the conservative Catholic college she attended.

> Growing up, I wish I had learned more about like being genderqueer, like being trans-masculine, not having fully transitioned or just knowing more about the options were. Like particularly in high school. . . . Because I feel like a lot of things would be different. My college years would have been different. Who knows if I would have chosen [name of college], probably not. But like now that I'm here I feel pretty isolated a lot of times, because the resources are just not here like the resource center in town does a lot with older transwomen and so like . . . and the church I go to, everyone's either a gay man or a lesbian. So it's still kind of . . . being genderqueer . . . there aren't really resources for me.

Clover remembered gender-related taunting, but for her it was the suffering of a male sexist gaze that first led her to choose androgynous clothing. She remembered:

> Boys would start paying attention to me all the time, and I didn't like that at all, so I was like what the fuck is wrong with my body? Why are people paying attention to me? . . . And I remember in seventh grade, seventh grade is when I really started dressing like a boy. I just like, I wore only Dickies and like, black T-shirts and my little leather punk jacket with my anarchy sign on it,. . . So, I started dressing like a boy to just not appear physically sexual at all to anyone. And also just to like, sort of slip by the radar like I didn't want attention from boys. And being the first girl getting it [puberty, breasts] that was hard because all the other girls hated me. And . . . like I didn't have that many friends to begin with, so then when I grew boobs all the girls were like, "Well fuck her, every boy wants to fuck her now." So then the few friends I did have were pissy that I had boobs, and I'm like, "I'm sorry! I had nothing to do with this. I don't even want this attention." And that's when I started dressing like a boy, essentially. I wore big baggy man work pants and converse and big baggy black hoodies and T-shirts, and I essentially was just trying to hide the fact that I was a woman. 'Cause I was the only woman in my grade. There was like maybe two other ones who were sorta getting to womanhood, but I was like . . . a woman physically . . . . That's the only time I really remember hating, hating, hating my body is because I didn't like the attention I got from it.

The irony, however, was that once Clover started dressing like a boy, to avoid boys stares and girls' jealousy, she started being bullied for looking masculine. Clearly she was damned if she did and damned if she didn't.

> One day we were in math class and she [her tormentor] was like still bugging me about being a boy and dating JOHN. And I'm a gay boy for Jake and all this stuff. And I don't remember exactly what she said, but she said something that pissed me off so bad to the point where I shoved her and she shoved me back. And then I took my math book and clocked her across the face with it, and then she punched me, and before we know it, we're on the floor grabbing each other and pulling hair and screaming and the teachers trying to separate us. And all of that shit. But yea, she never stopped giving me shit and she like even got pulled out of school a few times. . . . She always just was so, so terrible to me. So terrible.

Andy Jones also remembered being teased about her appearance. She was presumed to be a lesbian in high school because of how she dressed.

Everyone in high school thought I was a lesbian because I looked really lesbian, but I did have a boyfriend he just didn't go to school with me. He graduated ... so I had short hair, and they decided I was a lesbian so they clipped out all the woman seeking women personals and threw them at me and taped them on my desk and stuff and were like [cough], "lesbian," you know that kind of stuff like [cough], "you're a dyke."

Even friends sometimes do hurtful gender policing. While most of Susie Cue's friends now accept who she is, she still has some friends who refused to see her as she wanted to be seen.

I have friends who refuse to recognize that I like to be more androgynous in my personality I guess. Or friends who refuse my masculinity or some friends who refuse my femininity.

Eugene Martin had specific genderqueer criterion for the people she dated. As she told us:

I prefer dating someone who identifies as queer. I don't really like dating straight women or lesbians. [laughs] ... I don't want to date a lesbian because a lesbian, in my mind, is a woman identified person who wants to date another woman identified person. And, since I don't identify as a woman, even though I accept that I am female, um, like I don't want to be labeled as a lesbian. But, I don't want to date someone who identifies completely as straight either because I don't completely identify as a straight male, like with straight men either. So, I'd like to date a queer woman because it just makes more sense for me.

The transgender respondents talk more about being bullied for being nerdy, standoffish, or overweight than for gender nonconformity. Alice Weeks remembered being thrown "bodily into a closet" and having her "face slammed into a bench in the locker room" but downplayed the significance of these events because they were rare, while she was "verbally insulted fairly frequently." Even that verbal bullying was dismissed because she claims to have been able to deal with it easily and shrug it off. It is, of course, the case that Alice continues to have serious mental health issues so perhaps she has longer term effects of such bullying than she wants to admit. Salem Bee was bullied by girls throughout adolescence because he wasn't feminine and didn't fit in their circle. He was the focus of much abuse until one day he smashed one of the girl's face into her locker, and after that they left him alone. Amy Baker still feels bullied even on her college campus.

Gender policing, however, was not only enforced by the mainstream but, at least occasionally, also by members of the respondents' chosen peer group. Nick Cohen told us an interesting story about trying to be genderqueer in a mostly lesbian sports team where the women expected each other to identify as either femme or butch.

My rugby team really only knew me as super butch, and I'd been playing with them for a year. But we hadn't seen each other much outside of actual rugby functions when I was almost always in athletic gear, and even when we did it was casual social stuff. I would normally be in jeans and a plaid button up or something like that, backwards baseball cap . . . that's how they'd seen me. And then we had our annual semi-formal banquet. It was of course my first annual semi-formal with this team and I femmed it up. I wore a dress and heels and makeup and jewelry, and my team kind of freaked out. Like they weren't okay with it. Not that I was the only one there in a dress, about half of our team were femme. Most of the team was lesbian but you know at that banquet about half of them showed up in like vests and ties and fedoras and half showed up in dresses. And that was fine because the ones that were in dresses were the ones who always kind of looked femme when they weren't on the field. . . . . One of my closest friends on the team, who was just as butch as I was, had also come in a dress but as drag. Like she made a joke out of it. She and one of our other close friends on the team was usually really femme and they switched places for the night, and the femme girl dressed up as butch and the butch girl dressed up as femme, and it was a joke for them. And her reaction to me coming in a dress was kind of like "Oh, I didn't know you were coming in drag tonight too, ha, ha, ha." . . . But she knew that I wasn't in drag . . . it was a pointed comment of like, "Why are you dressed like that? You should be wearing a suit." . . . It's been a couple years, a few years since then, and I've, I don't know, I'm no longer comfortable wearing a dress even aside of the comments. And I'm not sure how much of that is just me becoming more comfortable with my trans masculine presentation and not wanting to go back, and how much of it is that I've internalized the disapproval of the queer community. For my original desire was to toe the line and kind of go on both sides. I'm really not sure.

The expectation that every person be masculine or feminine seems to shape behavior even in communities where masculine and feminine has been totally divorced from male and female bodies.

All of these *rebels* talked about the rudeness of strangers. Sometimes these were micro-aggressions involving people looking at them too long or with puzzled faces, but sometimes they were behaviors that threatened health and safety, such as being challenged when entering a women's restroom or dressing room in a clothing store. Clover Johnson talks about how her presentation of self confuses people.

Usually they looked at me trying to figure out if I was a boy or a girl. That's probably why they looked at me. They're like, "I can't tell 'cause she's got short hair and she wears boy's clothes, but those lips look kind of feminine. I think she's got tits under there."

Cary Van Pelt also remembers the stares, even short ones, as people try to figure him out.

A couple of times I've worn makeup in public, and I think people look at me two milliseconds longer than usual. . . . In the liberal environments that I stick to is such that I never get people screaming at me. But I do think people do look a little longer. Sometimes there is a little bit, not to say it is an angry look, but just . . . sort of . . . rolled in the eyes. There is some wariness sometimes. I don't know. The look like you're the other.

Sometimes when strangers create discomfort for these genderqueer *rebels*, they are not even aware they are doing so. Jes Simpson told us an anecdote about strangers presuming she is a man and the accompanying feeling that is easier to "act" like one than correct them.

I get called "sir" a lot . . . yeah . . . and when homeless people came up to me they ask for money, they're like, "Hey man, do you have a quarter or a cigarette?". . . I just really never had the desire to just want to be a man . . . I don't really want to pass. But it's just that a lot of times it's just easier for me to pass. . . . So sometimes I feel like yes, it [passing as a man] has some advantages and benefits that I can be perceived a man. Like it makes me a lot safer when I'm walking around at night by myself, and I never have to worry about you know, violence. Well less . . . not never but less. . . . And yeah um, but I don't really like how people treat me like a man because it's just . . . then I have to act like a man.

Respondents who shift their presentation of self from more or less masculine to more or less feminine notice a difference in how strangers treat them. Rhyn Black said:

I notice people like staring at my genitals or like my chest trying to figure out, like looking like are you a girl or are you a boy? I can't tell. You look kind of like a girl. Especially if I'm not wearing earrings because I wear earrings a lot but if I'm not wearing any earrings, I notice people like staring at me trying to figure it out. That's one thing too.

Sometimes "the look" is longer and accompanied by threats of violence or actual violence. Frankie Adams tells frightening stories about how strangers sometimes behave toward her. This story is about a man she met in a bar where she is known as a regular. Frankie now identifies as genderqueer but used to identify as a transboy and had even more serious trouble with strangers during that time of her life.

And I have one guy talk about basically like pulling down my pants and showing the panties underneath them, and I was just like are you kidding me right now? And this always happens in the same bar, because I only go to like one bar. So like it's my home, I used to work there, so I just grab security, so if that happens then okay. But if they hit me or swing at me, I'm going to hit them first or before I grab security . . . that happened a lot more when I was like actually boy identified. And like I have gotten into fist fights over it because people would like get so upset that they would try to hit me.

The frequency and form of strangers' negative reactions, including misreading genderqueer respondents appear to have a racialized form. Jes suggested that in the United States people presume an Asian man will be short and thin and so she is far more often mistaken for a man here than at home in Taiwan. Eugene Martin does not want to be a man nor tries to pass for one. But her very masculine style of dress has led her to feel racially profiled as a black man. She told us:

There was a white woman walking towards me, and she got off the sidewalk and started walking in the bike lane facing oncoming traffic. And as I was walking I was like, this is weird, and so we pass each other, and I thought I bet anything she got back on the sidewalk. And so I waited and then I turn around, she's back on the sidewalk . . . I felt profiled.

What is interesting here is that Eugene chuckled as she told this story, as if she was glad she has misled this racist woman. This happens rarely enough that it has yet to become a real problem but given what we know about how police sometimes profile black men, it is quite possible that it could become a serious problem sometime in the future.

There are a series of stories about problems entering bathrooms, with strangers challenging their right to be there, and another set of stories about feeling free to enter male bathrooms because they don't feel bound by the gender binary. The one male genderqueer respondent did not have this experience, never having been challenged going into a male bathroom or having tried to enter a female one. And the transwomen avoided bathrooms when possible and so told fewer stories about their experiences. Thus, these bathroom anecdotes are told primarily by female genderqueer respondents. It is important to note that the sheer quantity of these stories was not spontaneous: we had a vignette in the gender module that asked for reactions to a scenario when a person named Lisa was challenged about her right to be in a woman's bathroom by a stranger. The reaction to this question prompted the personal anecdotes. Some of these young females experienced this problem so often and so severely that they diligently tried to avoid using a public restroom. Others used the challenge as political theater, with the goal of confronting and educating strangers. Jes Simpson represents the former case, as she avoided female dressing rooms and public bathrooms as much as she could.

> I stopped doing that because that has been happening to me [being challenged] ever since I was very young, like a teenager. As early as sixth grade I have had older women seeing me in the women's room and like saying, "Little boy, you're not supposed to be in here." .... But then now I've learned not to ... to try not to go into the women's room. I try to use ... yeah like family restrooms and nongender-specific restrooms.

Similarly, Ali Kang told us she has faced this scenario as well. But she found a silver lining: easy access to the men's room when the women's room is crowded. Like Jes Simpson, she presumes that she is so often mistaken for a man because Americans presume Asian men are shorter.

> I go to a woman's bathroom and people will just like stare at me or they will look at the bathroom sign twice to make sure that they are at the right place.... No, they double check so if I'm on my way walking out and they are on their way walking in, I just give them a smile like yes, you are at the right place ... I get used to it. I will get used to it so don't really feel anything ... I look like a little boy. That's kind of funny. Yeah. But the good thing is whenever there is a long line in [the] women's bathroom, I can always go to [the] guy's .... They don't look at me at all. Guys, they don't care. And especially I'm Asian, and they think that Asian dudes are just smaller or tinier.

While Ali presumes she is mistaken for a man because she is Asian, many of our other genderqueer respondents, white and black, also had the same problem. Andy Jones told us that "middle-aged women" will say to her, "I didn't realize this was the men's restroom" when they spot her next to them. She referred to these as "little snotty comments that you would think an adult would be over by now." At least one of these *rebels*, Nick Cohen, used the occasion of disrupting public restrooms as political education, explaining to the men (or women) around her that she didn't believe in the "gender binary" and so could use either bathroom. Others just tried to defuse the situation quietly. Noelle Garcia used her most feminine voice when she felt disapproving eyes upon her. Eugene Martin told us she took off her vest, so her chest was visible, whenever someone seemed to be about to give her a hard time for being a man in the women's bathroom. Each of these respondents had their own strategies for dealing with this issue, but it made all of their lives more complicated. For those who avoided all single-sex public restrooms, this could become a health issue. As Eugene Martin explained, "In certain buildings, I just don't even bother using the restroom. I've developed a special bladder." Gender policing by strangers is an issue that nearly every one of these respondents considered a problem to be faced daily. The transgender respondents simply try to avoid restrooms or only use gender-neutral ones on their campuses.

Pushing Back

These *rebels* told more than seven times as many stories about rebelling against gender expectations as to conforming to them, and the stories about acquiescence were usually from childhood and early adolescence. The second theme that emerged was that they are consistently *pushing back* against the gender structure. They are rebelling against the gender structure of contemporary American society. Most of them are openly defiant and hoping to both live their lives without conforming to gendered expectations and, by doing so, to change the gender structure itself. Rhyn Black purposefully breaks gendered norms, trying to "undo gender" itself in her daily life. She explained:

> I'll be on the train, and I'll sit with my legs spread like leaning forward with my shoulders up just because it feels good especially when I'm wearing a dress. I love to dominate space in a dress because people are just like, you are not ladylike. I've seen people stare at me on the train. One of my like small social breaching experiences I can do without hurting or scaring people too badly. I like it.

Frankie Adams told us about how she shifted her activism from the traditional definition of social movement activities to insisting people deal with her genderqueer self, presuming it will dislodge stereotypes in their minds. Frankie said:

I used to do a lot of political activism, but I feel like my activism has definitely shifted, and its more in terms of like an awareness building, and that's just by like being me and like living life everyday. I mean, you can see, I'm a pretty loud person. I have a Mohawk that's pink and like I'm wearing pretty like, I guess, butch clothing today but like when I do my drag like when I do my like androgynous drag and like I take the CTA to my gigs, to my events, so like I CTA from the Southside an hour and a half to two hours to the Northside and then back, so that definitely like gets.

Frankie also told us about one success story of such interactional activism.

On New Year's, this boy comes up to me, I'm about to order a drink, and this boy comes up to me and is like what are you drinking. I'm like whiskey and coke. And he's like can I get you one. And I'm like, yeah sure. Then he's like, I find you really attractive, but I don't know which gender you are. . . . and so he asked me what gender are you. And I just raised my hands up like this, and I just give him this I don't know face and just kind of shrugged. So then we talked a little bit more, and then he asks me again and so then I just like kissed him on the cheek, and I walk away because that's just like how I do things, I guess. And he comes up to me maybe an hour later and he goes, you know what, I don't care, you're hot. And so I was like thank you! Why can't more people think like that? So that's like part of how my activism is too. Just slowly, you know, opening people's minds.

Nick Cohen makes a point of telling every restaurant manager where she eats that their bathrooms ought to be gender neutral, even though she was often met with blank stares in years before 2016. After political events in 2016 when North Carolina and Mississippi passed laws prohibiting transgender people from using restrooms based on identity, I would imagine the proprietors of these restaurants would now know what Nick was talking about. Clover Johnson enjoyed a sort of "in your face" everyday activism by confusing the people around her. She and her friends had changed the signs on bathrooms to indicate that they were gender neutral, and she passed the time near the entry waiting for men to go in.

I really wanted to see someone's reaction of like, the gender-neutral bathroom thing. So, Donny, Beverly, and I like hung out and were like staring at the door, waiting for people to go into it. The first guy walks up, looks at the door, reads gender neutral, and kinda shakes his head and just walks away, like he didn't even know what the fuck was going on. Like, I'm just not even going to deal with that. The second guy [laughs], the second guy used it and then like, didn't even notice because there was no girls in there. So, then the third guy comes and I was like, oh my god, I wanna fuck with him so bad. I just wanna like rock his gendered world right now! Like, I'm sure he's one of those guys that just thinks that girls are girls and guys are guys and that's that. Like, I wanna get in that bathroom and show him what a gender neutral bathroom is! So, he like, goes in the bathroom, and I was like, "Donna, Beverley, watch this." And I like go up really fast, and I get in the bathroom right behind him and he like, he's in the bathroom and I hop in right behind him and he looks and me and I just hop into the stall and I like, do my business and I come back out and he's still standing there, shocked. Like, has no idea if he should run, or you can tell he has the face of like, "Am I in a girls' bathroom? Did I just walk into the girls' bathroom?" . . . And he slowly came out after and like, looked back at the sign really hard and then like flipped up the piece of paper and was like [squints eyes and makes motion like she is repeatedly flipping up and down the piece of paper covering the sign that says "boys'"] "Whaaaaat?" and just walked away super confused. Like, he looked like he had been violated.

Frankie Adams wanted to bring her everyday activism into the beauty industry and make a career out of it.

I want to help change the norms in the beauty industry and like how heavily age-gendered it is and how there's these standards that nobody should be forced to look up to. And so like I want to go in there and like mess all that up, kind of.

Rhyn Black brought her feminist genderqueer standards to relationships with men, and if they weren't comfortable with her ignoring gendered traditions, they wouldn't remain a boyfriend for long.

I remember I was dating a guy this one time and we were cuddling and I wanted to like cuddle him. I wanted to be like the big spoon but he wouldn't let me. He was like no, that's my job. And I was like can you just, you can just like put your head on my chest, like we just had sex, like come on. And he just would not let me cuddle him. And I was like, wow, is your masculinity so fragile? This was after I got out into sociology and he was also a sociologist, oddly enough. Is your masculinity so fragile that you can't even fucking put your head on your partner's chest? Seriously? That relationship didn't last long.

Activism, in the more traditional sense, also figures centrally in many of these young people's lives. Alice Weeks, one of the transwomen, helped start a club for LGBTQ people on her campus and is a volunteer at the university sponsored LGBTQ Center. Clover Johnson also talked about her activist work with groups, called Feminists United and Are You Proud, to try to bring gender-neutral bathrooms across her college campus. Many were members of the LGBT groups in high school and college. Jes Simpson said she worked with a gay rights association in Taiwan.

> The very integral part of our work is taking phone calls from LGBT members in Taiwan. But we also do a lot of other work. . . . We have maybe six or eight working groups that work on family issues like coming out and LGBT members dealing with their families. Family is a very complicated issue in Taiwan and Asian culture. And we have education groups that we actually send LGBT volunteers to schools, public schools, or schools all over to give lectures or talks on LGBT issues.

All of these genderqueer and trans young people were very conscious that their lives embodied a critique of the gender structure. They were committed to standing up for their right to be different, as well as changing the world around them so that others now and in the future wouldn't have to face the kind of gender policing they take for granted comes with the territory in their lives. Salem Bee in particular doesn't mind being noticed as a transman; he's not in hiding and trying to pass. Instead his living openly as a transman everyday helps to critique a binary notion of gender.

Finding Supportive Social Networks

Every one of these *rebels* told story after story about gender policing and pushing back, but most had also by now found social settings where they felt supported and accepted for who they wanted to be. These stories of *supportive social networks* show the efficacy of these determined Millennials. They may have supportive close networks, loving partners, and good friends, but often they still struggle with parents or other family members. Another example of supportive networks that still police gender behavior is the sports team that we heard about from Nick Cohen. Those peers were very accepting of her butch appearance, and in that way, supportive of her identity but didn't allow for the gender fluidity she desired.

Some were lucky enough to have peers that accepted them from early childhood onward. For example, Rainbow Bright remembers that the boys she played football with all through childhood taught her how to play and eventually stopped insisting that she be excused from being tackled. She felt as soon as she proved she was a good player, they accepted her totally. Noelle Garcia found friends online to explore self-presentation styles that fit and became part of a genderqueer community, including traveling to a music festival for the queer community.

> I started talking to like other lesbians that were like around my age. There was like a social-networking site that was called Live Journal. So I was on Live Journal, and I had all these like lesbian friends in all of these different places. And they'd post pictures of themselves. And I'd be like oh that's . . . I like their style. And I'd be like okay, I'll wear like a shirt like that . . . this summer when I went on a trip with two of my close friends to Tennessee. We went to this awesome like queer festival. And I think that was the best experience of my life. . . . Well there were just people from all over the US that, you know, identified as queer and it was a very safe space, and people were just really comfortable with their bodies and like really friendly and it was just really nice to be there with people that I identify with that I don't really get to hang out with like that much around like in the city especially . . . . It was called Idapalooza.

Many of these respondents found community online. Andy Jones also told us about a community she'd first identified online. "There's a community called Autostraddle. I mean Autostraddle is a website but it's like female leaning queer, I mean news and social news sort of website, and they also have . . . a Chicago chapter that gets together and does things. And so I'm part of that." Rhyn Black also found support in a genderqueer discussion group. She told us that

> getting involved in queer groups and in a queer community . . . and then finally experimenting with identifying without female pronouns like in this gender-queer group that I went to, it's a really private sort of safe place and I . . . we went around in a circle and your preferred pronoun and for the first time ever, I said gender neutral just to see how it felt and it felt good. So then eventually, I went back to female and gender neutral but I like it. I think it was an intellectual broadening that got me to that point and really cultivat[ed] my critical thinking.

These rebel respondents talked about both college classrooms and LBGTQ organizations as places where they experienced supportive interaction and acceptance. Jes Simpson told us that the LGBTQ organization was her first stop both when she attended college in her own country and as a foreign student here in the United States. The first group of accepting friends Jes met was at a college, not her own, and they were a club that read about and studied gender issues. It was all very "academic" according to Jes and also the first place she felt accepted. When she studied abroad she told us:

> I looked up LGBT group before I arrived there, and I e-mailed them and I said that I'm an international student and I would be, you know, on campus at this time and I would really like to meet you . . . . I went to their office immediately and just sat in there for the entire afternoon. And there wasn't really anything going on, but I just sat there with a couple of people and just talked to them.

Andy Jones's story was similar to many others when she described the importance of a romantic partner in accepting her and supporting her genderqueer identity.

> My partner's been pretty instrumental in telling me that it's okay. And telling me that she still likes [me] even like when I was a very girly woman with very long hair and she identifies very strongly as a lesbian. And I was scared that if I'm looking more androgynous she would not like it but she says she says, "You're beautiful no matter how you look."

While all of these *rebels* talk about supportive social networks, there were still some bumps in the road to acceptance. The majority of these young people feel as if they have reinvented themselves at least once, and sometimes more often. Amy Weeks lost her very best friend when she came out as transgender, and a depression followed. But she picked herself up and went on to find a better fit with different friends, and now lives with two other transwomen in a polyamorous relationship. Salem Bee now has to contend, somewhat ironically, with a mother who thinks that as a man Salem is not masculine enough. Clover Johnson felt she had owned a different identity in high school and might yet reinvent herself years from now. Similarly, Eugene Martin complained that her family thinks she is a lesbian because they just can't "get anything regarding queerness." Frankie Adams also told us about how her identity has changed over time, and, because of that, Frankie shows empathy for her friends and family that have trouble keeping up.

> I would say [a friend Manny] is two or three years behind on my identity. So when I was identifying as like a transboy, you know as like a transguy, he thought that I was like . . . he was relating that to me being like lesbian. So when I was identifying as genderqueer, he finally got the trans thing. So I'm just waiting for him to catch up at least on this last part because I don't know where it's going to go from there. But he is trying. So like that's a thing.

As the quote indicates, while Frankie identifies as genderqueer today, she isn't sure where she might be tomorrow, having previously identified as transboy and a lesbian. Frankie wants friends and family to keep up with her identity but understands that might be difficult for them. Nick Cohen understands that asking for friends and family to understand entirely what genderqueer means will take time and emotional energy.

> It's really been only in the last year or two that I started explicitly using nongender pronouns even with my close friends. So it's something that has only come up with my family once or twice, and I'm just going to try and bring it to them gradually . . . . They don't understand what gender pronouns really are or why it matters to correctly gender somebody and why it hurts to misgender them. And I've been using female-gendered pronouns for so long that I'm willing to take it slow with them. My name is also an ongoing thing. I have a female name, and I've thought of trying to change it many, many times and I'm not brave enough yet. Maybe someday but not yet.

Andy Jones was somewhat like Nick, genderqueer by identity but not really "out" about it. She told us that even her partner was uncomfortable with the idea of gender-neutral pronouns. Her partner identified as a lesbian even though Andy did not.

> You know, I'm not really out as far as being gender queer. So I imagine if I ever am more serious about that, if I find out to be a strong enough part of my identity that I want to like have gender-neutral pronouns. That could be a struggle for a lot of people, my partner included . . . . So I could see that being a huge struggle, if I ever want to do that but don't know if I am that committed to it so I don't know.

Finally, while Rhyn Black feels her parents are a "safe space for my queerness," she finds that many others just can't accept her identity.

> There's a lot of people that don't understand my gender. Even when I try to explain it to them, it's like, are you . . . so wait, are you gay? And I'm like, well sometimes I'm gay, it depends on who my partner is, you know? . . . I don't always feel like a girl. I don't usually feel like a boy, but when I do feel more masculine, I want to feel free to express that. Sometimes, I just don't feel like either.

While the fluidity of identities was true for most of these respondents, it was not true for all. Three had been boyish girls who grew up quite directly into masculine lesbians. Some find it impossible to share their gender struggles with their parents at all. Jes Simpson told us that the day she had her breasts removed was the happiest day of her life, and that one bodily change made her comfortable. But now she feels as if she's hiding her true self from her parents.

> I feel like I'm in another closet now after the surgery . . . I don't think I could ever tell her [mother] . . . I've been big enough as a disappointment to her. It's like I am nothing that's she's wanted in a daughter . . . I can't take the last thing away . . . but to her . . . sex are the same things. Like my female . . . like being a woman . . . like I just can't tell her because if I told her that I had chest surgery then she would press on. She would ask more questions about it and about my gender like why I'm doing this and all those things. That she would feel like . . . like that's the one last thing she . . . like yeah, it's what she's given me and like she felt like she gave me a lot. She gave me a lot of things and like she wanted me to be all these things, and I didn't achieve any of them, and then I wanted to change, you know, like that thing . . . that mother-daughter relationship . . . well it wouldn't really change that but to her it just would be like changing my sex: one of the most fundamental things that she has given me and I didn't want.

The pain in Jes Simpson's story is undeniable. Even though she is now satisfied to be female, has a supportive partner, and identifies as a lesbian without the chest she so disliked, yet she fears letting her mother know because her mother might stop defining her as a daughter because she had removed her breasts.

These stories show us both how far we have come in accepting gender diversity and how far we have to go. Many of these rebel youth grew up in families where they were free to break gender norms and wear whatever clothing they wanted. Many of these females report their parents encouraged their athleticism, their interests whether gender typical or not, and allowed them to dress as they so choose. Most female *rebels* had been mistaken for boys sometime in their youth. There were others in this group, however, that were brought up in very traditional homes and felt restricted and oppressed by gender expectations from early childhood. The transwomen reported very unhappy childhoods where at least one parent was consistently pushing them to do more male activities. What makes this group unique is whether they came from supportive families or gender-traditional ones, they persisted in breaking gender norms, especially gender-typical presentations of self. They all faced negative sanctions, gender policing, from at least some adults in their lives, from doctors to teachers to bosses to strangers. Nevertheless they stuck to their own sense of authenticity and ignored gendered prescriptions they found uncomfortable. Most female *rebels* never did learn to look like a lady, and if they did, they rejected it as they aged.

They *pushed back*. The transgender respondents all first identified as gay or lesbian, and when that did not feel authentic, transitioned and report being far happier now. But they did not adopt essentialist gendered beliefs. The transwomen did not feel as if they had to present femininity to prove being female, nor did the transman try to hide aspects of femininity in his body movements. Many took strength from their identities as activists, as defiant *rebels* against gender constraints. Their lives were so far outside a gender binary that living everyday constituted activist moments of disrupting the gender structure by pushing back. While gender policing was often very painful for these emerging adults, some of them redefined such disruption as the political theater of activism and consciously tried to "undo gender" in the simple act of openly living between the binary.

WORLD VIEWS AND INSTITUTIONAL CONSTRAINTS
Or the Macro Level of Analysis

There were two major themes that emerged in the conversations about the macro level of analysis. The first was distinct from any other group in this research, the *rebels* told story after story about *institutional and organizational discrimination*. The 17 of them told 103 stories, an average of about 21 stories each. Nearly every organization one encounters is designed to differentiate by sex category, so a young person who rejects gender as a category, or changes categories, has continuing trouble fitting into institutional life. The second theme that emerged was that they all had *change the worldviews*, similar to the *innovators*, but positions held more fiercely and acted upon more often.

Institutional Discrimination

Every one of these young people at some point felt they'd experienced *institutional or organizational discrimination*. Several genderqueer respondents talked about how school always separated boys from girls. Suzie Jones remembered that was trouble for girls that were mostly comfortable "hanging out with the boys." These young people stopped activities they enjoyed because the organizations managing them insisted girls and boys fill different roles. For example, Rhyn Black quit ballet when she was told only the boys could really perform big fancy jumps, "like triple turns and axels," while she had to remain on point, which hurt her feet. And of course, they rebelled against single-sex sports. Andy Clover told the story of discovering the enforcement of gender after petitioning to join the football team:

> And they [school officials] were like, "You can't, you're a girl." So, me and two of
> the girls started a petition and there were only three signatures, ours, so we did-
> n't get to play football. Yeah, I remember being like, "This isn't fair, how come

I can't play football? Why do all my guy friends get to play a sport together and I can't join in? Why can't I go play with my guy friends?" It wasn't until I like got older that I realized boys played football and girls do cheerleading.

Of course, schools, sports, and extra-curricular activities are not the only places organized by sex category. Clothes stores are even more organized by presumptions about male and female differentiation than are schools. This was a problem for nearly every respondent. As Ali Kang remarked about Abercrombie & Fitch, "When you walk in the store it says 'dudes' and 'betty's.' It already separates into two categories." Andy Jones stated, "It is trouble finding clothes that fit . . . men's clothes don't fit me very well and girl's clothes are really girly [laughs], so that's sort of an issue." And, of course, schools that require dress codes were also a major sore spot for many of these respondents. Eugene Martin, for instance, participated in "power lifting" during high school but would never compete because she refused to wear the outfit. Jes Simpson suffered indignities of discipline because she disliked and refused to wear the dress required as a school uniform. What makes these respondents *rebels* is that when denied a place on the football team, they would protest and petition the officials. They find places to shop that allow them to feel comfortable, dressing in gender-atypical fashions, or they only shop online. They don't give in. They rebel.

The presumption that males should dress and behave as men and females as women pervades the world of work as well as school and clothing stores, with far more negative consequences for these respondents. Many of the females worry about the impact of not looking feminine on their job prospects. Ali Kang had decided to wear more feminine clothing during an internship at a financial firm. Nick Cohen negotiated with her employer about following the men's dress code instead of the women's and found a compromise, dressing according to the male code but without the tie. Frankie Adams is convinced that her failure to get a stable job has to do with her now being genderqueer.

It's definitely been a lot harder for me to find like a, I would say, like a stable job. Something that isn't like doing drives and hosting tables, things like that. I've definitely noticed a decrease in the ability to get a job. I can get an interview no problem, and I always can interview well, or so I've been told, but I never manage to land these jobs. So like the only possible thing I can think of is like how they're reading me.

Andy Jones is, however, very aware that she has the privilege of dressing in masculine clothes and being accepted far more than a male who chose to dress in more feminine attire.

I'm like I said trying to get a job and that job interview thing, it's a lot easier for a woman [than] for a man to dress the opposite gender, so for me to wear a men's suit isn't really that unusual. There's certain places that I'm sure would maybe give me a weird look, but I'm not particularly worried about it. . . . I mean, since the eighties probably women have been wearing men's style clothes to be taken seriously in the workplace, so I don't really think that I'd be necessarily persecuted. It's just an appearance.

What is interesting is that later on in the interview, Andy Jones referred to the organizational expectations of workplaces as the main reason she was not "out" as genderqueer publicly.

Getting a job is pretty important, and I feel like having a complicated gender identity could complicate getting a job. I definitely see that as maybe a side effect that I am not willing to take on right now, so that's maybe why I'm not out.

The *rebels* also reported feelings of discrimination by the medical system. For Eugene Martin, this has happened on several occasions. As mentioned, she believed a doctor tried to give her hormones to make her more feminine. Another way that Eugene feels discriminated against is that her desire to have smaller breasts, or no breasts at all, is a procedure not covered by insurance. Eugene Martin talks about her desire for breast reduction.

Well, actually, I saw my doctor a couple of years ago but my insurance . . . well, one, my doctor is skeezy, and two, my insurance wouldn't . . . I hadn't taken the proper measures yet, the proper steps. . . . But now like I have documented back pain and I have been to physical therapy so I'm like trying to do all of this to go around the . . . labeling it as a breast reduction. But otherwise, like I don't really have money right now because like I'm making ends meet. And so I can't really save up just yet. But hopefully this summer I'll be able to start saving.

The transgender respondents bemoan the prohibitive medical costs that influences their even considering surgeries. Costs also influence whether to go to college or save for medical care. Costs sometimes encouraged these emerging adults to stay in college because, as Alice Weeks noted, college health centers legally cannot behave in discriminatory ways, when most other medical providers can, and do.

And last, but not least, and perhaps most common was the complaint that nearly all buildings have single-sex bathrooms rather than gender-neutral ones. As Eugene

Martin said, "I'll go right before classes end so that I can . . . or like on certain floors of the student center . . . I'll go to like the third floor in the student center because no one ever uses that bathroom. So I just try to find gender-neutral bathrooms or just like ones that aren't frequented." Other genderqueer *rebels* who present themselves in traditionally masculine garb report similarly distressing circumstances on a daily basis. Frankie Adams's complicated story shows how the existence of single-sex bathrooms can impinge on female genderqueers safety whether they choose the men's or the women's restroom.

> There was this one time . . . at a concert, and so like I was like on my way to the girl's bathroom, and the guys were like why are you going to that bathroom? And so I just kept going to that bathroom. I'm not gonna like engage you all because you all are drunk and I don't want to and it's not a safe situation for me. And then went to the girl's bathroom and there was a line and the girl in front of me turns around and goes like asks me if I was a girl. And I was like uh, yeah. But like even though I identified at that time as like genderqueer and still do.

It is interesting that there were very few complaints about the rules and dictates of religious institutions, at least at the present time. Some of the genderqueer respondents and two of the transgender respondents had been stigmatized for their presumptive homosexuality by religious congregations, but as soon as they were able, they simply left those religions. These efficacious Millennials leave the institutions that are voluntary and discriminatory. Unfortunately, much of the public world is both discriminatory and mandatory.

Change the Worldviews

When it came to worldviews and cultural beliefs about the gender structure, the *rebels* were very like the *innovators*, none held essentialist or traditionally conservative beliefs about gender. Jes Simpson also sums up many comments when she said, "I think eliminating gender stereotypes is very important because a lot of times we really don't think about . . . how much we are programmed about gender." Cary Van Pelt is very enthusiastic about the Swedish school.

> At that age, education is what teaches you or trains people in society to categorize people into male and female camps. Teaching them not to value one thing over the other is very important, and giving boys and girls the freedom to express themselves however they wish is fundamental and an experience I wished I had.

Nick Cohen wants to raise entirely gender-free children but worries about the stigma they may already face with same-sex parents. Frankie Adams articulated an alternative way to conceptualize gender:

> The way that I see it is like it's a quote, I don't know exactly where it come from, but I know RuPaul is fairly known for saying it, but "you're born naked and the rest is drag." So pretty much everything anyone does, in a sense, is drag. It also kind of goes with Butler's gender as a performance theory.

So where did these *rebels* acquire worldviews so critical of the gender structure? Feeling constrained by the gender structure predisposes one to have a critical gaze, but how that develops into a critique of the gender binary is still an important question. Most told us that their views of the world were first discovered on the Internet, from friends, or from reading feminist texts in college. The Internet provided location-independent support and information, and this was important for many of them. Most of these Millennials are like Andy Jones who told us:

> The wonderful thing about the Internet is that there is always someone somewhere that you can talk to so even, I mean, I would say I was definitely not the only genderqueer person in Lincoln, Nebraska, when I lived there, but . . . there's not maybe like a large community. The whole queer community is sort of one big thing, which is cool. So maybe like that would be time when it was more accessible to talk to people online or read things online or whatever, but I've always since the Internet started when I was an early young teenager late elementary school, I've always had it there for me, thank goodness. There's always been someone somewhere.

Those who didn't learn a new way to think about gender from the Internet told us they learned about it reading feminist texts, usually, but not always, in college classrooms. Rhyn Black recalled her gender awakening, first in books, and then seeking out a queer community to explore more.

> I think that as I started to read more feminist theory, I started reading queer theory, and as much as I can criticize her, Judith Butler, reading Judith Butler really was like an enlightening thing for me. I think that sometimes she is a little idealistic. I think that she doesn't take into account that real world and accountability and people being like hey, but you're still a girl, but as far as a philosophy by which I live and understand my own life, I that that really had

a lot to do with it. So like reading, broadening my intellectual horizons, and finally moving to Chicago.

After doing this reading, Rhyn Black sought out a genderqueer support group. Clover Johnson told us similarly:

> The majority of my gender knowledge has come from the gender classes I've taken in like these past few semesters. Before that, I didn't know shit. I didn't know what intersectionality was or the difference between sex and gender, you know, all of that came from my college, yeah. From classes with teachers, good teachers.

These *rebels* were consistently critical of the gender structure, they wanted to *change the world* into a place without gender oppression. Whether they identified as genderqueer or not, they believed that norms that differentiated boys and girls, men and women, were oppressive. All were dedicated to a future where children would be free from gender restrictions and were critical of the gender policing that continues to plague each of them. These young *rebels* lived their own lives beyond the gender binary and were very critical of a gender structure that created the gender divide in the first place.

Divorce Bodies from Gender or Undo Gender?

At the individual level of analysis, we find *rebels* proud to *mix 'n' match* feminine and masculine personality characteristics, although they were concerned not to adopt the negative aspects of traditional masculinity. They rejected gendered cultural norms at the individual level and have refused to internalize them or follow them in their behaviors. They talked far more about adopting male-typed activities than female ones but did mix 'n' match their activities including those traditionally male and those traditionally female.

Unlike any other respondents in this research, they also rejected the gender structure at the individual level in a very embodied material way. The female respondents sometimes switched their gendered presentations of self, from day to day or over time. For some, a masculine or butch presentation of self is consistently what they intended. Most of the female *rebels* often, if not always, wore clothes purchased from the men's wear section. Some described their presentation of gendered bodies simply as masculine but more used the language of androgyny, or *between the binary*. Yet, these androgynous presentation styles were boyish enough to lead to many of them to be mistaken for males. Female bodies and male clothes may be one way to reach androgyny, but the common experience of their being mistaken for men suggests that the presentational self trends toward boyish, even if the body is female. It seems that in our society, even among *rebels*, what is labeled male is still conceptualized as androgynous, or human. What is traditionally masculine appears to be so desirable, so valued, in our world that it remains the ideal genderless category. It is a touch ironic that even among *rebels*, what is traditionally male is seen as generically human.

Most genderqueer respondents were comfortable in their bodies but not in the clothes that society presumed such bodies should wear. A few, however, were profoundly uncomfortable in their bodies, at least until they had altered their secondary-sex characteristics, for example, removed their breasts. Most, but not all, experienced fluidity in their identities, experimented with their sexual and gender labels, and expected they might continue to do so in the future. For the female *rebels* the materiality of living in a female body, especially in a culture that requires female bodies to be presented in feminine ways, was oppressive and the subject of much consternation and conversation. For the transgender respondents, hormones reshaped the materiality of their bodies in ways that helped them live their gender. These transgender Millennials were *rebels* in that they did not presume that being female meant they had to present themselves as traditionally feminine or being male meant they had to hide all evidence of femininity. All these *rebels* rejected the internalization of cultural femininity and masculinity into their definition of self and strove for integrative personalities *beyond gender binaries.*

What distinguishes this group of respondents from the rest, perhaps most strongly, is their rejection of the materiality of the gender binary at the individual level of analysis. They reject the societal norms that require females look feminine, that turn females into women. Instead, they either choose to present themselves as masculine females or attempt to present a self that is truly beyond the binary. Or they transition to being women but do not desire traditional femininity. They also reject, of course, the cultural believe that they should embody only feminine or masculine personality traits because they are reserved for one sex or the other. Nor do they limit their behaviors to those labeled for their sex. They repudiate both the material and cultural aspects of the gender structure at the individual level of analysis.

At the interactional level of analysis, *rebels* face *gender policing* and constantly navigate negative feedback, particularly from strangers and in their workplaces. Most of the *rebels* remembered being supported by parents to do activities they wanted to do as youngsters, and the women report being free to wear boyish clothing as children. It was peers and other adults in the public sphere that sometimes policed their presentations of self in youth. Some of these respondents had parents who totally allowed them to go their own way, to do boy or girl activities, and to dress however they wanted. Others had families that tried very hard to socialize them into gender-typical behaviors and dress patterns from early in their lives, without respite. The two transwomen were policed into doing more masculine activities, and mostly retreated into being solo actors, nerdy and alone. But these *rebels* don't acquiesce over time to gender policing, they *pushed back* on the boundaries of gender atypicality in the presentations of their bodies. *Rebels* report painful interactional skirmishes with teachers, doctors, bosses, as well as peers and family members. They worry about their ability to be who they want to be and still find and keep jobs, and have their medical choices respected. These *rebels* were remarkably efficacious; they transformed their bodies if they were uncomfortable within them; they found new *supportive peer groups* to support their self-identities and choices. These groups included feminist organizations, LGBTQ centers on college campuses, gay neighborhoods in urban centers, and carefully chosen partners, friends, and online communities. They rejected interactional expectations foisted on them by society; they did not acquiesce to cultural norms and. by doing so, perhaps changed those expectations, or at least, some of them hoped that was the case. They changed their material experiences of the world by rearranging the configuration of supportive versus critical others in their intimate networks and surrounded themselves with like-minded others whenever possible.

At the macro level of analysis, the entire social system or institutional rules and regulations designed around a gender binary feels oppressive to these respondents. Everyone had reported having experienced *institutional discrimination*. For young adults who reject the gender binary, schools, workplaces, medical systems, clothing stores, and bathrooms all conspire to deny them the right to live between maleness and femaleness, to be beyond woman or man. And yet most have found ways to navigate the world, and some even revel in their rebellion. They all reject the worldview that suggests women and men should live distinct lives, with different rules and regulations. Their worldview is one about *changing the world*. All share some commitment to a world where being labeled a male or female at birth does not require a set of behaviors or what clothes to wear. The material level of the social structure denied the *rebels* a place to be. Their sense of oppression is tied directly to everything from the architectural design of buildings without bathrooms designed for people like them to the clothing stores organized by sex. The material world oppresses them and, not surprisingly, they also reject the macro-ideological apparatus that justifies such a world. They reject cultural beliefs about sex and gender with great vehemence.

With cross-sectional interview data, I cannot make any arguments about how these young people came to experience the gender structure as they do or how they might change it. Their stories, however, do lead to some hypotheses. As Millennials they all grew up during the ongoing gender revolution. They had access from their early adolescence to the Internet, and many spoke about discovering ideas and communities online. Others spoke directly about reading feminist classics by Judith Butler and learning about the social construction of gender in college. The ability to imagine living between the binary existed in the cultural habitus in which they grew to young adulthood. Most, of course, had already felt oppressed by gendered rules during their childhood, but the ability to become *rebels* was at least aided and abetted, if not created, by the feminist and queer cultural images already widely available as they reached adolescence. These cultural products helped legitimate the lives of these Millennials as they rejected gender constraints. Once they became *rebels*, they changed the experiences of those they encountered simply by living as they chose. Some of them are very conscious and politically committed to living lives that help to queer the world around them, to queer gender, to "undo" gender as a heteronormative expectation. Others have few political goals but simply want to be free of gender constraints. Their stories suggest to me that the cultural production at the macro level helped legitimate feelings of constraint at the individual level, and that legitimation led to agentic decisions to be a rebel, to consciously try to change the interactional expectations for themselves and for others. Some try to change the cultural ideology with conscious political activity or by disrupting taken-for-granted expectations just by living between the binary. Others just want to be free to live the way that feels authentic.

All the *rebels* share the cultural commitment to a society where being labeled a male or female at birth does not require a set of behaviors or a required way to present one's body to the world. All share a goal to change the interactional level so others don't experience the push to do a gender that is the same as their sex. All share a cultural worldview antagonistic to the traditional gender structure. But, beyond that, there is some disagreement. Some are opposed to gender binaries, at least for themselves, and want a world without gender at all. Others are perfectly comfortable with gendered norms for bodily expression in the abstract, they just want those to be divorced from the actual physical sex of the body.

In the next chapter, we turn to the modal respondents in this study, those who are betwixt and between the categories of *true believers, innovators,* and *rebels.* They straddle the categories, sharing characteristics with some of each but without consistency across their interviews.

8

The Straddlers

LET ME BEGIN this chapter by introducing you to three of the *straddlers* in this study. No two or three respondents are the same, but a short biographical sketch of three young people will help introduce the concepts discussed in this chapter. Meet Tony Dentin, Giselle Hope, and James Williams.

Tony is a first-generation Albanian-American heterosexual male. He considers himself a religious Muslim and is engaged to his high school sweetheart. His parents were never very strict about anything, including dating. Although his fiancée is also an Albanian Muslim, he assured us that his parents didn't pressure him to marry within his own religious and ethnic community. He did grow up in a sex-segregated family. The men in his family spent their time together, without the women, hunting, fishing, and enjoying other outdoor activities. He does not consider himself a city person and hopes to move to a small, rural town where he can enjoy the great outdoors and practice his profession as an occupational therapist.

The strongest gender policing in Tony's life comes from his friends—other heterosexual men. When they hang out, they do stereotypically male activities like video gaming and hunting. Tony also enjoys hanging out with girls but for different reasons. Female friends help him with activities he considers feminine, like shopping, and he feels more comfortable talking about feelings with them. He is reluctant to share his emotions with male friends because they will judge him. He is sure that his male friends believe that "guys aren't supposed to have feelings." He knows this because sometimes he is picked on for being emotional and has learned to hide his feelings to avoid negative judgments by friends. When asked if he has to put on a front in the company of his male friends, he denies it. But later on in the interview he admits that it is necessary to pretend to have less intense feelings than actually exist so that he does "not sound feminine" to his friends.

Even though Tony participates in the reproduction of gender stereotypes, and lives by them, he rejects them in principle. In his worldview, gender stereotypes should not exist. For example, he doesn't think toys should be sorted by gender. He is knowledgeable and sophisticated when he talks ideologically about gender issues. For example, he knows that Easy Bake Ovens are pink to strengthen the gendered expectations that women should be wives, mothers, and primary caregivers who cook. He rejects the premise that women should be sole caretakers of families and the only ones who cook. As an individual, he is more emotionally sensitive, or in his own words "feminine," than most of his male friends, and he values that about himself. He believes in a world with far more gender equality than exists, one where he could more freely be himself and so rejects a macro-level worldview that relegates women to second-class citizenship. But he does not want to make waves. In his everyday social world where male behavior is policed, and his friends tease him when he shows his feelings, he tries hard to present himself as traditionally masculine and not show his sensitive side.

Tony straddles the gender structure because at the individual level he realizes that femininity and masculinity are not polar opposites and he can be both, and he believes in gender equality ideologically. And yet, he tries hard to meet masculine norms in his day-to-day life, to conform to gender expectations to avoid being hassled by his friends. His life illustrates the complications of living in a world where ideologies, perhaps first learned in university classrooms, and peer group pressures conflict. At both the individual and macro levels, he rejects gender inequality and even the reality of most sex differences, but at the interactional level, he tries hard to conform to avoid sanctions. He wants to go along to get along with his peers.

And now meet Giselle Hope. She is a 21-year-old white heterosexual female. Giselle's parents were strict about her doing chores and cleaning up around the house as she was growing up. Her mother decided on the rules in the family, but her father was the enforcer. Since Giselle was the oldest child, she was expected to watch over all of her siblings while their parents were at work. She was responsible for getting them ready for school, cooking for them, and was held responsible for their behavior. Giselle thinks of herself as a very good role model because she is hardworking, independent, and self-sufficient. Her parents expect her to finish college, get her own place, then get married, and have kids. Giselle is currently in college, majoring in nutrition and dietetics. Her future career plans are to either work with pregnant women or people recovering from eating disorders.

As a young child, Giselle was a tomboy and wore only shorts and T-shirts, which was appropriate for her favorite activities of running around outside and climbing trees. In childhood Giselle was involved in many sports including soccer and gymnastics. Giselle's mother did not approve of Giselle's tomboy childhood and constantly pressured her to be more feminine and have more same-sex friends. Giselle didn't have many girlfriends in grade school because she felt they were "catty," and so preferred to hang out with boys. By eight grade, Giselle finally acquiesced to her mother's insistence on femininity; she began to wear makeup and grew her hair long. She reported that as the time passed, she began to find these feminine activities routine and simple enough to accomplish. As she started to date, she liked the "advantage of being a girl" because she never has to "buy her own drinks or pay for dinner," as men do it for her.

And yet, Giselle also told stories with some pride about how she had ignored gender norms over her lifetime. She remembered in her childhood she was a flower girl at a wedding. Her grandmother told her to sit like a little lady in her white dress and not get dirty. But Giselle wanted to run around like her brothers and indeed got quite filthy. She was scolded and told to take better care of her clothes, an expectation she told us was never directed toward the boys in her family. Still, by now, her norm breaking has toned down considerably. In fact, when she talks about current norm breaking, she tells a story about drinking very dark beer, which she believes is a man's drink. She tells us that when men drink dark beer no one notices but when she does people always make comments about it. She seemed to enjoy this minor display of independence, as a reminder of her former self.

Giselle is clear that despite drinking dark beer, overall she accepts and endorses distinct norms for women and men. Her mother's socialization has been effective, and she agrees women should take the time to present themselves as feminine. At some points in the interview she called men who wear nail polish "weird" but later on claimed to accept other people's choices to do gender differently. She both accepts their right to do as they please, but at the same time judges them harshly.

Giselle's interview is full of inconsistencies, both within levels of analysis and between them. At the individual level of analysis, despite beginning life as a tomboy, she succumbed to her mother's gender-socialization practices by middle school and enjoys the privilege of being taken out on dates that come with free food and drink. In many ways she is a very traditional feminine woman at the individual level. But she really wants us to know that sometimes she isn't. She may present herself in very feminine ways, embody femininity at the individual level, but she holds onto some part of herself that rejects being entirely girly. She sees herself as independent and not simply following the rules. Still, she has adopted and internalized cultural meanings of gender and usually tries to act appropriately. At the interactional level, she wants to meet gender expectations most of the time, at least in settings with people who matter to her, like her parents. But she doesn't mind mildly shocking people, for example, by drinking dark beer. While the color of her beer may not seem particularly rebellious to others, the symbolic value she gives it is important, and a reminder that she retains the right to reject gendered norms that she finds unnecessary. At the ideological level, she primarily supports the gender structure, with different norms for women and men, but uses a libertarian ideology to claim that even though she thinks nonconformists are weird, they certainly have the right to be so. This mass of contradictions in her interview provides an example of a woman who straddles the gender structure, in her case, mostly traditional, but not a real *true believer*. She straddles the gender structure with contradictory answers in each level of analysis. She is individually mostly traditional, but not always. She mostly likes to meet interactional expectations except when she doesn't. She believes men and women should be different and accept different rules, but holds a libertarian philosophy so that she doesn't impose her beliefs on others, although she will judge them according to her personal standards.

Finally, meet James Williams. James is a transman who grew up in a middleclass African-American family with married parents who are still together. His dad is an ordained minister. He was raised within a strict conservative Evangelical Baptist tradition, and his parents strongly and vehemently imposed traditional gender socialization. James was assigned as a female at birth and was raised to be a Christian woman. He was not allowed to participate on a wrestling team, even though it was for girls. His parents decided wrestling was too masculine for their (then) daughter. After much insistence, he was allowed to take karate lessons and play with swords. However, his parents made it perfectly clear they'd prefer more feminine activities. In middle school, James identified as gay and realized that his church would not accept him. He began self-injuring and eventually confessed to cutting himself to a church-related counselor. Immediately his parents were informed, and his mother locked him in her car until he would tell her what was wrong. When he (then still presenting as a girl) admitted to being a lesbian, all hell broke loose. For a year and a half they required him to attend reparative counseling, which was over an hour drive each way every Monday. James recounted this experience:

> I would have my session with her, which generally comprised of reading about different people in the Bible and their sins and what they did and their flaws and how homosexuality is a flaw and they can fix it. How I was choosing to be gay so I could fit in. I had said that I really didn't fit in. I didn't fit in because I really didn't fit in with the boys and I didn't really fit in with the girls.

James was terrified he would get expelled from this therapy because he was sure his parents would make something even worse happen. They already would not let him leave the house alone, even to go to the mall. And so he cried, confessed, and stuck it out. At the same time, he continued to self-harm. As of the date of this interview, he barely kept contact with his parents, and, not surprisingly, he has not come out to them as transgender.

Very much like the other transgender respondents in this sample, James was bullied in adolescence, with "dyke talk" as he called it. Girls would take gym lockers as far from James as possible, and he described them simply as "mean." Although he doesn't talk very much about race, he mentioned that his was the only black family in a suburban neighborhood, so he grew up as the only black kid around. As a teenager he hated being forced to have his hair done and to wear a dress to church. When possible, he wore T-shirts and jeans. At college he discovered the LGBT Center and met his current boyfriend at a Gay Ice Cream Social on campus. He described the man he was dating as a "ferocious five-foot-one, half-white, half-Latino transman." James now has a bald head and enjoys that he is usually presumed male.

James seems to have clear ideas about how men and women are different. Boys like Pokemon and Power Rangers (and so did he). Girls think boys have "cooties." Differences remain in adulthood. Women, he believes, always have to be busy, chatting or moving around. Men, on the other hand, can sit quietly in a room. He's glad now to have the privilege to do the latter. In an interesting racialized experience of transition, James feels he has lost some kinds of privilege as he moved from living as a black woman to being a black man, thus facing more negative responses from others. On the whole, however, he is very pleased that he is now treated as a man. He enjoys the nasty looks he gets when he forgets to open a door for a woman, and he tries to remember to let "women and children" go first. He enjoys that nearly all men, especially black men, now acknowledge him in passing, which didn't happen before he transitioned. In the future, he'd very much like to have top surgery so that he can stop wearing a binder every day, but worries the cost is prohibitive.

Although James is quick to distinguish men's from women's behaviors and dispositions, he was very supportive of the Swedish school without gender pronouns. He said, "I think it brings up some great points. The fact they are not trying to force boys to play with trucks and girls to play with dolls. They're just putting everything together and letting kids be kids." He doesn't want to hide his status as a transman, although he enjoys passing as a man. In the future, he'd like to find some resources that help him or even allow him to reconcile his trans identity with a Christian one. For now, he claims no religion but continues to believe in God.

James straddles the gender structure because sometimes he answers questions just as *true believers* would, sometimes as an innovator, and often as a rebel. At the individual level, he clearly rejects the essentialist notion that material bodies must determine gender identity. He rejects the sex he was assigned and has transitioned to a man's life. And yet, at the cultural level of the individual dimension, he believes girls and boys, men and women, are different. He is just glad to be able to live the gender that is his authentic self-identity. At the interactional level, he wants to spend time with men, not women, and be part of male groups, and participate in segregated male space. He also enjoys the gendered expectations that men face, from being allowed to sit quietly, while women keep the conversation buzzing, to behaving chivalrously. He enjoys the cultural expectations of masculinity. And yet, at the ideological macro level, James critiques gender socialization for children and wants everyone free to choose their own path. He seems quite comfortable with the inconsistencies in his answers, as do the others in this straddler category.

In this chapter, I tell the story of the *straddlers*. What does it mean to straddle the gender structure? Think about what it looks to straddle a fence, with one leg on one side and one on another. Now the gender structure is that fence. Most of these young people have their feet firmly planted on one side when it comes to diligently trying to meet gender expectations because they fear the consequences, but then they put a foot on the other side when it comes to rejecting how the world should be. Some believe in a world without gender constraints and yet work hard to follow the existing rules to avoid censure. Others straddle this fence by rejecting sexism and a worldview that women and men are and should be different while following traditional religious beliefs about modesty and sexual restraint that differ for women and men. Still others straddle the gender structure by rejecting the sex category they were assigned at birth and living as the other gender, and so rejecting essentialist notions of material bodies, but holding expectations of gender that are sometimes traditional and sometimes rejecting gender stereotypes, and so full of contradictions.

I begin this chapter by introducing these 48 Millennials and provide a short portrait of who they are as a group, focusing on their understandings of the contemporary gender structure at the interactional level. These Millennials are inconsistent and so rather than organize this chapter by themes, it is organized around the levels of analysis. I flag individual respondent's inconsistencies as they appear. I start with the interactional level because one of the few things these young people have in common is their concern with others' expectations of them. Sometimes they work hard to conform, and sometimes not. But this concern about expectations, as well as some confusion as to what expectations currently exist, is a hallmark of this group.

What did their parents expect from them, allow for them? And what about peers? Do they remember peers teasing them for straying outside the gender box? After the interactional level of analysis section, I discuss the individual level of analysis. What do these young people tell us about their sense of themselves, how gendered are their activities, goals, and personalities? I end this chapter with a focus on the macro level, that is, ideologies and experience of gendered institutional constraints or opportunities. How do these young people understand the world around them, the cultural norms? What are their experiences of the sex-specific rules and regulations within institutions? What do they understand to be cultural beliefs about the role of women and men in society, and the extent to which they subscribe to it themselves? Are they constrained by the institutional gendered rules they identify? So, in this chapter, I will provide you with many examples of the contradictions offered from one level of analysis to the other.

As for most of the others in this full sample, these *straddlers* are ethnically, racially, and gender diverse. Slightly less than half are white (15 women, 1 transwoman, and 5 men). The next largest contingent are Latino/a (6 women and 5 men). There are 9 Asians and Asian-Americans (5 women and 4 men), three blacks (2 women and 1 transman), 1 mixed-race woman (Puerto Rican, black and Asian), and 1 mixed-race transman (Mexican and white). Two women identified their race as Middle Eastern. Some were raised in literalist religions, but few of them are practicing members of conservative religious groups at the present time. Half (24 of 48) of these young people are immigrants or children of immigrants, a ratio not very different from the sample as a whole. Most of these *straddlers* hold a sexual identity as heterosexual. There was one young man unsure about his sexual orientation, one bisexual woman, and one woman who declined to answer that question, indicating that she is at the very least uncomfortable with having to name her sexual identity. The three transgender respondents identify either as lesbian or queer/unsure. There were no identifiable differences by race or ethnicity in their stories.

These young people hold contradictory beliefs, and even when they seem consistent within their worldviews, those ideas are often in conflict with at least some of their lived experiences. Some have been raised with traditional gendered expectations, but most girls talk about being raised free to make their own choices on issues related to gender. The young men are far less likely to talk, and rarely do they boast, about breaking gender norms. Both young men and women are often unsure what the gender structure expects from them at the moment, and when they do have some ideas, they aren't sure how to live them or if they want to. Two of the three transgender respondents were subjected to reparative therapy when they identified as gay as teenagers.

TABLE 8.1
PROFILES OF *STRADDLERS*

No	Name	Sex	Sexual Identity	Race	Religion	Immigration Status
1	Adam Greene	Male	Heterosexual	Latino	None	Native-Born
2	Amy Lahey	Female	Refused	Asian	Indian	Child of immigrant
3	Andie Walsh	Female	Heterosexual	White	Catholic	Child of immigrant
4	Angelica Gallegos	Female	Heterosexual	Latina	Catholic	Native-Born
5	Ashley Martin	Female	Heterosexual	Latina	Catholic	Child of immigrant
6	Bill Cornell	Male	Heterosexual	Asian	Christian	Child of Immigrant
7	Brian Zen	Male	Heterosexual	Latino	Christian	Immigrant
8	Brook Mullen	Female	Heterosexual	White	Jewish	Native-Born
9	Carrie Smith	Female	Heterosexual	White	Catholic	Native-Born
10	Chanel Anthony	Female	Heterosexual	Black	Christian	Native-Born
11	Cindy Lauper	Transwoman	Homosexual	White	Wiccan	Native-Born
12	Danielle Dumelle	Female	Heterosexual	White	Catholic	Native-Born
13	Danny Donovan	Male	Heterosexual	White	Catholic	Native-Born
14	Desiree Valle	Female	Heterosexual	Mixed	Catholic	Native-Born
15	Gabby Garcia	Female	Heterosexual	Latina	None	Child of immigrant
16	Giselle Hope	Female	Heterosexual	White	Catholic	Native-Born
17	James Williams	Transman	Queer	Black	Spiritual	Native-Born
18	Jamsheed Raj	Male	Heterosexual	Asian	Hindu	Immigrant

	Name	Gender	Sexual Orientation	Race/Ethnicity	Religion	Immigration Status
19	Jane Court	Female	Heterosexual	Latina	Christian	Immigrant
20	Jane Smith	Female	Heterosexual	Asian	None	Immigrant
21	Jenny Baron	Female	Heterosexual	White	Catholic	Child of immigrant
22	Jenny Cuevas	Female	Heterosexual	Latina	Catholic	Native-Born
23	Jessica Brown	Female	Heterosexual	Black	None	Native-Born
24	John Paul	Male	Heterosexual	Latino	Catholic	Child of Immigrant
25	John Vick	Male	Unsure	Asian	Islam	Immigrant
26	Julie Richardson	Female	Heterosexual	White	Christian	Native-Born
27	Kira Sipkins	Female	Heterosexual	White	Bahai	Native-Born
28	Lily Castro	Female	Heterosexual	Latina	Unsure	Immigrant
29	Lizzie Foster	Female	Heterosexual	White	None	Immigrant
30	Mark Rose	Male	Heterosexual	White	Jehovah's Witness	Native-Born
31	Mckayla Soriano	Female	Heterosexual	Asian	Catholic	Child of immigrant
32	Miguel Barrea	Male	Heterosexual	Latino	None	Child of Immigrant
33	Mike Birchwood	Male	Heterosexual	Latino	Catholic	Child of Immigrant
34	Monica Adams	Female	Heterosexual	White	Catholic	Native-Born
35	Nancy Anderson	Female	Heterosexual	Asian	Islam	Immigrant
36	Pearl Smit	Female	Heterosexual	Asian	Hindu	Child of immigrant
37	Peter Steele	Male	Heterosexual	White	None	Native-Born

(continued)

TABLE 8.1
(CONTINUED)

No	Name	Sex	Sexual Identity	Race	Religion	Immigration Status
38	Phoebe Buffet	Female	Bisexual	White	None	Native-Born
39	Rebeka Kowalczyk	Female	Heterosexual	White	Catholic	Immigrant
40	Reese Smith	Female	Heterosexual	White	None	Native-Born
41	Sally Gries	Female	Heterosexual	White	Christian	Native-Born
42	Samantha Smith	Female	Heterosexual	Middle Eastern	Islam	Child of immigrant
43	Sebastian Blice	Male	Heterosexual	Asian	Catholic	Immigrant
44	Tim Drake	Male	Heterosexual	White	Unsure	Native-Born
45	Tim Lopez	Transman	Unsure	Mixed	None	Native-Born
46	Tony Dentin	Male	Heterosexual	White	Islam	Child of Immigrant
47	Tyra Banks	Female	Heterosexual	White	Catholic	Native-Born
48	Zolfa Merchant	Female	Heterosexual	Middle Eastern	Islam	Child of immigrant

What's Expected of Me?

Or the Interactional Level of Analysis

The women and men *straddlers* talk easily and often about how their parents raised them to be gender appropriate. Most of the men do not remember their parents explicitly trying to socialize them to be strong, tough, or silent men. The stories are more often about subtle, implicit gender training. Many men told us their parents wanted them to get a good job (i.e., become a breadwinner), marry, and settle down. They told stories about parents worrying that girls would distract them which would interfere with educational and professional aspirations. Peter Steele's mother's disapproval was very clear regarding his sexual relationship with a girlfriend while in college: "My mom was like, 'You guys can't have any kids even if it's accidentally, you've got one of two options, either adoption or abortion.'" He was not allowed to date at all, although he ignored that parental dictate. He claimed the rule against dating wasn't because his Hindu mother was so religious. He told us:

> She would disapprove of the fact of me having a girlfriend. Not the girl herself, but just the girlfriend aspect of it. She because, like I said, she wanted me to focus on school. Like, after I finish school, she wouldn't really care if I had a girlfriend. Just because if I had a job, then she'd be okay with it. But she wanted me to focus on school first and foremost. That's why I think she was very strict on that terms.

Nevertheless, Peter had one serious two-year relationship and everyone knew about his girlfriend—except his parents.

The socialization of the transmen was quite different. Both James Williams and Tim Lopez had been subjected to conversion therapy. While the religiously based conversion therapy was aimed to address their presumed homosexuality, it also attempted to divest them of their desire to be masculine. Deep antagonism developed between James and Tim and their parents around gender socialization as they rejected the feminine goals their parents held for them.

The other stories about parents focused mostly on them steering these young men to become successful wage earners. Bill Cornell's parents wanted to ensure he chose a major that made good money. As Bill said:

> Well, I applied to the school as a psych major . . . oh my parents were like, "How much money do you make as a psych major?" Money is an important thing for them. So yeah, now I am trying to pursue finance. Because math is a strong suit for me. People are like, "I can see you doing something like that."

The division of labor was gendered in most of these young men's homes, but the variety in their familial experiences is worth noting. Most of these men had mothers who did their laundry and prepared their meals. When chores were assigned, their sisters usually helped with the cooking and cleaning, while they were assigned yard work and taking out the trash. But Tony Dentin, who only had brothers, talked about taking turns doing their share of all the housework, including folding laundry. His mother also taught him how to sew.

While these young men did not remember strong and explicit attempts to create distinct rules for them versus their sisters, they did remember limits on how far their parents and teachers allowed them to stray from traditional male activities. Mark Rose loves to eat sweets and wanted to learn to make them. He wanted an Easy Bake Oven. His parents refused, making it clear that such toys were for girls. John Paul talks about censure from his family when he played with his sister's dolls, even if he played with them after playing sports:

> So after we [he and sister] played sports, we'd go inside and end up playing with her dolls. So I'd be playing with her dolls, and it'd be wrong when my other family came over and not just immediate family. Because every other guy kept asking why I was playing with dolls like that . . . . At the time I didn't understand it, and as an adult I think that just because it was a girly thing doesn't mean I'm going to become a girl or gay. Since that's pretty much what they insinuated by me playing with dolls.

Mark Rose told us that a teacher teased him for the bounce in his step, presumably because that seemed feminine. Tim Drake remembers wanting to paint his fingernails and being rebuffed by his mother, even though she relented a bit afterward.

> I remember when I was a kid, my mom was painting my sister's fingernails, and it was just me and my two sisters home, and I said, "Oh, I want my fingernails painted too." And she said, "No, you're a boy," and then I said, "Oh." And then she still ended up painting like my pinky. I don't remember what color. But that was kind of like the clue for me like hey, you're a boy.

More stories were told, with far more passion, about their peers' gender policing than about parents' restricting behavior. The breadth of what boys were teased for is breathtaking. These boys remembered being teased for everything from having good handwriting, long hair, salmon-colored shoes, to talking about feelings. Tony Dentin remembers it was in first grade when he learned that to be a boy he had to repress his feelings, play with guns, generally be tough, and choose clothes that showed his interest in sports.

Probably like first grade. I mean [he stops and thinks before continuing], just the whole boys don't cry type of mentality. Like boys are tough and boys are supposed to like dressing in guys clothes with like pictures of like a soccer ball or something like that. Playing with toy guns.

Here we see a set of contractions in young Tony Dentin's life. His parents relied on his and his brother's contribution to housework, taught him to sew, and raised their boys with few gender boundaries, but as soon as he hit elementary school, he learned quickly to do masculinity to fit in. Mark Rose was teased because he listened to bands more often liked by girls, and so came to think of music as a "guilty pleasure." Such teasing, and gender policing, didn't end with elementary school, although it certainly didn't always deter boys from doing what they wanted to do. John Paul informed us, "I ran a marathon, and before my marathon I went and got a massage, and a manicure and pedicure came with my massage. My guy friends did not let that down, but I mean I ran a marathon so they can kiss my ass."

Jamsheed Raj tells us about having to learn the gender coding of colors when he came to America. He learned through ridicule but decided to ignore the teasing.

I remember when I first came to America, and this is actually kind of interesting, because I got shoes that were salmon colored, so they were almost close to pink. . . . [laughs] So my cousins kinda started making fun of me for that, and I was like, I don't care, I mean, I don't really see it as a big deal, but I guess over here it is, but. Even now I still don't think it's that big of a deal. I have plenty of pink or purple dress shirts that I wear all the time, so. I mean, I don't see it as a big deal.

This next story is very interesting because you can trace, at least based on Tony Dentin's memory, the power of peer policing. He talks about what would happen if he told his friends his heart was broken when his girlfriend ended their relationship.

If you say something like, "Dude, she broke up with me, and like my heart's broken," like the first thing, I mean I know it's so horrible to say, but it's like, "Dude, you're so gay," but that's what they'll say, you know. But like girls, they'll like give you a hug and be like, "It's okay," and things like that.

Finally, Tony shows us that all this teasing works: when talking about his current relationships, this is how he describes his ability to talk about feelings.

Don't really like talking about my personal things so . . . even if I get into a problem or situation, I deal with it myself. Like I argue with my fiancée, she likes to talk about the issue, but I hate it. I can't do it. And so I keep more to myself.

Despite Tony Dentin's domestic abilities, and his early openness to his emotional self, by the time he's an emerging adult, peer policing has taken its toll, and he no longer is open to real intimacy with his fiancée.

These young men are sometimes proud that they had not caved in to pressure to restrict themselves to gendered norms. Jamsheed was glad he still had salmon shoes and colorful shirts. Adam Greene is glad he knows how to cook, and Bill Cornell still wears skinny jeans although teased for it. Tim Drake dyed his hair "purple and black and blue" despite his father's objections. Danny Donovan takes pride in his handwriting and won an award for it, despite others thinking it "girly."

The transmen, of course, tell very different stories. They were both brought up in gender-traditional households. James Williams is the child of an Evangelical Baptist minister and Tim Lopez was raised in an extended Latino family that sometimes expanded to 13 people in his household. Their parents were dismayed that their (then) daughters preferred masculine-type behaviors like football and wrestling and were shocked and appalled when they discovered their child was gay. As mentioned, both families required these young people to undergo conversion therapy, and both feel the negative psychological consequences into adulthood. Both James Williams and Tim Lopez rebelled against their parental socialization and pushed back. They now present as men, and everyone in the Lopez family accepts Tim as a man except an elderly grandmother. Unfortunately, James Williams's family has yet to come around, so he has very little contact with them.

Overall, most of these young male *straddlers* have been socialized explicitly by their parents to be breadwinners. Beyond that the messages are mixed from parents. But the message from their peers is clear: be tough, stoic guys. Nearly all of these young men related stories about peers policing them to remain in the small gendered box of boyhood. Sometimes it worked, and they learned to repress their feelings, or they grew a beard to signify masculinity to counteract their long hair. But sometimes they didn't cave in; they felt it possible to stick to their guns, cook and sew, and wear whatever color they wanted. While they were mostly socialized to be masculine by parents, teachers, and peers, they only sometimes learned their lessons, other times they resisted. In other words, they tell contradictory stories about how they dealt with the gendered expectations.

The women's stories were different. Nearly every woman had stories to tell about the expectations parents had for their presentation of self, including how they should dress and carry themselves. Most of the young women spoke of how their mothers dressed them up to look pretty, whether they liked it or not. They also told stories of being socialized to be feminine, to stay clean, to be modest, and to take care of others. And yet, many of the young women also tell stories about being allowed to wear boy's clothes and get dirty. Cindy Lauper, a transwomen, recalled her parents as very liberal, generally letting her do what she wanted, which was to have very long hair and dress "grunge." While Cindy remembers feeling "trapped in the wrong body," it wasn't because her parents denied her desire to play with whatever she wanted and to dress any way she pleased. And nearly every young woman talked about being expected to study hard and to succeed in the workplace. At least among this sample of mostly working-class young people, women are no longer raised exclusively to be wives and mothers. They are still raised to be feminine in style and demeanor as they succeed in their chosen careers.

As young girls, nearly all remembered being dressed up to appear pretty. Danielle Dumelle recalled: "I was always dressed girly. My mom always did my hair." Many had detailed memories about mother's and grandmother's socializing them into a feminine style of self-presentation. Monica Adams talked about a birthday party.

> My grandma is the theme of the evening, but I don't remember exactly how old I was, maybe like seven or eight or nine or somewhere around there. And I had this, like, really pretty, like, pink satin top and then it was like lace on the bottom of it . . . I liked this outfit. And my grandma had curled my hair and did my makeup for this party, and 'cause she would not go anywhere without doing makeup, and so if I like spent the day with her, we would do that. And she gave me a satin pillowcase . . . I think that's my first like girly memory.

Most of these young women felt a great deal of pressure to dress appropriately, even though that meant different things in different families. Jane Smith said, "coming from my family, no deep cut shirts, nothing that shows a lot of skin. That's from my family's point of view." She wants us to understand however, very clearly, that she does what she wants when she is not with them: "when I'm outside of home, I just wear whatever is comfortable." Ashley Martin, on the other hand, knows what her parents think is appropriate and submits to it. Ashley says she kind of knew what was appropriate and what was not, "But yeah, sometimes if my skirt was too short my mom would say, 'Change your skirt or your dad will tell you something.' You pretty much know what your parents expect of you." [laughs]

Gabby Garcia remembers a direct conflict with her father over his insisting she wear dresses, "When I was younger I didn't like dressing really girl. I never really liked dresses, even when I was in high school. My dad told me to wear a dress on graduation and he was really like, 'Why aren't you wearing a dress, why are you wearing pants?' And I'm like, 'Because it's more comfortable. I don't wanna wear a dress.' I ended up wearing a dress."

Now, not all of these young women's parents were so traditionally minded. Amy Lahey tells us she wore boys' clothes all the time and her parents didn't care, except they wanted her to leave her brother's wardrobe intact. There were many stories about wearing boys' clothes, particularly in middle school. Mckayla Soriano said:

> Oh, I guess in middle school, when I was just dressing like a boy. I would just always wear hoodies and sneakers and pants. I just didn't care, I wouldn't wear makeup or anything. I don't think people actually pointed that out, I think actually the only person was my mom, she pointed that out to me, like, why do you dress like that, you dress like a boy. [laughs] That's pretty much it.

While every woman had at least one and sometimes two or more stories to tell about how their parent's controlled, or tried to control, their attire, there were twice as many stories about their behavior being monitored and pressure exerted to be (not just look) feminine. These 31 women told us 104 stories about being treated differently from brothers and being restricted in their behavior because they were girls. The stories included not being allowed to date, to attend concerts, or to stay out late, as well as insisting they live at home during college. As young children, some of these girls weren't allowed to play football with their siblings and cousins, or to share their toy remote-controlled cars. Mothers and grandmothers insisted on buying dolls for both the girls who liked them and those who did not. Girls talked about their parents wanting to teach them to be nurturant, helpful, and understanding.

Gabby Garcia complained: "I think I am not more outgoing because of my parents. They didn't let me go out and stuff like that, and that kind of held me back from being able to explore." Several girls shared stories about mothers wanting them to play with dolls even though they weren't interested. Jenny Baron's quote is particularly illustrative.

> I didn't like Barbies and either did my sister. So we would always pull off all her clothes and pull of her head. So I mean my mom would be like, "Come on. Just play with the dolls." I guess that was kind of like an invitation that we're supposed to but we would always just pull of their heads. . . . [smiling widely] She [her mother] would just put their heads back on and try to dress them. Cuz she always wanted us . . . she never got to play with Barbie dolls because she was in Poland. So she was like, "Oh yah girls!" But we didn't want to. Me and my sister were really rough in tumble play. We liked to go outside and ride our bikes.

Nancy Anderson told us her parents were usually very supportive about her decisions, except for her choice to become skilled in karate.

> It was my passion, to grow some muscles. My mom was very . . . she didn't want me to do that because she was telling me that it's not feminine or when you do karate are you going to beat up some other people or what will you do with that, it is not fitting for a girl, these kinds of things. Other than that, they always support my decisions.

The daughters of immigrants often felt their parents "old world" ways were manifested in their childrearing philosophies. Jane Smith informed us of her parents wanting to raise an old-fashioned girl but notice that they also wanted her to study hard.

> I think they wanted me to be like a traditional girl. Like of the old custom, how do I say this? The quiet type who knows their place kind of thing. If I see a mess, I'll clean it up. Like a traditional housewife kind of girl. And I would clean up after people, and then mostly they want me to develop the habit of studying right after classes so I can have that in my head.

Jenny Baron also attributed her father's traditionalism to being

> old school Polish. Like the women is supposed to clean, and so if our rooms were dirty he was really mad. If we weren't helping around the house or helping my mom out. He didn't like that. Like if all we wanted to do is like be loud in the house, like if me and my sister wrestled, he would get really mad about that.

And yet, all of these women also informed us that their parents expected them to do well in school and get a good job. As Giselle Hope told us, her parents wanted her to understand "the value of hard work and maintaining your independence and being self-sufficient . . . I feel like they expected me to excel in college, get a good job, find a husband." These young women were expected to challenge aspects of a traditional gender structure that presumes men should be solo breadwinners. They were expected to have career aspirations while remaining feminine in their dress and demeanor. These young women believe their parents want them to remain feminine while successfully navigating the workplace.

What these life history interviews show is the inconsistency in the gender socialization these young women experienced as girls. For example, Phoebe Buffet told us about her parents giving her brother more freedoms at a younger age, "there was a double standard; he was allowed to go to concerts." But at another point in the interview, she praised her parents for allowing her the freedom to get dirty and play outside, unlike some of her friend's parents. Ashley Martin similarly talked about the complicated, and contradictory, messages she received from her parents:

And my mom, she always told me before you get married, you have to finish high school; you have to finish college. Because then you're going to be dependent on your husband, and then what if you get divorced?

The following anecdote told by Carrie Smith shows that fathers and mothers don't necessarily agree with one another about gender socialization. Carrie told us that when she "was younger [and] wanted to go out and shoot a gun with my dad, and he had told me that I was too young, and my mom had told him that if I would have been a boy, that I would have had a gun, my own gun for a couple years already."

Such contradictory stories don't end as the girls grow older. The stories continued, with the emphasis moving to complaints about brothers having later curfews and far less surveillance. A few quotes illustrate this very common complaint. Gabby Garcia told us:

My parents all the time tell me, "What are you a guy to be out late?" And my brother is always out super late, and sometimes he doesn't even come home till two days later. So how come he gets to stay out late. They say cuz he's a guy and I'm a girl. I can take care of myself; I'm more responsible than him. . . . That makes me really mad. Really just cuz I'm a girl? When I know I'm more responsible than him.

One young woman, Sally Gries, tells a particularly poignant story about her father not inviting her into the family business.

My dad used to joke about whenever I would ask if I could work for his construction company, and he would say no. I'd ask why and he would say, "Because you're a giiiirrrlll," he always said he was joking but I always knew there was some truth to that.

Of course, not all these girls told tales of being restricted. Some were raised by liberal parents. They were grateful their parents let them play outside and get dirty. Jessica Brown reported, "I mean everybody plays video games, snow ball fights, ran around, we all rode bikes . . . I did all of that and boys did that too. I mean it wasn't unusual for a girl to do that. There wasn't really much that I did that I wasn't supposed to do as a girl." Cindy Lauper's parents were very supportive of her education, both before and after her transition, and she is now working on a doctorate in English. She remembered growing up without their imposing gendered norms on her, without any sanctions from her parents when her hair was down to her waist (presenting as a man at that time). Despite wishing that hormone blockers had been available when she was a child, Cindy does not remember ever having been "angsty" or harassed by peers in high school. Although she had a rough and lonely childhood, with supportive parents she developed quite a lot of friends in high school and grew into feeling comfortable enough in her social world, even if not at ease about her gender.

Parents, of course, weren't the only examples of adult role models and authority figures that provided deep gender socialization. Monica Adams remembered the sexism of judges in debate contests.

> I think in my extracurricular activity of debate . . . I think that there are many occasions where I used attitude within the debate round or like a certain tone or certain shortness to what I was saying or took a jab at the other team, that I would get negative comments about because they thought I was being bitchy and inappropriate. When I think that they were very much like what my male competitors were doing. And a lot of times I would feed off of their aggression and their aggressiveness and so the more aggressive they were, the more aggressive I would be, and the harsher I would get judged by a lot of judges because I was not keeping my cool.

Religious young women told stories about youth group leaders and religious figures instilling gendered values. One example is when Giselle Hope talks about a youth group trip to Israel where she both had amazing experiences and learned about how to be a "good wife."

> When I went to Israel they separated the boys and the girls, and we had to go into this thing called the Mikva . . . it is where you go into the water and purify yourself, but they made the guys go in the water, and they didn't make the girls go into the water. But, yeah, it was an amazing experience though but, yeah, they really taught you a lot about how to be a good wife and stuff, it was very interesting.

Now it is possible that our questions led these young women to focus on the constraints of their girlhood rather than the opportunities. But it was very clear from the ease and quantity of their stories, that even as their parents wanted these girls to grow up to be successful workers, they continued to have different rules and regulations for their daughters and sons. Most of these parents encouraged their little girls to play with dolls, practice nurturing, keep their clothes clean, and avoid contact sports. But it is also the case, that these young women felt free to criticize these parental expectations and to reject them as often as not, at least in their recollections.

There were nearly as many stories about peer policing among young women as from their male counterparts. The women could recall teasing, rude remarks, and more subtle reactions to their behaviors, but unlike in family settings, where they often acquiesced, these women often recall sticking up for themselves rather than caving into peer pressure. The variety of behaviors that create negative peer reactions are wide and deep, including some I would never have guessed were perceived as gender violations, such as drinking dark beer or wearing a Bull's jacket. Other gender violations they report being sanctioned for by peers were more common, such as not wearing earrings or makeup, being promiscuous, playing soccer or football with guys, and not working at being "pretty" enough. Cindy Lauper, a transwoman, believes her bullying was only indirectly related to gender, in that she always felt she had a secret to hide, and so became a loner who didn't hang with the guys or share their interests.

The young women who were brought up in literalist religions and socialized with others in conservative faith traditions told stories about peers encouraging ladylike behavior. Monica Adams told us about a girls Christian club called Little Flowers. Its mission is to help girls grow "virtues." But she didn't like the group because they wanted everyone to have tea parties and wear dresses, so she quit. For girls raised outside of traditional faith communities, most of the stories told about peer policing by other girls were for how they looked rather than how they acted. But one exception was the shaming of promiscuity. Phoebe Buffet told us about breaking a gender norm and being punished for it by her peers.

> I guess being sexually promiscuous [is a gender violation]. That is another double standard . . . people would call me a whore and stuff. I don't . . . yeah, I guess that is kind of breaking a gender norm, because females are expected to not sleep around, you know, it's okay for males to do it, but not females.

For young female athletes, boys could be the problem. Boys sometimes ostracized the only girl on their team. Brook Mullen asserted the boys on her basketball team would "never pass me the ball, except a couple who were my friends before."

As the girls aged, they realized that being feminine was a requirement to having girlfriends, as well as boyfriends. As Pearl Smit said, "I guess that's when [high school] I realized that looks matter the most . . . girls will be friends with you if you dress girly. If you dress like a tomboy you won't be friends with any girls." And it is just at this age, at the end of middle school, most of the young tomboys began to dress in more feminine styles. The policing of peers was sometimes complicated, as this story from Phoebe Buffet shows. Phoebe still usually dressed down, without makeup, like a tomboy, and when she did put on earrings and eyeliner, then the teasing began. She told us:

> Someone's like, "Oh my god, you look like a girl! You're dressing like a girl" and I'm like . . . yeah?! Because usually I wear whatever, you know. Not whatever, but I'm not a girly girl. So people notice that about me, and they tell me when they're surprised because I dress up or when I look like a girly girl.

Clearly the message Phoebe is getting is that other young women notice that she doesn't dress in a feminine fashion very often, and so they needle her when she does; a not very subtle meta-message that she should conform more regularly.

The cruelty that girls remember from other girls includes everyday slights for not being pretty enough according to someone else's standards. These young women talked about being teased for being too fat, too thin, too tall, although not too short. Others remember being teased for having big noses or feet, or the clothes they wore. Several women talked about the effects of peer reactions to their presentation style and how they have learned to spend time and energy looking appropriate. Some enjoy this attention to appearance; others resent it. But nearly all feel the peer pressure to conform. Monica Adams talked about the work it takes to be a woman:

> I get my eyebrows waxed . . . . I mean I think there's a lot of things you do as a woman that you don't have to do if you're a man, like, I shave my legs, I don't know that I would otherwise. . . . I think the whole wearing makeup thing, men don't have to wear makeup to go dressed up, to like, go out but I feel if a woman goes out without wearing makeup, you're like not really dressed up. Or, just any of the societal expectations of what you're supposed to do as a woman.

Reese Smith also spoke of the ways women have to be appropriate.

> I feel like there are a lot of extra expectations placed on girls appearance wise, there is expectations to wear makeup, expectations to do your hair a certain way. There is expectations to wear this kind of dress and not that kind of dress and have different kinds of outfits and you know wear cute shoes and be trendy. I feel like guys don't have that same expectation. I think that that creates a huge difference in the culture in men and women. The fact that women are kind of expected to look and act and dress a certain way and keep up a level of

appearance that guys don't have that same expectation on them, and that is a huge difference.

Only one young woman, Jessica Brown told us about a group with feminist principles she joined and found helpful, Girls with Goals. She was encouraged to go to college, how to perform on a job interview, and think about life after graduation. There were very few other stories about feminist-inspired "girl power" experiences. Perhaps those are more available to suburban, middle-class white girls than the young women in this sample; many of them are ethnic minorities, who grew up in Chicago or immigrated recently to America.

The experiences of gendered expectations weren't limited to friends and peers. Several women told stories about strangers criticizing occupational choices and sexism in workplaces. For example Mckayla Soriano describes how people react when they find out she's going into the military:

> So many times I had people come up to me and say, "Oh, you don't look like . . .what, you wanna join the military? You don't seem like the kind of person to do that; you don't seem like a military girl." What is that supposed to mean? Just because I'm a girl, or because of my personality, or that I'm really girly about everything? . . . They don't expect me being all serious.

Gabby Garcia talked about the men she recently worked with at Dunkin' Donuts.

> There were probably three guys and the rest were females. They always expected us to do the mopping and the cleaning, and they just wanted to count the money. And there was this guy there that always used to give us orders and he wasn't the manager. One day I got really tired and said, "Why do you always have to tell us what to do, why don't you do it?" I just let the thing sit there, and I didn't do it. He said, "You know you have to do it to." I said, "I know I have to do it but so do you."

Cindy Lauper had a long cautionary tale about transitioning in the workplace. She had held a job as a middle school teacher for several years presenting as a man on the job, while presenting as a woman with her friends, but a man with her then partner and her family. She lived more than an hour from her workplace to avoid meeting anyone from her school while dressed as a woman. The complications eventually became too great and she broke off her relationship, resigned her job, and went back to graduate school. Upon arriving, she explained her gender to the graduate program director and has lived as a woman ever since, coming out to her family as well.

She wishes that there had been hormone blockers in her youth. She believes that would have spared her childhood loneliness and a helped her transition to being a woman, which took several years. Like other women, she now spends a good deal of time and money on her presentation of self.

The words shared in these interviews make it clear that we have a far way to go before young women do not face an avalanche of gendered expectations. Every young woman in this sample, most of whom are Millennials in college or recent graduates, are expected to become wage earners but that hasn't changed the expectations they face to be nice, well-behaved, and spend a great deal of time on their appearance. Indeed being a professional woman now includes attention to the appropriateness of one's demeanor and apparel. These young women face expectations to do gender appropriately from birth to their young adulthood. Many conform some of the time, others infrequently. We heard stories about gender socialization from parents and policing from peers from nearly every woman. These young women told many stories about rebelling rather than caving in to norms they reject. Nearly all feel free to criticize gendered expectations and to reject what strikes them as not worth doing. Still, the ease with which most of these girls told stories about their parents (and sometimes teachers) trying to mold them into a feminine box in childhood is striking. How much they internalize what they've been taught will be addressed in the section on the individual level of analysis. On the interactional level, these young women neither reproduce the gender structure completely nor do they reject all of it. Instead, they straddle the line even within this one level of analysis. And in doing so, may weaken the traditional macro-level norms that will exist in the future. Future expectations are created by today's behaviors.

Who I Am?

Or the Individual Level of Analysis

As in the previous section, here too, the stories are very different for the men and women. These men mostly tell stories about how they spend time at male-typed activities including playing with action figures, Power Rangers, working out, violent movies, doing the yard work, and all kinds of team sports. Adam Greene answered the question about what types of hobbies and games he liked with a list of sports, "soccer, uh, kickball, baseball, dodgeball, hide and go seek." Others played football and liked to break dance. Several liked video games and joined computer clubs at school. A few had joined gangs. Brian Zen told us about his normative boyhood:

> We were active and running around trying to be like tough and like aggressive . . . like wrestling . . . gaining more muscle, you know, trying to prove you

have strength like arm wrestling or just lifting weights or whatever. Just like guys are always trying to prove, to like, out masculine each other, so just doing things to prove strength.

Most of the childhoods sounded very boyish. Here is Tim Drake talking about his "nerdy" masculinity, still boyish if not in the image John Wayne.

I have a gigantic action figure collection . . . and that's pretty unheard of for a twenty-six-year-old man, but hey, no big deal. Uhm, also too, like I think that it's mainly a lot of my nerd traits that bleed into that, like I have a billion different comic books . . . I like monster movie genre, and I don't know just things of that nature and just your generally not norm sort of things.

Both transmen, James Williams and Tim Lopez, report male-typical interests in childhood, wrestling, football, shop classes, karate, sword fighting, and video games. But they were often forbidden from participating, although sometimes they persevered and were eventually allowed to follow their passions.

Although there were more than twice as many stories about activities that fit squarely in a masculine box than those that were nonconforming, 9 of the 14 men told stories about breaking gender norms. These stories were sometimes in the same sentence with accounts of gender typicality, showing that these men also break gender stereotypes, and by doing both, straddle the gender structure. For example, Tony Dentin told us he likes to

go hunting and fishing. I like prepare it like cutting and gutting it and I cook it. Like I help my mom with it. So I like doing that. My fiancée has no clue whatsoever how to cook, so I mean, I will show her what to do, and I don't mind sewing either. Like ripped shirts or something. I don't mind that either.

Here again, we see Tony Dentin both enjoying traditional masculinity but also being proud of his ability to sew and cook. Several of the other men like to cook. Jamsheed explains, "I cook, I clean the dishes, I'm not opposed to it at all." In fact, so many men were in his middle-school cooking class that Jamsheed wasn't sure this was a gender violation anymore. There were other accounts of gender violations that would never have occurred to me to be so coded if these men hadn't brought them up as such. For example, Peter Steele suggested that loving cats might be a gender violation, but he wasn't sure. Instead his love of "cute things" was what he views as the feminine side of himself. Boys who didn't like sports definitely saw themselves as outside of mainstream masculinity. Danny Donovan also thought his ability to write well and win a handwriting contest also made him unusual for a boy.

When these men talked about their personalities, it was usually in terms of traditional male traits: tough, silent, or aggressive. But it was a rare man that talked about their own personalities; this group of young men portrayed very little reflexivity about masculinity or the self. When asked about themselves, even directly about their masculinity, most responded in terms of what they did, not their internal sense of self. Brian Zen felt manly when his beard came in at a younger age then his friends. Besides facial hair, masculinity was about being muscular. Yet, not all boys felt similarly. For example, Tim Drake asserted his dislike of sports led him to a predominantly female friendship group, and he shares their interest in talking about others:

I never really cared about like sports much, and I felt like one of the girls because I liked to hang out with them and gossip and talk and stuff, and I was really big into that. Uhm, that's something that always carried over from that, I always have had more friends that were girls than guys. Uhm, so yeah, I just always identified with women more I guess.

Danny Donovan similarly told us he mostly hangs out with girls. He thinks this is because

we had the same personality traits I guess. After grade school I started to get along with girls. They were very some very strong friendships I have had. Just easier to talk to about feelings, emotions.

Jamsheed Raj also spoke of himself in almost the same words used to describe the nurturance measures on a feminine personality scale.

But the thing that I did like [about himself growing up] was the fact that I was very . . . caring. Because after coming from India, I realized that anytime somebody needed my help, I was always there. Just because I knew that at some point in life I would need somebody else's help, or I want somebody to be there for me. So I was always willing to help anybody that needed my help. Whether it'd be with homework, or with moving out, or moving things, doing a job or something of that sort, or switching shifts at work, I was very willing to accommodate people. Just because, like I said, it would help, later in life, if I needed help, I could count on somebody. I would say that's probably what I liked the most.

Both Tim Lopez and James Williams, transmen, were withdrawn as children and uninterested in typically feminine pursuits. This led to them both being the target of bullies and made their already lonesome lives even harder. Neither felt as if they belonged with the girls, but neither were they terribly sure they wanted to hang with the guys, especially as both identified for a time as lesbians during adolescence.

There wasn't very much talk about career goals, less than among the female *straddlers*. But when men did talk about it, the focus was on the ability to earn a good living, and most, but not all, wanted traditionally male jobs. These young men mentioned pharmacy, medicine, and music as professions but also social worker, counselor, and teacher.

At least some of these men believed they wanted the opportunity to make their own decisions about behavior society labeled as masculine or feminine. For example Jamsheed Rah asserted, "I don't want to act a certain way just because that's how I was brought up. I wanna have the opportunity to choose how I act." And yet, in what shows perfectly how conflicted *straddlers* can be, he embedded that sentence in a critique of the Swedish elementary school, which he (incorrectly) perceived as forcing boys to choose dolls instead of trucks. It seems the idea of a school that didn't organize children by gender so confused him that he didn't even understand the article accurately.

While there was considerably less talk about bodies by men than women in each group, every male straddler who talked about his body, save one, reported feeling bad about it. There was some talk about feeling awkward and voices cracking during puberty and positive experiences of feeling more grown up than peers when maturing before friends. Some thought they were too big or had floppy ears. Brian Zen, for example, said:

> I didn't really like my body, I guess . . . that could be part why I was shy too because I was, like, not confident in myself. So, like, yeah, like, self-image was a big thing. So yeah, I wasn't as comfortable . . . like [in] elementary, they used to make fun of me for well one, my ears because they're like big and kind of floppy right here so they would make fun of my ears. My weight also would be, they'd make fun of that too. Yeah. Mostly in elementary. At like high school, no, not anymore.

Similarly Mark Rose talked about being too heavy:

> When I was younger I was overweight, and then I lost a bunch of weight when I was an early teenager, and then I put a bunch of that weight back on, and now I'm just finally starting to lose it again. So I've always kind of had issues with that, just kind of really self-conscious with my weight.

Peter Steele talked about how being heavy affected his self-esteem as a child. At the time, he was on a weight loss and exercise program and dropped nearly 20 pounds. "At one point my self-esteem was so low that I couldn't even look at myself in the mirror. I thought that I was an ugly person."

Nearly as many men thought they were too thin as those who worried about being too fat. Miguel Barrea informed us:

> I didn't like being skinny—or at least as skinny as I was—I'm still skinny now, but that's the only thing I've ever not liked about myself is the fact that I'm always skinny, and it's really hard for me to gain weight because I have a high metabolism. So I mean even working out I would gain a little to no weight. As a child I'd eat a lot, and eat a lot, and eat a lot, and I would never gain weight.

As with the rest of the men in the sample, these male *straddlers*, whether they feel too fat or too thin, thought that working out and eating healthy was the way to fix the problem. The men usually told us about feeling bad about how they looked, but then explained that they worked out or dieted in order to be healthier. Peter Steele elaborated:

> I might want to build up some muscle. Not for the masculinity thing. I've heard that muscles actually protects like if you get involved in like a car accident or something it actually protects your organs from some damage. So I like that idea of it. And plus being able to lift objects more jobs would be available to me.

Tim Lopez is happier with his body now than before transition but doesn't think he is always "male passing" and would like to be. James Williams, however, is quite comfortable as a man and believes he passes without much trouble, and that pleases him greatly. Both use hormones, bind their breasts and hope eventually to have them removed. The one outlier in this group of young men was Danny Donovan, and he was very clear about his physique, "I always thought I was very handsome and had a great body."

These men are clearly masculine by many traditional standards but also sometimes reject the limits that masculinity might put on their behaviors and feelings. Many of them want to express their empathetic, emotional, and caring selves as well. They seemed to find it harder to talk about masculinity, and the ways they embody it, than the way masculinity hemmed them in and forced them to repress parts of themselves; for example, some thought they could only be their real self in the company of women. They did not frequently reject gender norms, but their stories showed how hard those norms were to follow and sometimes how painful.

Next we hear from the women. First about their activities, then their sense of selves, including their bodies. When they were girls they liked everything from playing with dolls, arts and crafts, hopscotch, jumping rope, volleyball to sleepovers with friends. They liked their Barbie dolls and Poly Pockets. The young women spoke of enjoying styling their hair, shopping, manicures and pedicures, and getting all dolled up. They told stories about the time and work it takes to look feminine: shaving legs, waxing eyebrows, and wearing makeup. The work needed to do femininity was sometimes fully embraced, enjoyed, and viewed as part of the self; other times the talk was tinged with annoyance at how much effort it takes to be a woman.

While we heard story after story about traditional gender socialization from these women, when they actually talked about their activities, they talked more about doing activities that did not conform to gender norms than about those that did. While most of the women in this group told us stories about gender-conforming and nonconforming activities, only six young female *straddlers* told us they primarily spent time in feminine activities, while 14 emphasized more typically male activities. Cindy Lauper, the one transwoman, remembers herself as an antisocial child who mostly read, played video games, and stayed far away from traditional masculine activities. She felt as if she had a secret to hide, her true gender, and so didn't want to interact much with others. The fact that she was beat up and bullied so badly that her parents pulled her out of school and homeschooled for a year must have also had an effect, but one she preferred not to discuss in-depth. By high school, Cindy was popular in the "alternative crowd," with flowing waist-long hair.

Some women saw themselves as "all girl." As Brook Mullen tells us about her childhood, "I was definitely society's norm as to what a girl would typically do." Pearl Smit was also a girly girl: "I wore like princess clothes . . . like big poofy gowns and tiaras [laughs] . . . I would wear these every day." Mckayla Soriana defines being girly by color: "I love the color pink. Most of the stuff I have is pink. My laptop, my phone color, everything is just bright and sticks out to people." Cindy Lauper very much wants to be more girly than she was when transitioning began. She has had breast enlargements, takes estrogen, and has had electrolysis on her face, which she vividly talks about as incredibly painful. But she now can live her life feeling authentic as a woman.

Several of the young women told us that being a girl in their family meant sharing their mother's domestic labor. Lily Castro said:

During the summer when we weren't in school, I would help my mom cook her lunch; help her make rice. She would work the night shift so while she was sleeping, I would cook rice; she would take water, like flavored water, so I would make it for her rice, and sometimes I would even help her cook lunch for us. I would take care of my brother while she was working and my dad was working

Monica Adams told us a similar story, but she did even more care-work for her many siblings.

I'm the second of nine, and I'm the oldest girl by a lot, like ten years. So, I pretty much was a second mom to my siblings . . . I would help clean a lot more than most people because it bothered me that the house was so messy all the time.

Despite these stories about traditionally feminine activities, we heard even more about typically masculine activities. Many of these women seem to take great pride in doing whatever they wanted to do, even if it was traditionally meant for men, and maybe more so because it was. These women enjoy working out, weightlifting, playing all kinds of sports including basketball and baseball, sometimes on male teams. As children, they remembered enjoying remote-controlled cars, video games, computers, climbing trees, wearing boys' clothes, and karate. One young woman was proud she spit when she wanted to even though condemned for doing so. They told stories about going bungee jumping and using zip lines. Several made a point of telling us they hated hopscotch, ice skating, dolls, wearing skirts, dresses, tutus, and even earrings. Phoebe Buffet explained, "You can't play soccer or do a cartwheel in a skirt." Chanel Anthony said, "I liked to fight a lot and start things, and, yeah, I was a bully at first." She assured us she was "well past it now."

Many of these girls were remarkably, and articulately, proud of themselves for breaking gender norms. Rebeka Kowalczyk told us:

I'm really like a daredevil. I would do things that a lot [of] girls probably wouldn't do. . . . Girls like going skiing or doing like winter sports but I like doing bungee jumping . . . what's it called where you have like the obstacle course, like ropes on top like zip lining, what's that thing called.

Similarly, Phoebe Buffet bragged that she liked to "burp out loud, that's not girly, I spit, that's not girly, I drink a lot, that's not, you know . . . girly. I wear a lot of T-shirts, but I don't care." Tyra Banks is a proud member of the NRA who also bragged that "sometimes I fart really loud." Nancy Anderson attributes her passion for karate to wanting to grow some muscles. Desiree Valle told us, "There was a time when I cut my hair really short, and I shaved the back of my head." Clearly this was not a typical hairstyle in her world, but a pushback against enforced femininity.

The following quote is a perfect illustration of how these girls enjoyed bragging about breaking gender norms even though they simultaneously described themselves as very feminine. Brook Mullen, who remembered being a girly girl told us she was

> a bigger athlete than my brother was and enjoyed playing sports . . . basketball, baseball . . . I didn't enjoy, ughh [says in disgust], I didn't enjoy ice-skating. [laughs], I hated wearing, I HATED wearing the tutus and the outfits. I did not enjoy dancing since I did not have a beat back then . . . I played on an all-boys basketball team. I was the only girl playing and you know, my performance was in some ways better than the boys I was playing with.

This self-declared girly girl also said she "loved remote-controlled cars, and every Chanukah I would ask for a remote-controlled car. Um, or like Stretch Man Armstrong." And she got them. Gabby Garcia also didn't like the girls toys she was expected to play with:

> I didn't really like playing with dolls or cars; it was more like active. I wanted to be running around and playing catch. I hated the whole idea of playing with dolls and sitting down. It was stupid to me.

Jenny Baron felt similarly. When she was young, Jenny told us her "favorite thing to do was climb trees. . . . We use to ride our bikes or rollerblades. And be active and not play with dolls." Later in the interview, we found out that Jenny is one of the few women in our sample who thinks being a housewife is an ideal career choice. Once again, showing the complicated and inconsistent meanings of gender at the individual level.

These women told us about their life goals, and here, too, there were those who hope to do work that has traditionally been defined as feminine, such as working with children, event planning, or interior design. Only two named motherhood as one of their career goals. Other women wanted more traditional careers. As Desiree Valle told us:

> Yeah, I love children, I want to work with children, I want of course I want to be a mother to my children. I have lots of children in my family, children are a part of me.

Jenny Barron stated her dream job when she was little was to be a doctor, but now she mostly wants to be a mother. She was very clear that she wanted at least one of her daughters to be a princess "to wear like ballerina tutus. . . . The rest can be like a tomboy for all care. I just want like one princess" and explained that this desire for a "princess" daughter is because she was the opposite and disappointed her mother with her disdain for dolls. So the one woman who most defines motherhood as a job is the one who told us she really disliked playing with dolls.

Most women wanted to earn a living in careers without a great deal of concern whether they were jobs stereotypically male or female. In fact, it is not clear that these women even conceptualize traditionally male jobs as for men. For example, becoming a doctor is no longer seen as breaking a gender norm at all. Jane Court hopes to be a doctor and her role model was a woman TV doctor. Jane told us:

> I've been wanting to be a doctor since I was little. . . . Pediatrician . . . I think I've always been interested in the medical field. I don't know why. I mean since I was little, like for Halloween my mom dressed me up as a little nurse, and then a couple years later I was dressed up as a surgeon, and I guess all these things have kind of added up. I grew up watching Doctor Jeanne, medical examiner, so I mean, Discovery Health Channel was like my go-to channel.

Nancy Anderson decided in high school what she wanted to do.

> When I was graduating high school, I remember I was telling myself I am going to be an ambassador and deal in international relations with other people and ultimately that's what I, that's the way in which I went. I took my bachelor's in international relations and my master's is international studies. I still want to do that and use my knowledge and realize in a practical way.

Others chose work that, by now, has no real gendered meaning, such as visual arts and design, physical therapist, or a business owner.

Gender at the individual level among female *straddlers* is very inconsistent. Most of these women described masculine and feminine aspects to their personalities. There are also often inconsistencies between how these female *straddlers* describe their psychological traits and what they like to do. Overall we had nearly the same number of self-descriptions as feminine as masculine (57 versus 54 quotes). Thirty-six described themselves in at least some feminine terms, and thirty-four described themselves at least once with a masculine personality adjective. The most common presentation style is to present with both masculine and feminine personality traits. For example, Desiree Valle, the women in the quote that loves children and feels they are a part of her also asserted:

> I am very aggressive . . . . Umm, I would say there was this one time where I got into an argument with this one girl, and I didn't like the way she spoke to me, so I just grabbed her very aggressively and I hit her.

So Desiree adores children and hopes to work with them and sees her personality as very aggressive. Many other women in this straddler group describe themselves as masculine as they are feminine. Reese Smith said:

> I have always gotten along a bit easier with guys than I do girls. I get along with girls too, but I have just found guys are just less generally speaking, catty, drama-filled that kind of thing.

Phoebe Buffet described herself in typically masculine terms, such as avoiding emotional conversation. "I have feelings, I just don't express them. So I don't really like when people are whinny or complaining." Similarly Reese Smith said:

> I am not good at figuring out sorting out my feelings, my emotions, why I am feeling this way? If I am sad, if I have any negative emotion, I get angry. I get mad and I kind of pout about it. I am not good at sorting out from being jealous from being sad from being any other negative thing that is going on.

While Phoebe and Reese sound like emotionally repressed men, others talk about masculine traits as more agentic, they just like to be in control. Brook Mullen likes to be the pursuer in heterosexual dating relationships, "I like the chase, and once I get the person I get uninterested." Monica Adams told us she is "a pretty confident and independent person. And in whatever group I was in, I was usually leading it, or if I wasn't actually leading it, I had a lot of influence over whoever was actually leading it. . . I was a pretty influential individual." This is the same Monica Adams raised to be a good wife and mother and who wants a husband with a good income. Contradictions abound in her interview.

The descriptions these women provided of their masculine selves were detailed and full of pride. Giselle Hope elaborated:

> I feel like I am always independent because I don't like relying on people, and I feel like it is good to always do things for yourself, and that was the way I was brought up. I was brought up taught that you need to do be able to do anything yourself.

Jessica Brown told us she goes beyond simply being independent. She is usually in charge.

> In a group situation or in my relationships, I am the dominant force in the relationship. [laughs] I have to organize things, and I have to be the one to say, well

this is where we should go, this is how the money should go . . . I like being in control and organizing and making sure things are okay.

While some of these women think of themselves in primarily feminine terms, they often hedged their feminine descriptions with a qualification. Danielle Dumelle, who was quite comfortable with her mother dressing her up in girly outfits, assured us she is not aggressive but contradicts herself by also assuring us she can be, if needed.

> I'm really don't consider myself aggressive at all. I just feel like if somebody starts talking to me aggressively, then I just automatically start being aggressive too, but I never try to enter any situation being aggressive. So that's why I don't really consider myself aggressive, too much . . . . When it comes to my daughter, I'm always gentle and loving and things like that.

Mckayla Soriano believes women and men are essentially different and described herself as feminine, without qualification. Similarly Kira Sipkins defined herself as very feminine by saying, "I am a very caring person, I'm a gentle person . . . I'm really girly." Reese Smith, despite her earlier disclosure that she likes men better than women because that avoids the "drama" she sees among girlfriends, told us about her caring, domestic nurturing self: "I am good at cleaning. I am good at doing things that were asked of me. . . . Every time I make a decision for the, I would say ninety-nine percent of the time, I always have other people in mind."

While many of the women, like Reese Smith, provided contradictory information in their interviews without realizing it, others reflected on their lives and saw their contradictory aspects in a developmental framework as phases of life. Monica Adams told us this about herself and her gender.

> It would definitely depend on the phase . . . I was a girly girl when I was younger. I loved dresses . . . I would wear skirts and I would wear dresses . . .I would go shopping, and I would have tea parties with my friends and . . . we would do our nails . . . . I liked talking about boys and talking about crushes . . . . Just very stereotypical things that I thought a girl, like, that's what girls were supposed to do. When I was being a tomboy, I basically would just wear like, whatever my older brother was wearing because we were so close in age, that, it was just easy for me to do that. So, like, just gym shorts, or I loved scrunchy pants or squishy pants, like the athletic kind that made noise when you walked, loved those always with T-shirts, never with anything fitted. And in those times, I hated getting dressed up to go to a fancy thing. I didn't like tea parties, I was really big

into soccer at that time, I loved being outside, I loved being with the boys. And when you're with the boys, you don't talk about crushes on the boys.

Later in the interview Monica said she is now quite consciously looking for a man so she doesn't really have to worry about supporting herself. So she has changed her ideas more than once.

While I didn't begin this project with a particular interest in how the respondents talked about their bodies, the topic was so common and so heart-wrenching that it is clearly important to these women's lives and central to how they experience the gender structure. Of 15 quotes initially coded as positive toward the body, only three were really entirely positive. These 31 young women told us 42 stories about not liking their bodies; 25 women told us stories only about not liking their bodies, that is, they said nothing positive.

All but one of these women felt badly about their bodies. More than half (18) felt too fat; only one worried about being skinny. Six of the women felt too tall, only one worried about being too short. The variety of other bodily parts they didn't like included their breasts, teeth, hair, and nose. I could have written a full book about the negative feelings these young women express toward their bodies. A few quotes will have to illustrate the breadth of this discontent with their bodies. Jane Court said:

> I had really curly hair, like curlier than I have now, so I always hated my hair. I had glasses, so I didn't like glasses. I had very very messed up teeth. [laughs] I was a little bit chubby, so I was kinda like all those things added together.

Julie Richardson worried about her height, and her weight, and then was teased for how she looked in a cheerleader's costume:

> It wasn't until seventh grade I realized something. . . . That's the age I was being told, "Oh, you're kind of fat," or I got those comments about being chunkier and not being the skinniest girl in the world . . . I wouldn't say I am super tall but I am five-foot eight, so I was always one of the taller, girls and my friends are like five-foot two, five-foot three, so I would always kind of tower over them. I was always the awkward girl in the room full of short like small girls that are probably all size zero, and I don't think I was ever size zero. . . . I was never like obese or a big girl, but I was compared to people I was around. I was bigger. I mean I was playing softball and basketball my whole life, and then I got to middle school, and I decided to be a cheerleader so the shape of my body was

built to be a basketball player and not built to be a cheerleader . . . I got a lot of harassment from that [how she looked a cheerleader outfit] and that kind of steamed my insecurities.

Pearl Smit's story represents many in that she tried to fix her weight problem, and it illustrates how her self-esteem depends on her weight.

I got to a point where I was like fatter, but then I lost weight so at *that* time I felt really good, but now I feel like I'm fat again, I guess. There was a point where I thought I was fatter looking.

Jenny Baron and Kira Sipkins showed viscerally how dislike for one's body led to drug abuse and an eating disorder, respectively. Jenny told us:

I didn't like my body which was kind of the reason I went into drugs, which was to stop eating. I always thought I was really big and now that I think about it, I am not that . . . I was never that big. So I don't know what my problem was. It was when I quit gymnastics. I just started smoking, just pot, and eating. And I kinda gained some weight. And then I started doing other drugs and I was like, "Oh, I'm not hungry ever. Oh! I am never hungry!" [she says this still enthusiastically] . . . I'm still body conscious because my mom, sister, and dad are all really overweight. But I just, I eat really small meals. And I go to the gym. It used to be the only constant thing in my head. It was like, "Oh my god, I am so big!" But now, it's not that big of a deal anymore.

Kira Sipkins explains the history and consequences of her eating disorder.

When I was thirteen, I had an eating disorder, and my parents knew, and I would be lying about it you know. . . . I was in the shower and I was washing my hair and an enormous clump of hair came onto my hands, and I literally flipped a shit and I went crazy, and I was, I went nuts like I can't explain to you. I lost all sort of femininity, sexuality, self-worth that I had. I felt like I was nothing because . . . I had no idea how much hair mattered until I lost it. And I lost it because . . . of an eating disorder and having too much stress. I induced it so I hated myself because I felt like I did it to myself.

Later on Kira Sipkins asserted her eating disorder was in the past, as she said, "I love my body, and I don't fixate on it anymore. All I care about is being healthy."

Even when women told us something positive about their bodies, it was usually embedded in another ambiguous, if not downright negative comment. For example, Phoebe Buffet said:

> In high school I was less tall and lanky than I used to be, so I thought I was getting fat. Looking back on that I was not fat, at all. [laughs] *I think I liked my body in high school*, I felt like I was tall, I played sports, I felt that I had nice legs, nice breasts. I just didn't like my face, actually. I thought that I had an ugly face. I didn't like my hair either. I straightened it every single day, which would take a while.

The only unadulterated positive comment about her body was from Nancy Anderson who told us, "I didn't have any complexes as far as psychological complexes, feeling bad about physical appearance. I don't have any issues with that. I am skinny, I guess it is the gift of Mother Nature or whatever." [laughs]

We see in this section the work it takes to appropriately present a woman's body. Some enjoy the process; others do not. But almost no one feels good enough when it comes to their bodies. While most of these women internalize the lessons learned from other's expectations about their looks, they have not restricted themselves to either entirely masculine or feminine self-definition, nor do they restrict themselves to traditionally feminine activities. Indeed, they enjoy almost as many traditionally masculine as feminine pursuits.

Both the men and women tell stories full of contradictions between the interactional, individual and macro level of analyses. Within the interactional level, many prefer the company of others of their own sex and so help to recreate mostly sex-segregated material spaces for leisure. But they also often pick and choose from which cultural gendered expectations they want to follow and which they reject. And we have seen that there are often contradictions between how they see themselves and the interactional standards they believe exist in the world around them. Now to the macro level of analysis.

HOW GENDER SHOULD BE
Or the Macro Level of Analysis

Now that we know how these young *straddlers* perceive the expectations they face in their social worlds, and how they see themselves as masculine or feminine (or not), we move to a discussion of how they understand the gender ideology as it exists in our society, the degree to which they agree with their view of societal norms, and if they believe institutions formally regulate and constrain them because of their sex category, whether they are men or women. This is a macro level of analysis because it is an exploration of how these young adults understand the contemporary cultural logic of gender. How do they understand the societal worldview embedded in the gender structure. And do they adopt the cultural logics or not?

We begin with the men. They found it hard to talk about these abstract issues, and so there are few responses to code for them. The two transmen had far more to say about the gender structure than others: they were generally in agreement that gender differences do exist and probably should. Tim Lopez could recount how different it was to play sports with guys and girls. With the guys you played to win. With the girls, well, he had to goad them:

> I was very much like . . . we're not done. We need to finish this game. We need to pull it together, get shit together, we have to finish this . . . I wasn't content being somebody who sat back and waited for that to happen . . . . Girls just really didn't like me because [they thought] you are way too intense about this.

From such experiences, Tim Lopez became convinced that guys are competitive and want to win and the women, not so much. Women in Tim's experience are passive and don't always voice their opinions whereas guys shout out what they want. Tim Lopez is glad that he now gets to talk guy talk and doesn't have to translate his thoughts for a female communication style that always frustrated him. He just likes to "bark" commands, and he believed women need to be dealt with in a more polite manner. Tim enjoys masculinity. James Williams presumes men and women are different, and he is glad to do the heavy lifting at work and being treated like one of the guys.

One thing was very clear: men did not feel constrained by social institutions because they were men, with one exception. Mark Rose believed that the Bible required male dominance in families.

> Well the source of the arrangement [gender] is the Bible, and I do give that authority, so I don't claim to be smarter than God and say that his arrangement for males as taking the lead is wrong. So if that's what it is, that's what it is. So I don't think there really can be anything done with that.

Mark Rose exemplifies the category of straddler. His religious beliefs justify male dominance, he generally believes that pink is for girls and blue is for boys, and wouldn't want to see a kindergarten try to change that. Yet he is a supporter of gender-neutral marketing for something like an Easy Bake Oven; in fact, as mentioned, he always wanted one. He also sees himself as different from other boys because he doesn't like sports and, as we saw in his quote about his personality, he sees himself as emotionally more like women than other men.

> I now kinda feel like girls are more empathetic than guys, they can really kind of understand emotionally situations more and relate to them, and that's something I feel like I can do well. And just kind of empathize with people on their emotional issues and really kind of understand what they're going through, more than maybe your average guy would.

While Mark is quite conservative at the macro-ideological level and supports gendered expectations at the interactional level, he knows, at some gut level, that he is not just like the other guys and does not seem too worried about that.

The most common ideological stance taken by these male *straddlers* is best described as libertarian. Even though they often state they would not personally break most gender norms, especially about bodily presentation, they refuse to endorse societal norms that forbid stigmatized behavior. For example, Bill Cornell responds to the question about the J.Crew ad with a mother painting her son's nails pink by both providing negative judgment and claiming not to do so.

> Guys don't paint their toes. Like there might be speculation like, "Maybe this kid is gay. Pink is his favorite color." There is no problem. I guess. So I guess. So then, that makes people think that maybe being gay is a bad controversy or something like that. . . . If you want to, go ahead. I don't really care. It is not something [laughs] that I would want to do, maybe? I actually say maybe very loosely. It is not something I would ever want to do. But if someone else wants to do it. I am not going to judge. Go ahead. You know.

John Vick similarly articulates this libertarian streak among these men who straddle the gender structure as he talked about boys painting their fingernails.

> Some people say it's just not normal that kid's being painted with the pink nail polish, because pink is, it's general, pink is for the girls. And blue is for boys. It's just normal that people think it's not normal, yeah. It just represents for a different gender or a different stuff. . . . It's not my choice or it's not your choice to decide what guys should wear or do, or what they should do. In this case it is painting toenails, or whatever it is, yeah. It's not my choice, if you want to do it, yeah do it, go ahead do it.

John Vick really disliked the idea of the Swedish kindergarten that did not use gender pronouns. He told us:

> I always think it's fine to be gay or bi or whatever, but like I feel like when you are young like that you are a him and you are a her. You are a boy and you are a girl and that's that. I don't really agree with them calling them kids . . . It's just not normal. In a sense it's good but it's just not normal.

Most of these *straddlers* refuse to endorse any notion that traditional gendered norms should be enforced in our society even though they mostly lived by them. With the exception of one man with a literalist Christian belief system, none of these men experienced any social institution as gendered, it was simply not within their consciousness to think about institutional constraint (or privilege) in that way. They mostly adopted worldviews that accepted gendered norms as normal and legitimate, but they did not live entirely by such rules, and they also rejected them when they so desired. Even when these Millennials espoused very traditional gendered beliefs, they didn't necessarily live by them. Even when they claim to critique gendered worldviews, and support a more feminist future, they often lived very gendered lives comfortably.

Now we take a look at the women *straddlers*. The women in this category had three distinct worldviews. Some held very conservative beliefs about gender, particularly around women and men's material bodily presentations, yet, still, often broke social norms despite this. They thought girls should be feminine and boys masculine, and disapproved of gender-bending but told some stories of challenging gender in their lives despite their ideology. Others were critical of stereotyping and considered themselves very open-minded, but they disapproved of making waves and worried what other people think and so (at the interactional level) played by it very safe, by the rules. Finally, there are some women who endorse feminist social change at the societal level and yet hope to lead traditional lives and describe themselves in stereotypically gendered ways.

The first group of women sounded like *true believers* of the gender structure, and they were concerned that people should present themselves appropriately. For instance, Amy Lahey was not only upset at the J.Crew ad of a mother painting her son's nails, she concocted a story to put the blame on the mother:

> It's not like his favorite color was pink. His mom wants him to like put on nail polish, like she's the one doing it. Like he's little, he's not going to know what is right, what a guy does, what a girl does. He learns when he gets older, but she just wants him to be like a girl . . . . The mom is trying to make the boy into

the girl, which is not right because it's not like he wants to do it; you know, his mom is doing it.

Here, Amy Lahey's attitudes are far more conservative than you'd expect given she'd been allowed to dress boyish and get dirty, and do what she wanted when a young girl. Sally Gries also critiques this ad, believing that the mother was "a mom that really desired a daughter and got a son." Similarly, Rebeka Kowalczyk thinks the mom in the J.Crew ad is wrong and suggests that she may lead her child to want to change his sexuality, or even his sex, when he grows up.

> So, it's kind of like saying, I guess, the, advertisement is kind of pointing out the child is going more like feminine . . . when they grow up they can be gay or bi . . . I mean, these days anyone's permitted to believe whatever they want, but I don't think boys should paint their nails . . . I think it's just weird. It's just my personal opinion . . . . It's just, it's kind of like a girlish thing. . . . Men are supposed to be you know [clears her throat], men are supposed to be like masculine figure, the person that's like serious, and that kind of just makes them look girly.

As might be expected, Rebeka also thought the kindergarten that didn't use pronouns was "weird."

Brook Mullen presumes that the Swedish kindergarten was designed to make transgender children comfortable. She totally missed the possibility that the school is trying to open up options for every child.

> I don't understand why they chose the whole non-pronoun thing. Like they said it's causing stereotypes by calling them their gender, and I get that because, in some cases if certain children are confused about their genders, you know, it's automatically putting them in a certain category. But then it's also like not giving them a sense of identity . . . but what percentage of people, or children of that school, are gender confused?

While Amy, Rebeka, and Brook are clearly supporters of the gendered status quo, others in this group were not. The "don't make waves" women are not judgmental, but they worry about the risk of being social outcasts or raising children who might be. These women who just don't want to make waves also thought people who consciously chose to break norms should expect a negative response. For example, Tyra Banks tells us that the J.Crew ad upset people because "boys aren't supposed to like pink. And . . . people get upset when things aren't how they're traditionally supposed to be. When things aren't the way that society deems normal, people get pissed off." Carrie Smith agreed and explained, "I would say that society thinks it's not appropriate for a young boy, child, to have his toenails painted." Jane Court concurred, being explicit that while she might not agree with them, it's what "people" think.

> It's not so much as like what I would think. It's probably what getting made fun of by other people, 'cause people don't think what I think. I mean, I think little things like this . . . shouldn't be such a big deal. So, but then it's not what I think, it's what other people think, 'cause they might not have the same mentality as I do. So it's more like, don't do this because other people won't think of it the same way as I do. . . . I think people make too much of a big deal about this whole color pink thing and this whole nail polish thing.

Jane Court does not endorse gender stereotypes but still ridicules the ideals of the Swedish school. She believes we have already moved beyond gendered expectations and should go no further because sex differences exist:

> I feel like if we just start eliminating those words [male and female pronouns] from our vocabulary, we just kind of like, blend. Obviously there are differences between the two sexes. I don't mean, like it says right here, society expects girls to be girly, nice, and pretty and boys to be manly, rough, and outgoing. I don't know. I feel like we've kind of grown out of that a little . . . I don't feel like that's the expectation any more. Maybe like at some point, but men aren't supposed to cry? I feel like people are realizing that that's absurd, like crying. So I feel like instead of like trying to make it neutral, trying, we should be trying to explain that, like, there are differences that it doesn't have to be like this way, but it doesn't mean that it should blend in together, into one category, to men and women.

Reese Smith talked about the consequences for a young boy who others will not like. (It's interesting to notice that Reese chose a gender-neutral pseudonym for herself.)

> So, it probably caused a lot of controversy because I think people really shy away from males who identify more as a female, not even more as a female but identify more with what is considered female, hobbies, interests, likes, dislikes, and vice versa. Females who identify more male, likes, dislikes, hobbies.

Julie Richardson further discusses the closed-minded people that have to be taken into account, for example, when women dress in men's clothes—as Lisa did in our scenario. As with the other women in this straddler group, Julie would not intervene even if she felt sorry for Lisa. She told us why.

> I think I would just kind of ignore the situation. Unfortunately in the world, there are very many closed-minded people. They get this idea that all women are supposed to look like woman, and you don't really play in the fact that, like, there are people that don't feel comfortable and don't think they were meant to be a woman. . . . Maybe they are straight, but that's the way they like to dress. . . . I don't know I mean . . . I guess, that's just how I feel.

There was evidence of a libertarian streak in some of the women *straddlers* as well as their male counterparts. Jenny Cuevas uses libertarian rhetoric to accept behavior but sounds as if she is badly disguising disapproval of a boy painting his toenails.

> I mean it obviously, like I said, I'm very open so I don't having anything to say bad about it because everybody chooses what they want to do. But I could see that it would bring controversy to those people that are opposed to gays and lesbians. I would say because here's a mom who is teaching . . . the little boy to be girly at such a young age, and they could even criticize her for doing that and confusing the little boy as in to be feminine . . . . I could totally see that that's what the critics . . . . are talking about. But in my opinion I don't really have anything to say you know. Everybody raises their own children the way they want to.

There were, of course, also women in this group who wholeheartedly supported moving beyond having gendered social norms. Not all of them were totally comfortable with gender-bending, but they want to be. For example, Julie Richardson thought the nail painting ad was adorable:

> I think it's cute. It's a bonding thing for me . . . it's hard to say one time painting your toes or it's hard to say doing that is going to affect whatever. . . . I mean it gives the child a better like . . . okay, freedom to be who they want to be and not feel like a pressure to be a certain way or do certain things. I honestly in a certain way kind of like it because I feel like it helps give them a sense of freedom and knowing that like . . . going against stereotypes or going against what everyone else expects of you is okay and like if you're happy. So I think that's kind of cool. It's hard because you grow up thinking that, okay, only girls do this, so seeing it is just weird because it's not something you usually see. I don't

think that boys can't do it; I just think that it's not as accepted as it is for girls just because of stereotypes of society. So like if I was to see it, then I would kind of be caught off guard and start questioning you know like the original things you would question. Like you're gay or straight.

Other women are more wholeheartedly supportive of changing the gender structure. For example, Amy Leahy would want to send her kids to a school like the Swedish one in the article we had her read.

Yeah, because then they are like not being separated, like girls only play with this, you know? They can play with whatever they want, because when you're little it's not like you know what you're doing, it's just like hey there's a car, like, I mean just play with it. Yeah, I would.

Similarly, Jenny Baron doesn't even like that the ad was controversial and told us, "I feel like they are being dumb if it is causing controversy." Gabby Garcia thinks the Swedish school is a good thing and spoke of boys painting their nails as well, and cites a sociology class for broadening her opinions.

A lot of girls like cars and boys like dolls. So, I don't see anything wrong with that. It's all what society wants you to play with. If you're a boy and you have to play with boy toys, but I feel like they should be able to play with whatever toys they want.... Well, I mean boys do paint their nails even if they're straight. You know the rockers. I mean when I was younger I would think this was wrong but now that I took a sociology class, and I've been thinking everything over. There should be nothing wrong with it; it's society that wants you to separate female and male, the genders. So painting nails, I don't see it as a big deal.

Here we see Gabby, raised in traditional norms, and policed by family and peers, struggling with integrating new ideas learned in class into her life. Jane Smith, too, despite having been raised to be a traditional "old world" girl who mostly complied with her family's wishes, is against a society that says,

"This is what guys should do, this is what girls should do." I wouldn't mind a guy doing ballet; I wouldn't mind a girl doing martial arts. I know a lot of people seem to have a bad impression of . . . guys taking girls' roles. Like guys taking ballet. A lot of people seem to have a bad impression, and I don't know why. That's one of the reason, I don't want my children to be sexist I guess—girls should be just like this, guys should be just like this.

Jane, traditional in her life, straddles the gender structure by believing in a world that should be different. Phoebe Buffet not only thinks that the Swedish school with no pronouns is a good idea but she has also worked at a school that attempted to do something similar in the United States.

> I think that's a really neat idea, and I wish we would adopt that here. I actually worked at a preschool, and we would call them all friends, we would never say, "Hey guys, come here!" We would say, "Hey friends, come here." I mean it's great to let boys play with whatever they want, let girls play with whatever they want. To teach kids at a young age that it's okay to cry, no matter what gender you are, it's okay to begin to whatever, no matter what gender you are.

In another part of the interview, Phoebe made clear how sad she thought it was that the masculine-looking Lisa in our scenario was treated so poorly when she simply wanted to use the restroom, and she praised the existence of gender-neutral bathrooms on some university campuses. Angelica Gallegos agreed that forcing children into gender boxes is a bad idea. She said, "It's kind of like a girl can do whatever a guy can do, and a guy can do whatever a girl can do, so it's not like its demeaning."

Cindy Lauper, having crossed the gender divide, has complicated and conflicting gender views. She was opposed to "everyone going gender neutral." She herself is "fairly feminine" but realizes that not all transwomen are. Very much like many others in this sample, she has libertarian tendencies, although phrases her response somewhat differently than most. Cindy wants everyone to have the freedom to be anywhere they so desire on a "gender as a spectrum." She wants it clear that she doesn't think there is "anything wrong with masculinity or femininity. And I don't think there's a problem with being a woman who identifies or a man who identifies as very masculine." Still, she is opposed to "everyone going gender neutral." So while embracing femininity herself, she wants everyone to have the freedom to choose but wouldn't like it if everyone were to "undo" gender.

Some, but less than half, of these millennial *straddlers* could identify macro-level institutional and organizational constraints or opportunities they faced because of their sex. Such recognition was not limited to those women ideologically opposed to these constraints existing. The institutions mentioned by these women included sports (inside and outside school settings), religion, and the workplace. Phoebe Buffet reported an experience when she wanted to play sports with men and was denied: "Yeah, I wanted to play football. I always thought that would be fun. I wanted to play guys' lacrosse, because they can hit each other. But, yeah. Not allowed to . . . I didn't pursue it, I knew that wasn't an option." From sports to religion, these young women felt institutional constraints on their activities. Monica Adams told us:

> I was an altar server, it's like a kid who helps with Mass, and, in my parish, and especially in my family, it was okay for girls to be altar servers. But in a lot of the conservative parishes [yawns] with a lot of the homeschoolers, that was totally wrong to have a girl because they see it as the altar servers are supposed to be like practicing to see if they want to be priests, and since in the Catholic Church women can't be priests, I was pretending to do something that I could never do. And the logical leap for them was that I wanted to be a priest and I was trying to change the Church's teachings. That was very frustrating to me at lots of times because in no way did I ever want to A. change the Church's teachings or B. I can't imagine being a priest, even if you could as a woman. I don't, couldn't imagine it. So, that would be one. If I was a boy, I would have been fine [yawns] . . . and I was an altar server from like second grade all the way through high school, and so I got a lot of flak about it, but.

Several of the women discuss apparent gender inequality in the workplace. Since most hadn't had full-time positions yet, the constraints were still abstract. Reese Smith complained "that women receive a lower pay grade than men if they do the same job. That bothers me." Brook Mullen talks about what she and other women like her will need to do when they get to the workplace to overcome gender inequality.

> I definitely think it's very important for women, especially in the workplace, to not play that innocent female role. Like you want to establish that you're a strong woman, you know, and that you're not going to get walked over, all walked over on, or walked all over on.

The few women in the sample already out of school and working in a career had a different experience. Jessica Brown thinks there are particular opportunities available to women because of their gendered skills. Jessica told us:

> In my job women are more likely to become higher up because we have better communicating skills. We have better salesman skills. It's easier for a woman to sell something to a man or even to a woman than it is for a man to sell something to a woman or to another man. So it's a lot easier to get promoted at my job as a woman.

Jessica doesn't provide any evidence to back up her claims, but it would be interesting to know the sex ratio of the management in her firm and industry. Cindy

Lauper mentions the discrimination in our medical care systems, as many people, she believes, have trouble with insurance covering hormones and surgeries required for transitioning.

In summary, these *straddlers*, men and women, sometimes support traditional gender beliefs despite breaking norms themselves. Sometimes they disagree with gendered expectations but find comfort in staying within societal rules. Others are outspoken feminists who remain contentedly living safely within gendered norms. What these *straddlers* all have in common is that their answers are inconsistent across their individual identities, the expectations they experienced from others, and their beliefs—across the three levels of the gender structure.

SUMMARY: CONFUSION IS THE NEW NORMAL

The men and women tell very different tales about the gendered expectations they face. The men remembered parents who wanted them to grow up to earn a living, but beyond that, the expectations about masculinity were subtle. They were expected to do the male-typed household tasks, but not always. They barely remember any gendered rules that differentiated them from their sisters. Men don't remember being raised to be boys; they simply see themselves as the norm, the generic human being. The transmen remember painful childhoods where their parents tried to coerce them into both heterosexuality and gender conformity.

What a difference a female standpoint makes. The girls remembered parental pressure to become feminine women. Whereas the boys remembered some pressure regarding how they should act, they told almost no stories about being socialized how to look. The women tell nearly as many stories about socialization regarding appropriate dress and self-presentation as about socialization to behave appropriately. The transwoman, unlike many others, had parents who let her be the quiet loner that avoided masculine pursuits entirely. She felt no gender socialization pressure. But most of the women remember stories of their brothers' relative freedom, later curfews, and less supervision. Overall, the women have far more memories of parental constraints and explicit socialization than the men. From their disparate memories, it is hard to imagine that these young women and men grew up in similar families at all. The girls experienced and remembered a great deal of gendered rules where boys had freedoms they did not, while boys didn't notice gender inequality in their families.

When it came to peer policing, however, the men understood themselves to be at least as constrained as the women, and maybe more so. The men told painful stories about being teased and ridiculed by other boys for a slight deviation from masculinity, in dress or behavior. The transmen's pain was inflicted more by their parents and churches than by peers, although female peers bullied them for not fitting into the girls' world. For the other men, peer pressure stings more today than any memory of parental socialization. We do not know if peer policing stings more than the parental socialization because it was delivered with viciousness, while parents' were more likely to mold gender behavior with warmth and rewards.

What is clear is that these young men and women have experienced strong and ongoing pressure to become who they are today. And yet, they all believe they are capable of rejecting gender socialization whenever they choose. Most of these *straddlers* accept some of the traditional gender structure while rejecting other aspects. The men certainly see themselves as far more traditionally masculine than feminine, and tell more stories about doing male-typical than female-typical activities. But most of them also either talk about doing activities more typically done by women or they describe their personalities in terms of nurturance and empathy, and they realize that makes them more like women than most of the guys they know. The women, on the other hand, talk just slightly more about nonconforming gender behaviors than traditional ones, and they often sound proud of themselves for breaking barriers. They also describe their personalities with nearly as many masculine traits as feminine ones.

Women talk far more about their bodies. As children, and even as young adults, they are pressured to do the work it takes to present a feminine body—with waxed eyebrows, painted nails, hair well styled, and a thin body. And that's before the effort it takes to shop for a cute wardrobe. Many of the women enjoy this process, while some enjoy parts of it, but also resent the time it takes. Some resent the work it takes to do gender entirely. Both men and women tell stories about disliking their bodies. Only the transgender respondents have narratives about bodies that have overtly happy endings, or at least positive framing of the current journey. For most men, weight is a problem on both ends: they worry about being too thin and too fat. Women, it seems, can never be too thin but worry tremendously about being too fat. But it's not just weight that bothers these young people; there is a range of complaints about their bodies. It was a rare person in this group who feels at home in his or her skin.

Straddlers no longer presume families should have male breadwinners and domestic mothers. What everyone in this chapter has in common is that there is internal inconsistency in their responses. That is perhaps the **only** commonality among these *straddlers*: their narratives are inconsistent from one moment to the next in the interview. The inconsistency exists often within one level of analysis. Most of the women describe inconsistent messages about what it means to be a woman; the women describe being taught to be career focused and independent, while at the same time they are expected to be warm, people-oriented, thin, and well-coifed. How these inconsistencies evolve over time, if they do, will help shape the stories of these Millennials' lives. The *innovators* and *rebels* also mix 'n' match from masculine- and feminine-typed behaviors and personalities, but they do so consciously and with positive reflexivity. They are proud to do so. These *straddlers* sound unsure and confused. But they are, after all, still emerging adults, and perhaps a better way to think of the inconsistencies is that they are still struggling with the complicated world around them and still weaving together who they will become as full-fledged adults.

When reading one person's interview across individual, interactional, and macro levels of analysis, the inconsistencies are even sharper. Some women are proud to say they overcame and ignored traditional gender socialization, but then they espouse conservative gender politics. Others sound feminist while never challenging gender boundaries. Both women and men often have very libertarian views toward gender expression, but hold fast to their own gendered selves and express some disdain for those who are gender nonconformists.

With these data, based on life history interviews, I cannot formally address causality at all. But I can use the data to hypothesize, to speculate on the causal directionality of change across levels of analysis. The stories do lead to some hypotheses. These young people were mostly raised by parents with traditional gender expectations, although this was remembered far more vividly by women than men. The peer pressure to "do gender" traditionally was strong for both men and women. All this pressure from interactional expectations seems to have been partially effective with *straddlers* internalizing and expressing gendered selves. But not entirely, many of these young people also rejected aspects of traditional masculinity and femininity for themselves. They sometimes, yet inconsistently, adopted traditional worldviews about gender. Alternative ideologies were vying with traditional gender ones for their attention: the individualist ideology of upward mobility was widely shared by women and men, the libertarian attitude toward free choice for all was widely endorsed, and together these beliefs overcame any gendered expectations for women to opt out of the labor force for motherhood. Will these young people pick and choose among gendered expectations, and will the new patterns change the gender structure for the future? How will they reconcile critical views of gender often learned in college classrooms with the identities that their parents helped shape over two decades? Time will tell.

If, once upon a time, the gender structure in America was a seamless system with boys and girls raised for traditional lives—internalizing gendered personalities, and endorsing separate spheres for their lives—that world is shattered beyond recognition. The majority of young people in this unrepresentative sample are full of contradictions as to just what the norms are; who they are supposed to become; who they want to become; and how they think the world does, and ought, to operate. Their contradictions simply mirror the world around them, still in flux, the products of a yet incomplete gender revolution. The best phrase to sum up this chapter is confused searching. These Millennials are still emerging into adulthood and wrestling with learning how to reconcile a gender structure that itself is complicated and chaotic. With that, we move to the next chapter where we compare Millennials in each category and later to a conclusion where I propose a future that may lead to a more just world for us all.

9

Bringing Gender into the Emerging Adulthood Literature

WHERE DO THE MILLENNIALS STAND?

IN THIS CHAPTER we return to questions raised earlier about the Millennials as a generation. We begin here with a summary of the conclusions from the data chapters. After the summary, I highlight important theoretical themes that appear for all the different types of Millennials. In every chapter, the relationship between gendered identities and sexuality emerges as a central theme, as does the subjective negativity respondents feel toward their bodies. These narratives also help us understand something important about contemporary meanings attached to masculinities and femininities, as well as to the powerful role of culture to frame understandings about the self. This chapter ends by returning to a focus on gender as a social structure, and the way it operates at this historical point for the millennial generation as they emerge from adolescence into adulthood, and how these young people may affect the future of gender itself. These data illustrate that conceptualizing gender as a social structure helps us better understand the complex reality of these young people's lives and their ability to change the future.

We know that the transition to adulthood is now longer than ever before and if family patterns are any indication, far more class differentiated. Most college-educated Millennials will remain footloose and fancy free through much of their 20s. Kimmel (2016) even claims that 30 is the new 20, that is, when Millennials will end their transition into adulthood and settle down with careers and families. The respondents in this study are mostly working and lower middle class but decidedly and hopefully upwardly mobile. Most of them are still in college, and so their trajectories are not entirely clear. They certainly hope to be in the category of college-educated Millennials. And they do appear on track. No one in this sample is through school, in a stable career, and raising a family. So while raised as working class, they are following the trajectory the American dream has taught them for upward mobility through education.

What is very clear is that the interviews analyzed in this book have definitely included the identity seeking that is the hallmark of the new developmental stage of emerging adulthood. Here we have focused on a topic that barely has been noticed in either the life course or the Millennial research—the gender structure. This is the life stage where decisions are made that will make it possible for women to compete in the public sphere equally with male colleagues, or not. This is the moment in the life cycle where people are choosing life partners, to share work and family equally with them, or not. And this is the life stage for many women who do not go to college when they become mothers, with or without husbands. This is also when some of our respondents begin to question their gender identities and adopt new ones, such as genderqueer. How is it that gender could have been so absent from thinking about a new stage of human development and from questions about generational identities? Gender is indeed front and center in this stage of life, and with this work, I bring it to the forefront of our understanding of emerging adulthood.

The great debate in the millennial literature is whether this will be the next great generation or an entitled generation full of people who put "me" first. It is in some ways too early to tell whether they will become the next "great" generation solving social problems as Winograd and Hais (2011) argue or whether they are the "me" generation Twenge (2014) describes. There is some support for both arguments in their stories. Yet, I don't think we can really know the answer until they have actually emerged into adulthood and made the life choices that will define their paths. But perhaps this debate is really irrelevant to my respondents. In this sample of working- and middle-class Millennials, most are simply striving to get into the labor force and start a career that allows them to support themselves and perhaps a family.

Still, we know from the polls and rallies that Millennials turned out in 2016 to support Bernie Sanders in the Democratic presidential primaries, and this may indicate a politically activist generation. The media suggests, however, that Sanders supporters were often white and middle class, and the respondents in this study are not.[1] There is yet no research on the mammoth women's marches all over the United States (and the world) the day after Donald Trump's election, but my personal experience in Washington, DC and my study of the pictures posted from elsewhere show the Millennials might have woken up to the issues of gender inequality that, until that point, many had taken for granted as an earlier generation's problem. Some *rebels* and *innovators* in this research are involved in anti-violence against women movements or LGBTQ collective action. Beyond that, we heard very little about commitment to other social movements. But then we asked far more questions about gender than any other social inequality. Even in terms of changing the gender structure, most of these *innovators* and *rebels* held somewhat individualist views of promoting change. *Innovators* believed that if they lived egalitarian lives, where they share the responsibility for working and raising a family, the world will change because of it. The *rebels*, while perhaps the most revolutionary gender actors, also often hold an individualist philosophy. Those with a genderqueer identity and the transgender respondents who do not want to "pass" entirely but to display their identities believe that by doing so, they challenge—on a political level—the social construction of gender as a binary attached to sexed bodies. And surely they do. Just as surely, this is a social change strategy that is influenced by neoliberal ideas about individual responsibility. The most common social change strategy appears to be that at the individual level, these Millennials hope to change the expectations of others, and the institutional rules will have to follow, as will the changed meanings of gender as well. In addition, however, *innovators* and *rebels* often engage in Internet activism, something done as an individual to change others' opinions. On the Internet, they join communities of like-minded others, and they debate with friends and family whose views differ. Perhaps then, this is a self-centered generation that hopes to make social change by living the lives they feel entitled to. A "me" generation trying to change the world by being authentic to their own identities, not caving in, and thus demanding change from the ground up. As mentioned, there is little published research yet on the mammoth women's marches the day after Donald Trump was inaugurated, but my experience in DC and my observation of the pictures from across the country suggest that the Millennials were out in full force. It maybe that the election of an openly sexist president who bragged about "grabbing pussy" has woken the Millennials to the danger of a focus only on the self, without political mobilization. I withhold judgment as to whether they are the next great generation, to see how efficacious change from the ground up really is, and whether these young people become active in support of women's rights now that they are so threatened by our federal government. Of course, not all the respondents care about gender equality. I summarize main findings from the last few chapters to remind the reader of the variability in the experiences of today's Millennials.

CONSERVING THE GENDER STRUCTURE FOR THE NEXT GENERATION

Perhaps the hallmark of *true believers* is the consistency in their interviews. They were raised to be traditional men and women and they become so. They do not feel pressured to comply with parental expectations because they have internalized self-identities that embrace traditional masculinity or femininity. In addition, they adopt ideological beliefs that naturalize essential differences between the sexes. Their worldviews match their practice and their internalized identities. Smooth gender sailing.

Not only do these *true believers* reject the need for feminist social change, they affirmatively disapprove when people break gender norms in either their activities or presentations of self. And while they claim to support free choice for themselves and others, they nevertheless judge others who break gender norms. While these Millennials identify actual, usually religious, rules and regulations that require sex-differentiated behaviors, such rules are not experienced as oppressive because they hold cultural beliefs that legitimate differential opportunities for women and men, and even justify some forms of male privilege.

At the interactional level, the *true believers* are far more likely than any others to choose sex-segregated activities, in their families and in their social lives. In that way, their material experiences of everyday life are more gendered than most. The interactional expectations they face in their personal lives are far more traditional than for any other respondents. Both men and women face explicit and deliberate gender socialization, and this really sets them apart from the rest of the sample. The women have far more stories to tell than the men about explicit gender socialization, having faced more daily restrictions and constraints, legitimated by religious doctrine. They were raised to be feminine women and masculine men and so, they too expect others, at least in their own social networks, to behave in similar ways.

At the individual level, *true believers* have internalized the feminine or masculine selves their parent's wanted them to be. Parents socialized women to be respectful, modest, and domestic, and they try to be so. The young men were taught to be tough, emotionally repressed, and skilled at masculine tasks, such as home and car repair, and so they are. While some of the women occasionally chafe at the greater freedoms of their brothers, few complain seriously or try to change the rules their parents enforce. Few deviate enough from gender rules to have stories of peers policing their behavior. They also work hard to carry their bodies in gendered fashion. It isn't obvious if their strong discomfort with their bodies is related to the hyper concern with being gendered, but stories full of angst about being too heavy or too skinny, too short, or too hairy do appear in many of their narratives. It is important to understand that whatever role gender socialization might have played in the women's lives, they are quite committed to making their own decisions and experience their choices as personal agency. This is a hallmark of all the respondents in the study; the almost religious belief in their ability to be individuals and make a free choice about their lives, including gender norms.

At the macro-cultural level, their ideologies legitimate the lives they expect to live. For women, religion is usually the basis of their stated beliefs about gender. Men more often rely on biological essentialism for their beliefs in sex differences. Neither women nor men critique norms or actual religious dictates that subordinate women or expect different obligations from girls and boys or husbands and wives. And yet, no one argued that women's sole role should be motherhood or that women should not work for pay. Even traditional ideology now includes women's labor force participation.

These interviews provide strong evidence for the link among literalist religions, heteronormativity, and homophobia. The Millennials in this study who hold a sacred explanation for sex differences totally conflate sexuality and gender normativity. They worry that if we eliminate gender socialization, and allow men and women to be more alike, homosexuality will rise, and that, they believe, would be very bad for society. They understand sex as an ascribed characteristic that does and should become gender, so that men and women become different kinds of people, who are exclusively heterosexual. Not one true believer identified as gay, and most disapproved of homosexuality entirely. We cannot know definitively where their worldview comes from, but we do know that their parents raised them in literalist faith traditions and are mostly believers themselves. We can trace the respondents' stories from their parents' cultural logics and their religious organizations rules and regulations (the macro level) to the expectations they faced during parental gender-socialization patterns (the interactional level). In this developmental moment, emerging into adulthood, it appears that their parents were successful raising children who shared their beliefs. While life history data does not allow for tracing causality, the hypotheses I take from these interviews is that the macro worldviews of parents are indeed transmitted to children through their socialization practices, and these young people have adopted their parent's worldview. They do not feel oppressed by religious gendered regulation. Thus, the hypothesis based on their stories is that the causality flows from macro through interactional to individuals in these lives.

And yet, we also see the 21st-century American individual ideologies of free choice, individualism, and upward mobility for both sexes. No woman or man suggested college-educated women should identify being a mother as a primary career goal. Most of the respondents, of course, were in college and so self-selected to be career oriented. Some may indeed become full-time mothers when juggling child-rearing with paid labor becomes a reality in their lives. Still, not long ago, traditional women and men believed children needed a mother at home full time and a married woman should plan a life devoted to her family. These young people, while holding close to the gender structure they inherited, are also adapting it because they accept the reality that most women today work for a living. The gender structure is dynamic as even *true believers* hold competing cultural logics and, by doing so, both support and begin to change the contours of a gendered worldview. While even *true believers* modify the world, they do so far less than many others in this research, as the summary of the *innovators* shows.

FEMINIST FUTURES ENVISIONED

Most of the *innovators*, both women and men, had experienced some gender norms as personally oppressive, even if temporarily, during childhood or adolescence. Personal experience helped solidify ideologies consistently critical of the gender structure. Every innovator was critical of rules that differentiated boys and girls. Many of the women had grown up in liberal homes where they were encouraged to be all they could be and remember being free from gendered constraints. Those who remember strong gender socialization, often the young men, regretted they hadn't been free to develop all facets of themselves. All of the *innovators* intended to raise their children without gendered restrictions. They were critical of gender policing, personally experienced or not. Whether these young *innovators* were openly radical or quietly resistant, they were opposed to the gender structure that required different lives for women and men. But they did not conceptualize their innovation as rejection of the gender binary. They wanted to undo gender, so that being a man or woman wasn't confined by gendered expectations.

At the macro level, they rejected the cultural worldview that men and women were and should be different, and they also rejected the existence of rules or regulations that create inequality in a real material sense between the sexes. They believed that women should have equal opportunity in the labor force, and that men had the responsibility to co-parent their children, and not to leave nurturing to mothers. But they had yet to experience much formal gender discrimination. Schools seemed, to them, to be meritocratic, and women were competing quite well with the men in their classes. At this point in their lives, however, they couldn't really identify any material rules that they had experienced as oppressing women, although they most certainly could identify sexist cultural beliefs, workplace policies, and media portrayals.

At the individual level, the men and women *innovators* tell somewhat different stories about who they are and want to be. Both sexes talk about participating in stereotypical male- and female-typical activities. They all feel comfortable mixing and matching stereotypically masculine and feminine traits into their self-descriptions. But here a difference emerges. The women are very proud to mix and match male and female behaviors and personality traits, and feel as if they are better people for doing so. This is true for the men as well. And yet, the men are also hesitant to proudly own their masculine personality traits. They are acutely aware that traditional masculinity is often oppressive to women, and they do not want to replicate that. As with most of the other respondents, in every group, the *innovators* talked a great deal about how their bodies were not quite good enough, although these narratives were not openly linked to gender. But of course, the standards by which they were judging their bodies were entirely gendered. This did not, however, lead to a rejection of the embodiment of gender by women and men and their different standards for beauty or bodily presentation.

The interactional expectations during childhood were experienced quite differently for the women and men. Despite most of the female *innovators* having remembered childhood free from oppressive gender socialization, or perhaps because of that, many had been mistaken for boys routinely during childhood. Puberty changed all that, as they were strongly encouraged to look more like "ladies" and over time did so. The men remembered far more oppressive childhoods. They had been fiercely policed for any behavior strictly beyond traditional boyhood activities by peers and family. Such sanctions against gender nonconformity could not be distinguished, by the men themselves or by me when analyzing their stories, from sanctions against presumed homosexuality. Even the slightest gender nonconformity was understood by those around them to be an indicator of being gay, from wanting to take a ballet class to joining a volleyball team. This was true for straight and gay men, but the shaming was reported as far more painful by the gay men, as they knew they were being punished for being who they really were. The straight men found it far easier to ignore the policing, and some even developed an ironic attitude followed by exaggerated gender-bending and/or identification with a feminist social movement. The gender expectations for male *innovators* were far narrower than for female ones.

By this developmental stage, all *innovators* had rebelled against sanctions for gender nonconformity and had sought out supportive peer groups including feminist organizations, LGBTQ centers on college campuses, gay neighborhoods in urban centers, and carefully chosen partners, friends, and online communities. All were efficacious enough to find social support so that the daily experiences in their material worlds were more supportive than not. We cannot know whether these women will face pushback in their careers because of the well-documented cognitive gender bias against females who are powerful actors. My hope is that they will be as effective in the labor force as they have been thus far in their lives. All these *innovators* have rebelled against the internalization of cultural femininity and masculinity into their definition of self and strive for integrative personalities beyond gender binaries while still accepting gender differences in self-presentation without comment.

My analysis leads to some tentative hypotheses. Millennials all grew up during the ongoing gender revolution. The *innovators* took advantage of this historical moment. They had Internet access from early adolescence onward—some do not even remember the time before the Internet became available—and many spoke about discovering ideas and feminist-leaning communities online. Many told about discovering feminists writers such as Judith Butler. Others learned about the social construction of gender in college classrooms and tell how profoundly that affected them. Such cultural ideas helped initiate and/or legitimate innovative behavior as they rejected gendered expectations. The feminist-inspired cultural changes already in the air during their lives helped make rebellion easier. They hope to continue to alter expectations simply by living their innovative lives. Some, but not most, were explicitly political in their goals to "undo" gender beyond heteronormative expectations. My hypothesis about *innovators* is that the cultural changes already afoot at the macro level legitimated their sense of oppression at the individual level when they were required to stay inside a masculine or feminine box. Their sense of legitimated anger at lingering sexist expectations helped them make agentic decisions to be *innovators* and to consciously try to change the interactional expectations for themselves and for others.

All shared the vision of a world where being labeled a male or female at birth did not shape future possibilities in any way. All expected to help change the world or the expectations related to gender, at least, simply by being who they are. They wanted to embody the change that they hope to see. All shared a cultural worldview antagonistic to the traditional gender structure. These *innovators* do not reject their sex, just the belief that sex should matter for how they live their lives. This is much the same message the second wave of feminism has been preaching for decades but is now the air these Millennials choose to breathe. Feminism has been mainstreamed but perhaps so taken for granted that these Millennials forgot it was a social movement. Of course, these data were collected before a qualified woman lost the presidency to an openly misogynist man who campaigned on reducing women's rights to control their bodies. So perhaps these young feminists are now more political than when these data were collected. The feminist background is also the taken-forgranted reality of the *rebels*, but they move in a different direction.

REBEL CRITIQUE: DIVORCE BODIES FROM GENDER OR REJECT GENDER?

All the *rebels* share the cultural commitment to a society where being labeled a male or female at birth does not require any set of behaviors. This is also true for the *innovators*. But the *rebels* go further. They also want a society where being labeled a male or female at birth does not necessitate any particular way to present one's body to the world or to identify with a particular gender. They do not want to have to do gender in accordance with biological sex. This is a worldview totally antagonistic to the traditional gender structure. But, beyond these statements, there is some variation within the *rebels*. Some are opposed to gender binaries themselves, at least for themselves, and want a world without gender at all. Others are perfectly comfortable with gendered norms for bodily expression in the abstract, they just want those to be divorced from the actual physical sex of the body.

At the individual level of analysis, the *rebels* are proud to mix 'n' match feminine and masculine personality characteristics, although like the male *innovators*, they are fearful about adopting hegemonic masculinity, because they do not want to show any hint of sexism. *Rebels* talked far more about adopting male-typed activities than female ones but did mix 'n' match their activities to include those traditionally male and those traditionally female. Unlike any other respondents in this research, they also rejected the gender structure at the individual level in a very embodied, material way. Some of the female respondents sometimes switched their gendered presentations of self, from outfit to outfit, or day to day. For some females, a masculine or butch presentation of self is how they wanted to be seen and remembered that to have been so since childhood. Other female-bodied genderqueer persons presented themselves primarily in masculine attire but considered themselves androgynous, or between the binary because of the mix of their female body with male-typical clothing. Yet, these androgynous presentation styles were boyish enough that many were mistaken for males. Female bodies and male clothes may be one way to enact androgyny, but the common experience of their being mistaken for men suggests that the presentational self trends toward masculine even if the body is female. Male is still considered the unmarked version of humanity, and this seems true even among *rebels*. What looks masculine is called androgynous, generic human. Maleness is still so valued in our world that it remains the presumptive ideal genderless category. It is ironic that even *among rebels,* what is traditionally male is seen as generically human. Ironic, and a strong illustration of the power of sexism that shows the embedded strength of male privilege even in the 21st-century *rebels'* unconscious imagination.

While the genderqueer *rebels* were more comfortable in their bodies than with the clothes available for them, other *rebels* were profoundly dissatisfied with their bodies, at least until they had altered some secondary-sex characteristics, for example, removing their breasts. Most, but not all, experienced fluidity in their identities, experimented with their sexual and gender labels, and expected they might continue to do so. For the female *rebels*, the materiality of living in a female body, especially in a culture that requires female bodies to be presented in feminine ways, was oppressive and the subject of much consternation and conversation. For the transgender women and man, hormones helped reshape the materiality of their bodies in ways that helped them live their gender. They were *rebels* in that they did not presume that being female meant they had to present themselves as traditionally feminine, not did being male mean they had to hide evidence of femininity. All these *rebels* rejected the internalization of cultural femininity and masculinity into their definition of self and strove for integrative personalities beyond gender binaries. All the *rebels* rejected the gender binary, including the transgender respondents who were not trying to pass, but to break free of the exclusive one they had been labeled at birth.

The *rebels* are different from all others in this research because of their rejection of the materiality of the gender binary. They reject the social rules that that turn females into women, or males into men. Instead, they either choose to present themselves as masculine females, feminine males, or someone truly between the binary. Or they transition to being women but do not desire traditional femininity, nor do they care that they are identifiable as transgender women. They reject the idea that behaviors or personality traits are typically reserved for one sex or the other. They repudiate both the material and cultural aspects of the gender structure at the individual level of analysis.

At the interactional level of analysis, *rebels* face constant gender policing and withstand negative feedback, particularly from strangers and in their workplaces. Most of the *rebels* remembered being supported by parents to pursue activities they wanted to do as youngsters, and the females reported wearing such boyish clothes when children they were often mistaken for boys. With a few notable exceptions, it was peers and non-family members that sanctioned them for gender nonconformity in youth. There were some, though, whose families tried very hard to pressure them toward gender typicality from early childhood through the present. They report painful interactional skirmishes with teachers, doctors, bosses, as well as peers and family members. The two transwomen were forced to try more masculine activities in childhood, and between parental coercion and peer sanctions, both retreated into being introverted, nerdy, and lonely. But none of these *rebels* acquiesce to gender policing. They all stand up for themselves and push the boundaries, in behaviors, personalities, and how they present their bodies.

These *rebels* were remarkably efficacious. If they were uncomfortable in their bodies, they changed them. If they were being bullied by peers, they searched for new supportive networks including feminist organizations, LGBTQ centers on college campuses, gay neighborhoods in urban centers, and very carefully chosen partners, friends, and online communities. When they rejected gendered expectations, they hoped to change those expectations for others. Still, they worried about the future, their ability to be who they want to be, find and keep jobs, and have their medical choices respected.

At the macro level of analysis, the entire social system, every part of it, presumes only two genders, stable throughout a lifetime, with no one in the middle. This constantly feels oppressive to the *rebels*. Every single one reported having experienced institutional discrimination. If you reject gender as a binary or the sex on your birth certificate, schools, workplaces, medical systems, clothing stores, and bathrooms all are designed to ignore your existence. And yet, all are navigating this hostile world, and some even seem to revel in their rebellion. Their ideological commitment is to changing the world so that being labeled a male or female at birth does not require any set of behaviors or clothes or ways of being. They reject cultural beliefs about sex and gender with great vehemence.

I cannot make causal arguments with such data, but these analyses do lead to some hypotheses. Millennials grew up surrounded with much information about gender and feminism, particularly from online sources. Most had access from their early adolescence to ideas about gender. As they aged, they discovered on campus and online communities about gender rebellion, transitioning, and what it means to be genderqueer. The ability to imagine living between the binary existed in the cultural habitus in which they grew to young adulthood. This wouldn't have mattered to them if they had not already felt oppressed by gendered rules. Life as a rebel was shaped by the feminist and queer cultural products that existed as they emerge into adulthood. Just as they rejected gender as a binary, most have also rejected a binary definition of sexuality as either gay or straight. While all hope to change the expectations of those around them simply by living their lives, some are very politically committed to queering gender so that it has nothing to do with sex of the body. Others want to "undo" gender as a heteronormative expectation and live between the genders or beyond it entirely. Some have few political goals, but simply want to be free of gender constraints they find so oppressive. At the individual level, these respondents feel oppressed, and the cultural products at the macro level helped give voice to that oppression, which led to agentic actions that allow them freedom to navigate their daily lives, and they hope to change the interactional expectations of those around them by living the lives they chose. Once again, I remind you these data were collected in a different, if very recent, political moment, when laws were beginning to change to honor the needs of genderqueer and transgender people. It is possible that these *rebels* have become more political in this historical moment of government backlash against feminism. While the *rebels* were quite sure of their rejection of gender, the *straddlers* were not quite sure about anything related to gender.

CONFUSION IS THE NEW NORMAL

The *straddlers* tell very different tales about the gendered expectations they face. The rest of the respondents tell a consistent gender tale while these respondents do not.

The men remembered parents who wanted them to grow up to earn a living, but beyond that, the expectations about masculinity were subtle. They were expected to do the male-typed household tasks, but not always. They barely remember any gendered rules that differentiated them from their sisters. Men don't remember being raised to be boys; they simply see themselves as the norm, the generic human being. What a difference a female standpoint makes. The girls remembered strong parental pressure to become feminine women. Whereas the boys remember some pressure on how they should act, they tell almost no stories about being taught how to look. The women tell nearly as many socialization stories about looking good as about behaving like a lady. Most of the women also tell stories of their brothers' relative freedom, later curfews, and less supervision. Overall, the women have far more memories of parental constraints and explicit socialization than did the men. From their disparate memories, it is hard to imagine that these young women and men grew up in similar families at all. Girls experience and remember a great deal of gendered rules where boys had freedoms they did not, and boys didn't notice any gender inequality in their families. The transgender respondents had far different stories to tell. The straddler who is a transwoman, had parents who let her be the quiet loner she wanted to be, and so avoided childhood masculine pursuits entirely, and remembered no coercive gender socialization at all. The transmen had far more painful childhood memories, with parents trying to coerce them into both heterosexuality and gender conformity. The transmen's parents wanted their girls to be heteronormative girls and not lesbians. But eventually came to accept them as sons.

While parental gender socialization was remembered far more vividly, and oppressively, by girls and transmen (who were presenting as girls when being socialized), males remembered far more sanctions for gender nonconformity from their peers than do females. Men believed their peers constrained them to stay in gendered boxes. These *straddlers* told painful stories about being teased and ridiculed, especially boy on boy, for any slight deviation from masculinity in dress or behavior. Stories of peer pressure were told with more pain than the memories of parental socialization. Perhaps peers deliver sanctions with viciousness, while parents' try to mold behavior with more warmth and sometimes with rewards. The *straddlers* have all experienced strong and ongoing pressure to be gender appropriate.

All these respondents believe that whatever their socialization, they are capable of rejecting gender norms if and when they choose to do so. Most accept some of the traditional gender structure while rejecting other aspects. The men are more traditionally masculine than feminine and do stereotypically male rather than female activities. And yet, they also cross boundaries and do some female activities or describe their personalities as feminine in some ways. Some claim to be more empathetic than your typical guy. The women talk as much, or more, about nonconforming gender behaviors than conforming ones and sound proud of themselves. Similarly, they describe themselves with as nearly as many masculine traits as feminine ones.

Straddler women talk far more about their bodies than do the men. They tell stories about being pressured to wax eyebrows, paint nails, style hair, and diet. All that body modification work has to happen before the investment of time and money to shop for a wardrobe. Many of the women enjoy this process and others enjoy parts of it but at the same time resent the effort. A few seriously resent the work it takes to do femininity. The men don't tell stories about the work it takes to be masculine, although perhaps some of them do such work at the gym. Both men and women talk about disliking their bodies. For most men, weight is a problem on both ends: they worry about being too thin and too fat. Women, it seems, can never be too thin but worry tremendously about being too fat. But it's not just weight that bothers these young people; there is a whole range of complaints about their bodies. Only the transgender respondents have narratives about bodies that have overtly happy endings or at least positive framing of the current journey.

What *straddlers* have in common is that there is no consistency in their responses. The **only** commonality is that their narratives are inconsistent from one moment to the next in the interview. The inconsistency exists often within one level of analysis. One man tells us he only has stereotypically male hobbies and interests and then describes his personality as empathetic and people-oriented. A woman tells us she adores children and wants a career nurturing them, and soon thereafter informs us that she's aggressive and has engaged in physical fights. But that is merely one example of inconsistency in these stories. Most of the women describe very inconsistent socialization about what it means to be a woman. The women describe being taught to be career focused and independent, while at the same time expected to be warm, people-oriented, thin, and well-coifed. Their inconsistencies grow to the point of confusion as the interviews progressed. While *innovators* are proud to mix 'n' match from masculine and feminine-typed behaviors and personalities as well, this source of pride is absent among *straddlers*. When looking across answers at the individual, interactional, and macro levels of analysis, the *straddlers'* answers are almost chaotic. Some women are proud to say they overcame gender socialization, but then go on to espouse conservative gender ideology. Others talk like feminists but never challenge any gender norms. Many have very libertarian views toward gender expression but hold fast to their own gendered selves and express disdain for those who are gender nonconformists. These respondents sound unsure and confused. But they are emerging as adults, and perhaps a better way to think of the inconsistencies are that they are still struggling with the complicated world around them and in the process of designing who they want to be as full-fledged adults. .

As I reiterate regularly, I cannot answer causal questions. Here, with so few patterns beyond inconsistency, I have not even a hypothesis. These *straddlers* were mostly raised by parents with traditional gender expectations, although this was remembered far more vividly by men than women. The peer pressure to "do gender" traditionally was strong for both men and women, although peer pressure seemed stronger for the men. All this pressure was somewhat effective with *straddlers* internalizing and expressing gendered selves, but not entirely, as they do reject some aspects of gender for themselves. They adopt some liberal ideologies, and then contradict themselves with conservative or essentialist beliefs. The ideology of upward mobility and libertarian attitude toward free choice was widely shared and so left little room for the expectation that women should opt out of the labor force for motherhood. These emerging adults reflect the world around them, a world with a gender revolution still ongoing, with the future still unclear. Will these young people pick and choose among gendered expectations, and will the new patterns change the gender structure for the future? How will they reconcile critical views of gender often learned in college classrooms or through their experiences with the identities which their parents helped shape over two decades of life? Time will tell.

The gender structure in America was once more stable, with boys and girls raised for traditional lives, internalizing gendered personalities, and endorsing separate spheres for their lives. By now that world is shattered beyond recognition. The majority of young people in this unrepresentative sample are full of contradictions as to just what the norms are, who they are supposed to become, who they want to become, and how they think the world does, and ought, to operate. Their contradictions simply mirror the world around them, still in flux, the product of a yet incomplete gender revolution. The best phrase to sum up the experiences of *straddlers* is confused and still searching. These Millennials are still emerging into adulthood, and wrestling with learning how to reconcile a gender structure that is complicated and currently chaotic.

THE LIMITS OF A VOLUNTEER SAMPLE

As I have reminded the reader throughout this book, this sample is entirely voluntary and cannot be generalized. I searched high and low for a nationally representative quantitative data set that had measures of the individual, interactional, and macro levels of analysis. None exists. In that search, I did find another voluntary sample of college students, but larger and with quantitative data. The data is called Future Pathway. This data set was originally collected by Caroll Serin and Susan Silbey to study what effects the choice of college majors. The five-year longitudinal panel

data of over 700 men and women is described more fully in Cech (2013). Future
Pathways has measures of individual gendered identities, expectations about same-
sex others' behaviors, and ideological worldviews. The respondents in their research
came from East Coast colleges and universities, although various types of institutions, including University of Massachusetts, Amherst, MIT, Franklin W. Olin
College of Engineering, and Smith College. When I analyzed the data to estimate
the percentage of students in each category, the percentage of students in each category was radically different from the sample analyzed in this book. When I looked
for respondents in the Future Pathways study who were *true believers*, I selected
for respondents that saw themselves as feminine women or masculine men, that
expected others of their same-sex to behave within gender stereotyped patterns, and
reported worldviews that endorsed distinct roles for women and men. Only six men
fell in the category. When I selected for people who might be *innovators* and *rebels*,
because they had very liberal worldviews on gender equality, I found tremendous
sex differences with 23% of the women and only 8% of the men. Those numbers suggest that, at least in this East Coast sample of college students, women are far more
likely to be *innovators* or *rebels* than men. Of course, not all of those women with
very liberal ideologies will be either *innovators* or *rebels*, some might be *straddlers*,
but that is the upper limit, since no one without a liberal ideology could qualify as
an innovator or rebel. If such a sex difference exists, the heterosexual women are
going to find it difficult to find egalitarian men to marry. Clearly future research
is needed with nationally random samples. Without it, we cannot know the percentage of Millennials in each group, and how that differs by class status, racial and
ethnic identity, and, of course, sex itself. So even with these quantitative data, we do
not know how many Millennials are in each group. What else might we learn from
the qualitative data reported throughout this book?

SEXUALITIES

As in much research on gender, the link among gendered selves, identities, performances, and sexuality is complicated, but present. Every true believer identified
their sexual orientation as straight. These young people who believe in gender difference and a traditional gender structure presume heteronormativity is required
as part of a normative gender identity. These *true believers* presume that attraction
to the opposite sex is part of conforming to normative femininity or masculinity.
Crawley et al. (2007) explain this by describing how gender is regulated by creating
a belief in conformity among sex of the body, gender, and sexual orientation: if you
are male, you must be masculine and interested in women. My hypothesis is that if

someone is raised as a true believer and begins to feel attraction to a person of the same sex, he or she questions this gender box of conformity and therefore begins to question the gender structure itself and becomes a straddler.

Most of the *straddlers* were also heterosexuals, but here we had a little more variation, with five responding they were bisexual, queer, unsure, or wouldn't answer the question. Still approximately 90% of the *straddlers* claimed a heterosexual identity. This was not true for the *innovators*, where half identified as straight. Eleven claimed a heterosexual identity and the other ten offered a variety of other identities including queer, unsure, bisexual, and gay/homosexual. Not one rebel identified as heterosexual. Here identifying as gay or homosexual was also minority choice, with only about a quarter clearly doing so (n = 4). Most of the *rebels* not only rejected gender categories, they also rejected binaries more generally, including the binary of straight or gay. Two of the transwomen were in polyamorous relationships with other transgender women. The terms used for sexual self-identification included pansexual, queer, bisexual, and bi-curious. The most often used sexual identity was queer (n = 7). The data suggest a strong correlation between rejecting the gender structure and exploring sexual identities beyond heterosexual. It may be that those who have opted out of traditional gender expectations are open to more fluid understandings of sexuality. Or it may be that those who experience sexual fluidity in desire or nonheterosexual desire are more likely to reject the gender structure. With these data, I cannot begin to sort out this puzzle, but these data show that as Millennials become more radically rejecting of the gender binary, so, too, they are far less likely to identify as straight sexually. Relying on research based on the National Surveys of Family Growth with representative cohort data from 1966 to 1995, we do know that over time more women, but not men, have bisexual identities and are more likely to have sex with same-sex partners (England et al. 2016).

BODIES

One commonality across the vast majority of the Millennials interviewed for this book was dissatisfaction with their bodies. The questions are why and whether this is new in American society. None of the other research on Millennials focuses on the topic or even mentions it. Is it simply part of a developmental stage of emerging adulthood? Or is there something about American culture, and the gender structure, right now, that triggers insecurity about the appropriateness of one's body? Perhaps the focus on health these days has the unintended consequence of creating body-image issues for emerging adults. More research is needed to address this question that unexpectedly came up in this research. My hypothesis is that as the differences in girls' and boys' lives decreases, and gender expectations begin to converge, the one clear way left to "do gender" is with the body. And so, the body itself becomes more problematic, carries more weight, so to speak, to signify becoming an appropriately gendered adult. Nearly all the respondents in this research were dissatisfied with their bodies and mostly appreciated them only after at least some attempt at intervention. Perhaps our bodies are becoming more commodified in post-industrial society, and advanced capitalism has succeeded in objectifying ourselves to the point of needing a constant stream of new products and self-help programs to accept our material selves. Future research is much needed because the pain in the respondents' stories was loud and clear when it came to talking about their bodies.

For those *innovators* who identify between the binary, or across it, bodies are central to their identity struggles. Many of those between the binary shop primarily in men's departments and presume that female bodies dressed in male clothing are androgynous. Still, they often tell stories about being mistaken for boys or men. Why is it that some people who opt for androgyny are mistaken for males? My analysis is that even among the rebellious of Millennials there remains an unreflective, perhaps unconscious, androcentrism where what is male is seen as generically human, while anything female, or feminine, is marked as only for women. There were also a few respondents whose strategy for living between the binary was to dress feminine sometimes and masculine at other times, or to mix up feminine and masculine signifiers in one outfit. But the hidden message that presenting as masculine was somehow generically human was hard to miss when interviewing respondents assigned female at birth who identify as genderqueer but are often mistaken for boys or men. For the *rebels* who do present between the binary, the future remains unclear. While there may be little discrimination against genderqueer presentation, for example, as a barista in a coffeehouse or on college campuses, how well non-binary presentations of self will be accepted in either blue-collar or professional occupations is unknown.

CONTEMPORARY MEANINGS OF MASCULINITY, FEMININITY AND BETWEEN THE BINARY

Distilled to the basics, femininity has come to mean empathy and nurturance, traits needed for caretaking, while masculinity is about agency, traits needed for leadership. But, of course, meanings attached to masculinities and femininities are elaborated, accepted, rejected, and adapted continually. And as meanings change, so too does the gender structure. Every time Millennials reject expectations for gender stereotypes or refuse to choose gendered activities, they presume they will change the world for themselves and for those that come after. Whether individuals changing their own lives, that is, rejecting masculinity or femininity, is an effective way to make social change is unclear.

We must remember, however, that masculinity and femininity are not simply equivalent—separate but equal. Masculinity is far more highly valued symbolically, but also in real ways. Men make more money, hold more power, and have more prestige. But not all men. Connell's work (1987; 1995) showed how hegemonic masculinity was the ideal type; the well-rewarded masculinity owned by the men who run the show. This is the masculinity of the mostly white, elite men who fill the halls of Congress and the board rooms. Other masculinities may trump femininity but are still subordinated to hegemonic masculinity, which involves repressing emotions in the service of economic success. The mostly working-class majority-minority men in this sample are unlikely to emerge into an adulthood of hegemonic masculinity. Indeed, it is unclear to me whether most of them even want to. They want good jobs and stable economic lives, but only the *true believers* seem to aspire to the traditional masculinity of this sort. The rest, even the *straddlers*, want to develop aspects that are stereotypically feminine, while the *innovators* and *rebels* demand the right to do so. While most of the men may want traditionally tough bodies, and are therefore disappointed with the ones they have, most have personal goals for a broader definition of masculinity. Anderson (2002; 2009) offers a new conceptualization of "inclusive masculinity" in which men incorporate same-sex emotional and physical intimacy into their lives. Most of the men in this sample are incorporating aspects of what we now call feminine traits into their repertoire of behaviors, and this may allow them to move beyond homophobia. Not all the men in this research portray inclusive masculinity, but many of the *straddlers* and the *innovators* do. The *rebels*, of course, go beyond this and question the need for labeling aspects of the human experience by gender at all. Many of the men in this research are actively exploring alternative, or even hybrid, forms of masculinities, as Pascoe and Bridges (2015) suggest is common and necessary in today's world.

It is worth noting that the innovator women incorporate some aspects of masculinity into their lives. Some also value aspects of femininity, but many reject anything pink and value the masculine over the feminine. Similarly, the female *rebels*, those who articulate the desire to live between the binary, usually appear masculine, at least somewhat boyish. It seems that for these reflexively feminist and political radical Millennials what is generically male is perceived as the unmarked androgynous human. Presuming the masculine to be generically human can be seen in how uniforms are adopted when women enter traditionally male jobs. One example of this is when male-only restaurants hire women as servers. They are dressed as men, and waiter attire becomes wait staff attire. Never could we imagine men join-ing a female occupation, such as nursing, and being required to wear a dress or even a nurse's cap. In a patriarchal world, men's status pervades our understanding of the human. God may be genderless but is traditionally imagined and referred to as "he." Mankind is presumed to include women, even if it doesn't linguistically do so. With such cultural baggage, is it surprising that when young people want to go beyond gender, they do so without noticing that a generic human being doesn't necessarily look male?

What do these Millennials teach us about contemporary femininity? While the *true believers* espouse gender traditional ideals about how women should act, the rest of the sample does not. Women are proud of incorporating stereotypically male personality traits and behaviors into their definition of themselves. What remains most marked as feminine is the body, the heels and hose, the accessories and the diets. As women move into more highly valued male territory, it seems as if the way they continue to "do gender" is with the body. A woman may be the CEO, but she still wears high heels, which does not allow her to move quickly, effortlessly, or per-haps without pain. She certainly cannot run from an assailant or fight back easily if attacked. Femininity is devalued culturally, but women need to prove their fem-ininity with their bodies to be accepted as professionals. As gender stereotypes for behavior are reduced, it seems as if the requirements to embody gender in presen-tation increases. With such exaggerated requirements for embodied gender, so too does dissatisfaction with our bodies grow.

MOVING TOWARD THE FUTURE

The Millennials are living through interesting times. The world has changed a great deal since the second wave of feminism. Millennials grew up in an era with many new opportunities for girls, yet still many expectations are attached to gender. They were raised by baby boomer parents who lived through the activist, historical times of the second wave of feminism. Many were raised by parents who were conscious to let their children, at least their girls, go beyond gendered boundaries. All the respon-dents are in that new stage of development called emerging adulthood, still strug-gling with who they want to be. They live in a world framed by neoliberal beliefs where individuals are presumed responsible for their lives, where change is presumed to come from individual agency. Some are perfectly satisfied with the world as they find it. Others are not. Even those who hope to change the world often seem to think that can be done entirely by living authentic lives beyond gender stereotypes or gender. In the next chapter, we return to a deeper consideration of gender as a social structure and the implications of the framework for feminist social change. I make an argument that to move beyond gender inequality, we must be able to imagine a world beyond gender itself. Furthermore, for Millennials to be effective actors in social change, they must go beyond their individualism and join others in future feminist social movements.

Getting to a Utopian World Beyond Gender

IN THIS BOOK I have argued that gender is a social structure that has implications for individual identities, social expectations, and the macro organization of institutions and cultural logics in which they are embedded. I began with a presentation of the history of gender scholarship and then presented a theoretical argument that revised my earlier writings. I used this theoretical framework to help us understand today's emerging adults, the Millennials. I have now spent all these pages convincing the reader that the gender structure exists, and that young people today struggle with the constraints it imposes on them. There is no one path they follow, even though most of these young people lived in Chicagoland or surrounding university towns. They already struggle with what gender means in their lives and have yet to face the institutional constraints of trying to juggle work and parenting. My closing argument is that confining people to gender expectations and organizing society around gender categories has pernicious effects on women and men, and those who would rather not have to identify as either.

In this last chapter, I return to my major theoretical takeaway messages and their implications for the possibility of making feminist social change. What can we learn from Millennials, and where should we go from here? After a brief discussion of how the Millennials in this research project think about social change, I integrate the empirical research from this project with other research on current gender controversies, focusing on the incompatibilities of expectations and realities at different levels of the gender structure, what Connell (1987) has called "crises tendencies."

Such crises tendencies provide leverage for activists to push for social change. I call attention to the contemporary social movements now agitating for a more feminist and gender-inclusive society. Some activists are pushing for women's rights, others for the right to exist on a gender spectrum rather than within the categories of stereotypical masculinity or femininity. While some of these social movements may seem to conflict with one another, a gender structure framework allows us to see seemingly contradictory movements not as antagonistic but rather as a tapestry, each one taking aim at a different part of our complex gender structure. Once I've discussed contemporary movements primarily active in the United States, I turn to research that helps identify what factors seem effective as proximate causes for social change. For this, I turn to social science research and try to use it in the service of social change. I offer evidence from the research to suggest where we ought to go from here. I conclude this chapter with a call for a fourth wave of feminism with the utopian goal to dismantle the gender structure entirely. If the gender structure constrains human freedom, then to move forward to a more just society, we must move beyond gender itself.

WHAT DO WE LEARN FROM MILLENNIALS ABOUT SOCIAL CHANGE?

The empirical evidence in this book is based on life history interviews with 116 Millennials. Many Millennials today are confused about the gender structure, with little consistency in their answers to our questions. They have inherited a culture much changed from the 1950s *Leave It To Beaver* homemaker-breadwinner, sex-segregated America. Men's and women's lives are far more alike than they used to be. Women, even very traditional *true believers* in socially important differences between themselves and men, expect to be paid workers for most or all of their lives. The stark public-private division between female homemakers and male breadwinners is a distant memory. Separate spheres as an ideology or even partial reality should be studied only in history courses. It's simply no longer relevant to young people's lives. In this research, the expectation that women should remain outside the labor force was not a part of these women's narratives. But what comes next? That's the question. The *rebels* and *innovators* in this sample are questioning gender socialization, social norms and expectations, and the worldview and societal structures that require females to become feminine women and males to become masculine men. They expect to change the gender structure by rebelling against it as individuals, sometimes by disentangling gender from bodies, sometimes simply by ignoring it, and other times by organizing with others to change it. Feminist change is in the air, influencing the contour of their lives, more than as a distinct social movement. While the second wave of feminism didn't finish a gender revolution, many of those feminists are the mothers of today's Millennials. Some of the Millennials carry on their struggles, and others are just confused. Still others adopt what has been called egalitarian essentialism both expecting and desiring gender equality in the labor force but still holding onto beliefs, often supported by religious doctrine, that men and women are inherently different.

In this volunteer and non-representative sample, many of the *rebels* and *innovators* felt that by rejecting the expectations they disliked, they were changing them, and when enough people individually rebelled, they believed the world would change. In theoretical language, many of the *rebels* and *innovators* seemed to believe that effective change could happen regarding gender oppression by rejecting interactional-level expectations with their own counter-normative behavior at the individual level. These respondents expect gender demands to recede as more people ignore them. The implicit social change strategy often offered by the respondents begins with individual action. At the individual level of analysis, they reject interactional expectations by innovating or rebelling, and presume their individual actions will eventually reverberate to change what others expect, and then the larger cultural beliefs as well. This is a domino theory of social change starting with the self. The individual would change the interactional, which—presumably, eventually—would change how children are raised in the future, and how our institutions are organized. We didn't ask direct questions about political or social movement activity in our interviews, but if face-to-face political activity were an important part of these young people's lives, we would have heard more about it than we did. A few of the respondents were active in LGBT or anti-violence against women movements, but not that many. More were online activists. Millennials have been raised in an individualist era, when social programs have dissolved in favor of "personal responsibility." Thus many think of taking personal responsibility for their actions, presenting their bodies as they desire, and following or ignoring gendered expectations as the way to make change.

This focus on the self is an implicit if unreflective consequence of a neoliberal ideology that has enveloped this generation from birth. While there is no one definition of neoliberalism, the implications of neoliberalism involve shifting the expectations for solving social problems to personal responsibility and choices. Solutions to social issues, such as gender oppression, are conceptualized as being the responsibility of individual's self-help, self-empowerment, and self-reliance efforts (Peters 2001). Neoliberalism justifies an individualist ideology where each of us takes personal responsibility for all aspects of our lives. If we are oppressed, we must shake off the shackles as strong isolated actors. In a neoliberal philosophy, social structure recedes into the murky irrelevant background. Millennials grew up in this era in which power to shape one's life is presumed to rest primarily, and rightly, with each individual. When it comes to the gender structure, it seems that the young people in this study have imbued neoliberalism in the air around them. While many are confused by a gender structure that they somewhat disagree with, those who innovate or rebel against the gender structure do so primarily as individuals, not as part of formal social movements. While American ideology has always tended to be individualist, social movements in the past have been far more tied to collective struggle, from unions to the civil rights movement to the second wave of feminism.

Social movements involving Millennials, of course, still exist today. As Milkman (2017) illustrates, Black Lives Matter, Occupy Wall Street, Dreamers who fight for immigration rights, and the campus-based movement against sexual assault are all led by college-educated Millennials. These movements bridge the cyberspace and face-to-face divide naturally because the leadership is made up of digital natives who organize online and protest in person. Another commonality of these Millennial-led movements is their commitment to intersectionality, that is, the realization that experiences of inequality are multidimensional and cross identity categories (Milkman 2017). Intersectional feminism has been integrated into the Black Lives Matter's and the Dreamer's movements organically. Milkman's research suggests many of the leaders in those movements are queer women committed to an intersectional analysis. While sexual assault is a feminist issue to the core, Milkman's research suggests that many of the privileged, white heterosexual women who led this charge denied being feminists at the start but came to hold that identity as their activities progressed. In all these movements, cyber mobilization has the advantage of information spread at the speed of light, but the weakness of little organizational infrastructure that still remains after even a successful event to push for legislative or political change. Although these movements have been led by college-educated Millennials, the working-class respondents in this research did not report much participation in them. Perhaps this will change after the dramatic and well-attended women's marches immediately after the inauguration of Trump as president of the United States.

While the respondents in my study were not often active participants in face-to-face social movements, many reported that online activism had helped shape their worldviews. They had learned about gender on the Internet, joining communities of like-minded others and also confronting those with whom they disagree. The influence of ideas floating around on the Internet and the power of online activism exist concurrently with the individualist, almost libertarian, ideology that often pervaded the interviews with Millennials. In the research presented here, both *innovators* and *rebels* wanted to change the gender structure. The common theme was a belief in change that began with the individual. By living their lives beyond the rules they disagreed with, they would shake up the interactional expectations around gender, and eventually the world itself. The *innovators* ideologies were very similar to second wave feminists in ideology, although most did not actively participate in face-to-face mobilizations on any regular basis. Feminism has gone mainstream in the *innovators'* lives. A strong commitment to social movement activity was not common among either *innovators* or *rebels*. Individual decisions about the self seemed to many of these millennial respondents their contribution to changing gender oppression.

When it comes to changes in the gender structure, the *rebels* seem to be a uniquely millennial phenomenon. These young people rejected gender at the individual level, but beyond the cultural beliefs about their personalities, they also rejected the expectations about bodily presentations. Some even wanted to escape from the category of man and woman, both in how they act and how they dress and identify. In some ways, the *rebels* signify a new step in the gender revolution, a millennial one. While there clearly have been transgender men and women throughout time, this is the first moment in history where young people are confronting gender oppression by trying to step outside the binary. The *rebels* very existence shows the power of ideas, as nearly all of them first encountered the possibility of living between the binary from online sources or in college classrooms. The rest of the sample was also cognizant of the social change happening around them. In a technologically fast-paced world, where economic and political changes have propelled women into the labor force, and waves of feminism have politicized sexual inequality, nearly all of these Millennials, except the *true believers*, talked about changing expectations full of inconsistencies across and within levels of analysis.

Indeed, we swim in contradictions. The 2016 presidential election had a politically experienced strong white woman in pants debate a rich white business man who bragged about grabbing women's pussy without consent. So are women world leaders or sexual objects without the right to contest male sexual aggression? Contradictions such as these destabilize the taken-for-granted presumptions within gender structure and open the possibility for change, perhaps toward a more radical gender revolution. All of these interviews happened, of course, before Donald Trump became president of the United States of America. And with his presidency, the gender contradictions skyrocketed to national prominence. The contradiction between the progress on gender equality made in the last 50 years and the right-wing attempt to "make American great *again*" with its backward-looking goal to recreate an era when men were heads of households and women had no right to control their own fertility has become hotly contested. Millennials showed out in droves for the women's marches all over the world to proclaim their support for gender equality and the right to gender diversity. The marches had strong intersectional mission statements, and Millennials were out in force, as were people of all ages.[1] The question remains, of course, if those events will evolve into successful social movement activity that elects progressive feminist candidates in the future. What kinds of crises tendencies now exist and their consequences so far are highlighted using my own and others research below.

INDIVIDUAL LEVEL OF ANALYSIS:
INNOVATIVE AND REBELLIOUS YOUTH

In this book, we have met a few young people disrupting norms about the gender binary itself, chafing at the confinement of the gender structure and demanding the freedom to be queer not just in their sexuality but in their gender as well. Before this book, there has been very little research on genderqueer Millennials (but see Factor and Rothblum 2008; Shotwell and Sangrey 2009), and most of that is about their status as at-risk adolescents (Smalley et al. 2015). Previous reports are primarily journalistic (Conlin 2011; Herman 2015), and much writing has appeared on blogs. Every day more blogs are written by people identifying as genderqueer[2] and/ or transgender.[3] High school students are requesting the right to choose their own pronoun; college students are demanding all-gender bathrooms and dormitories, and Australia now offers passports with an "other category." Intersex activists are demanding a third sex on passports and driver's licenses. Some young men in Japan are, like the *rebels* in this research, ignoring gender norms in bodily presentation, wearing makeup and high heels and promoting a genderless "danshi" concept of personhood without reference to gender category.[4] The State of Oregon now accepts genderqueer as a gender category. This rejection of gender as a primary status is distinct from sexual identities. In my small and non-representative sample, genderqueer youth have a variety of sexual identities. Some are straight; some are gay. The issue at hand is the rejection of the expectations that belong to the status of woman or man. We have no good data on whether the number of people who find gender identity constraining has increased. What we do know is their demands to be seen and heard and accepted have. While trans activists have been making waves since Stonewall, the growth of an identity of genderqueer and a growing public acceptance of trans identities is new. In the past, there was not much critique of the binary categorizations of women and men; people labeled medically as "transsexuals" were reported to want to be the other sex—or at least that's what they told medical gatekeepers who required such a belief to allow access to surgery. Today, we see development of new kinds of identities and demands for new pronouns: *hir, zir, s/he,* or *they* to apply to individuals who reject the categorization of male and female. The desire for a new pronoun suggests that these people are rejecting not just gender but being categorized as male or female as well. This kind of linguistic activism by people who are genderqueer creates a crisis tendency because rejecting the binary destabilizes gender essentialism. Those who are *rebels* can be seen as revolutionary actors at the individual level. They defy gender as a binary. The question remains, of course, whether individual action alone can effectively make social change.

While language is in flux today, we see transgender identity or the phrase "trans*" being adopted both by those who critique the gender binary and those who accept the binary and want to travel across it (McKenna and Kessler 2006 discuss these multiple meanings of "trans"). Transgender people have traditionally desired to define their own sex because they have believed they were born in the wrong body (Gagné et al. 1997; 1998). Even when transgender persons believe in the gender binary, their very existence calls into question the necessary correlation between biological sex (as in genitalia and secondary-sex characteristics), the sex one claims, and preference for gender presentation of self and sex-typed behavioral norms (Crawley et al. 2007). With current medical technologies, people can identify with a sex or gender and then (with enough wealth or good health insurance) create the body that suits their identity. Such fluidity necessarily raises the question for all of us: Why must our lives be organized by the legal and bureaucratic binary system that relegates everyone to one of two categories based originally on genitalia observed at birth? The Internet, with the instant availability of writing and videos questioning the gender binary, has surely facilitated the pace of change.

Much questioning and defying gender today is occurring online. Some bloggers are calling not for the end of gender, but for the queering of gender and its association with sex category. Costello (2011) makes the distinction between binary-identified trans people and genderqueer people, who may or may not be trans. Costello writes that people with genderqueer identities deserve respect from the binary-identified, but that those who can pass within the binary should acknowledge their privilege when doing so. Second, Ward (2011) writes that she is co-parent with a woman known at home as Dad. Ward argues that totally dissolving the gendered "Mom and Dad" concept was not realistic in their home town, but that they queer the concept by putting a woman into the role. Those on the gender vanguard, like public sociology bloggers Costello and Ward, occupy and enlarge the fissures in the gender structure. They may pay a price for deviating from norms, depending on their community, but their writings increase the crisis tendencies that may quicken change for the rest of us.

The materiality of bodies is of central concern at the individual level of analysis. The most coercive gendered practice that remains legal at the individual level is when medical authorities surgically alter bodies of intersex children to force them into a sex binary, even at the expense of the potential for future sexual pleasure. Intersex scholar and activist Georgiann Davis argues to stop such surgeries and allow intersex children to grow up with the bodies with which they were born. Her research on intersexuality illustrates just how slippery cultural definitions of sexuality and gender are: the intersex social movement is fighting to change the very language for bodies born beyond the binary from disorder to diversity (Davis 2015; Dreger 2009; Preves 2003). It is only gender essentialist ideology that justifies surgery to shoehorn a baby into the gender binary. If a fundamental right is bodily integrity, then intersex children should have the freedom to live in their bodies until they are mature enough to make their own decisions. Social movements about bodies are cracking the gender structure itself.

Ending surgery for babies born beyond the sex binary and allowing surgery for those who desire different bodies is really two sides of the same coin, allowing people to exist along a sex and gender spectrum (Davis et al. 2016) or to reject gender constraints entirely. Why should women who want flat chests or differently shaped genitals have to present themselves with a psychiatric diagnosis of gender dysphoria to be allowed the freedom to change their bodies? Women who want smaller, or larger, breasts for aesthetic reasons do not have to claim a mental illness to justify the surgery, nor do those who want differently shaped noses or eyes. Some of the *rebels* in my sample changed their bodies to live in them comfortably. Others sometimes bound their breasts. Others mixed and matched their gender presentations by outfit, by article, or clothing. Using their bodies, with surgery or by presentation of self, to make their lives feel authentic illustrates the complexity of the social and medical construction of gender itself. Our bodies (are) ourselves (1971) is a phrase first coined by the Boston Women's Health Collective nearly half a century ago. But our bodies cannot be ourselves unless everyone is allowed the freedom to present bodies that align with identities. The call to use technologically sophisticated medical procedures to claim a sex or gender is one easily identified crisis tendency in today's gender structure.

Rebellion, however, against gendered bodies needn't be so radical to be meaningful. The *innovators* in this sample do not challenge the gender binary at the material dimension of the individual level of analysis, yet they challenge the stereotypes attached to the categories. Women who engage in more activities that are traditionally masculine than feminine, and men that self-reflexively rebel against hegemonic masculinity and develop their emotional sensitivity are also—at the individual level—challenging the gender system. Women who have path-breaking careers in male-dominated fields are challenging stereotypes. We've yet to see very many men knocking down the doors to lower paying women's jobs, but we are beginning to see some men move into caretaking roles in their households. And now some girls are demanding to join the Boy Scouts (Melendez 2015). Hopefully they will succeed and overcome the gender discrimination that keeps them out. Young girls now assert that their bodies are tough enough for the activities presumed appropriate only for boys. Millennial women have even joined combat units in the Marines.

Even the most traditionally gendered men and women, very comfortable in their bodies, often feel contradictory longings to sometimes behave in ways that are not typical for their gender. Women who refuse to discipline their bodies into feminine styles are challenging others to see femininity as a social construction. Just as when women first started wearing pants instead of dresses, and were demanding freedom of movement, women today who allow themselves to be bossy and aggressive challenge the gender structure when they deviate from stereotypical presentations of self and behavioral expectations. Even the *straddlers* in my sample, most of whom had deeply gendered selves, felt contradictions between their selves, the expectations they faced, and the cultural constructs around them. The *true believers* in my sample do not reject gender as an organizing principle or even experience inconsistencies in the gender structure, so it is important to remember that some Millennials fully accept religious ideologies that include gender essentialist beliefs. Still, the more openly we address contradictions, the more we destabilize the gender structure.

An explosion of gender identities and individuals challenging gender norms leads to questioning whether we need gender categories at all. While everyone but those born with intersex traits can be identified at birth as male or female, why should any of us have to conform to gendered expectations imposed on us because of our genitalia? Every time I fly, I wish I had the right to refuse to answer the gender question. Why do they ask me my gender? I am a female and would gladly testify to that for the purposes of identification and security, but what has my gender have to do with my status as a passenger? Should more feminine women get better seats? Do I deserve a window seat because I am assertive and have spent a lifetime breaking gender norms, or does that get me the back of the cabin? *Rebels* are clearly challenging the gender structure, from the ground up, but so are the *innovators* in this sample. And even the *straddlers* sometimes ignore the gender structure when they cannot reconcile the contradictions that exist between individual, interactional, and macro levels of their lives.

INTERACTIONAL EXPECTATIONS: NEW ELASTICITY IN GENDER STEREOTYPES

The stereotypes that drive gender expectations—women nurture, men are better leaders, and so forth—are being eroded on a daily basis. Women are now more likely to graduate college than men (Diprete and Buchmann 2013) and are the higher income earners in 38% of heterosexual marriages (Bureau of Labor Statistics 2015). While the expectation that men be breadwinners has not disappeared, the presumption that married women do not have to work for a living is, as the sample in this book has shown, a fading, if not dead, expectation. Jacobs and Gerson (2005) show that the expectations about which parent should compromise their career for childcare is far more complex than in the past, with income-earning potential considered along with gender stereotypes about nurturing. The fact that same-sex marriage is legal in the United States and many, but certainly not all, countries and children in these countries can have married parents of the same sex challenges the taken-for-granted belief that children need male and female parental figures. Such a change has major implications for our ideas about gender. All of these changes destabilize the gender structure, creating crises tendencies.

Changes are happening around the globe, with governments endorsing policies and programs to change gender expectations, to support women's equality. Sweden has moved quite deliberately to challenge stereotypes. In one government-sponsored program, Swedish elementary schools are to avoid using gendered pronouns entirely (Hebblethwaite 2011). The Swedes have also created a new non-gendered pronoun, "hen."[5] In Zambia (Evans 2015) the government has instituted "gender sensitization" curriculum in the schools to explicitly change stereotypes about women, to help students see girls as equal to boys. In Italy as well, gender equity temporarily entered the public school curriculum (Kirchgaessner 2015) even if it was highly contested, and then defeated by the Vatican (Abatecola 2015). In the United States, the disparity of women and men majoring in science, technology, and math, and the resultant lack of gender diversity among faculty in universities, has been identified as a national crises. To change this, the National Science Foundation awarded millions of dollars in ADVANCE grants for gender transformation projects on American university campuses.[6] These projects address many levels of the gender structure but include a focus on changing the cognitive bias women students and faculty face from their peers and superiors (Bilimoria and Liang 2012; Risman and Adkins 2014). These grants also sometimes attempt to change the material aspect of the interactional level of analysis by supporting female hires to change the sex ratio within science departments.

Technology companies are realizing the need to hire more women and people of color, because diverse workforces have positive benefits for the bottom line (Herring 2009). Some companies are hiring consultants to design workplace interventions to lessen the consequences of cognitive bias for their female employees (an example is the Voice & Influence Program at the Clayman Institute for Gender Research at Stanford University).[7] Public pressure has even led some big box stores, Target, for example, to stop identifying toys, or toy aisles, by sex. They've started marketing toys to children instead of specifically to boys or girls. Gillam and Wooden (2008) analyzed masculinity in Disney/Pixar films and argue that most of the modern male characters start out insensitive "alpha" men but over the film the flaws of traditional masculinity, loneliness and vulnerability to emasculation, become clear, and the characters ultimately accept a more sensitive "feminine" version of themselves. Perhaps these films are baby steps toward promoting a new kind of masculinity. Of course, change is slow and comes in fits and starts. In 2016, America elected a man that embodies traditional masculinity who is proud of never changing diapers and judges women by their body parts. But then again, backlash always seems to follow progress toward equality, and perhaps this electoral acceptance of Trump's misogyny is at least partly a kind of political backlash to feminism.

Traditional gender expectations have hardly disappeared. Overall, toys are now more gendered than ever before in history (Sweet 2014). On Disney's website, all toys are either for boys and girls, and none for both (Auster and Mansbach, 2012). Cohen (2013) has analyzed the portrayal of women and men in Disney cartoons and finds the sexual dimorphism (the size difference between men and women) so exaggerated as to be ridiculous. He argues that the presentation of women as tiny supports a belief in male dominance and female fragility.[8] Similarly, the existence of Boys and Girls Scouts as different organization shows that de jure segregation remains quite legal by sex long after it has been legally forbidden by race. The very existence of all-male fraternities and all-female sororities shows how deeply gendered expectations are embedded in our consciousness and our society. Even in congregations with female clergy, churches often still have sisterhoods and brotherhoods with sex-segregated tasks such as the women baking holiday treats and the men keeping the grounds. All of these contradictory expectations now coexist. How ironic is it for a female rabbi to lead a congregation where the sisterhood is still expected to bake cookies. Target sells toys to children, but many parents only buy dolls for girls. Girls love to camp but can't join the Boy Scouts to do so. Contemporary expectations are in flux, creating ever more moments with crises tendencies.

MACRO LEVEL: BIG IDEAS AND ORGANIZATIONAL STRUCTURE MATTER

Crises tendencies around changing expectations do not exist in a vacuum. There are also contradictions in how society is organized, and the worldviews and beliefs that legitimate our everyday lives. There has been much success in legal systems throughout Western democracies to remedy gender discrimination in formal rules and regulations in the United States. Hiring notices no longer indicate whether the company desires a man or a woman. Divorce laws are gender neutral. Women and men compete for spaces in graduate school and career opportunities. And yet, divorced women with children are likely to be less wealthy than their ex-husbands (Jenkins 2008). Women still face barriers in male-dominated fields, and occupations are still gender segregated. Formal rules do not end sexism, but they are a start.

The Clayman Center at Stanford University has created a series of videotapes for the public (http://gender.stanford.edu/rrwvideobook) that highlights why we need to redesign workplaces to further actual material change in the rules and procedures in government and business. These videos illustrate why traditional organizational designs don't work anymore: the intended employee pool of male breadwinners with domestic wives exists no longer, but the workplace policies are still designed for them. Any workplace that requires eight or more hours a day and 50 weeks a year presumes the worker has no other moral or practical responsibilities, no caretaking work for anyone at all. When workers do have caretaking responsibilities beyond the workplace, we see a crisis tendency ready to ignite into flames. Most Millennials, and certainly those in this research, have yet to face the conflict between employment and caretaking. Most of them have not yet had children, aging parents, or even very sick friends who need their time and attention. Nor have most of the women yet faced cognitive bias in male-dominated workplaces or in leadership roles. What makes the videos produced by the Clayman Center powerful is that these videotapes are designed for the people who run today's technology companies, for business men and women. Hopefully, these technology leaders will realize that change is coming and be ahead of the curve.

Some religious denominations also want to be in front of social change. The more liberal denominations of historically patriarchal religions, Judaism and Christianity, now routinely ordain women clergy. By 2018, we take this for granted, but given the historical power of patriarchy in beliefs about God, this is really a significant step forward toward gender equality in the 20th century. In my childhood, women's primary role in congregations was to serve pastries at the "Oneg Shabbat," the reception following a Sabbath service. Women were never allowed to lead a congregation, nor were we permitted to read from the Torah. Recently, I heard a young child raised in a congregation with only female rabbis ask her parents if men can be rabbis. What a new world that is from the history of Judaism. And yet, of course, only liberal denominations worldwide endorse female leadership. As in business and government, change is uneven.

One sphere where feminism has seemingly failed miserably, despite very hard work by many activists, is to lessen the commodification of women's bodies. On this cultural domain feminists have made little progress. We have increasing numbers of women in leadership positions, and increasingly egalitarian attitudes and yet, the market for women's bodies remains strong. In fact, commercialization appears to be increasing, encompassing ever younger girls (Levin and Kilbourne 2008). Perhaps the sexual objectification of women is a backlash to the increasing power of women (Faludi 2000). One faint glimmer of hope is that very ubiquitous commercialization of female bodies has lessened the taboo of nudity, and thus its profitability. Recently Playboy has decided to stop publishing nude bodies, and in 2015 the nude calendar published by Pirelli has become obsolete, and instead of pin-ups they are publishing "sheroes," highlighting important women such as musician Yoko Ono and author Fran Lebowitz. Nudity simply isn't profitable with so much hardcore pornography available for free at the tap of a finger. The contradiction between women's increasing (if not fast enough) political leadership and the market for commodified female bodies is striking. But bodies are now controversial not only because of commodification of women but also by virtue of the bathroom wars.

We have seen a public battle over access to bathrooms that has resulted in 2016 in cross-filed lawsuits between the US government under President Obama and the state of North Carolina. This is manifestation of a cultural divide in our worldviews, the ideological justifications for our social institutions. In 2015, a law was passed in North Carolina, HB2,[9] requiring people to use bathrooms that matched their birth certificates, even if at odds with their gender identities. Mississippi followed with a similar new law. As of this writing in 2017, the State of Texas is threatening to enact such a law as well. Another lawsuit was filed in 2016 by parents in Illinois to protest new regulations promulgated by the Obama administration that allowed schoolchildren to use bathrooms and locker rooms that match their gender, even if different from the sex on their birth certificate. The former governor of North Carolina, Pat McCrory, who started these bathroom wars was voted out of office, replaced in 2017 by the state's form attorney general, Roy Cooper, who fought the bathroom bill and repealed at least most of it within a few months after the election. Why these laws now? And of course, in 2017, we saw the Trump administration retreat from protecting the civil rights of transgender and gender non-conforming people. Is this really only about what bathrooms transgender people use? Not at all. This is the perfect storm of a crisis tendency at the cultural level of the macro dimension gender structure. What is at stake is whether the government can enforce the gender structure on each of us, require that we follow the norms to act, dress, and identify with the sex we were assigned at birth. Why must female-bodied people look and act like girls? The underlying issue at stake is how could we continue to have a society where women earn far less than men if we didn't construct dramatic difference between the sexes? If we accept that gender and sex identified at birth are not necessarily the same, the gender structure foundation is cracked for good.

The war about bathrooms is a battle about enforcing the gender structure, with its binary sex categories. For conservatives this is a war worth waging because they know that requiring sex difference and sex segregation is necessary to justify gender itself, and women's place in society subordinate to men. As sociologists have long argued (Lorber 1994; Padavic and Reskin 2002), an important reason for dividing the work of men and women, in the labor force and in families, is to ensure that the sexes are believed to be different enough to justify male privilege. When conservatives, like former Governor McCrory of North Carolina, talk about protecting "women and children" he is infantilizing women into a category collapsed with children instead of treating them like adults, as adult as men. Sex segregation, including in bathrooms, is at least partly sexism masquerading as chivalry. When we debate men and women's bathrooms, what we are really talking about is that outer area where we wash our hands, with those who have (or are presumed to have) similar body plumbing. Most stalls, after all, are already designed for just one of us at a time to protect our privacy. If each gender needs its own washrooms, we need more than two because in today's world, we no longer have just two genders. In the past there were only men and women, or at least everyone else was stigmatized enough to stay out of the public eye. But now the gender structure is being challenged, and people with a variety of gender identities have come out of the closest. If we acknowledge that gender is not a binary, then how can we have two and only two kinds of bathrooms? Think of the cost to business and government of constructing bathrooms for men, women, transmen, transwomen, genderqueer, agender, and whatever other identities bloom in the future. Who can afford bathrooms for them all? But then again, the war about bathrooms is really a battle to enforce the gender structure and force us all to remain in our gendered places.

This war on bathrooms is really a moment in history, an open controversy about whether politicians and governments can enforce the gender binary, and therefore the gender structure itself. President Trump proudly promises to turn the clock back to a time when America was great for white men, when women knew their place, and other categories remained hidden in their closets. Can he succeed? I hope not. Feminist and gender-inclusive social movements seem to be swelling in size both on the streets and on the Internet since his election. A debate about bathrooms, and gender, destabilizes the status quo but does not determine what comes next. Whether the cultural direction continues toward gender equality depends, at least partly, on the effectiveness of feminist and gender-inclusive social movements. Where are they now, and are they working in coalition or not?

GENDER-INCLUSIVE AND FEMINIST SOCIAL MOVEMENTS TODAY

While there may has been little high-profile, face-to-face feminist social movement organizing in this century, there have been many branches of feminism moving forward in the 21st century. Queer politics is alive and well, diversifying from a focus on the deconstruction of categories to the celebration of an explosion of new gender categories (Gamson 1995; Steele 2011). Third-wave feminism is alive and well online (Crossley 2015). If all some Millennials do is share posts online, we could hardly call that a social movement. But often Crossley tells us that cyber-feminism goes hand-in-hand with actual protests.[10] Milkman (2017) illustrates how campus activism against sexual violence started locally but became a national movement by organizing online, eventually changing national policy, at least under the Obama administration, although those changes have recently been revoked by Betsy Devos in the Trump administration. In the aftermath of the 2016 election, thousands of feminists across age, race, and geography joined together in FaceBook (FB) feminism, in groups like Pantsuit Nation and Nasty Women, and created the largest marches in history, not only in Washington, DC, but all over America, in small and big cities, and even across the world. Cyber-feminism became an effective tool to organize a face-to-face protest. FB feminism becomes a real social movement when it is used to organize a mass protest. Still, online feminism is only effective at changing people's minds if we talk to others different from ourselves, but the growing political polarization in America makes that unlikely. The growing polarization of America is perhaps best exemplified by juxtaposing queer politics to the right tilt of American politics in 2018.

Queer theory, and politics based on it, originally posited that sex and gender identity boundaries were socially constructed and thus should be deconstructed. Gamson (1995) identified a paradox built into queer politics: a movement whose goal is to destabilize, deconstruct, and blur categories required identity categories to mobilize members to the cause. But this hasn't slowed the growth and vitality of queer politics. Instead, this paradox has been solved by a celebration of the multiplicity of gender and sexual identities that can coexist under the category of "queer." We have increased numbers of categories and fluidity between them, and the multiplicity of identities have bonded in coalition to support the queering of America. Scholar activists and bloggers (e.g., Costello, http://trans-fusion.blogspot.com/) regularly demand rights for those beyond the binary, whether genderqueer, intersex, transgender, or any combination thereof. In an essay in one of my other books, Dozier (2015) writes about being a "guy mom," a transgender man who identifies as his children's mother and considers this a contribution to queering parenthood. People with complex queer identities are now part of a queer movement as the fight for equal rights for gays and lesbians had expanded to a movement for LGBTQI (lesbian, gay, bisexual, transgender, queer, and intersex) and sometimes A for (agender, asexual, or ally). Whether more and fluid categories are steps en route to the deconstruction of categories remains an open question.

Millennials' focus on individual authenticity, emphasizing personal freedom to choose identity, pushing the queer politics demand for new choices in pronouns due to the increasing number of gender categories. Since most of these demands have successfully gone public after the interviews for this book were complete, I don't use such pronouns to describe my respondents because they were not doing so when we interviewed them. But I am quite sure many of the *rebels* we interviewed, some of whom were considering new pronouns, have by now taken the leap. I know that at least two have done so. Individuals who choose to go by *ze* and *zir* or a singular *they* shake up the binary logic that sex category can only be a dichotomy, with males and females. In that way they hope to change interactional expectations, and therefore crack the foundation of the gender binary. For some this is a deliberately political act, for others, a route to personal authenticity and for some both. But by opting out of categories that feel constraining, these *rebels* do not challenge the stereotypes that define the categories. The stereotypes attached to female and male remain intact and just as constraining to those who use them. The new alternative pronouns of linguistic choice birth one more gender category, as a personal option for individuals, but do not challenge what gender categories that already exist mean. New pronouns may ease the pain of gender oppression for those who use them. But whether ze or zir will be treated by others face-to-face as a new gender category or simply whatever gender (man or woman) they appear to others is as an empirical question. Perhaps we will now have three gender stereotypes to attach to people, he, she, and singular they/ze.

Are those Millennials who use new pronouns and reject the identity of male or female social activists in an unstructured queer mobilization from the ground up? Or is a third, between the gender binary identity, one more personal solution to social issues in a neoliberal world where everyone has the responsibility only to and for themselves? Perhaps both are true. This is all so new, there is little research to draw on. But the success of activists who require space for those between the binary can be readily seen in every campus building with all-gender restrooms. The unanswered question is whether new pronoun choice is a political act, a social movement of individual rebellion, or a new category that simply allows liberty for some without threatening the larger meaning or structure of gender itself. Can the gender structure simply adapt to a third category but continue to constrain our identities, interactions, and social institutions? Or will a demand to reject the binary destabilize gender itself? Only time will tell.

Whether the transgender rights movement is part of queer politics is unclear, although transgender activists are clearly in the coalition with genderqueer Millennials to fight for all gender bathrooms and the right to use their bathroom of choice. In my very small and totally unrepresentative sample of transgender Millennials, some were *rebels*, fully aligned with queer politics who wanted the freedom to live between a gender binary. Others fully supported a gender binary and just wanted to be on the other side of the divide. Still, the right to live openly as the gender of identity is a fight that has finally come out of the closet and is winning public acceptance, at least in more liberal pockets of America. Universities are beginning to offer gender-affirmation surgery in their health packages. The Obama administration issued executive orders supporting the rights of transgender youth to equal opportunity in educational settings. Acceptance of gender freedoms is hotly debated. Some have argued that conservative backlash to the protections offered by the Obama administration helped elect Donald Trump to the presidency. President Trump has retracted the executive orders that provide civil rights for transgender people. What the government cannot do with a flick of the pen is turn back the cultural acceptance and the increasing acceptance by some of the public that allows transgender people to live as they identify, at home, at work, and in their schools (Meadow 2012; also see Schilt 2011). There are now progressive parents that allow even their young children to live as the gender of their identity (Meadow 2012). Clearly the freedom to identify as genderqueer, or between the binary, or to cross the binary as transgender has made progress in the 21st century.

While feminists of all stripes generally support a gender-inclusive world, some feminists have critiqued the individualism behind the social movements focused primarily on gender identities. Nancy Fraser (2015) argues that today's third-wave activists embrace of free choice rhetoric helps show how the personal is political, but the strong focus on identity also sometimes clouds a concern with stratification and inequality. Sheila Jeffreys (2014) critiques the underlying presumptions of transgender politics. Jeffreys argues there is a theoretical conflict between social constructionist feminism and transgender activism. She notes that many feminist writers, myself included (Lorber 1994; Martin 2004; Risman 2004), conceptualize gender as a socially constructed stratification system that disadvantages women as a class. For this reason, feminists seek to overturn gender as a stratification system. Jeffrey argues that at least some transgender activists assume gender—at least their own—is essentialist, built into their very bodies. At the individual level, it clearly cannot to be denied. Jeffreys argues that the gender boxes that feminists have been trying to escape seem to be those (at least some) transgender women like Caitlin Jenner desire to decorate and inhabit for themselves. Transgender activists consider Jeffreys, a self-identified lesbian feminist, a "terf" or "trans-exclusionary radical feminist" and protest her at every opportunity. This firestorm of conflict with practical implications remains simmering today, and sometimes bursts into transphobic flames. For example, Jeffreys argues that transwomen are not "really" women, and so she wants them excluded from female-only spaces such as domestic violence centers and jails. This is, of course, the very definition of transphobic. Transgender activists protest such transphobia, and everyone should wonder why Jeffrys believes she has the right to impose a gender identity on anyone else. Few academic feminist writers agree with Jeffreys, and I certainly do not. Gender identity, however it is formed, is deeply held and can only be determined by the individual him-, her-, their- or their self. The central issue Jeffrey raises remains, however. Does social constructionism necessarily conflict with transgender activists claim to an essentialist gendered identity? This is an intelligible question only if we consider what is socially constructed less than real and therefore less essentially an aspect of ourselves. As Wade has argued (2013), science has moved beyond an either/or version of nature/nurture as neither exists without the other. A basic principle of sociology (called the Thomas Theorem) is that just because something is socially constructed does not make it any less real in its consequences. I return at the end of the chapter to this conflict between social constructionism and essentialist beliefs about the self to suggest a way beyond this volatile conflict in my admittedly utopian social movement strategy offered in conclusion.

Transgender activists, queer theorists, and feminists of every wave do a great deal of their mobilizing on the Internet in the 21st century. Feminist bloggers and feminist sites seem ubiquitous on Facebook, Twitter, Instagram, and everywhere else. Internet feminism has a far wider scope, creating communities among those far apart, but also rallying those on campus to show up for actual events. Crossley (2015) argues that Facebook feminism is an important facet of Millennials' social movement activism. Online feminism is incredibly diverse. There are sites for feminists of color (e.g., blackfeminists.blogspot.com; www.latinafeminism.com), many of which critique a feminism that focuses mostly on white women's issues. Other sites, such as Bitchmedia, are truly multicultural. Strong online communities may empower feminists of this generation, and, increasingly, older ones as well, to raise their issues with those who disagree, friends, families, and others. It may be more likely for activists to raise others' consciousness with Internet dialogue than at rallies. And then again, if online communities only involve others like ourselves, we simply amplify an echo chamber. Perhaps online communities are also a refuge from the pain of working and living near people whose values are antithetical to one's own, and so these communities act as shelters and sources of regeneration. Many of the *rebels* and *innovators* in this research mention their online reading and communities as places of learning and discovery about gender, and now so too do their elders as they use the Internet to respond to the fear of a misogynist president.

The 21st century has also seen a revival of professional-class feminism, with calls for women to "lean in" (Sandberg 2013) and for social policy to build an "infrastructure of care" (Slaughter 2015). This is a renewed attempt to jump-start a more traditional version of feminism for professional-class women who want equal access to leadership roles in business and government. Facebook executive Sheryl Sandberg (2013) has self-consciously tried to create 21st-century consciousness-raising groups where women encourage each other to "lean in" to their jobs, to take their rightful place in the running of corporations. Sandberg's acknowledges that workplaces are not family friendly and advises women to take control of their personal lives by picking an equal partner. She counsels women to actively manage cognitive bias and stereotypes. Her advice sounds as individualist, as neoliberal, as any version of millennial identity feminism. Sandberg suggests that women often undercut themselves by presuming that they cannot have both workplace success and motherhood and so do not give their careers a chance to flourish. She cites research (e.g., Elsesser and Lever 2011) that suggests women begin to downsize their careers because they sense that powerful women are disliked by others, and they have internalized the need to please. She argues that women themselves need to close the "leadership ambition gap" (p. 12). The advice to "lean in" is particularly poignant in the anecdotes Sandberg shares about young women so terrified about how they were going to balance their work and their families that they jump onto a self-inflicted mommy track even before they have a serious boyfriend. She argues that not much has changed with societal expectations of parenthood. When a man has a baby everyone congratulates him. When a woman has a baby everyone asks her what she is going to do about her work. Thus, the expectations and options are still far different for mothers and fathers. Sandberg argues that women should keep their eyes on the prize, and see their careers as a long-term investment, even if they occasionally have to take a short detour. There is an implicit argument within Sandberg's book about female leadership: with women at the top, attention to gender bias, and attention to work-family conflicts will come. That, of course, is an empirical question, as not all women are feminists and many men are. What makes this book different is the "lean in" communities that Sandberg is organizing; groups of women talking about gender in their lives. They may be very privileged women, who have choices most others can only dream about, but the successful instigation of new consciousness-raising groups is a remarkable feat. Whether they help women navigate the road to success is an open question. And whether more women in high places helps the rest of us is even more of an unknown.

At about the same time Sandberg was urging women to lean in, Marie Anne Slaughter wrote a 2012 *Atlantic* article titled "Why Women Still Can't Have It All." She now regrets the title and that the article focused on women rather than caregivers. In the book that grew from that article, Slaughter (2015) focuses on the systematic ways that workplaces privilege people who are not caretakers, and make it impossible for anyone to consistently, throughout the entire life course, commit themselves to "leaning in" at work if they have responsibilities for anyone other than one's self. Almost everyone with responsibilities to take care of another human being at some time needs to "lean out," especially when the best laid plans are toppled by a chronically ill child, a chronically ill elderly parent, or even the unexpected death of a partner. Slaughter argues that gender inequality exists not because women don't lean in, but because workplaces and career structures are designed for people (read men) who leave the important work of caring for other people to unemployed or less career committed partners (read wives). Slaughter makes a powerful, and very sociological, argument that to move forward we must redesign our whole society, to make workplaces organized so that caretakers can succeed within them, and to insist that males take their rightful place in society as equal caretakers. While Slaughter never uses the language of the gender structure, she is arguing that we must begin change at the interactional and macro levels, and not with the individual. One year after the unexpected death of her husband, Sheryl Sandberg wrote a blog on Mother's Day which acknowledged Slaughter's arguments that we need to "re-think our public and corporate workforce policies" to broaden our understanding of how families really operate.[11] Sandberg now better understands the work-family conflict. The fight between whether women need to "lean in" or we need an infrastructure of care is illusory. We need both. This recognition of the complexity of inequality is not new. Women's movements have always been multifaceted.

Walby's (2011) book *The Future of Feminism* illustrates that women's movements have never been single issue. According to Walby, feminism has never been stronger, at least in the European Union. Feminism is now diffuse, built into the missions of many NGO missions, and housed in government agencies. Feminist ideas have moved from margin to center in many places. Sweden has announced it will have a feminist foreign policy. Margot Wallstrom, Sweden's top diplomat in 2017, suggests that means asking these questions: Do women have equal rights? Are women at the decision-making table? And, are resources equitably distributed to women.[12] Feminists are not interested in gender alone, however. Feminists now collaborate with other social movements for equality, with activists concerned with economic and racial progress. Walby reminds us that feminism is vital and has made much progress in fighting for women's equality, and for changing stratification structures that include but are not limited to gender. First-wave feminists helped secure women's rights to access the public sphere. Second-wave feminism discovered that the personal was political. The phrase coined by Hillary Rodham Clinton that "women's rights are human rights" shows the progress of feminism in the 20th century. The third wave of feminism was built on the intersection with other social movements at home and across the world and has successfully complicated the movement, consciously focusing on intersecting gender with race, class, sexualities, and national inequalities. Walby hopes that the next push within feminism will be to shape stronger and more caring social democratic politics. At the current moment, at the start of 2018, with conservative parties gaining strength across Europe, I hope the progressive social democracies remain strong so that feminism can remain mainstreamed within them. And yet, in my utopian dreams I have even higher hopes for the fourth wave of feminism.

So are social movements, second-wave feminists, queer politics, transgender rights, third-wave feminists, women of color feminism, professional-class feminism in conflict with one another? Are their priorities so different as to clash? I think not. One implication of conceptualizing gender as a social structure is that we can understand social movements not as either/or but instead as a both/and. There is no reason to argue about whether gender is internalized into the self or a product of expectations of others. It is both. It is not useful to argue whether women should lean in or organizations must change to accommodate people who are caretakers as well as workers. Both must happen. It is clear that gender inequality works differently for poor and rich women, for white and non-white women, for Americans and for Europeans. Our analyses must be both universal but also contextualized. We must change culture and social policy. Ideological change is necessary before citizens will vote for social policies that benefit caretakers who also work for pay. It isn't attitudes that must change or policies. It is both. Is there an inherent conflict between the feminist social constructionist critique of gender stereotypes and some transgender activists' belief in essentialist gender identities? Such a conflict only exists if you presume that just because something is socially constructed it is not real. Sociologists argue just the opposite, race is socially constructed and a powerful stratification system in America. So too for gender. Our task remains, however, to try to understand how change happens, when it happens, and when it does not. We cannot successfully dismantle the gender structure without understanding where leverage exists to make change.

At any given moment, for any given question, empirical research can help identify proximate and contextual causal mechanisms. What variables in any setting are most responsible for what happens next? If women want to be top management, in a particular context, are they held back more because they face strong cognitive bias, or does the requirement for 70 hours a week face-time disadvantage caretakers so completely that they leave before they face bias? By conceptualizing gender as a social structure, we can try to disentangle what particular aspects of gender at each level of analysis are most consequential in a specific context without pretending that other factors are not also involved. Empirical evidence is always place based and local, yet it remains necessary to look for empirical evidence with implications that may apply to similar contexts. What follows is some research findings that help identify possible causal mechanisms that may successfully trigger social change, and also findings that suggest social change paths unlikely to be fruitful. My vision is that changing one part of the structure will cause a cascade, like dominoes, throughout, and perhaps even crack the foundation to its core.

FACTORS THAT MAY HELP CRACK THE GENDER STRUCTURE

Few research projects try to sort out whether change, or for that matter, the status quo, can be attributed to individual, interactional, or macro-level explanations. Most research focuses only on one level and so cannot really address complexity of the gender structure. But for research to help us identify how to promote change, we need to think more causally across levels of analysis, to identify mechanisms that are at work in a specific context. Here I highlight research projects, both qualitative and quantitative, that help disentangle what explains change across levels of analysis. This research covers a variety of topics: whether internalized gendered selves drive sex segregation in the labor force, sexual assault on campus, the conditions under which governmental programs can be effective at promoting gender equality, and how anti-LGBT social movements successfully went offshore, taking their homophobia to other countries. I use these studies to identify some proximate causal explanations for change in feminist social directions and return to these mechanisms in the final section where I suggest a future for feminist activism.

An important question to solve is why we have such a sex-segregated labor force even though so many women go to college. The gender revolution has been very successful in offering women an equal chance for an education. In fact, women are now the winners of the educational sweepstakes, at least as measured by who gets college degrees. Unfortunately, college majors and subsequent occupational sex segregation has remained powerful and, with it, economic inequality between the sexes. Why do we see such sex segregation across majors, and then consequently in the labor force? Cech (2013) analyzed longitudinal data from the Future Plans Study on four college campuses in the Northeast corridor of the United States to test whether individual's beliefs about their own gendered personalities (rating one's emotionality, systematic nature, and people orientation) or their social and political beliefs about gender itself (do they hold feminist ideology) was more predictive of choosing a sex-typed college major. Her research is a test of the power of the cultural aspect of the individual level of analysis, internalized gendered selves, versus students' cultural beliefs at the macro level about feminist ideology as determinants of choosing sex-typed college majors. Do women who see themselves as more feminine choose female-dominated jobs? What about men who see themselves as more feminine, are they more likely to pursue jobs usually held by women? Conversely, are women who see themselves as more masculine more likely to enter male-dominated jobs? The quick answer to these questions is yes. Men and women who rate themselves as more feminine (more emotional, less systematic, and people oriented) as sophomores are more likely to enter careers or graduate school in fields that are female-dominated and stereotypically women's occupations. Similarly, women and men who rate themselves as less feminine (less emotional, more systematic, not so people oriented) as sophomores are more likely to enter male-dominated professions. Are feminists, of either sex, more likely to break gender norms and choose an occupation in which they are the minority? The answer is no for both women and men. Feminist women were not more likely to be scientists. Nor were feminist men more likely to go into nursing. Gendered selves were more predictive of college majors than feminist political beliefs.

Cech argues that the power of internalized gender preferences for college majors reproduces sex segregation in these fields and reinforces the cultural stereotype that, for example, engineering is masculine and nursing is feminine. This research shows the power of gender socialization and the importance gendered selves for life trajectory. In theoretical terms, Cech's research suggests that the individual level of analysis, how we raise our children, remains very important for reproducing gender inequality. Gender socialization has profound effects on the gender structure. Even when political beliefs about gender change, internalized masculinity and femininity continue to influence occupational choices. As long as students are free to choose their own fields of study, and no one would hope otherwise, we cannot fully address occupational segregation until we change the way we raise our boys and girls. But this research goes further; it suggests that the cultural dimension at the individual level of analysis, gendered selves, was more powerful than cultural beliefs at the macro level of political ideology. Feminists were not any more likely to choose nontraditional careers than anyone else. It would be quicker to be able to make social change if we could do so simply by changing hiring practices, but this research suggests we cannot succeed unless we also address gender socialization.

Charles and Bradley (2009) use cross-national data and report similar findings, the importance of gendered selves to occupational sex segregation. They find that educational sex segregation actually increases in the most wealthy, modern postindustrial societies. Using cross-national data from 44 countries, they find that sex-typing of majors is stronger in more economically developed contexts. The most technologically advanced and economically successful societies are those that also most value self-expression and individualism. As long as gender socialization remains strong in these societies, women and men use their freedom to choose gendered careers. This "choice" may be steered by mentors, and hostile classrooms, but by the 21st century, there are also strong peer networks and "women in science" programs on college campuses to encourage women's participation in science, technology, engineering, and math. These programs are yet to be entirely effective, and the answer to why is that gendered selves have the freedom to flourish even when young men and women have the formal freedom to make nontraditional career choices. This research contrasts the power of cultural beliefs internalized at the individual level of analysis with the opportunities opened up at the material level of the gender structure when jobs are no longer formally sex-typed in modern, technologically advanced economies. This research also indicates that we cannot ignore the individual level of analysis if we hope to reduce gender inequality in occupational settings or more broadly to dismantle the gender structure. When young people are raised to be feminine women and masculine men, and then given free choice for college majors and careers, they are free to express their gendered selves and do so. But is this all that's going on? The research on sexual violence on college campuses suggest that women's options are limited by far more than their internalized sense of self.

Nearly one-fifth of American female college students report having been victims of sexual violence (Fisher et al. 2000). Armstrong, Hamilton, and Sweeney (2006) use data from a nine-month ethnographic observation and interviews with women who lived on one floor of a dormitory to show that sexual assault was as much an outcome of processes at the interactional and organizational levels of campus life as about individual's bad choices. While most explanations for sexual violence focus on bad apple men and women who are not careful enough, Armstrong et al. show that other levels of the gender structure are involved. Their analysis points to the importance to look beyond just the individual level of analysis to understand how to make social change. Women and men come to college ready to "party" and expect to do so in gendered ways (Wade 2017). Students also follow gendered scripts that represent the expectations held for them at the cultural dimension of the interactional level of analysis. Peer sexual culture is gendered. The men earned prestige by securing sex from high-status women, while the women earned respect by getting attention from high-status men. Finally, and perhaps most important, at the institutional material level of analysis, the university rules pushed parties off campus because they enforced alcohol restrictions in dormitories At the same time, the "Greek" system institutionalized gender-specific organizational policies. The fraternity system allows men the freedom to have alcohol in their houses, but the Panhellenic system that regulates women's residences does not. Fraternity houses then become the place for parties, and the men control the events with little university oversight. The men control the material space where the social scene operates. They stage parties with themes that subordinate women such as "Pimps and Hos, Victoria Secret and Playboy Mansion" (p. 489). The men call the shots. They invite women and control the physical space and the alcohol. Armstrong et al. write, "socialization processes influenced gendered selves, while cultural expectations reproduce gender inequality in interaction. At the institutional level, organizational practices, rules, resource distributions and ideologies reproduce gender inequality" (p. 485). They suggest that university policies that try to end campus assault simply by teaching women to "be careful" are bound to fail, because the interactional expectations and organizational design are powerful engines that create a context that promotes violence against women. To reduce such violence effectively, we need to address policies beyond retraining individuals and focus on the interactional and institutional levels of analysis concurrently. If I were designing such a policy, I'd start by changing the venue of the parties, to spaces controlled by women. In addition, perhaps create "lean in" style consciousness-raising groups designed to change sexual scripts and expectations around consent for erotic activity. From this research, we see that even though gender socialization matters, so does the interactional peer cultures and the material dimensions of institutional organizational design.

Another kind of research suggests that we are unlikely to successfully change gender beliefs about the self at the individual level unless the actual division of labor in the public sphere at the macro level of workplace organization changes as well (Evans 2015). The country of Zambia undertook an ambitious "gender sensitization program" that Evans documents with ethnography, life history interviews, and group conversations with over 200 Zambian men and women. The goal of this social change intervention, shared by NGOs and local government, was both to decrease domestic violence and increase women's representation in electoral politics. A gender sensitization curriculum was institutionalized into secondary schools for well over a decade. Students were taught about the social construction of gender and how some laws and customs could discriminate against women. All young teens were taught the difference between" sex roles" and "gender roles," the former defined as biological and the latter as social constructions. There were also egalitarian gender messages on the radio and television. This intervention was widespread; only 6 of 200 of the participants had not heard of this attempt at social change.

To understand the efficacy of the curriculum and the public service announcements, Evans visited gender sensitization classes at three schools for over three months. Does teaching about gender this way change minds? Do young women see themselves as having more rights and freedoms after taking these classes and hearing these state-sponsored messages? Evans finds that gender sensitization alone provides information but rarely changes women's beliefs about themselves. When gender sensitization does make a difference is when it is paired with actual organizational changes in the gender division of labor, especially when adult women are seen as competent in male-dominated work settings before messages about equality between the sexes are broadcast. That is, it is only when some women have already broken into male-dominated jobs that educational messages actually changed teenagers beliefs about their own possibilities. Without changing division of labor in local settings, the gender equality messages were resisted as a "northern imposition." Feminist messages inconsistent with personal observations were rejected. Evans concludes, "endorsement of egalitarian discourses generally appears contingent upon exposure to flexibility in gender divisions of labor" (p. 18).

Theoretically, the take-home message from this research on Zambia is that an attempt to change cultural beliefs about gendered selves at the individual level and even changing political cultural ideologies at the macro level fail in isolation from actual material changes in the macro organizational material structures that matter, in this case, the workplace. Changing the material aspect of the social institutions, reducing sex segregation in the labor force, seems a necessary precursor for effectively changing girl's beliefs about their opportunities, at least in this research in Zambia. This study highlights the centrality of the material organization of the macro level of the economy. The implication is that to make effective social change, we cannot start by only changing worldviews, but must instead also change reality simultaneously, if not before. In this research, change in the gendered division of labor had to precede educational curriculum about gender equality to shift cultural ideas about gendered selves and interactional expectations. How to make change remains elusive if women have to desire to break into gender-segregated spaces while they need to be in such spaces before feminist messages are successful. The gender structure is self-reinforcing, and it also changes continuously.

Another example of empirical evidence that helps to disentangle how change can happen in the gender structure is about a homophobic social movement that has at least mostly failed in America, but appears to be successfully reinventing itself around the world, that is the social movement to change gay people's sexual orientation. Robinson and Spivey (2007) studied the politics of the ex-gay movement, a loose network of religious, pseudo-scientific therapeutic and political organizations that advocates re-educating homosexuals into heterosexuality. They analyzed texts produced by these movement actors and evaluated their acceptance by target audiences by levels of the gender structure. At the individual level, the texts frame mothers as responsible for causing gender deficits in their sons, which are represented as the root cause of homosexuality. They define gender nonconformity as an individual personality disorder that is a precursor of homosexuality and advocate treating it as a disease. But this movement isn't only about individual "illness," it also advocates using social interaction and expectations to change behavior. They argue that appropriate resocialization can "heal" men of homosexuality. Ironically, these therapies depend on accepting the performative character of gender. Their goal is to teach homosexual men to "do masculinity" to recover heterosexual desire. Men are taught to mimic stereotypical masculine behavioral styles, to shun everything feminine, and to marry and become fathers. Without intention, these now reputed therapies presume the social construction of sexuality and its relationship to gender; they presume teaching masculinity will create heterosexuality. Several of the gay men and transwomen in the research reported in this book were sent to such therapies, where they were taught to be more masculine. They all still report great pain from the experience.

At the macro level of analysis, these organizations promote books for parents in order to create anti-gay cultural worldviews. These social movement actors also try to create social policy at the institutional level to support regulations that are "pro-family," which they define as anti-feminist, anti-gay, heterosexual families. While this movement seemed to be gaining influence decades ago, with the rise of the Promise Keepers, a male Christianity promoting group, they have clearly lost the battle to control the culture in contemporary American society. This movement appears to have failed in "blue" states and the cities of America, but who knows about the future, as proponents are now in the executive office. Vice President Pence was once a supporter, and may still be, and certainly some of the voters who supported him are.

But anti-gay "Christians" have not disappeared. The movement has moved offshore establishing a worldwide network of anti-gay, conservative, "Christian" institutions trying to influence the global culture. Robinson and Spivey's (2007) analysis shows this social movement at least partially succeeded by attending to every level of the gender structure—individual, interactional, and macro concurrently. Its influence is still felt elsewhere around the world (Robinson and Spivey 2015). What can we learn from the successes of an anti-gay social movement? This research suggests that a powerful social movement needs to address the individual level of analysis, the internalization of gender, the interactional level of social scripts enforced by friends and family, and also the macro level with attempts to change laws and cultural beliefs at the same time. Perhaps feminists can learn strategy from the sophistication of this homophobic social movement. We feminists need to attack every level of the gender structure and not argue about which one matters most.

We clearly need more research like these studies that focus on comparing the causal power of different aspects of the gender structure. But there are lessons here: although sociologists have focused much research on the importance of "doing gender" at the interactional level, we must not short change the power of gender socialization. We need to raise our children without boxing them into gender stereotypes. Their occupational choices depend on it as do their future incomes. But then again, we cannot only focus on gender socialization because interactional scripts matter as well. And the Zambian gender sensitization programs suggest that without material change at the level of workplaces, school-based curriculums will not be successful at changing gendered cultural beliefs or beliefs about the self. A social movement must attend to all three levels of analysis; the anti-gay movement still promoting homophobia overseas illustrates this well. The lesson is that we must have a both/and strategy. Social movements can try to intervene to change the gender structure, and the opportunity to do so occurs most often when one aspect of the gender structure is out of synch with another. In this next section and concluding section, I argue that we should leverage such discrepancies to destabilize the gender structure entirely, to move toward a post-gender society.

A BOLD CALL FOR A SOCIAL MOVEMENT TO DISMANTLE THE GENDER STRUCTURE

I concluded an earlier book published at the end of the 20th century (Risman, 1998) with the argument that

> we have come as far as we can with incremental change. To get to the next stage, to move fully toward justice for women and men, we must dare a moment of gender vertigo. My hope is that when the spinning ends, we will be in a post-gendered society that is one step closer to a just world. (p. 162)

At the time, I could have never imagined that I would be predicting just what was about to happen in the 21st century: the development of genderqueer identities, young people who declare they are neither men nor women but between or beyond a binary. People without a gender do indeed make us dizzy. For many, transgender women and men who are openly living the gender of their identity, and not their ascribed sex, are also challenging previous notions of sex and gender consistency and making some of the rest of the country dizzy. The world is indeed at a moment of *Gender Vertigo* (Risman 1998). Even *National Geographic* has a full issue devoted to gender because they noticed that in 2017 beliefs about gender were rapidly shifting.[13]

I conclude with my admittedly utopian dream, a feminist strategy to move us toward a post-gender society. It may seem naïve to envision a world without gender at the moment an openly misogynist anti-feminist man is president of the United States. And yet, without dreams, without vision, we cannot act strategically. If we are ever to move forward to a more just world, we must have effective social movements with clear goals. My own findings in this book have solidified my commitment to a world without gender, where we are truly free from the constraints of the sex we have been ascribed at birth. I share many values with feminists worldwide, but this argument is controversial even among feminists.[14] We must move beyond the first three waves of feminism to a 21st -century feminist movement that rejects gender as a primary organizational category for social life, we must start a movement to overturn gender as a social structure.

The goal of a world beyond gender is not widely shared, even by women's rights activists. In fact, disagreements among those who share a commitment to gender equality are deep and wide. Feminists with essentialist leanings argue that physical experiences of menstruation and (for some) birth and lactation are so materially significant for psychic development that males and females are inherently different. Essentialist feminists believe these different potentialities should be equally valued and rewarded (Laws 1990; Martin 1987; O'Brien 1981). Transgender activists argue that gender identity transcends bodily differences. Others, more symbolically focused, argue that gender is so deeply built into the structures of thought and language that we can never deny it, but must revalue the feminine (Chodorow 1978; Gilligan 1982). Others (e.g., Orloff 2009) argue that gender is so firmly entrenched within personal identities that no democratic process could ever lead to a society that would desire to go beyond gender. That may be so, but we will never know unless we create a conversation about it.

A caveat before I proceed. I cannot envision strategies to move to a society beyond gender for any place where women do not have basic human rights. In that sense, I acknowledge here a modernist view of human societies. Women must first be seen as human beings with political rights before we can envision a post-gender utopia. The utopian vision I offer and particularly the strategies to get there are narrowly path-dependent, applicable only to 21st-century Western democracies (Ferree 2009). Acknowledging my standpoint as scholar in the Global North, I limit my proposals for feminist strategies to societies where women have the technological abilities and legal rights to control their fertility and to participate in the public and political sphere. At this point, that includes the United States, but if a future Supreme Court removes women's right to control our fertility, the possibility of moving beyond gender will be impeded. The current right to control fertility is clearly unequally distributed in every society and more available to privileged women than others. Given the Millennials in this book are all American, the utopian focus for imagining a more just world for Western countries is no more narrow than the research reported here.

My utopian vision builds on the successes of every wave of generations of activists before me. Feminism as a social movement has strategically attacked both material inequality between the sexes and androcentric cultural beliefs. Feminism's most basic goal has always been to reallocate rewards to improve the quality of women's lives, whether or not that changed their position in the social structure (e.g., wages for housewives did not seek to change women's responsibility for homemaking). Affirmative action and recruitment of women into male-dominated jobs has moved beyond increasing the quality of women's lives, as they have traditionally been defined, toward mainstreaming women into societal positions of power and prestige. The feminisms of the 20th century was a precursor to a gender movement, necessary but not sufficient for liberation from gender itself. No explicit feminist political social movement organizations have attacked the use of gender as a cultural category.[15] Indeed, some feminist theorists have argued quite the contrary, that erasing the cultural and institutional practices of gender would be not only be impossible but also unwanted by women as well as men (Shalev 2009; Orloff 2009). I hope my work contributes to a positive post-gender queer alternative future. I hope to persuade those of you who have never considered a post-gender world as a possibility, as well as those now opposed to the concept, by suggesting here that the very existence of gender categories oppresses as it imposes different socialization and interactional expectations on everyone before she or he knows that they can conceptualize the possibility of alternative options.

We have had successful waves of feminism in the past and recent LGBTQ movement successes as well. There are now sufficient cracks in the foundation of our gender structure, more than enough crises tendencies, for me to believe such a movement to dismantle the gender structure is possible, if not plausible. The fourth wave of feminism must remain intersectional as a movement to end oppression. I have argued that the bathroom wars are a symbol of the first battles for the destruction of gender as a social structure. And yet I caution that this movement to eradicate gender must necessarily work for slow metamorphosis, a cacophony of simultaneous strategies at the level of individual, interactional, and institutional levels to undo and dismantle gender (Deutsch 2007; Lorber 2005). A social movement to eradicate gender will have strong opposition—persuasion not coercion is required. This change, eventually a true revolution, may take generations.

My goal here is to jump-start change, to add fuel to the several small fires that continue to push the boundaries of our gender structure. I will not duplicate the old the sameness/difference debate that has divided feminists in the past (Foster 1999). Instead, I follow Walby's transformational (2011) feminist policies and use the both/and model suggested by Collins (1998). Women need not become more like men in contemporary society, nor do we need some version of women's values as in maternalist politics. Rather than androcentrism or gynocentrism, we need a society where both caring work and economic production are equally rewarded, and women, men, and others are equally involved in both. I envision a new society not by integrating women into the male-dominated sectors, nor revaluing what has traditionally been labeled as feminine but rather by banishing the constraints of femininity for females and masculinity for males, by designing social organizations for people without regard of the sex they were ascribed upon birth.

My utopian vision, and my call for a fourth wave of feminism, includes benefits for women, men, and those between the binary, but it is not a blueprint for every needed social justice beyond the inequities around gender. Gender is only one of many dimensions of inequality along which privilege occurs. We must always take into account intersectional domains of inequality (Collins 1990; McCall 2005), and I am fully aware that the utopian vision laid here attacks gender inequality but will not by itself decrease racial or class inequality. This narrow project does not even scratch the surface of the utopian imagination for how to decrease growing income inequality, racial inequality, xenophobia, or how to attack other sources of unearned privilege. Each system of inequality has a different history and therefore different, though related, solutions. We must have a both/and orientation, destabilizing gender while also finding ways to address other axis of inequality. I see this work as one piece of a very complicated puzzle. But each piece of a puzzle matters even if many pieces are necessary to create a more just world.

The traditional goal of feminism has been to eliminate the substantial inequalities between women and men. This is, of course, an important goal but should be an intermediate goal on a route to actual liberation from gender constraints, to a world where gender as a social structure no longer exists. Liberation from gender oppression will only come to be when gender is no longer an important classification category for individuals, no longer a scaffolding for expectations faced during social interaction, no longer a cultural rhetoric supporting inequality, no longer embedded in social organizations. This goal of liberation from gender cannot be deduced from evidence; rather, it is based on moral values.

As my following argument is more normative than scientific, I depend upon queer philosopher scholar activists for the ethical bases of this call to arms. In Miqqi Alicia Gilbert's (2009) article entitled "Defeating Bigenderism" s/he makes a philosophical argument for ending gender as we know it (pronoun used by author on website). As an activist in the transgender community, Gilbert is a regular columnist for *Transgender Tapestry*, the magazine of the International Foundation for Gender Education. Gilbert argues that Butler (1990) was right that throughout history we have needed to preform gender to be intelligible as a person, but it is inaccurate to believe that doing so is logically a necessity for human interaction. S/he calls it "systemic bigenderism" when sex, sex category, and gender are presumed synonymous and imply heteronormativity. S/he argues, as has Lorber before her (1994), that the division of the world into the binary of woman and men is what allows sexism to exist. Gilbert argues that "the banishment of bigenderism and heteronormativity would logically also eliminate homophobia and transphobia" (p. 98). It is the tyranny of systemic bigenderism, according to Gilbert, that allows for the slurs that regularly face those who do not meet gender normativity, such as sissy, tomboy, fag, or tranny. While discussing a variety of possible systems that might follow systematic bigenderism, Gilbert proposes non-genderism, which "entails no binary distinction and no societal valuation making masculine more highly valued than feminine" (p. 107). S/he argues that only non-genderism can reach an ideal that eliminates sexism, heterosexism, homophobia, transphobia, and sexual discrimination. It is interesting to note that in this philosophical treatise, Gilbert cites many feminist sociologists and psychologists. Indeed she uses the work of feminist psychologist Sandra Bem (1993), who envisioned a world beyond androcentrism and gender polarization, a world where the distinction between the sexes no longer organized culture or psyche. Gilbert assures the reader that erotic pleasure does not have to depend on difference by disclosing a life as a committed cross-dresser who enjoys dirty dancing with both sexes, and with others whose genital status are unimportant to her. Gilbert's arguments build on my earlier work, and my arguments now also build upon Gilbert's.

Nicholas (2014) furthers Gilbert's argument in zer book on queer post-gender ethics. Ze (the pronoun used for all human beings in the Nicholas book) argues that bigenderism limits human freedom. Indeed, Nicholas uses similar distinctions between material and cultural aspects of gender as do I, arguing that they are co-constitutive, and even the material realities of our bodies would change without the cultural meaning we now use to construct them. But Nicholas goes beyond the claim that the gender structure creates difference to make an ethical case for why the "transcendence of sexual difference is preferable to other possible corollaries" (p. 51). Nicholas argues for a post-gender society rather than one that simply revalues the feminine. Ze argues everyone ought to be able to be perceived without reference to reified identities and accompanying stereotypes about sexual or gender categories. Only a society without reified gender and sexual identities holds the possibility for individuals to construct themselves freely. Nicholas' proposal for a post-gender ethics includes queer pedagogy and gender-neutral child-rearing. To restate this argument with my theoretical language: Nicholas argues that a queer ethics concerned with the creation of a just society requires intervention at the macro level of ideological ideas, teaching with a queer pedagogy, and also socializing children at the interactional level to think about themselves as children, not as boys and girls, with the hope that a new generation can grow up with individual-level identities not tied to the sex-based material reality of their bodies. Only then will children be free to choose from the wide range of human possibilities and unconstrained by categorical identities. This utopian realism is offered in the spirit of freedom, with the stipulation that it can never be imposed on people who already have investments in their sex/gender identities. And so Nicholas argues that this ideal could allow a multiplicity of behaviors and expressions within it. The difference being, however, that these characteristics lose their sex/gendered significance. . . . The vision of androgynous ethics or queer sociality that I am proposing is not one of sameness to replace difference, but of limitless proliferated differences, united around broad values. (p. 206)

While Nicholas, Gilbert, myself, Lorber, and others have written about the need to end gender as we know it, there has never been a social movement to dismantle gender. This is my call for such a movement, as both an intellectual agenda and a volley in feminist politics. While others have fought for gender equality, and written about a society without gender, I end with a call for a social movement to dismantle gender as a social structure. I envision a society where as philosopher Susan Okin has written, "one's sex would have no more relevance than one's eye color or the length of one's toes" (1989, p. 171).

The philosophers mentioned help provide a framework for imagining a just world beyond gender. But it is social scientific research, my own and others, that provide empirical evidence for efficacious possible strategies. The research reviewed in this chapter that weighs the power of change at the different levels of analysis provides two clear lessons. First, we cannot ignore the power of gender socialization. A goal to move beyond gender at the individual level is a goal for the long haul, including raising children free from gendered stereotypes. Sociologists often worry that focusing on individuals is "blaming the victim" and that a more sociological way forward is to focus only on changing institutions. But the research on college majors both here and cross-nationally suggests we cannot ignore the power of the gender structure to become internalized within us. It is not blaming a victim for admitting the power of internalized oppression, and that is the definition of gender socialization, training people to fit into social roles entirely because of the sex they were identified at birth. Second, the research on gender sensitization programs and the ex-gay social movement suggest that we must have a multidimensional strategy. Trying to change cultural ideas isn't effective without material changes in the division of labor. What we can learn from social movements, even ones we disagree with, is that any movement is stronger with strategies to change individuals, social expectations, cultural worldviews, and material organizational reality. I take both of these lessons into consideration as I suggest a feminist strategy for the 21st century to end gender as a social structure. Following the theoretical framework of this book, I proceed to imagine what must happen at each level of the gender structure, differentiating when appropriate between material and cultural dimensions.

Much conversation and social movement energy today is around gender as an identity, at the individual level of analysis. I have been critical of those whose only focus is here, and at the same time, critical of feminist sociologists who ignore the individual level. A broad social movement needs action by the individuals who feel oppressed, people who push back. Individual action makes sense to Millennials, who were raised in a neoliberal era. Individuals pushing the boundaries, those going beyond gender norms is necessary, although by itself insufficient to effectively make social change. Still, at the least, individuals ought to have the freedom to choose their own identity, to live what they feel are authentic lives. From the research reported in this book, it is clear that this has both material and cultural ramifications. At the cultural level, we now have a smorgasbord of categories, in addition to male/man and female/woman. We need to have a box on surveys for "other" with the possibility of write-in identities, and then eventually we will be able to do a qualitative analyses to clarify which identities are shared widely enough for long enough to become themselves new formal categories. Eventually, this may sort itself out into the categories that remain from one generation to the next with others falling by the wayside. Who knows how many sex or gender categories will we end up with eventually from the ground up? We must be clear when we mean sex (male or female, ascribed at birth or medically constructed) or gender (feminine or masculine), which are often related but not synonymous. No one should be asked their gender in order to fly in an airplane, although security questions might include sex category. We must stop assuming that being female is the same as being feminine or "doing gender" as a woman. We already have more than two sex categories as intersex people should not be pigeon-holed into male or female sex when they are not either. We already have many more than two gender categories if possibilities offered on social media or dating sites are an indication.

Does it really matter how many categories exist if those categories do not carry with them expectations, opportunities, and constraints? We have little good scientific knowledge of why people identify as one sex category or gender rather than another. Perhaps this is primarily cultural, perhaps more materially embedded in the nature of bodies. And surely, the materiality of bodies matters a great deal to individuals. All adults should have the right to choose the medical procedures they need to shape their bodies to match their identities. Why should we require people to have a medical diagnosts if they want their breasts removed for identity purposes, but allow women who want to augment their breasts for aesthetic reasons to do so without a mental health diagnosis? Gender as a social structure organizes our imagination and constrains our choices, and any strategy to move beyond it must allow adults free choices at the individual level about identity, personality, and presentation of the body.

Will gender identities matter, or be so significant, if we remove expectations attached to them? I do not think it likely we will entirely eliminate the categories of male or female, since both reproductive activities and medical interventions are related to the materiality of bodies, although the likelihood of adding categories for inter-sex or other categories seems likely. But simply having more categories does not, by itself, address the issue of a gender structure. We could have a gender structure with four or more categories, each constrained by expectations, constraints, and oppor-tunities. How important would sex identities be if they were not embedded in a stratification system that both privileges men and constrains everyone by gender expectations attached to the categories themselves? That is a question for research-ers of the future. For now, I suggest we let a thousand categories flourish because, at the moment, that's what freedom feels like for individuals oppressed by gender categories. If we explode a binary of sex, we might simply end up with a system of more but equally oppressive categories unless we also eliminate the gender expecta-tions attached to categories. And that brings us to the interactional level of analysis.

At the interactional level, we ought to destroy social expectations attached to male or female bodies and to people who identify as men and women (or new gender categories such as genderqueer for that matter). Any classification of some human attributes as masculine and some as feminine, and the concomitant gendering of people and social institutions, oppresses all human beings and renders social inter-action inherently coercive. As long as all babies born with male genitalia are shaped and pressured to be masculine and infants born with female genitalia are shaped and pressured to be feminine, no one is actually free. Femininity and masculinity are not equally rewarded or valued, nor given the history of patriarchy will they ever be. But even more importantly, there is no reason that people born with differently shaped genitals, and corresponding secondary-sex characteristics, should be even slightly steered into different kinds of clothes, behaviors, or identities. Such categorization of expectations limits human freedom, boxing us into cultural interactional scripts. The material level of sex segregation at the interactional level matters as well. We must eradicate segregation so that workplaces and public spaces are not designated primarily for one sex or the other. If gender is no longer tied to the sex of the body, and gender stereotypes cease to exist, so would the possibility of male- and female-dominated professions, playgrounds with mostly female caretakers, and single-sex bathrooms. The material dimension of the interactional level of the gender structure justifies sex segregation and that too would end in a post-gender society. Sex-segre-gated bathrooms would be unknown.

Much change has happened at the formal institutional level of the macro structure in modern, post-industrial societies, including the United States. Most legal doc-trines are now gender neutral, including divorce laws, as are workplace policies. Of course, there are still religious institutions where leadership roles are limited to men, including the Catholic Church, but then again, there are many religious denomi-nations that have become gender egalitarian decades ago. While formal policy becomes more egalitarian, the actual distribution of wealth and power in contemporary American society still tilts strongly male. Material equality remains a feminist goal shared by all waves of feminism. Where I go further as a proponent of a new wave of feminism is to suggest we develop a cultural worldview that totally erases the distinctive live trajectories of people based on their identity as male, female, or any other sex or gender category. I suggest we transform our society so that both caring work and economic production are equally rewarded, where women and men (and any other identity categories that people adopt) are involved in both. As long as mostly men have wives who do the caretaking work of society, men will continue to control the public sphere with the power to decide all of our fates. We need public policy that requires the private sector to allow workers to remain income earners and caretakers over their life course. These can be policies such as paid family leave, short-term, or part-time employment when family demands are high, available affordable daycare, and school days synched with the normative workweek. We need to redesign social organizations for a post-gender world.

Changing social organizations is a necessary but insufficient goal for a movement to end gender at the macro level. We need to begin to develop a post-gender cultural worldview that does not provide ideological justification for sex-segregated policies, gender expectations, or socialization. This is a tall order, and not something I consider likely in the near future but a goal nonetheless. It is perhaps the most radical of all the changes necessary. It entails creating a culture that does not divide human beings into a binary around sex status or gender identity and does not categorize individuals for purposes of socialization, schooling, careers, or caretaking responsibilities by sex category or gender identity. To end sexism, we must end the presumption that what sex is ascribed at birth or gender identity held has any importance for the rest of one's life. Simply, we need a culture that is post-gender, where there are no expectations for a child, teen, or adult simply because of the sex category they claim or the gender identity they hold. I would expect the importance of gender identities to wither as gender expectations at the interactional level cease to exist. Without gendered norms for anything from clothes to personality traits, what would be the basis for any justifications for cognitive bias or for social organization based on sex category? But then again, if gender identity (being a woman or a man) remained important to some individuals, it would no longer be the basis for the organization of anyone's life or inequality between those who hold a male or female sex status.

Here is a quick summary of my strategy for a social movement to end gender as a social structure. First, encourage what has already begun with the explosion of the sex and gender binary categories. Sex categories of male or female must expand to include intersex and be available to anyone who wants to own them, whether so labelled at birth or not. With technology today, people can create bodies to display the sex they claim. Gender identities are also exploding from woman and man to genderqueer, agender, and pangender, as well as others only now being imagined. At the individual level, let a thousand identities bloom, for without the sex/gender binary, the gender structure becomes far weaker. How many identities will remain over time is an empirical question, as to their importance in a world without gender as a structure, but that is a research project for the future, perhaps for the 23rd century. At the interactional level, we must cease and desist to have any expectations of people because of their sex category or gender identity. This will not be easy, we have yet to solve the problem of unconscious bias, and may not do so as long as sex and gender are so correlated, but without ceasing such expectations and the physical manifestation of sex segregation that accompanies them, gender inequality cannot be overcome. And at the macro level, we not only need gender-free formal rules and regulations, we also need to redesign our social organizations so that caretaking and economic labor are no longer incompatible. We need to begin to create a culture of equality that doesn't dichotomize the world into the masculine and the feminine, where no presumptions exist between skills, tastes, presentation of self, or competence simply because of sex category or gender identity.

THE DOMINO EFFECT

How do we start toward this utopian world? For people who have the privilege to do so, the time is ripe to take risks. For some, it might be as easy as refusing to wear "feminine" shoes that hurt, to stop dieting to meet a beauty standard designed for a male gaze rather than eating to have a healthy body, to opt out of traditional femininity if and when it chafes. Recently, I've been reading social media complaints by men about the requirement to do masculinity by wearing uncomfortable suits and ties. Why should there be gendered standards for professional dress? Women wear pantsuits because they are comfortable but have not adopted the less desirable tie. Why shouldn't men stop wearing them? Everyone could work in more comfortable, more gender-neutral, professional clothes. People can undo gender in their private lives as well (Risman 2009). Women can take the lead in heterosexual relationships, and men can learn the art of following. Of course, individuals cannot make change in isolation from changes in expectations and institutions. The Millennials seem to focus solely on the individual, and that strategy is unlikely to work. When individuals take risks, they are far more likely to be successful, rather than defeated, if they are part of social movements. It is up to those who seek a post-gender world to work toward it.

What would prompt a social movement that supported individuals changing themselves, changing the expectations for others, and widespread changes in cultural beliefs and organizing social institutions? One part of the answer is the increasing dissatisfaction with the gender structure voiced by the *rebels* and *innovators* in this research. The push from young people who identify as genderqueer, trans activists, and heterosexual couples who share or reverse family roles all chip away at the existence of gender as a permanent category that does and should shape human life. While much dissatisfaction is felt, it is not necessarily now, or yet, linked to the existence of a gender structure. My goal is to illustrate how the contemporary dissatisfaction with many aspects of family and work lives can be traced to the gender structure, that is, the presumption that sex ascribed at birth determines a gendered life trajectory. Every presumption that there are two and only two sexes, two and only two genders, and that these sexes and genders are different should be interrogated. Every questioning moment is a small drip of water helping to move mountains of tradition (Sullivan 2006). Once such questioning is related to the very existence of a gender structure, perhaps a vibrant social movement will once again emerge.

As much as I advocate a new movement to eradicate gender, I do not suggest that a fast paced radical social change to move beyond gender is either possible or desirable. Nor can such change be imposed from the top down. I do not believe that any but the most draconian anti-democratic society could impose a totally post-gender imprint in any institution, workplace, or religion. Nor could change be imposed on intimate relationships in private space. Gender is too close to home, a source of comfort to many (although pain to others) and inequality. While some people at the gender-protesting vanguard don't want freedom *from* gender, but freedom *with* gender, queering and multiplying genders can be conceptualized as part of an evolutionary process toward dissolving the binary (Lorber 1994). Gender nonconforming individuals certainly raise others' consciousness by pushing at gender binaries with and without conscious political intent.

A serious jump-start toward this utopian vision requires a renewed social movement to press for freedom from gender and to support those who walk the walk in their personal lives. We need to make overt genderism as politically impolite as racism or sexism. To move toward a sustained metamorphosis in society we need to experiment with post-gender institutions at the margins of today's world: couples creating households without using hetero-gendered scripts or perhaps networks of people who create chosen families with shared caretaking duties. Experimental attempts at post-gender lifestyles further destabilize taken-for-granted assumptions about gender. People on the margins not only think the impossible but sometimes make it appear plausible. For permanent change, however, cultural meaning systems have to be transformed at the center and not just at the margins. Sex declared at birth should no longer be used to create gender, and the correlation between the two need no longer exist. We should have new pronouns that do not indicate gender, but not just for those who are genderqueer, for all of us. None of us should be labeled in writing for our gender any more than our marital status. Why not Mx. instead of Mr. or Ms.? Perhaps "they" instead of his or her for us all? I have no strong arguments for one way or another of de-gendering our language, but I want to remind us that English is a relatively gender-neutral language and it is within our ability to revise it to be entirely post-gender. It may take generations before this happens but little change can happen unless we all risk undoing gender when, as individuals, the gender structure constrains us. But atomized individuals rebelling are unlikely to make social change. We need a social movement to nurture activists on the outside and leaders on the inside who inhabit organizations from the bottom up, and move up the ranks so they can institutionalize change eventually from the top down. I hope I have moved you, the reader, to at least consider the possibility that a future without gender allows for the most flowering of human potential, the freedom for people to develop without being categorized into the life of a she or a he or even a ze. I urge those of us who teach and study in universities to redouble our efforts to critically analyze the roots of gender oppression, to re-conceptualize discomfort with gender constraints as a critique of the gender structure itself. We need feminist scholarship both inside Women and Gender Studies Programs and beyond them to continue to shed light on how gender itself challenges our ability to be free human beings.

To move beyond a world where gender is a social structure, we need to envision a multigenerational strategy that seeks to create a better world for our children and their children. The strategies I have suggested require a strong and sustained social movement, and even with that, resistance and backlash are to be expected. My hope is for social change that is reiterative, dynamic, and creative. Institutional changes open up possibilities for cultural changes and the reverse. Once women are allowed into powerful spaces previously forbidden, younger women take for granted their right to such positions. As women in newly opened spaces juggle the incompatibilities of traditional female responsibilities and economic labor, they begin to notice that organizations are no longer peopled by workers with wives. Research shows us that when women reach leadership in organizations, sex segregation decreases and women's chances improve (Stainback et al. 2016). Change reverberates across levels of analysis, from individuals to expectations to cultural meaning, to organizations, and back to individuals, or to interactional expectations. I have no ability to forecast the directionality or pace of such reverberations of gender changes, except to hope for a continued domino effect and ever-growing momentum. And how might such a feminist movement reach beyond the liberal echo chambers of society to those beyond it? Here the reality that women and LGTBQ people are embedded in all families brings possibilities. In every extended family there is someone who chafes at the gender structure, and it is to them we must hold out an analysis and then to those who love them. Causation is recursive, material changes allow for cultural ones that will spur future material ones. And the cycle continues, with one change spawning future ones, until—perhaps—gender becomes a dim memory. Fourth-wave feminism may not succeed, but we will never know if we do not try.

Might there be unintended consequences of a feminist social movement aiming at a post-gender society? At the individual level, most of us are very attached to our gendered selves, and if change at this level were somehow instituted quickly (e.g., no men's or women's departments in clothing stores), many of us would feel disoriented and reject this as a sign of progress. When expectations for behavior change quickly, it becomes uncomfortable to enter a setting unsure of how to meet normative requirements, without knowing what others expect from us. And yet, pushing the envelope about expectations around caretaking or leadership activities can indeed provide a needed support for men and women held back by current norms. Perhaps the most serious unintended consequence of moving too far too fast, in this new feminist direction, is to create an illusion that we live in a post-gender world long before we do, which will lead anti-feminists to declare victory and the end of need for more social change.

So I end this book with a call for a fourth wave of feminism, a social movement for a just world, a world beyond gender. We will surely still have a kaleidoscope of ways to present our bodies, from colorful hair, to dresses, to ties and jewelry, but none of that needs to be understood as gender or linked to certain kinds of bodies. I ask feminists to leave behind what I consider an intermediate stage of merely aiming for equality between women and men, far before we have achieved it. Let's dream bigger, aim higher, for what seems an impossible goal—a world where people are not forced to live constrained inside one sex category, where expectations for interaction are not based on gender identity, where social life is organized to combine productive paid work with the unpaid but equally important work of social reproduction and caring for our loved ones.

While it is true that most of us can hardly imagine a society with such freedom, my goal in this book is to provide such imagination, to be a utopian realist (Nicholas 2014). I have provided an analysis showing how gender is a social structure and how this shapes the lives of Millennials today. Some Millennials are pushing back against the gender structure, and it is to them I dedicate this book, and my proposal for a fourth wave of feminism. I hope to have freed your imagination just enough so you too can dream of a society without gender as a social structure. Twentieth-century feminism fought hard, and often successfully, for women's rights. The 21st-century movement must go further—to imagine a world free from gender itself.

GROWING UP IN THE 21ST CENTURY: INTERVIEW SCHEDULE

MODULE 1: LIFE HISTORY/BACKGROUND

Thank you for being willing to talk with us. Remind me here, on tape, the name you'd like us to refer to you as; make up any first and last name that you'd like.

I'll begin by asking you some questions about your family.

FAMILY

- Tell me a little bit about your family: how many family members you have, and their relationship to you. You may include anyone whom you consider to be a family member, whether related by blood or marriage or not related.
- Did your family change over time, that is, who you lived with? If so, how?
- Where were your parents born? What country or countries are they citizens of?
- Were you raised in a religion? If so, what one?
- (If self and/or parents born outside the US) When did you/your parents move to the United States? What were the circumstances that brought you here?
- (Ask for each parent/guardian) What is the highest level of education your (mom/dad/other) completed?
- Is your (mom/dad/other) working now? (If so) What does s/he do?
  o What other jobs have they had in the past?

BACKGROUND ABOUT YOURSELF

- How old are you? (In what year were you born?)
- Where were you born?
- Your sex?
- Your race?
- Your sexual orientation?
- Your religion now?
- What country or countries are you a citizen of?
- What is the highest level of education that you've completed? (If in college, what year are you?)
- Are you working now? (If so) What do you do?
- Where do currently live? (If a student, probe for on or off campus)
- Who lives with you?
- Do you have any children?
- What languages do you speak? Do you speak a different language in different settings, like home, school, or work?

Now I'm going to ask you a few questions about what things were like at home as you were growing up.

- What sorts of things were your parents strict about?
- What sorts of activities did your parents disapprove of? Did you ever do any of these activities?
  - o Tell me about a time when your parents confronted you about something you did that they disapproved of.
- What responsibilities did you have at home as you were growing up?
- Did you ever feel like you were treated differently from your siblings? (By parent(s), other family members, others? Probe for chores, curfews, dress codes)
- What do you think your parents most wanted you to learn from them when you were growing up? Are those same things important to you now?
- What were some things that you liked and disliked about yourself as you were growing up?
- What did you like to wear? What activities did you enjoy? What activities did you not enjoy?
- What expectations did you have for your future?
- What expectations did others have for you? (Probe: parents, teachers, coaches, peers, religious leaders, others)
- How did you feel about your body as you were growing up? (Probe: If your feelings about your body changed significantly at any point, tell me about that.)

- Describe a moment in your life that stands out as an especially positive experience. What happened, when and where, who was involved, and what were you thinking and feeling?

- Describe a moment in your life that stands out as a low point. What happened, where and when, who was involved, and what were you thinking and feeling?

- If you could relive any part of your life, what part would it be and why? Is there anything you would change? What would it be?

- Tell me about your first crush. When was it? What happened?

- Tell me about another crush or romantic relationship that was really important to you.

- Have you ever had a romantic relationship with someone that your family or friends did not approve of? (If so, probe for details about who disapproved, why, and how they handled that)

- Are you in a romantic relationship now? If so, tell me about that relationship.

- How would you describe your ideal partner? (Probe for ideal characteristics of future partner)

- What online social media do you use?
  - o Tell me about the social media that you used/use most frequently. What did/do you use it for?
  - o Are there any friends or communities you get together with only on-line?

- Tell me about the friends you spent time with face-to-face in high school. What do you do with them?

- Tell me about any organized groups you belonged to before college (such as sports teams, Boy or Girl Scouts, youth group, etc.).

- Were there any activities you wanted to participate in, but weren't allowed to?

- Tell me about an organization that you were a part of that really mattered to you or affected your life in an important way. (Probe: when and how did you join this organization? What are some things you liked/disliked about it?)

SCHOOL

- Tell me about the school(s) you went to. Did you go to school close to home, or did you commute a long distance to get to school? (Probe for racial makeup of school)

- Did you have any favorite teachers? What did you like about them?

- Do you think your teachers expected you to succeed? (Probe: Did your teachers help you when you needed it?)

- Did you do any extracurricular activities organized by any of your schools (e.g., sports teams, clubs, band?)

- Have you ever been an international student? If so, tell me about it.

- Tell me about a situation (in school or outside of school) where you felt that you were picked on. (Probe: How often did this happen? Were there any consequences for the people who picked on you?)

- Tell me about a situation (in school or outside of school) where you and your friends were picking on somebody else. Why? What happened?
- If you are in college now, what's your major? What job would you like to have after college? Do you plan on going to graduate school?

NEIGHBORHOODS/CRIME AND SAFETY

- Tell me about the neighborhood(s) where you grew up. (Probe: Did you live in urban, suburban, or rural areas?)
- How would you describe the racial and ethnic makeup of your neighborhood(s)?
- How safe or unsafe did you feel living in these neighborhood(s)?
- How would you describe your overall experiences with the police?
- Tell me about a specific time that you interacted with a police officer. What happened?

TRANSITION: NOW WE'RE GOING TO TALK ABOUT SOME CURRENT EVENTS THAT WE WANT TO GET YOUR POINT OF VIEW ON.

Module #2: Gender Meanings

1. Please read the following news article about a preschool in Sweden that uses no gender pronouns when they refer to their own students. [http://www.nytimes.com/2012/11/14/world/europe/swedish-school-de-emphasizes-gender-lines.html
   - What is your overall impression of this school?
   - Would you have wanted to attend a school like this one?
   - If you had a child in the future (or if you have a child now), would you want your child to attend a school like this one? Why or why not?
2. I'm going to read you a vignette, and then ask you your opinion about it:
   Lisa is a woman in her early 20s. With her hair cut short and wearing clothing that she bought from the men's department, Lisa is frequently mistaken for a man. While traveling, she stops by a roadside restroom. As she enters the restroom, another woman mistakes Lisa for a man, telling her that "this is the *woman's* restroom," and threatens to call security on Lisa if she doesn't leave. After encountering this situation numerous times, Lisa begins avoiding public restrooms and locker rooms altogether.
   - What would you have done if you'd seen this happen?
   - Have you ever been in a situation like this one, as either actor?
   - How do you think Lisa should handle this situation?
3. I'm going to show you a recent J Crew advertisement which caused some controversy. [Advertisement appears in chapter 4.]
   - Why do you think it caused controversy?
   - How do you feel about it?
   - Do you think boys as well as girls should be permitted to paint their toenails? How about their fingernails?

- Think about a time when you did something that would have not even been noticed if you had been a boy (or a girl) but was unusual because you did it.
- What was it you did? How did your parents react? How did your peers react? How did you feel about it?
- How about as a teenager? Do you have any experience with breaking traditions or rules that had to do with being a boy or a girl? If so, please tell me about it.
- How about now as an adult? If so, please tell me about it.
- Are there ways you'd like to dress or behave that you don't? (Probe re: fear of negative reactions or discrimination)
- What are your thoughts generally about this? Should this oven be made?
- Why do you think they only make pink ovens?
- Did you know any kids growing up that wanted to play with toys marketed usually to the other sex? If so, please tell me about it. What did other kids say about this child?
- Tell me about time when you, a family member, or a friend got a toy that some people thought was inappropriate for their gender.
- Did you want any toys that were marketed to the other sex? If so, what happened?
- At this point in your life, are there activities you like to do that few others of your sex enjoy? (Probe)

We are going to end the interview with a few more questions about your own experiences.

4. Think back in time to when you were a small child. What's your earliest recollection when you recognized that you were a (girl/boy/another gender)? How did you feel about that?
   a. **Ask as appropriate:** Have you ever considered identifying in some other way? Did you do it? Why/not? Please walk me through that decision process.
5. What are some ways that you felt similar to (other little boys/little girls) as you were growing up? What are some ways that you felt different from (other little boys/little girls)?
6. What are some ways that you felt similar to (boys/girls—gender they don't identify as) as you were growing up—that is, what are some things you think you had in common with girls? What are some ways that you felt different from (boys/girls)?
7. Tell me a story about a time when you wanted to do something that mostly only (boys or girls) do. What happened? (Probe school, relationships, hobbies)
8. Have you made any changes to your body for gender-related reasons? (Probe for what changes, when, why, whether others were supportive or unsupportive)
9. Are there any changes you'd like to make, but haven't?
   a. If so, do you anticipate being able to do this someday? (Probe for when/why not, and steps needed to make this happen)

10. **Ask as appropriate:** Are there people in your life who refuse to recognize your gender? How have you handled that? Has your approach to this issue changed over time? How so?

11. Have you faced any unique challenges or opportunities because of your gender? (Probe: socially, at work, in your healthcare, in your education, in your family)

12. **Ask as appropriate:** Where do you get gender-related resources and information?
    a. Are there resources that have been particularly important for you?
    b. What about online social media, such as forums or social networks—have these been resources for you? How so?
    c. Are there resources you needed, but didn't have access to?

CONCLUSION

Those are all the questions that I have prepared for us today. Before we wrap up, is there anything else you'd like to add? Are there important aspects of your life that were not touched on by this interview?

CODING SCHEME: GENDER STRUCTURE THEMES

INDIVIDUAL LEVEL CODES: ALL ABOUT INTERNAL SELF

IL Body
  IL Body Pro
  IL Body Con
IL Femininity   self-evaluation of personality
IL Masculinity   self-evaluation of personality
IL Personal Gender Beliefs
  IL Beliefs essentialism
  IL Beliefs constructionist
  IL Beliefs liberal (liberal attitudes about gender equality—I don't believe a woman's role
    is to be a stay at home mom)
  IL Beliefs conservative (conservative attitudes about gender equality—I believe a wom-
    an's role is a homemaker)
IL Gender Related Activity
  IL activity conforming to sex at birth
  IL activity non-conformity to sex at birth
IL Gender related goals
  IL goals conforming
  IL goals non-conforming

INTERACTIONAL LEVEL CODES: ONLY FROM SOCIAL INTERACTION

Int Expectations—Dress	parents/peers make clear dress appropriate
Int Expectations—Behavior	parents/peers make clear behavior norms
Int Policing gender norms	anyone enforce/make them do it
Int Acquiesce to norms	mention of giving in to norms
Int Rebellion from norms	mention of breaking norms
Int Support for Rebellion	elder, peer or community supporting

MACRO: SOCIETAL LEVEL (ORG/RELIGION/SCHOOL)

Mac rule/regs that constrain re gender	discussion of official policy re gender
Mac cultural beliefs on societal level	interpretation of societal beliefs
Mac liberal	
Mac conservative	

NOTES

CHAPTER 1

1. According to a Pew Research Center report (2015) many Millennials do not embrace this label given to their generation by academics and marketers. Only 40% embrace their generational title. Still, it is the generational title by which they have become known and I will use the term to refer to them.

CHAPTER 2

1. Some of the arguments presented in this chapter were presented in an earlier version in Risman and Davis 2013, and others in an earlier version in Risman 2017.

2. While women entering the academy might not have led to more research on gender, many of the women who entered the academy were also involved in the women's liberation movement of that decade and brought their questions about women's subordination and gender inequality to their academic work. Social experiences often influence scientific ideas (Sprague 2016).

3. It is true that psychologists have not made this transition, as a major journal in that field is *Sex Roles*. My explanation for this is that they study, primarily, the individual, the means by which culture gets inside us, and so the language is not so inaccurate for them. And yet, the language of roles even there seems to imply that the roles attached to sex are somehow consistent across time, race, ethnicity, and class. At this writing, there is conversation about changing the title of this journal for just these issues.

CHAPTER 3

1. Joyce A. Martin et al., 2015, "Births: Final Statistics for 2013," *National Vital Statistics Reports* 64 (1), http://www.cdc.gov/nchs/data/nvsr/nvsr64/nvsr64_01.pdf.

CHAPTER 4

1. See the following for an article about the school: John Tagliabue, "Swedish School's Big Lesson Begins with Dropping Personal Pronouns," *New York Times*, November 13, 2012, http://www.nytimes.com/2012/11/14/world/europe/swedish-school-de-emphasizes-gender-lines.html.

CHAPTER 9

1. See the following article about young peoples' support for Bernie Sanders: Jeff Stein, "Bernie Sanders's base isn't the working class. It's young people," *Vox*, May 19, 2016, http://www.vox.com/2016/5/19/11649054/bernie-sanders-working-class-base.

CHAPTER 10

1. See the Women's March website for learn about their mission: Women's March,"Our Mission," *Women's March*, https://www.womensmarch.com/mission.

2. See the following webpage from Androgyne Online for their description of androgyny: *Androgyne Online*, http://androgyne.ocatch.com/.

3. See this blog written by a "proud married gender queer transwoman": Lilith Routh, "A Gender Queer View," *A Gender Queer View*, http://genderqueerview.blogspot.com/.

4. http://nyti.ms/2iMIBdo.

5. See this article about the use of gender-neutral pronouns in Sweden: Kevin Matthews, "Sweden Adopts a Gender-Neutral Pronoun," *Care2*, April 17, 2017, http://www.care2.com/causes/sweden-adopts-a-gender-neutral-pronoun.html.

6. See this webpage for more information on National Science Foundation ADVANCE Programs: National Science Foundation, "ADVANCE: Increasing the Participation of Women in Academic Science and Engineering (ADVANCE)," http://www.nsf.gov/funding/pgm_summ.jsp?pims_id=5383.

7. See this page on Stanford University's website for more information on their Center for the Advancement of Women's Leadership: Stanford Center for the Advancement of Women's Leadership, Stanford University, http://gender.stanford.edu/voice-influence.

8. See this post in the blog *The Society Pages* about gender dimorphism in the Disney Film, *Frozen*: Philip Cohen, "'Help, My Eyeball is Bigger than My Wrist!': Gender Dimorphism in Frozen," *The Society Pages*, December 17, 2013, https://thesocietypages.org/socimages/2013/12/17/help-my-eyeball-is-bigger-than-my-wrist-gender-dimorphism-in-frozen/.

9. HB2 allows far more discrimination than around gender but that is not our focus here.

10. There are some Millennials who have taken to calling themselves the "fourth wave." How they are different from the third is not clear, as they too are digital natives who integrate intersectionality into their identity as feminists. See this example of a fourth-wave online journal (https://thefourthwavepitt.com/). In the book, I shall adopt this fourth-wave metaphor and bring my own

meaning to it. I hope and believe my use of the term incorporates what is important to those who currently use the label.

11. See this page on Facebook to view Sheryl Sandberg's Mother's Day post: Sheryl Sandberg, May 6, 2016, https://www.facebook.com/sheryl/posts/10156819553860177.

12. See this article in the *New York Times* for Wallstrom's views on Feminism, Trump, and Sweden's Future: Somini Sengupta, "Margot Wallstrom on Feminism, Trump and Sweden's Future," December 18, 2016, http://www.nytimes.com/2016/12/18/world/europe/margot-wallstrom-on-feminism-trump-and-swedens-future.html.

13. See the following response from Susan Goldberg on why National Geographic put a transgender girl on the cover of its magazine: Susan Goldberg, "Why We Put a Transgender Girls on the Cover of National Geographic," *National Geographic Magazine*, January 2017, http://www.nationalgeographic.com/magazine/2017/01/editors-note-gender/.

14. A first early version of this utopian argument was coauthored with Judith Lorber and Jessica Holden Sherwood and prepared for an invited session that was part of the Envision Real Utopias project formulated by Erik Olin Wright and highlighted as the theme of the 2012 American Sociological Association meetings. It was controversial then and remains so.

15. It is the case that feminist theorists such as Judith Butler (1990) have created deconstructionist enthusiasms within the academy. Other theorists, particularly Judith Lorber (1994; 2005), have also argued to deconstruct gender.

REFERENCES

Abbatecola, Emanuela. 2015. "Donna Faber: Male Jobs, Sexism and Other Stereotypes." Presented at University of Illinois at Chicago, August 27.

Acker, Joan. 1990. "Hierarchies, Jobs, Bodies: A Theory of Gendered Organizations." *Gender & Society* 4: 139–158.

———. 1992. "From Sex Roles to Gendered Institutions." *Contemporary Sociology* 21: 565–569.

———. 2006. "Inequality Regimes Gender, Class, and Race in Organizations." *Gender & Society* 20: 441–464.

Adams, Julia, and Tasleem Padamsee. 2001. "Signs and Regimes: Rereading Feminist Work on Welfare States." *Social Politics: International Studies in Gender, State & Society* 8: 1–23.

Ahearn, Laura M. 2001. "Language and Agency." *Annual Review of Anthropology* 30: 109–137.

Anderson, Eric. 2002. "Openly Gay Athletes: Contesting Hegemonic Masculinity in a Homophobic Environment." *Gender & Society* 16: 860–877.

———. 2009. *Inclusive Masculinity: The Changing Nature of Masculinities.* New York: Routledge.

———. 2012. "Shifting Masculinities in Anglo-American Countries." *Masculinities and Social Change* 1: 20–40.

Armstrong, Elizabeth A., Laura Hamilton, and Brian Sweeney. 2006. "Sexual Assault on Campus: A Multilevel, Integrative Approach to Party Rape." *Social Problems* 53: 483–499.

Arnett, Jeffrey Jensen. 2000. "Emerging Adulthood: A Theory of Development from the Late Teens Through the Twenties." *American Psychologist* 55 (5): 469–480.

———. 2015. *Emerging Adulthood: The Winding Road from the Late Teens Through the Twenties.* 2nd ed. Cambridge: Oxford University Press.

Arnold A. P., and R. A. Gorski. 1984. "Gonadal-Steroid Induction of Structural Sex-Differences in the Central Nervous System." *Annual Review of Neuroscience* 7: 413–442.

Arum, Richard, and Josipa Roksa. 2011. *Academically Adrift: Limited Learning on College Campuses.* Chicago: University of Chicago Press.

Auster, Carol J., and Claire S. Mansbach. 2012. "The Gender Marketing of Toys: An Analysis of Color and Type of Toy on the Disney Store Website." *Sex Roles* 67: 375–388.

Bandura A., and R. Waters. 1963. *Social Learning and Personality.* New York: Holt, Rinehart and Winston.

Bell, W. B. 1916. *The Sex Complex: A Study of the Relationship of the Internal Secretions to the Female Characteristics and Functions in Health and Disease.* London: Baillière, Tindall & Cox.

Bem, Sandra. 1974. "The Measurement of Psychological Androgyny." *Journal of Consulting and Clinical Psychology* 42: 65–82.

———. 1981. "Gender Schema Theory: A Cognitive Account of Sex Typing." *Psychological Review* 88: 354–364.

———. 1993. *The Lenses of Gender: Transforming the Debate on Sexual Inequality.* New Haven, CT: Yale University Press.

Berger, Peter L., and Thomas Luckmann. 1966. *The Social Construction of Reality: A Treatise in the Sociology of Knowledge.* Garden City, NY: Anchor Books.

Bianchi, Suzanne M., Melissa A. Milkie, Liana C. Sayer, and John P. Robinson. 2000. "Is Anyone Doing the Housework? Trends in the Gender Division of Household Labor." *Social Forces* 79: 191–228.

Bilimoria, Diana, and Xiangfen Liang. 2012. *Gender Equity in Science and Engineering: Advancing Change in Higher Education.* New York: Routledge.

Bittman Michael, Paula England, Liana Sayer, Nancy Folbre, and George Matheson. 2003. "When Does Gender Trump Money? Bargaining and Time in Household Work." *American Journal of Sociology* 109: 186–214.

Blair-Loy, M. 2005. *Competing Devotions.* Cambridge, MA: Harvard University Press.

Blau, Peter. 1977. *Inequality and Heterogeneity: A Primitive Theory of Social Structure.* New York: Free Press.

Booth, Alan, Douglas Granger, Allan Mazur, and Katie Kivlighan. 2006. "Testosterone and Social Behavior." *Social Forces* 85: 167–191.

Booth, Alan, Greg Shelley, Allan Mazur, Gary Tharp, and Roger Kittock. 1989. "Testosterone and Winning and Losing in Human Competition." *Hormones and Behavior* 23: 556–571.

Bourdieu, Pierre. 1988. *Outline of a Theory of Practice.* Cambridge, MA: Cambridge University Press.

Brizendine, Louann. 2006. *The Female Brain.* New York: Morgan Road Books.

Broido, Ellen M. 2004. "Understanding Diversity in Millennial Students." *New Directions for Student Services* 106 (Summer): 73–85.

Browne, Irene, and Paula England. 1997. "Oppression from Within and Without in Sociological Theories: An Application to Gender." *Current Perspectives in Social Theory* 17: 77–104.

Brush, Lisa D. 2002. "Changing the Subject: Gender and Welfare Regime Studies." *Social Politics: International Studies in Gender, State & Society* 9: 161–186.

Budig, Michelle. 2002. "Male Advantage and the Gender Composition of Jobs: Who Rides the Glass Escalator?" *Social Problems* 49: 258–277.

Budig, Michelle, and Paula England. 2001. "The Wage Penalty for Motherhood." *American Sociological Review* 66: 204–225.

Budig, Michelle, Joya Misra, and Irene Boeckmann. 2012. "The Motherhood Penalty in Cross-National Perspective: The Importance of Work–Family Policies and Cultural Attitudes." *Social Politics: International Studies in Gender, State and Society* 19: 163–193.

Bureau of Labor Statistics. 2015. "Wives Who Earn More than Their Husbands." June. https://data.bls.gov/search/query/results?cx=013738036195919377644%3A6ihohfrgl50&q=wives+who+earn+more+than+their+husbands.

Burt, Ronald S. 1982. *Toward a Structural Theory of Action: Network Models of Social Structure, Perception, and Action.* New York: Academic Press.

Butler Judith. 1990. *Gender Trouble: Feminism and the Subversion of Identity.* New York: Routledge.

———. 2004. *Undoing Gender.* New York: Routledge.

Bystydzienski, Jill M., and Sharon R. Bird, eds. 2006. *Removing Barriers: Women in Academic Science, Technology, Engineering, and Mathematics.* Bloomington: Indiana University Press.

Cahill, Larry. 2003. "Sex- and Hemisphere-Related Influences on the Neurobiology of Emotionally Influenced Memory." *Progress in Neuropsychopharmacology and Biological Psychiatry* 27: 1235–1241.

Carlson, Daniel. 2017. "A View from Above: How Structural Barriers to Sharing Unpaid Work at Home May Lead to 'Egalitarian Essentialism' in Youth." Online Symposium published by the Council on Contemporary Families. https://contemporaryfamilies.org/4-carlson-egalitarian-essentialism-in-youth/.

Cech, Erin A. 2013. "The Self-Expressive Edge of Occupational Sex Segregation." *American Journal of Sociology* 119: 747–789.

Charles, Maria, and Karen Bradley. 2009. "Indulging Our Gendered Selves? Sex Segregation by Field of Study in 44 Countries." *American Journal of Sociology* 114: 924–976.

Cherlin, Andrew J. 2014. *Labor's Love Lost: The Rise and Fall of the Working-Class Family in America.* New York: Russell Sage Foundation.

Chodorow, Nancy. 1978. *The Reproduction of Mothering.* Updated edition. Berkeley: University of California Press, 1999.

Choi, Namok, and Dale R. Fuqua. 2003. "The Structure of the Bem Sex Role Inventory: A Summary Report of 23 Validation Studies." *Educational and Psychological Measurement* 63: 872–887.

Choi, Namok, and Jody L. Newman. 2008. "The Bem Sex-Role Inventory: Continuing Theoretical Problems." *Educational and Psychological Measurement* 68: 800–881.

Cinamon, Rachel Gali. 2006. "Anticipated Work-Family Conflict." *Career Development Quarterly* 54: 202–215.

Collaer M. L., and M. Hines. 1995. "Human Behavioral Sex Differences: A Role for Gonadal Hormones During Early Development?" *Psychological Bulletin* 118: 55–107.

Cohen, Philip N. 2013. "Disney's Dimorphism: Help My Eyeball Is Bigger than My Wrist." https://familyinequality.wordpress.com/2013/12/16/disneys-dimorphism-help-my-eyeball-is-bigger-than-my-wrist-edition/.

———. 2014. *The Family: Diversity, Inequality and Social Change.* New York: W. W. Norton.

Collins, Patricia Hill. 1998. *Fighting Words: Black Women and the Search for Justice.* Minneapolis: University of Minnesota Press.

———. 2000. *Black Feminist Thought.* 2nd ed. New York: Routledge.

Conlin, Jennifer. 2011. "The Freedom to Choose Your Pronoun." *New York Times*, September 30. http://www.nytimes.com/2011/10/02/fashion/choosing-a-pronoun-he-she-or-other-after-curfew.html.

Connell R. W. 1987. *Gender and Power: Society, the Person, and Sexual Politics*. Palo Alto, CA: Stanford University Press.

———. 1995. *Masculinities*. Berkeley: University of California Press.

Cooke B., C. D. Hegstrom, L. S. Villeneuve, and S. M. Breedlove. 1998. "Sexual Differentiation of the Vertebrate Brain: Principles and Mechanisms." *Frontiers in Neuroendocrinology* 19: 323–362.

Correll, Shelley J. 2004. "Constraints into Preferences: Gender, Status, and Emerging Career Aspirations." *American Sociological Review* 69 (1): 93–113.

Costello, Carrie Yang. 2004. "Cosmetic Genital Surgery Performed Upon Children." In Robert Perrucci, Kathleen Ferraro, JoAnn Miller, and Paula C. Rodriguez Rust, eds., *Solutions: Agenda for Social Justice 2004*. Knoxville, TN: Society for the Study of Social Problems, 81–86.

Costello, Cary Gabriel. 2011. "Genderqueer Individuals and the Trans Umbrella." http://trans-fusion.blogspot.com/2011/10/genderqueer-individuals-and-trans.html.

Crawley, Sara, Lara Foley, and Constance Shehan. 2007. *Gendering Bodies*. Lanham, MD: Rowman and Littlefield.

Crenshaw, Kimberle W. 1989. "Demarginalizing the Intersection of Race and Sex: A Black Feminist Critique of Antidiscrimination Doctrine, Feminist Theory and Antiracist Politics." *The University of Chicago Legal Forum* 1: 139–167.

Crossley, Alison Dahl. 2015. "Facebook Feminism: Social Media, Blogs and New Technologies of Contemporary U.S. Feminism." *Mobilization* 20: 253–268.

Daniel Béland. 2005. "Ideas and Social Policy: An Institutionalist Perspective." *Social Policy & Administration* 39: 1–18.

———. 2009. "Gender, Ideational Analysis, and Social Policy." *Social Politics* 16: 558–581.

David Karoly, John Freud, and Samuel Elxevier De Jongh. 1934. "Conditions of Hypertrophy of Seminal Vesicles in Rats: The Effect of Derivatives of Oestrone (menoformon)." *Biochemical Journal* 28: 1360–1367.

David, Georgiann, Jodie Dewey, and Erin c. Murphy. 2016. "Giving Sex: Deconstructing Intersex and Trans Medicalization Practices." *Gender & Society* 30 (3): 490–514.

Davis, Georgiann. 2011. "'DSD Is a Perfectly Fine Term': Reasserting Medical Authority through a Shift in Intersex Terminology." In P. J. McGann and David J. Hutson, eds., *Advances in Medical Sociology*, vol. 12: *Sociology of Diagnosis*. Bingley, UK: Emerald Group, 155—182.

———. 2015. *Contesting Intersex: The Dubious Diagnosis*. New York: New York University Press.

Davis, Shannon N., and Theodore N. Greenstein. 2013. "Why Study Housework? Cleaning as a Window into Power in Couples." *Journal of Family Theory & Review* 5: 63–71.

Davis, Shannon N., and Barbara J. Risman. 2014. "Feminists Wrestle with Testosterone: Hormones, Socialization and Cultural Interactionism as Predictors of Women's Gendered Selves." *Social Science Research* 49: 110–125.

D'Augelli, Anthony R., Arnold H. Grossman, and Michael T. Starks. 2008. "Families of Gay, Lesbian, and Bisexual Youth: What Do Parents and Siblings Know and How Do They React?" *Journal of GLBT Family Studies* 4 (1): 95–115.

Deaux, Kay, and Branda Major. 1987. "Putting Gender into Context: An Interactive Model of Gender-Related Behavior." *Psychological Review* 94 (3): 369–389.

Deutsch, Francine M. 2007. "Undoing Gender." *Gender & Society* 21: 106–127.

Diamond, Milton. 2009. "Clinical Implications of the Organizational and Activational Effects of Hormones." *Hormones and Behaviors* 55: 621–632.

Dietert, Michelle, and Dianne Dentice. 2013. "Growing Up Trans: Socialization and the Gender Binary." *Journal of GLBT Family Studies* 9: 24–42.

Diprete, Thomas A., and Claudia Buchmann. 2013. *The Rise of Women: The Growing Gender Gap in Education and What It Means for American Schools.* New York: Russell Sage Foundation.

Donnelly, Kristin, Jean M. Twenge, Malissa A. Clark, Samia K. Shaikh, Angela Beiler-May, and Nathan T. Carter. 2015. "Attitudes Toward Women's Work and Family Roles in the United States, 1976-2013." *Psychology of Women Quarterly.* doi:10.1177/0361684315590774.

Dozier, Raine. 2015. "The Power of Queer: How 'Guy Moms' Challenge Heteronormative Assumptions about Motherhood and Family." In Barbara Risman and Virginia Rutter, eds., *Families as They Really Are.* New York: W. W. Norton, 458–476.

Dreger, Alice. 2009. "Gender Identity Disorder in Childhood: Inconclusive Advise to Parents." *Hastings Center Report* 39: 26–29.

Dyson, Tim. 2012. "Causes and Consequences of Skewed Sex Ratios." *Annual Review of Sociology* 38: 443–461.

Eagen. Kevin, Jennifer B. Lozano, Sylvia Hurtado, and Matthew H. Case. 2013. *The American Freshman: National Norms Fall 2013.* Los Angeles: Higher Education Research Institute at UCLA.

Eagly, Alice H., and Linda L Carli. 2003. "The Female Leadership Advantage: An Evaluation of the Evidence." *The Leadership Quarterly* 14: 807–834.

Edwards Allen L., and Clark D. Ashworth. 1977. "A Replication Study of Item Selection for the Bem Sex Role Inventory." *Applied Psychological Measurement* 1: 501–507.

Ehrensaft, Diane. 2011. *Gender Born, Gender Made: Raising Healthy Gender-Nonconforming Children.* New York: The Experiment.

Elsesser, Kim M., and Janet Lever. 2011. "Does Gender Bias Against Female Leaders Persist? Quantitative and Qualitative Data from a Large-Scale Survey." *Human Relations* 64: 1555–1578.

Ely, Robin, and Irene Padavic. 2007. "A Feminist Analysis of Organizational Research on Sex Differences." *Academy of Management Review* 32: 1121–1143.

Ely, Robin J., Pamela Stone, and Colleen Ammerman. 2014. "Rethink What You 'Know' About High-Achieving Women." *Harvard Business Review.* https://hbr.org/2014/12/rethink-what-you-know-about-high-achieving-women.

England, Paula. 2010. "The Gender Revolution: Uneven and Stalled." *Gender & Society* 24: 149–66.

———. 2016. "Sometimes the Social Becomes Personal Gender, Class, and Sexualities." *American Sociological Review* 81: 4–28.

England, Paula, Paul Allison, Su Li, Noah Mark, Jennifer Thompson, Michelle J. Budig, and Han Sun. 2007. "Why Are Some Academic Fields Tipping Toward Female? The Sex Composition of U.S. Fields of Doctoral Degree Receipt, 1971-2002." *Sociology of Education* 80: 23–42.

England, Paula, Emma Mischel, and Monica. C. Caudillo. 2016. "Increases in Sex with Same-Sex Partners and Bisexual Identity Among Cohorts of Women (but not men). *Sociological Science* 3: 951–970.

Epstein Cynthia F. 1988. *Deceptive Distinctions: Sex, Gender, and the Social Order.* New Haven, CT: Yale University Press.

Epstein, Steven. 1996. *Impure Science: AIDS, Activism, and the Politics of Knowledge.* Berkeley: University of California Press.

Evans, H. M. 1939. "Endocrine Glands: Gonads, Pituitary and Adrenals." *Annual Review of Physiology* 1: 577–652.

Evans, Alice C. 2015. "Gender Sensitisation in the Zambian Copperbelt." *GeoForum* 59: 12–20.

Factor, Rhonda J., and Esther Rothblum.2008. "Exploring Gender Identity and Community Among Three Groups of Transgender Individuals in the United States: MTFs, FTMs, and Genderqueers." *Health Sociology Review* 17: 235.

Faludi, Susan.2000. *Stiffed: The Betrayal of the American Man.* New York: Perennial.

Fausto-Sterling, Anne. 2000. *Sexing the Body: Gender Politics and the Construction of Sexuality.* New York: Basic Books.

Ferree, Myra Marx. 1990. "Beyond Separate Spheres: Feminism and Family Research." *Journal of Marriage and the Family* 52: 866–884.

———. 2009. "An American Road Map? Framing Feminist Goals in a Liberal Landscape." In J. C. Gornick and M. K. Meyers, eds., *Gender Equality: Transforming Family Divisions of Labor.* London: Verso, 283–315.

Ferree, Myra Marx, and Elaine J. Hall. 1996. "Rethinking Stratification from a Feminist Perspective: Gender, Race, and Class in Mainstream Textbooks." *American Sociological Review* 61: 929–950.

Fine, Cordelia. 2011. *Delusions of Gender: The Real Science Behind Sex Differences.* New York: W. W. Norton.

———. 2017. *Testosterone Rex: Myths of Sex, Science and Society.* New York: W.W. Norton.

Fisher, Bonnie S., Fancis T. Cullen, and Michael G. Turner. 2000. *The Sexual Victimization of College Women.* Washington, DC: U.S. Department of Justice.

Fiske, Susan T. 1993. "Controlling Other People: The Impact of Power on Stereotyping." *American Psychologist* 48: 621–628.

———. 1998. "Stereotyping, Prejudice, and Discrimination." In D. T. Gilbert, S. T. Fiske, and G. Lindzey, eds., *Handbook of Social Psychology.* 4th ed. New York: McGraw-Hill, vol. 2, 357–411.

———. 2001. "Effects of Power on Bias: Power Explains and Maintains Individual, Group, and Societal Disparities." In A. Y. Lee-Chai and J. A. Bargh, eds., *The Use and Abuse of Power.* Philadelphia: Psychology Press, 181–193.

Fiske, Susan T., and Laura E. Stevens. 1993. "What's So Special about Sex? Gender Stereotyping and Discrimination." In S. Oskamp and M. Costanzo, eds., *Gender Issues in Contemporary Society.* Thousand Oaks, CA: Sage, vol. 6. 173–196.

Foster, Johanna. 1999. "An Invitation to Dialogue: Clarifying the Position of Feminist Gender Theory in Relation to Sexual Difference Theory." *Gender & Society* 13: 431–456.

Foucault, Michel. 1978. *From the History of Sexuality,* vol. 1: *An Introduction.* Harmondsworth, NY: Penguin.

Frank, Robert T. 1929. *The Female Sex Hormone.* Baltimore, MD: Charles C. Thomas.

Fraser, Nancy. 2015. "How Feminism Became Capitalism's Handmaiden—and How to Reclaim It." *The Guardian,* October 14. http://www.theguardian.com/commentisfree/2013/oct/14/feminism-capitalist-handmaiden-neoliberal.

Freese, Jeremy, Jui-Chung Allen Li, and Lisa D. Wade. 2003. "The Potential Relevances of Biology to Social Inquiry." *Annual Review of Sociology* 29: 233–256.

Furstenberg, Frank F. Jr.,2017. "The Use and Abuse of Millennials as an Analytic Category." Online Symposium published by the Council on Contemporary Families. https://contemporaryfamilies.org/8-furstenberg-millennials-analytic-category/.

————. 2010. "On a New Schedule: Transitions to Adulthood and Family Change." *Future of Children* 20: 67–87.

Furstenberg, Frank F., Jr., C. Vonnie, C. Mcloyd, Ruben G. Rumbaut, and Richard A. Settersten. 2004. "Growing Up Is Hard to Do." *Contexts* 3: 33–41.

Fussell, Elizabeth, and Frank F. Furstenberg Jr. 2005. "The Transition to Adulthood During the Twentieth Century: Race, Nativity and Gender." In R. A. Settersen, Jr., F. F. Furstenberg, Jr. and R. G. Rumbaunt, eds., *On the Frontier of Adulthood: Theory, Research and Public Policy*. Chicago: University of Chicago Press, 29–75.

Gagné, Patricia, and Richard Tewksbury. 1998. "Conformity Pressures and Gender Resistance Among Transgendered Individuals." *Social Problems* 45: 81–101.

Gagné, Patricia, Richard Tewksbury, and Deanna McGaughey. 1997. "Coming Out and Crossing Over: Identity Formation and Proclamation in a Transgender Community." *Gender & Society* 11: 478–508.

Gamson, Joshua. 1995. "Must Identity Movements Self-Destruct? A Queer Dilemma." *Social Problems* 42: 390–407.

Garcia, Lorena. 2012. *Respect Yourself, Protect Yourself: Latina Girls and Sexual Identity*. New York: New York University Press.

Garcia-Retamero, Rocio, and Esther López-Zafra. 2006. "Prejudice Against Women in Male-Congenial Environments: Perceptions of Gender Role Congruity in Leadership." *Sex Roles* 55: 51–61.

Garofalo, Robert, Joanne Deleon, Elizabeth Osmer, Mary Doll, and Gary W. Harper. 2006. "Overlooked, Misunderstood, and At-Risk: Exploring the Lives and HIV Risk of Ethnic Minority Male-to-Female Transgender Youth." *Journal of Adolescent Health* 38 (3): 230–236.

Gerson Kathleen. 1985. *Hard Choices: How Women Decide About Work, Career, and Motherhood*. Berkeley: University of California Press.

————. 2010. *The Unfinished Revolution: Coming of Age in a New Era of Gender, Work, and Family*. Cambridge, MA: Oxford University Press.

Gettler, Lee T., Thomas W. McDade, Alan B. Feranil, and Christopher W. Kuzawa. 2011. "Longitudinal Evidence that Fatherhood Decreases Testosterone in Human Males." *PNAS* 108 (39): 16194–16199.

Gherardi, Silvia. 1995. *Gender, Symbolism and Organizational Cultures*. London: Sage.

Gherardi, Silvia, and Barbara Poggio. 2007. *Gendertelling in Organizations: Narratives from Male-Dominated Environments*. Copenhangen: Copenhagen Business School Press.

Giddens Anthony. 1984. *The Constitution of Society: Outline of the Theory of Structuration*. Berkeley: University of California Press.

————. 1991. *Modernity and Self-Identity: Self and Society in Late Modern Age*. Stanford: Stanford University Press.

Gilbert, Miqqu Alicia. 2009. "Defeating Bigenderism: Challenging Gender Assumptions in the Twenty-First Century." *Hypatia* 24: 93–112.

Gill Sandra, Jean Stockard, Miriam Johnson, and Suzanne Williams. 1987. "Measuring Gender Differences: The Expressive Dimension and Critique of Androgyny Scales." *Sex Roles* 17: 375–400.

Gillam, Ken, and Shannon Wooden. 2008. "Post-Princess Models of Gender: The New Man in Disney/Pixar." *Journal of Popular Film and Television* 36: 2–8.

Gilligan, Carol. 1982. *In a Different Voice: Psychological Theory and Women's Development.* Cambridge, MA: Harvard University Press.

Grossman, Arnold H., and Anthony D'Augelli. 2006. "Transgender Youth: Invisible and Vulnerable." *Journal of Homosexuality* 51 (1): 111–128.

Grossman, A. H., A. R. D'Augelli, and J. A. Frank. 2011. "Aspects of Psychological Resilience among Transgender Youth." *Journal of LGBT Youth* 8: 103–115.

Grossman, A. H., Anthony D'Augelli, Tamika Jarrett Howell, and Steven Hubbard. 2005. "Parents' Reactions to Transgender Youths' Gender Nonconforming Expression and Identity." *Journal of Gay and Lesbian Social Services* 18 (1): 3–16.

Grossman, Arnold H., Anthony R. D'Augelli, and Nickolas Salter. 2006a. "Male-to-Female Transgender Youth: Gender Expression Milestones, Gender Atypicality, Victimization, and Parents' Responses." *Journal of GLBT Family Studies* 2 (1): 71–92.

Grossman, Arnold, Anthony D'Augelli, Nicholas Salter, and Steven Hubbard. 2006b. "Comparing Gender Expression, Gender Nonconformity, and Parents' Responses of Female-to-Male and Male-to-Female Transgender Youth." *Journal of LGBT Issues in Counseling* 1 (1): 41–59.

Haddad, Yvonne Yazbeck, Jane I. Smith, and Katheleen M. Moore. 2006. *Muslim Women in America: The Challenge of Islamic Identity Today.* Cambridge: Oxford University Press.

Halpern, Carolyn Tucker. 2012. "Affirmation of a Development Systems Approach to Genetics." *Behavioral and Brain Sciences* 35 (5): 367.

Harris, A. 1990. "Race and Essentialism in Feminist Legal Theory." *Stanford Law Review* 42: 581–616.

Hays, Sharon. 1994. "Structure and Agency and the Sticky Problem of Culture." *Sociological Theory* 12: 57–72.

———. 1998. *The Cultural Contradictions of Motherhood.* New Haven, CT: Yale University Press.

Hebblethwaite, Cordelia. 2011. "Sweden's 'Gender-Neutral' Preschool." BBC. July 8. http://www.bbc.co.uk/news/world-europe-14038419.

Heilman, Madeline, and Alice H. Eagly. 2008. "Gender Stereotypes Are Alive, Well, and Busy Producing Workplace Discrimination." *Industrial and Organizational Psychology* 1: 393–398.

Herman, Barbara. 2015. "Bruce Jenner's Diana Sawyer Interview: A Watershed Movement for Transgender and Genderqueer Visibility." *International Business Times*, April 24. http://www.ibtimes.com/bruce-jenners-diane-sawyer-interview-watershed-moment-transgender-genderqueer-1895969.

Herring, Cedric. 2009. "Does Diversity Pay? Race, Gender and the Business Case for Diversity." *American Sociological Review* 74: 208–224.

Hoffman Rose Marie, and L. DiAnne Borders. 2001. "Twenty-Five Years After the Bem Sex Role Inventory: A Reassessment and New Issues Regarding Classification Variability." *Measurement and Evaluation in Counseling and Development* 34: 39–55.

Hollander, Jocelyn A. 2013. "'I Demand More of People' Accountability, Interaction, and Gender Change." *Gender & Society* 27: 5–29.

Holterhus Paul-Martin, Jan-Hendrik Bebermeier, Ralf Werner, Janos Demeter, Annette Richter-Unruh, Gunnar Cario, Mahesh Appari, Reiner Siebert, Felix Riepe, James D. Brooks, and Olaf Hiort. 2009. "Disorders of Sex Development Expose Transcriptional Autonomy of Genetic Sex and Androgen-Programmed Hormonal Sex in Human Blood Leukocytes." *BMC Genomics* 10: 292–304.

Horn, Stacey S. 2007. "Adolescents' Acceptance of Same-Sex Peers Based on Sexual Orientation and Gender Expression." *Journal of Youth and Adolescence*, 36 (3): 363–371.

Howe, Neil, and William Strauss. 1991. *Generations: The History of America's Future, 1584-2069*. New York: William Morrow.

———. 1997. *The Fourth Turning: What the Cycles of History Tell Us About America's Next Rendezvous with Destiny*. New York: Broadway Books.

Hrabovszky, Zolton, and John M. Hutson. 2002. "Androgen Imprinting of the Brain in Animal Models and Humans with Intersex Disorders: Review and Recommendations." *The Journal of Urology* 168: 2142–2148.

Ingraham Chrys. 1994. "The Heterosexual Imaginary: Feminist Sociology and Theories of Gender." *Sociological Theory* 12: 203–219.

Jacobs, Jerry A., and Kathleen Gerson. 2005. *The Time Divide: Work, Family, and Gender Inequality*. Cambridge, MA: Harvard University Press.

Jeffreys, Sheila. 2014. *Gender Hurts: A Feminist Analysis of the Politics of Transgenderism*. New York: Routledge.

Jenkins, Stephen P. 2008. "Marital Splits and Income Changes over the Longer Term." ISER Working Paper No. 2008-07.

Jones, Nikki. 2009. *Between Good and Ghetto: African American Girls and Inner-City Violence*. Newark, NJ: Rutgers University Press.

Jordan-Young Rebecca M. 2010. *Brainstorm: The Flaws in the Science of Sex Differences*. Cambridge, MA: Harvard University Press.

Kan Man Yee, Oriel Sullivan, and Jonathan Gershuny. 2011. "Gender Convergence in Domestic Work: Discerning the Effects of Interactional and Institutional Barriers from Large-Scale Data." *Sociology* 45: 234–251.

Kane, Emily W. 2006. "'No Way My Boys Are Going to Be Like That!': Parents' Responses to Children's Gender Nonconformity." *Gender & Society* 20: 149–176.

———. 2012. *The Gender Trap: Parents and the Pitfalls of Raising Boys and Girls*. New York: New York University Press.

Kanter, Rosabeth Moss. 1977. *Men and Women of the Corporation*. New York: Basic Books.

Kaufman, Debra R. 1991. *Rachel's Daughters: Newly Orthodox Jewish Women*. New Brunswick, NJ: Rutgers University Press.

Kawashima-Ginsberg, Kei. 2017. "How Gender Mattered to Millennials in the 2016 Election and Beyond." Online Symposium published by the Council on Contemporary Families. https://contemporaryfamilies.org/kawashima-ginsberg-gender-millennials-2016-election-and-beyond/.

Kimmel, Michael. 2008. *Guyland: The Perilous World Where Boys Become Men*. New York: Harper Perennial.

———. 2016. "Guyland: Gendering the Transition to Adulthood." In C. J. Pascoe and Tristan Bridges, eds., *Exploring Masculinities: Identity, Inequality, Continuity and Change*. New York: Oxford University Press.

King, Deborah K. 1988. "Multiple Jeopardy, Multiple Consciousness: The Context of a Black Feminist Ideology." *Signs* 14: 42–72.

Kirchgaessner, Stephanie. 2015. "School Plan to Change Gender Stereotypes Causes Storm in Italy." *The Guardian*, March 10. http://www.theguardian.com/world/2015/mar/10/school-plan-change-gender-stereotypes-storm-italy.

Kohlberg, L. 1966. "A Cognitive-Developmental Analysis of Children's Sex-Role Concepts and Attitudes." In E. E. Maccoby, ed., *The Development of Sex Differences*. Stanford: Stanford University Press, 82–173.

Kondo, Dorinne K. 1990. *Crafting Selves: Power, Gender and Discourses of Identity in a Japanese Workplace*. Chicago: University of Chicago Press.

Laws, Sophie. 1990. *Issues of Blood: The Politics of Menstruation*. London: Macmillan.

Laqueur E, E. Dingemanse, P. C. Hart, and S. E. Jongh. 1927. "Female Sex Hormone in Urine of Men." *Klinische Wochenschrift* 6: 859.

Lareau, Annette. 2003. *Unequal Childhoods: Class, Race, and Family Life*. Berkeley: University of California Press.

Lever, Janet. 1974. *Games Children Play: Sex Differences and the Development of Role Skills*. New Haven, CT: Yale University Press.

Levin, Diane E., and Jean Kilbourne. 2008. *So Sexy So Soon: The New Sexualized Childhood, and What Parents Can Do to Protect Their Kids*. New York: Ballantine.

Levitt Heidi M., Elisabeth A. Gerrish, and Katherine R. Hiestand. 2003. "The Misunderstood Gender: A Model of Modern Femme Identity." *Sex Roles* 48: 99–113.

Lillie, Frank R. 1939. "Biological Introduction." In E. Allen ed., *Sex and Internal Secretions*. 2nd ed. Baltimore, MD: Williams & Wilkins.

Lippa Richard A. 2005. *Gender, Nature and Nurture*. New York: Psychology Press.

Locksley Anne, and Mary E. Colten. 1979. "Psychological Androgyny: A Case of Mistaken Identity?" *Journal of Personality and Social Psychology* 37: 1017–1031.

Lopata Helena Z., and Barrie Thorne. 1978. "On the Term 'Sex Roles.'" *Signs* 3: 718–721.

Lorber, Judith. 1994. *Paradoxes of Gender*. New Haven, CT: Yale University Press.

———. 1996. "Beyond the Binaries: Depolarizing the Categories of Sex, Sexuality, and Gender." *Sociological Inquiry* 66: 143–159.

———. 2005. *Breaking the Bowls: Degendering and Feminist Change*. New York: W.W. Norton.

Lorde, Audre. 1984. *Sister Outsider*. Trumansburg, NY: Crossing Press Feminist Series.

MacDonald, Cameron Lynne. 2011. *Shadow Mothers: Nannies, Au Pairs, and the Micropolitics of Mothering*. Berkeley: University of California Press.

MacKinnon, Catharine A. 1982. "Feminism, Marxism, Method, and the State." *Signs* 7: 515–544.

Mannheim, Karl. 1927. "The Problem of Generations." In *Essays in the Sociology of Knowledge*. London: Routledge & Kegan Paul.

Martin, Emily. 1987. *The Woman in the Body: A Cultural Analysis of Reproduction*. Boston: Beacon.

Martin, Karin A. 1998. "Becoming a Gendered Body: Practices of Preschools." *American Sociological Review* 63: 494–511.

Martin, Patricia Yancey. 2003. "Said and Done vs. Saying and Doing: Gender Practices/Practicing Gender and Work." *Gender & Society* 17: 342–366.

———. 2004. "Gender as Social Institution." *Social Forces* 82: 1249–1273.

———. 2006. "Practicing Gender at Work: Further Thoughts on Reflexivity." *Gender, Work and Organization* 13: 254–275.

Mayhew, Bruce. 1980. "Structuralism vs. Individualist, Part I: Shadowboxing in the Dark." *Social Forces* 59: 335–375.

McCall, Leslie. 2005. "The Complexity of Intersectionality." *Signs* 30: 1771–1800.

———. 2015. "Beyond the Work/Family Debate: Gender and Class Inequalities in Resource Pooling." Sociologists for Women in Society Annual Meeting, February 19-22, Washington, DC.

McGuire, Jenifer K., Charles R. Anderson, Russell B. Toomey, and Stephen T. Russell. 2010. "School Climate for Transgender Youth: A Mixed Method Investigation of Student Experiences and School Responses." *Journal of Youth and Adolescence* 39 (10): 1175–1188.

McKenna, Wendy, and Suzanne Kessler. 2006. "Transgendering: Blurring the Boundaries of Gender." In Kathy Davis, Mary Evans, Judith Lorber, eds., *Handbook of Gender and Women's Studies*. London: Sage, 342–355.

Meadow, Tey. 2010. "A Rose Is a Rose': On Producing Legal Gender Classifications." *Gender & Society* 24: 814.

———. 2011. "'Deep Down Where the Music Plays': How Parents Account For Childhood Gender Variance." *Sexualities* 14: 725–747.

Melendez, Lyanne. 2015. "Santa Rosa Girls Fight to Join Local Boy Scout Troop." *ABC News*, November 11. http://abc7news.com/society/santa-rosa-girls-fight-to-join-local-boy-scout-troop-/1080330/

Milkman, Ruth. 2017. "A New Political Generation: Millennials and the Post-2008 Wave of Protest." *American Sociological Review* 82 (1): 1–31.

Moen, Phyllis, Erin L. Kelly, Wen Fan, Shi-Rong Lee, David Almeida, Ellen Ernst Kossek, and Orfeu M. Buxton. 2016. "Does a Flexibility/Support Organizational Initiative Improve High-Tech Employees' Well-Being? Evidence from the Work, Family, and Health Network." *American Sociological Review* 81: 134–164.

Mohanty, Chandra. 2003. *Feminism Without Borders: Decolonizing Theory, Practicing Solidarity*. Durham, NC: Duke University Press.

Money, John. 1965. *Sex Research: New Developments*. New York: Holt, Rinehart and Winston.

Nakano Glenn, Evelyn. 1992. "From Servitude to Service Work: Historical Continuities in the Racial Division of Paid Reproductive Labor." *Signs* 18: 1–43.

———. 1999. "The Social Construction and Institutionalization of Gender and Race: An Integrative Framework." In M. M. Ferree, J. Lober, and B. Hess, eds., *The Gender Lens: Revisioning Gender*. Lanham, MD: Rowman and Littlefield, 3–43.

———. 2010. *Forced to Care: Coercion and Caregiving in America*. Cambridge, MA: Harvard University Press.

Nicholas, Lucy. 2014. *Queer Post-gender Ethics: The Shape of Selves to Come*. Hampshire, UK: Palgrave Macmillan.

O'Brien, Mary. 1981. *The Politics of Reproduction*. New York: Routledge.

O'Connor, Julia S., Ann Shola Orloff, and Sheila Shaver. 1999. *States, Markets, Families: Gender, Liberalism and Social Policy in Australia, Canada, Great Britain and the United States*. Cambridge, UK: Cambridge University Press.

Okin, Susan Moller. 1989. *Justice, Gender, and the Family*. New York: Basic Books.

Orloff, Ann Shola. 2009. "Should Feminists Aim for Gender Symmetry? Why a Dual-Earner/ Dual-Caregiver Society is Not Every Feminist's Utopia." In Janet Gornick and Marcia K Meyers, eds., *Gender Equality*. London: Verso, 129–157.

Oudshoorn, Nelly. 1994. *Beyond the Natural Body: An Archeology of Sex Hormones*. London: Routledge.

Padamsee, Tasleem J. 2009. "Culture in Connection: Re-Contextualizing Ideational Processes in the Analysis of Policy Development." *Social Politics* 16: 413–445.

Padavic, Irene, and Barbara Reskin. 2002. *Women and Men at Work*. Thousand Oaks, CA: Sage.

Paechter, Carrie F. 2007. *Being Boys Being Girls: Learning Masculinities and Femininities*. New York: Open University Press.

Parkes, A. S. 1938. "Terminology of Sex Hormones." *Nature* 141: 12.

Parsons Talcott, and Robert Freed Bales. 1955. *Family, Socialization, and Interaction Process.* Glencoe, IL: Free Press.

Pascoe, C. J. 2007. *Dude, You're a Fag: Masculinity and Sexuality in High School.* Berkeley: University of California Press.

Pascoe, C. J., and Tristan Bridges, eds. 2015. *Exploring Masculinities: Identity, Inequality, Continuity and Change.* Cambridge, MA: Oxford University Press.

Pedhazur Elazar J., and Toby J. Tetenbaum. 1979. "Bem Sex Role Inventory: A Theoretical and Methodological Critique." *Journal of Personality and Social Psychology* 37: 996–1016.

Pepin, Joanna, and David Cotter. 2017. "Trending Towards Traditionalism? Changes in Youths' Gender Ideology." Online Symposium published by the Council on Contemporary Families. https://contemporaryfamilies.org/2-pepin-cotter-traditionalism/.

Peters, M. A. 2001. *Poststructuralism, Marxism, and Neoliberalism: Between Theory and Politics.* New York: Rowman and Littlefield.

Perrin, Andrew J., and Hedwig Lee. 2007. "The Undertheorized Environment: Sociological Theory and the Ontology of Behavioral Genetics." *Sociological Perspectives* 50: 303–322.

Pew Research Center. 2014. "Record Share of Americans Have Never Married." http://www.pewsocialtrends.org/2014/09/24/record-share-of-americans-have-never-married/

———. 2015. "Most Millennials Resist the 'Millennial' Label." http://www.people-press.org/2015/09/03/most-millennials-resist-the-millennial-label/.

———. 2016. "For the First Time in Modern Era Living with Parents Edges out Other Living Arrangements." http://www.pewsocialtrends.org/2016/05/24/for-first-time-in-modern-era-living-with-parents-edges-out-other-living-arrangements-for-18-to-34-year-olds/

Pfannkuche, Kristina, Anke Bouma, and Ton Groothuis. 2009. "Does Testosterone Affect Lateralization of Brain and Behavior?" *Philosophical Transactions of the Royal Society* 364: 929–942.

Pfau-Effinger, Birgit. 1998. "Gender Cultures and the Gender Arrangement—A Theoretical Framework for Cross-National Gender Research." *Innovations: The European Journal of Social Sciences* 11: 147–166.

Phoenix Charles H., Robert W. Goy, Arnold A. Gerall, and William C. Young. 1959. "Organizing Action of Prenatally Administered Testosterone Propionate on the Tissues Medicating Mating Behavior in the Female Guinea Pig." *Endocrinology* 65: 369–382.

Pierotti, Rachael S. 2013. "Increasing Rejection of Intimate Partner Violence Evidence of Global Cultural Diffusion." *American Sociological Review* 78: 240–265.

Poggio, Barbara. 2006. "Outline of a Theory of Gender Practices." *Gender, Work, and Organization* 13: 225–233.

Preves, Sharon E. 2003. *Intersex and Identity: The Contested Self.* New Jersey, NJ: Rutgers University Press.

Rich, Adrienne. 1980. "Compulsory Heterosexuality and Lesbian Existence." *Signs* 5: 631–660.

Ridgeway, Cecilia L. 1991. "The Social Construction of Status Value: Gender and Other Nominal Characteristics." *Social Forces* 70: 367–386.

———. 2001. "Gender, Status, and Leadership." *Journal of Social Issues* 57: 637–655.

———. 2011. *Framed By Gender: How Gender Inequality Persists in the Modern World.* New York: Oxford University Press.

Ridgeway, Cecilia L., and Shelly Correll. 2004. "Unpacking the Gender System: A Theoretical Perspective on Gender Beliefs and Social Relations." *Gender & Society* 18: 510–531.

———. 2006. "Consensus and the Creation of Status Beliefs." *Social Forces* 85: 431–454.

Rieger, Gerulf, and Ritch Savin-Williams. 2012. "Gender Nonconformity, Sexual Orientation, and Psychological Well-Being." *Archives of Sexual Behavior* 41: 611–621.

Risman, Barbara J. 1987. "Intimate Relationships from a Microstructural Perspective: Men Who Mother." *Gender and Society* 1: 6–32.

———.1998. *Gender Vertigo: American Families in Transition*. New Haven, CT: Yale University Press.

———. 2001. "Calling the Bluff of Value-Free Science." *American Sociological Review* 66: 605–611.

———.2004. "Gender as a Social Structure: Theory Wrestling with Activism." *Gender & Society* 18: 429–451.

———. 2009. "From Doing to Undoing: Gender as We Know It." *Gender & Society* 23: 81–84.

———. 2011. "Gender as Structure or Trump Card?" *Journal of Family Theory and Review* 3: 18–22.

———. 2017. "Are Millennials Cracking the Gender Structure? *Social Currents* 4: 208–227.

Risman, Barbara J., and Timothy Adkins. 2014. "The Goal of Gender Transformation in American Universities: Toward Social Justice for Women in the Academy." In J. Shefner, H. F. Dahms, R. E. Jones, and A. Jalata, eds., *Social Justice and the University: Globalization, Human Rights and the Future of Democracy*. New York: Palgrave Macmillian, 99–113.

Risman, Barbara J., and Georgiann Davis. 2013. "From Sex Roles to Gender Structure." *Current Sociology Review* 61: 733–755.

Risman, Barbara J., and Elizabeth K. Seale. 2010. "Betwixt and Between: Gender Contradictions among Middle Schoolers." In B. J. Risman, ed., *Families as They Really Are*. New York: W. W. Norton, 340–361.

Risman, Barbara J., Ray Sin, and Buddy Scarborough. 2017. "Millennials: Not Pushing the Envelope, Not Rejecting the Gender Revolution." https://thesocietypages.org/families/2017/04/18/millennials-not-pushing-the-envelope-not-rejecting-the-gender-revolution/.

Ritter, Barbara A., and Janice D. Yoder. 2004. "Gender Differences in Leader Emergence Persist Even for Dominant Women: An Updated Confirmation of Role Congruity Theory." *Psychology of Women Quarterly* 28: 187–193.

Robinson, Christine M., and Sue E. Spivey. 2007. "The Politics of Masculinity and the Ex-Gay Movement." *Gender & Society* 21: 650–675.

———. 2015. "Putting Lesbians in Their Place: Deconstructing Ex-Gay Discourses of Female Homosexuality in a Global Context." *Social Science* 4: 879–908.

Robnett, Rachael D., and Campbell Leaper. 2013. "'Girls Don't Propose! Ew.' A Mixed-Methods Examination of Marriage Tradition Preferences and Benevolent Sexism in Emerging Adults." *Journal of Adolescent Research* 28: 96–121.

Rojek, Chris, and Bryan Turner. 2000. "Decorative Sociology: Towards a Critique of the Cultural Turn." *The Sociological Review* 48: 629–48.

Rosenblitt, Jon C., Soler Hosanna, Stacey E. Johnson, and David M. Quadagno. 2001. "Sensation Seeking and Hormones in Men and Women: Exploring the Link." *Hormones and Behavior* 40: 396–402.

Rubin Gayle. 1975. "The Traffic in Women: Notes on the Political Economy Sex." In R. Reiter, ed., *Toward an Anthropology of Women*. New York: Monthly Review Press, 157–210.

Rudman, Laurie A., and Kris Mescher. 2013. "Penalizing Men Who Request a Family Leave: Is Flexibility Stigma a Femininity Stigma?: Feminizing Male Leave Requesters." *Journal of Social Issues* 69 (2): 322–340.

Rytina, Steven, Peter M. Blau, Terry Blum, and Joseph Schwartz. 1988. "Inequality and Intermarriage: A Paradox of Motive and Constraint." *Social Forces* 66: 645–675.

Saltzburg, Susan, and Tarama Davis. 2010. "Co-Authoring Gender-Queer Youth Identities: Discursive Tellings and Retellings." *Journal of Ethnic and Cultural Diversity in Social Work* 19 (2): 87–108.

Sandberg, Sheryl. 2013. *Lean In: Women, Work and the Will to Lead.* New York: Knopf.

Schilt, Kristen. 2011. *Just One of the Guys?: Transgender Men and the Persistence of Gender Inequality.* Chicago: University of Chicago Press.

Schilt, Kristen, and Laurel Westbrook. 2009. "Doing Gender, Doing Heteronormativity 'Gender Normals,' Transgender People, and the Social Maintenance of Heterosexuality." *Gender & Society* 23: 440–464.

Schippers, Mimi. 2007. "Recovering the Feminine Other: Masculinity, Femininity, and Gender Hegemony." *Theory and Society* 36: 85–102.

Schwalbe, Michael, Sandra Godwin, Daphne Holden, Douglas Schrock, Shealy Thompson, and Michele Wolkomir. 2000. "Generic Processes in the Reproduction of Inequality: An Interactionist Analysis." *Social Forces* 79: 419–542.

Seidman, Steven, ed. 1996. *Queer Theory/Sociology.* Malden, MA: Blackwell.

Settersten Richard A., Jr., and Barbara Ray. 2010. "What's Going on with Young People Today? The Long and Twisted Path to Adulthood." *Future of Children* 20: 19–41.

Shalev, Michael. 2009. "Class Divisions of Women." In Janet Gornick and Marcia K. Meyers, eds., *Gender Equality.* London: Verso, 255–282.

Shanahan, Michael J. 2000. "Pathways to Adulthood in Changing Societies: Variability and Mechanisms in Life Course Perspective." *Annual Review of Sociology* 26: 667–692.

Shotwell, Alexis, and Trevor Sangrey. 2009. "Resisting Definition: Gendering Through Interaction and Relational Selfhood." *Hypatia* 24: 56–76.

Siebke, H. 1931. "Presence of Androkinin in Female Organism." *Archiv für Gynaekologie* 146: 417–462.

Slaughter, Marie-Anne. 2015. *Unfinished Business: Women, Men, Work, Family.* New York: Random House.

Smalley, K. Bryant, Jacob C. Warren, and K. Nikki Barefoot. 2015. "Differences in Health Risk Behaviors Across Understudied LGBT Subgroups." *Health Psychology.* OnlineFirst. http://www.ncbi.nlm.nih.gov/pubmed/26375040.

Smelser, Neil J., ed. 1988. "Social Structure." In *Handbook of Sociology.* Thousand Oaks, CA: Sage, 103–129.

Spence, Janet T., Robert L. Helmreich, and Carole K. Holahan. 1975. "Negative and Positive Components of Psychological Masculinity and Femininity and Their Relationships to Self-Reports of Neurotic and Acting Out Behaviors." *Journal of Personality and Social Psychology* 37: 1673–1682.

Spence, Janet T., Robert L. Helmreich, and Joy Stapp. 1975. "Ratings of Self and Peers on Sex Role Attributes and their Relation to Self-Esteem and Conceptions of Masculinity and Femininity." *Journal of Personality and Social Psychology* 32: 29–39.

Stacey, Judith. 1990. *Brave New Families: Stories of Domestic Upheaval in Late Twentieth-Century America*. New York: Basic Books.

Stainback, Kevin, Sibyl Kleiner, and Sherl Skaggs. 2016. "Women in Power: Undoing or Redoing Gendered Organization? *Gender & Society* 30: 109–135.

Steele, Sarah M. 2011. "Queering Intersectionality: Practical Politics and Southerners on New Ground." M.A. dissertation, Department of Women's Studies, University of Florida, Gainsville.

Stockard, Jean, and Miriam M. Johnson. 1980. *Sex Roles: Sex Inequality and Sex Role Development*. Englewood Cliffs, NJ: Prentice Hall.

Stryker, Robin, and Pamela Wald. 2009. "Redefining Compassion to Reform Welfare: How Supporters of 1990s US Federal Welfare Reform Aimed for the Moral High Ground." *Social Politics: International Studies in Gender, State & Society* 16: 519–557.

Sullivan, Oriel. 2006. *Changing Gender Relations, Changing Families: Tracing the Pace of Change over Time*. Lanham, MD: Rowman and Littlefield.

Sweet, Elizabeth. 2014. "Toys Are More Divided by Gender Now Than They Were 50 Years Ago." *The Atlantic*, December 9. http://www.theatlantic.com/business/archive/2014/12/toys-are-more-divided-by-gender-now-than-they-were-50-years-ago/383556/.

Swidler, Ann. 1986. "Culture in Action: Symbols and Strategies." *American Sociological Review* 51: 273–286.

Taylor, Marylee C., and Judith A. Hall. 1982. "Psychological Androgyny: Theories, Methods, and Conclusions." *Psychological Bulletin* 92: 347–366.

Terman, Lewis M. and Catharine Cox Miles. 1936. *Sex and Personality: Studies in Masculinity and Femininity*. New York: McGraw Hill.

Tichenor, Veronica Jaris. 2005. *Earning More and Getting Less: Why Successful Wives Can't Buy Equality*. New Brunswick, NJ: Rutgers University Press.

Torkelson, Jason. 2012. "A Queer Vision of Emerging Adulthood: Seeing Sexuality in the Transition to Adulthood." *Sexual Research & Social Policy* 9: 132–142.

Twenge, Jean M. 1997. "Changes in Masculine and Feminine Traits over Time: A Meta-Analysis." *Sex Roles* 36: 305–325.

———. 2014. *Generation Me: Why Today's Young Americans Are More Confident, Assertive, Entitled—and More Miserable Than Ever Before*. 2nd ed. New York: Atria Books.

Twenge, Jean M., W. Keith Campbell, and Brittany Gentile. 2012. "Generational Increases in Agentic Self-Evaluations Among American College Students, 1966–2009." *Self and Identity* 11 (4): 409–427.

Udry Richard J. 2000. "Biological Limits of Gender Construction." *American Sociological Review* 65: 443–457.

Wade, Lisa. 2013. "The New Science of Sex Difference." *Sociology Compass* 7 (4): 278–293.

———. 2017. *American Hookup: The New Culture of Sex on Campus*. New York: W. W. Norton.

Walby, Sylvia. 2011. *The Future of Feminism*. New York: Polity.

Ward, Jane. 2011. "Queer Parenting for Heteros (& anyone else who wants to teach kids that being queer is awesome)." http://feministpigs.blogspot.com/2011/10/queer-parenting-for-heteros-anyone-else.html.

Warner, Michael. 1993. *Fear of a Queer Planet: Queer Politics and Social Theory*. Minneapolis: University of Minnesota Press.

Waters, Mary C., Patrick J. Carr, Maria J. Kefalas, and Jennifer Holdaway. 2011. *Coming of Age in America: The Transition to Adulthood in the Twenty-First Century*. Berkeley: University of California Press.

Weitzman, Lenore J. 1979. *Sex Role Socialization: A Focus on Women*. Palo Alto, CA: Mayfield.

Weitzman, Lenore J., Deborah Eifler, Elizabeth Hokada, and Catherine Ross. 1972. "Sex-Role Socialization in Picture Books for Preschool Children." *American Journal of Sociology* 7: 1125–1150.

West, Candace, and Don H. Zimmerman. 1987. "Doing Gender." *Gender & Society* 1: 125–151.

Westbrook, Laurel, and Kristen Schilt. 2014. "Doing Gender, Determining Gender Transgender People, Gender Panics, and the Maintenance of the Sex/Gender/Sexuality System." *Gender & Society* 28: 32–57.

White, Martha Sturm. 1979. "Measuring Androgyny in Adulthood." *Psychology of Women Quarterly* 3: 293–307.

Wilkins, Amy C. 2012. "Becoming Black Women: Intimate Stories and Intersectional Identities." *Social Psychological Quarterly* 53: 173–196.

Williams, Christine. 1992. "The Glass Escalator: Hidden Advantages for Men in the 'Female' Professions." *Social Problems* 39: 253–267.

Williams, Joan C. 2001. *Unbending Gender: Why Family and Work Conflict and What to Do About It*. New York: Oxford University Press.

Wingfield, Adia Harvey. 2009. "Racializing the Glass Escalator." *Gender & Society* 23: 5–26.

Winograd, Morley, and Michael D. Hais. 2011. *Millennial Momentum: How a New Generation is Remaking America*. New Brunswick, NJ: Rutgers University Press.

Wyss, Shannon E. 2004. "'This was my hell': The Violence Experienced by Gender Nonconforming Youth in US High Schools." *International Journal of Qualitative Studies in Education* 17 (5): 709–730.

Young, Robert, and Helen Sweeting. 2004. "Adolescent Bullying, Relationships, Psychological Well-Being, and Gender-Atypical Behavior: A Gender Diagnosticity Approach." *Sex Roles* 50 (7/8): 525–537.

Zelditch, Morris. 1955. "Role Differentiation in the Nuclear Family: A Comparative Study." In T. Parsons and R. Bales, ed., *Family, Socialization, and Interaction Process*. Glencoe, IL: Free Press, 307–352.

Zimmer Lynn. 1988. "Tokenism and Women in the Workplace: The Limits of Gender-Neutral Theory." *Social Problems* 35: 64–77.

Zondek, Bernhard. 1934. "Oestrogenic Hormone in the Urine of the Stallion." *Nature* 133: 494.

INDEX